The *Sams Teach Yourself in 24 Hours* Series

Sams Teach Yourself in 24 Hours books provide quick and easy answers in a proven step-by-step approach that works for you. In just 24 sessions of one ho or less, you will tackle every task you need to get the results you want. Let ou experienced authors present the most accurate information to get you reliabl answers—fast!

Useful Data Dictionary Views

Lock Activity

DATA DICTIONARY VIEW	INFORMATION PROVIDED
DBA_WAITERS	Sessions waiting for locks and sessions that hold locks
DBA_LOCKS	Locks and latches
DBA_DML_LOCKS	DML locks
DBA_BLOCKERS	Sessions that hold locks requested by other sessions
DBA_DDL_LOCKS	DDL locks

Database Security

DATA DICTIONARY VIEW	INFORMATION PROVIDED
DBA_ROLES	Database roles
DBA_PROFILES	Database profiles
DBA_USERS	Database users
DBA_SYS_PRIVS	System privileges granted to users and roles
DBA_ROLE_PRIVS	Roles granted to users and other roles
DBA_TAB_PRIVS	Grants on objects

Object Partitions

DATA DICTIONARY VIEW	INFORMATION PROVIDED
DBA_PART_KEY_COLUMNS	Columns that form the partitioning key for partitioned objects
DBA_PART_TABLES	Partition-level information for partitioned tables
DBA_PART_INDEXES	Partition-level information for partitioned indexes
DBA_TAB_PARTITIONS	Partition-level information, storage information, and partition statistics generated by ANALYZE for partitioned tables
DBA_IND_PARTITIONS	Partition-level information, storage information, and partition statistics generated by ANALYZE for partitioned indexes
DBA_PART_HISTOGRAMS	Histogram data for histograms on partitioned objects

SAMS Teach Yourself Oracle8i on Windows NT in 24 Hours

Distributed Databases

DATA DICTIONARY VIEW	INFORMATION PROVIDED
DBA_SNAPSHOTS	All snapshots in the database
DBA_SNAPSHOT_REFRESH_TIMES	Snapshot refreshes
DBA_JOBS	All jobs in the database
DBA_JOBS_RUNNING	Jobs now running
DBA_2PC_PENDING	Distributed transactions awaiting completion
DBA_REFRESH	Refresh groups
DBA_SNAPSHOT_LOGS	Snapshot logs
DBA_DB_LINKS	Database links
DBA_REFRESH_CHILDREN	Objects in the refresh groups

Procedures and Triggers

DATA DICTIONARY VIEW	INFORMATION PROVIDED
DBA_TRIGGERS	Database triggers
DBA_OBJECT_SIZE	Size of various PL/SQL objects
DBA_SOURCE	Source of all database objects
DBA_ERRORS	Errors in the current database objects
DBA_DEPENDENCIES	Dependencies between the various database objects

Database Storage

DATA DICTIONARY VIEW	INFORMATION PROVIDED
DBA_TABLESPACES	Tablespaces
DBA_ROLLBACK_SEGS	Rollback segments
DBA_EXTENTS	Extents that comprise the segments
DBA_FREE_SPACE	Free extents in the database segments
DBA_TS_QUOTAS	Tablespace quotas for the various users
DBA_SEGMENTS	The various database segments
DBA_DATA_FILES	The database files

Meghraj Thakkar

SAMS
Teach Yourself

Oracle8i™ on Windows NT®
in 24 Hours

SAMS

A Division of Macmillan Computer Publishing
201 West 103rd St., Indianapolis, Indiana, 46290 USA

Sams Teach Yourself Oracle8i™ on Windows NT® in 24 Hours

Copyright © 1999 by Sams Publishing

International Standard Book Number: 0-672-31578-5

Library of Congress Catalog Card Number: 99-60196

Printed in the United States of America

First Printing: May 1999

01 00   4   3   2

Trademarks

All terms mentioned in this book that are known to be trademarks or service marks have been appropriately capitalized. Sams Publishing cannot attest to the accuracy of this information. Use of a term in this book should not be regarded as affecting the validity of any trademark or service mark.

Oracle8i is a trademark of Oracle Corporation.

Windows NT is a registered trademark of Microsoft Corporation.

Warning and Disclaimer

Every effort has been made to make this book as complete and as accurate as possible, but no warranty or fitness is implied. The information provided is on an "as is" basis. The author and the publisher shall have neither liability or responsibility to any person or entity with respect to any loss or damages arising from the information contained in this book.

ASSOCIATE PUBLISHER
Michael Stephens

ACQUISITIONS EDITOR
Angela C. Kozlowski

DEVELOPMENT EDITOR
Susan Shaw Dunn

MANAGING EDITOR
Jodi Jensen

PROJECT EDITOR
Tonya Simpson

INDEXER
Kevin Fulcher

PROOFREADER
Jill Mazurczyk

TECHNICAL EDITOR
Joseph Duer

INTERIOR DESIGN
Gary Adair

COVER DESIGN
Aren Howell

COPY WRITER
Eric Borgert

LAYOUT TECHNICIANS
Ayanna Lacey
Heather Hiatt Miller
Amy Parker

Contents at a Glance

Table of Contents

Dedication

To my son, Varun, who has brought so much joy to my life.

Acknowledgments

I want to thank my parents for always being a source of inspiration to me; my wife, Komal, for her belief in everything I do; and my brothers Krishnaraj, Jayraj, and Ramraj for their undying support and encouragement.

Tell Us What You Think!

As the reader of this book, *you* are our most important critic and commentator. We value your opinion and want to know what we're doing right, what we could do better, what areas you'd like to see us publish in, and any other words of wisdom you're willing to pass our way.

As an Associate Publisher for Sams Publishing, I welcome your comments. You can fax, email, or write me directly to let me know what you did or didn't like about this book—as well as what we can do to make our books stronger.

Please note that I cannot help you with technical problems related to the topic of this book, and that due to the high volume of mail I receive, I might not be able to reply to every message.

When you write, please be sure to include this book's title and author as well as your name and phone or fax number. I will carefully review your comments and share them with the author and editors who worked on the book.

Fax: 317-581-4770

Email: mstephens@mcp.com

Mail: Michael Stephens
            Associate Publisher
            Sams Publishing
            201 West 103rd Street
            Indianapolis, IN 46290 USA

Introduction

Sams Teach Yourself Oracle8i on Windows NT in 24 Hours is a valuable asset if you're planning to work with Oracle on Windows NT. Although it focuses on helping those of you who are just beginning to use Oracle on Windows NT, even experienced Oracle/Windows NT professionals can benefit from the tuning, troubleshooting, and clustering solutions presented.

Some books discuss generic Oracle capabilities, and others discuss Windows NT. This book specifically discusses using Oracle on Windows NT. You will use the GUI Windows NT tools for managing Oracle databases, and you will implement various strategies for efficient integration of Oracle with Windows NT.

Many projects and corporations have recognized the benefits of using Windows NT instead of UNIX as their enterprise platform. Reading this book will make transition from the UNIX environment easy. You will learn the variations you might encounter when using Oracle on Windows NT, rather than in a UNIX environment. Also, you will discover how easy it is to migrate from Microsoft SQL Server databases to Oracle databases.

Who Should Use This Book?

This book is ideal for the following readers:

- DBAs whose companies are installing or upgrading to Oracle on Windows NT systems
- Windows NT administrators new to databases
- DBAs who are new to Oracle
- First-time DBAs in a new office
- DBAs developing a new database for a Web site

Some knowledge of Windows NT or general database knowledge (Access, SQL Server, and so forth) is expected.

How This Book Is Organized

The book is designed to teach you topics in a series of lessons, each of which should take an hour (or less) to learn. All books in the *Sams Teach Yourself* series enable you to start working and become productive with the product as quickly as possible. This will do that for you, too!

The lessons are categorized as follows:

- Part I, "Getting Started with Oracle on Windows NT" (Hours 1–4), gets you up and running quickly with Oracle on Windows NT. You learn about the Windows NT architecture and how Oracle is used with Windows NT, become familiar with Windows NT tools that you can use to manipulate and integrate Oracle on Windows NT, configure Windows NT to work optimally with Oracle, and install Oracle on the Windows NT platform.
- Part II, "Building Databases" (Hours 5–8), helps you quickly migrate your Oracle7 databases to Oracle8i, convert existing SQL Server databases to Oracle8i, create new Oracle databases, and integrate Oracle databases with Windows NT.
- Part III, "Working with Oracle Utilities" (Hours 9–12), shows how you can easily manipulate information by using graphical tools such as the Oracle Enterprise Manager. You also work with objects in Oracle8i.
- Part IV, "Protecting Your Database" (Hours 13–16), shows you various ways in which you can protect your data and recover from various scenarios of data loss.
- Part V, "Tuning and Troubleshooting the Databases" (Hours 17–20), is where you learn tuning techniques for optimizing Oracle's performance on Windows NT. You also learn various troubleshooting techniques for improving performance and diagnosing other problems.
- Part VI, "Windows NT Clustering Solutions and the World Wide Web" (Hours 21–24), shows you how to use Oracle Fail Safe and Oracle Parallel Server—the Windows NT clustering solutions for Oracle. You also work with Oracle8i's Internet capabilities.

Each lesson starts with an overview of its topic so that you can determine whether it is relevant to your needs or interests. Each lesson concludes with a set of questions and answers, as well as a quiz—just to make sure you were paying attention! (The answers to the quiz questions can be found in Appendix A, in case you need them.)

Conventions Used in This Book

You will find the following typographical conventions throughout the book:

- Commands and output appear in a special `monospaced` font.
- *`Italicized monospace`* words indicate placeholders that you must replace with the appropriate values.
- Words that you type appear in a **`bold monospaced`** font.
- If a task requires you to choose from a menu, the book separates menu commands with a comma. For example, "Choose File, New" means to choose the New command from the File menu.

The lessons contain the following special elements as well:

Notes present interesting informative asides related to the discussion.

Tips offer advice or describe an easier way of doing something.

Cautions alert you to possible problems and instruct you how to avoid or fix them.

 This special icon indicates a new term that's defined and explained in a paragraph. The term being defined is formatted in *italic*.

 The Input icon identifies code that you yourself must type. It usually appears next to a code listing.

 The Output icon identifies the output produced by running the code.

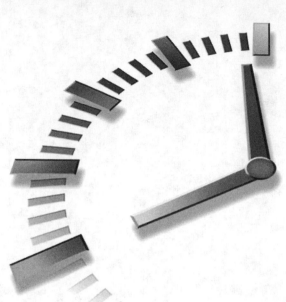

PART I

Getting Started with Oracle on Windows NT

Hour

HOUR 1

Understanding the Architecture of Windows NT and Oracle8i

Windows NT is rapidly becoming the operating system of choice for enterprise solutions. With the advent of Oracle8i, Windows NT administrators and Oracle DBAs can cooperate in many ways to allow Oracle to run efficiently on Windows NT. Windows NT is a tier 1 port for Oracle, meaning that Oracle's new releases and capabilities are quickly available on Windows NT, compared with Oracle's availability on other platforms.

This lesson begins by describing the architecture of Windows NT that an Oracle DBA should be aware of and then describes the architecture of Oracle8i on Windows NT, which is essential to make the most of Oracle8i on Windows NT.

In this hour, you will learn the following:

- Windows NT architecture
- The architecture of Oracle8i on Windows NT
- How an Oracle instance runs as a service on Windows NT
- The physical structure of Oracle8i
- The logical structure of Oracle8i

Windows NT Basics

Windows NT provides a cost-effective solution to information management. It's easy to administer and provides GUI tools to further simplify management. Windows NT security is provided through a mandatory logon procedure, which assigns a security identifier to every user process; this identifier stays attached to the process throughout its lifetime on Windows NT.

Windows NT supports FAT, HPFS, NTFS, and CDFS file systems. NTFS provides file-level security and allows different disk configurations for fault tolerance.

Windows NT also allows user groups to simplify user management. Through Oracle8i's multi-threaded server feature, a large number of users can be supported. Windows NT is a multi-threaded and preemptive multitasking operating system. A group of Windows NT servers and workstations can be connected to form a workgroup or a domain (different domain models can be used, based on the need). Windows NT uses the concept of *trust* to provide flexibility in administration of resources and users.

Windows NT Architecture

Windows NT has several important features:

- Symmetric multiprocessing operating system—This allows the processors to be used by application software and the operating system simultaneously. An asymmetric multiprocessing system assigns operating system functions to one processor and applications to other processors.
- Can run on Alpha, Intel, Mips, and PowerPC—Because Windows NT hides the complexities by using a component called the *hardware abstraction layer* (HAL). Except for the HAL, the Windows NT source code is shared across all platforms; therefore, Oracle can easily port the database software across all Windows NT platforms.

- Accesses up to 4GB of RAM—Each process is allocated a unique virtual address space. Each process gets 2GB for itself and another 2GB that it shares with other system processes.

- Virtual memory—Windows NT uses a 32-bit linear address space. Virtual memory is used, and the virtual memory manager uses demand paging and LRU algorithm to swap pages between the RAM and the paging file to support multiprocessing.

- Supports four file systems: FAT, HPFS, NTFS, and CDFS—FAT allows filenames up to 255 characters long, including spaces and multiple periods. Filenames aren't case sensitive but do preserve case. FAT has a minimal overhead and is preferred for disk partitions smaller than 200MB. FAT doesn't provide any file-level security. Each long filename has an equivalent 8.3 short name.

  The HPFS file system is for people who are transitioning from OS/2 to Windows NT. It supports filenames up to 254 characters long. It's not case sensitive but preserves the case. HPFS partitions can't be created using Windows NT.

  NTFS file system allows filenames up to 255 characters. It provides file-level security. NTFS isn't case-sensitive but preserves case. NTFS supports file compression. It's recommended for partitions at least 50MB in size.

> To convert FAT or HPFS to an NTFS file system, use the convert.exe utility:
>
> ```
> convert c: /fs:ntfs
> ```
>
> You can't use convert.exe to convert NTFS to FAT or HPFS, however.

  The CDFS file system is used for the CD-ROM format.

- Threads are scheduled—A *thread* is the smallest unit of execution. Windows NT schedules threads instead of processes. Because of the multi-threaded feature, thread switching is fast, and overall performance is improved.

- Uses different modes of execution—Threads on Windows NT can be run in one of the various privilege levels of the processor. Based on a thread's priority, it may or may not be able to access certain resources on the system. A Windows NT process may be running in user mode or kernel mode. Nonprivileged user mode processes usually comprise user applications; they must call system services to access system resources. On the other hand, kernel mode processes are privileged. The Windows NT executive service runs in privileged mode. Processes running in kernel mode have access to system memory and hardware. Kernel mode allows the Windows NT executive service to perform thread scheduling, interrupt handling, exception handling, I/O, networking, security, and so on.

- Modular architecture—Windows NT's architecture allows a network component to be replaced with a newer version without affecting the other network components. New components can be integrated with the default network components. Figure 1.1 shows the major components that comprise the Windows NT architecture.

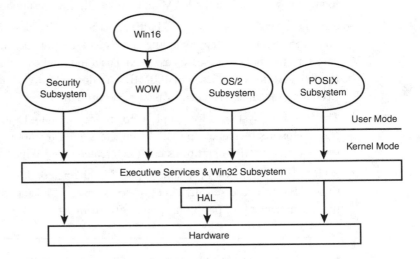

FIGURE 1.1

Windows NT architecture components.

The major components of the Windows NT architecture are as follows:

Component	Function
Executive managers	A set of modules to manage I/O, objects, security, processes, virtual memory, and graphics
Microkernel	Performs operating system functions such as thread scheduling and interrupt handling
Device drivers	Control access to the hardware devices
Hardware abstraction layer (HAL)	Makes Windows NT portable by isolating hardware differences

- Built-in networking—Such networking allows Windows NT to interoperate in many network environments simultaneously without additional software requirements. Windows NT includes four transport protocols:

Protocol	Description
NetBEUI (NetBIOS Extended User Interface)	Ideal for fast performance on small LANs. Requires a small memory overhead but is nonroutable.
NWLink	The NDIS-compliant version of Novell's IPX/SPX. Routable but requires the use of a redirector such as Microsoft's Client Service for NetWare (CSNW) to access file and print services.
TCP/IP	The most popular transport protocol. Routable and should be used for internetworking. Supports Simple Network Management Protocol (SNMP), Dynamic Host Configuration Protocol (DHCP), and Windows Internet Name Service (WINS).
Data Link Control (DLC)	Provides applications with direct access only to the data link layer and therefore isn't used for session communication between Windows NT machines. Should be installed only on computers that need access to IBM mainframes or print to HP printers connected directly to the network.

- Use of subsystems to support applications—Windows NT uses subsystems to support various applications. For example, a POSIX subsystem supports POSIX applications, and an OS/2 subsystem supports OS/2 applications. Windows 32-bit applications run in a Win32 subsystem, which also provides all the graphics to the various other subsystems.

NEW TERM Win16 on Win32 (WOW) is a 32-bit user mode program that allows 16-bit applications to be run in a 32-bit environment. Win16 applications make use of a Windows NT virtual DOS machine (NTVDM). WOW performs a function called *thunking* to translate 16-bit calls to 32-bit calls. The overhead of thunking is offset by the speed advantage of running applications in a 32-bit environment. By default, all Win16 applications run in a single NTVDM.

Memory isn't shared between applications running in WOW and other Windows NT applications. However, a failure of one Win16 application can cause the failure of all other Win16 applications running in the same NTVDM.

Oracle8i Architecture on Windows NT

Oracle uses the Windows NT multi-threaded model by running the Oracle server executable as a process and running the background "processes" as threads. If you have multiple instances of Oracle on Windows NT, there's one server process for each instance (and corresponding threads).

Windows NT reserves 2GB of address space for each process, and system resources use 2GB (which is shared by all processes). Each Oracle instance therefore has 2GB of address space, which puts a serious limit on the number of concurrent users. The stack for every thread consists of two components: the reserved space and the committed space. The number of concurrent connections is directly related to the stack space and the type of work performed by the threads. Now, Oracle8i on Windows NT is linked in the default way, using 1MB of reserved space. Oracle8i on Windows NT and Net8 provide four possible solutions to achieve more concurrent connections per each Oracle8i instance:

- *Multi-Threaded Server (MTS)* allows many user threads to share very few server threads. The user threads connect to a dispatcher process, which routes client requests to the next available server thread, thereby supporting more users.

- *Connection Manager* concentrates multiple clients into a single multiplexed data connection, even if the clients use different protocols. It's ideal for users who need to use the applications continuously.

- *Connection pooling* places idle users in suspended mode and reassigns their physical connections until they become active again. It's ideal for users who need to be logged on all the times but don't have to really use the application.

- *Orastack* allows customers to change the amount of default reserved stack space used by each Oracle thread. Use this utility with caution.

The architecture of Oracle RDBMS comprises two parts:

- The *Oracle instance* consists of the background processes (threads) and memory structures such as the SGA and PGA. Each component will be discussed in greater detail.

- The *Oracle database* consists of physical components such as datafiles, control files, redo log files, initialization files, and archive logs. It also consists of the logical components such as tables, constraints, and so forth. Each component is discussed in greater detail later.

Each Oracle instance is identified by a unique system identifier (SID).

Oracle instances run on Windows NT as services and can interact with theoperating system.

Windows NT Services

Because an Oracle instance runs as a service in Windows NT, you can use it to automatically start the database without users logging on to the system. For every Oracle instance on Windows NT is an OracleServiceSID service and an optional OracleStartSID service (present only if configured for autostart). The OracleServiceSID is the Oracle instance, and the OracleStartSID is used to automatically start the database on server boot.

If the OracleStartSID service isn't seen in Windows NT's Control Panel Services tool, run the instance manager and edit the instance to create the missing service.

Background Processes and Threads

On Windows NT, Oracle background processes run as threads, which Windows NT uses for scheduling purposes. Threads also can improve performance because of the fast context switching that can occur. An Oracle instance consists of several required threads and can have other optional threads:

- The required SMON thread, also referred to as the *system monitor*, is responsible for performing instance recovery, coalescing free extents, and reclaiming space used by temporary segments.

- The required PMON thread, also referred to as the *process monitor*, is responsible for performing thread recovery for failed threads, releasing system resources held by these threads, rolling back aborted transactions, and restarting shared servers and dispatchers.
- The required DBWR thread, also referred to as the *database writer*, is responsible for writing modified database buffers from the database buffer cache to the datafiles on disk, reducing disk I/O, improving the cache hit ratio by using an LRU (least frequently used) algorithm to retain frequently accessed database blocks, and performing *checkpoint*, the process of writing modified database buffers (committed and uncommitted data) to the datafiles so that they're updated.
- The required LGWR thread, also referred to as the *log writer*, is responsible for writing redo log buffers to redo log files when a commit is issued or when the redo log buffer is one-third full. It can determine the checkpoint frequency.

 The init.ora parameter LOG_CHECKPOINT_INTERVAL sets the threshold for the number of redo log buffers that need to be filled, after which a checkpoint occurs—unless LOG_CHECKPOINT_TIMEOUT occurs earlier, in which case the checkpoint also occurs earlier.

- The optional RECO thread, also referred to as the *recovery* process, is responsible for the recovery of failed distributed transactions. It resolves in-doubt transactions.
- The optional ARCH thread, also referred to as the *archiver* process, is responsible for the archiving of redo log files to archive logs on disk or tape.
- The optional CKPT thread, also referred to as the *checkpoint* process, is responsible for updating the datafiles and control file with the new log file control number.
- The optional LCKn thread communicates with the distributed lock manager in a parallel server environment to maintain concurrency control.
- Qnnn is an optional parallel query process used during the execution of parallel operations.
- SNPn is an optional snapshot process used for refreshing snapshots.
- Optional shadow threads are created for every user connection to the database. Such threads can read directly from the database but write only to the SGA.

When a checkpoint occurs, the following is performed:

- LGWR signals DBWR to write the modified database buffer blocks to the datafiles on disk.
- CKPT updates the headers of all datafiles and control files to indicate that a checkpoint has occurred. This is necessary so that all the files are in sync.

> In the absence of a CKPT thread, the LGWR thread updates headers for datafiles and control files. In heavily used databases, use CKPT to relieve LGWR's load and improve overall system performance.

Checkpoints automatically occur under the following situations:

- When a log switch occurs
- When an online backup starts
- When a database is shut down
- When a tablespace is taken offline
- As specified by LOG_CHECKPOINT_INTERVAL and LOG_CHECKPOINT_TIMEOUT parameters

Oracle Memory Structures

 The *shared global area* (SGA) is a major part of an Oracle instance and consists of several components:

- A fixed part that contains the internal Oracle structures.
- A variable part that contains the data dictionary cache and shared and private SQL areas. The shared SQL area (also referred to as the *library cache*) contains parsed SQL statements and their execution plan. The size of the shared pool is determined by the SHARED_POOL initialization parameter.
- A database buffer cache that contains the database buffers. The DB_BLOCK_SIZE and DB_BLOCK_BUFFERS parameters determine the size of the cache. Database buffers store information that's read from or written to the database. The DBWR is responsible for writing the modified database buffers to the datafiles on disk.

- A redo log buffer records all changes made to the database. It functions in a circular manner, and its size is determined by the LOG_BUFFER initialization parameter.
  LGWR is responsible for writing the information from the redo log buffer to the redo
  log files. The redo log buffer also keeps track of checkpoints that have occurred.
  Redo logs are used during database recovery.

NEW TERM The *program global area* (PGA) is a fixed size structure in memory that's created when a user connects to the database. It contains the user stack space and
private SQL area (unless Multi-Threaded Server is used, in which case the private SQL
area is part of the SGA). Figure 1.2 shows the Oracle8i architecture on Windows NT.

FIGURE 1.2

*The Oracle8i
architecture on
Windows NT.*

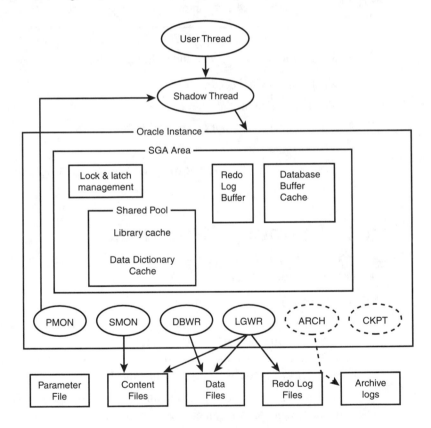

Database Files

Several file types associated with the database constitute the physical components: the initialization file, control files, redo logs, archive log files, and datafiles.

Initialization File

The initialization parameter file (init*SID*.ora) contains the parameters to initialize the database when it starts up. This file is read-only during database startup. Changes made to the initialization file take effect when the database is restarted.

You can get a feel for what the initialization file looks like and contains by looking at the following sample file:

```
db_name = test
instance_name = test
service_names = test
db_files = 2048
control_files = ("c:\database\test\control01.ctl",
➥" c:\database\test \control02.ctl")

db_file_multiblock_read_count = 8

db_block_buffers = 6400

shared_pool_size = 90000000

log_checkpoint_interval = 10000
log_checkpoint_timeout = 0

processes = 50

parallel_max_servers = 5

log_buffer = 32768

max_dump_file_size = 10240   # limit trace file size to 5M each

global_names = true

background_dump_dest = c:\database\test\bdump
user_dump_dest = c:\database\test\udump

db_block_size = 8192

remote_login_passwordfile = shared

compatible = 8.1.5.0.0
sort_area_size = 100000
```

Information in the init*SID*.ora file can include the following:

- A parameter to specify the size of the SGA, such as `shared_pool_size`, `db_block_buffers`, and `log_buffer`
- Parameters to perform database tuning
- An event to generate database tracing for diagnostic purposes
- Location of control files

Control Files

The control file associated with a database contains pointers to the locations of other files (such as datafiles and redo log files) that make up the database.

 Mirror your control file because without a valid control file, the database won't know how to locate the database files.

The contents of a control file include

- System change number (SCN)
- Location of datafiles
- Location of redo log files
- Database name
- Database size

 Keep all the database files—datafiles, redo logs, and control files—synchronized with one another; otherwise, the database might not start.

You can use `alter database backup controlfile to trace` to generate a trace file in the dump destination that contains the `create controlfile` command, as follows.

```
# The following commands will create a new control file and use it
# to open the database.
# Data used by the recovery manager will be lost. Additional logs
# may be required for media recovery of offline datafiles. Use this
# only if the current version of all online logs are available.
```

```
STARTUP NOMOUNT
CREATE CONTROLFILE REUSE DATABASE "TEST" NORESETLOGS ARCHIVELOG
    MAXLOGFILES 32
    MAXLOGMEMBERS 2
    MAXDATAFILES 254
    MAXINSTANCES 1
    MAXLOGHISTORY 226
LOGFILE
  GROUP 1 'C:\DATABASE\TEST\REDO01.LOG'  SIZE 1M,
  GROUP 2 'C:\DATABASE\TEST\REDO02.LOG'  SIZE 1M
DATAFILE
  'c:\database\test\SYSTEM01.DBF',
  'c:\database\test\RBS01.DBF',
  'c:\database\test\USERS01.DBF',
  'c:\database\test\TEMP01.DBF',
  'c:\database\test\INDX01.DBF',
CHARACTER SET WE8ISO8859P1
;
# Recovery is required if any of the datafiles are restored backups,
# or if the last shutdown was not normal or immediate.
RECOVER DATABASE
# All logs need archiving and a log switch is needed.
ALTER SYSTEM ARCHIVE LOG ALL;
# Database can now be opened normally.
ALTER DATABASE OPEN;
# No tempfile entries found to add.
#
```

Redo Logs

The redo logs are a very important component of the database and are used during database recovery. Redo logs record all the changes made to the database and the checkpoint information.

At least two redo logs are written in a circular fashion. You should multiplex the redo logs and place the groups on separate disks so that you have more than one copy in case there's a problem with one set of redo logs. When the redo logs are multiplexed, each set of redo log files are grouped, and the groups are written to simultaneously.

Archived Log Files

Because redo logs are written in a circular fashion, unless you archive them, they eventually will be overwritten. You should run the database in archivelog mode, which will copy the redo log files before they arc overwritten. Running the database in archivelog mode also allows you to make hot backups.

The archive process should be fast; otherwise, LGWR might have to wait for the process to finish archiving the redo. While LGWR is waiting, database activity stops.

Datafiles

The datafiles associated with a database contain the data. Database information is contained in tables and indexes. You should spread the datafiles across all the available disks, ensuring that the tables and indexes are separate so that the I/O is balanced and no "hot" disks can act as a bottleneck.

Naming the datafiles is a matter of personal choice, but you should follow some naming conventions so that the files can be easily managed. OFA guidelines for naming datafiles suggest that they be named so that

- They can be distinguished from other files on the system.
- Files of one database can be distinguished from files of other databases.
- They can be easily distinguished from control files and redo log files.
- You can easily associate datafiles with tablespaces.

Logical Database Components

You've seen that the database's physical components contain various files such as the control files, parameter files, redo logs, archive logs, and datafiles. Logically, however, the data is stored in the database in tablespaces.

Data Blocks

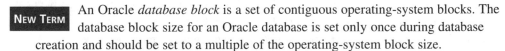 An Oracle *database block* is a set of contiguous operating-system blocks. The database block size for an Oracle database is set only once during database creation and should be set to a multiple of the operating-system block size.

The OS block size for Intel NT is 4KB, whereas for DEC Alpha it's 8KB. If you want to change the database block size for a database after it's created, you have to re-create the database; otherwise, the database may get corrupted.

1

A *data block* is the smallest unit of data storage. Each block in the database buffer is the size of a data block. A data block can't span datafiles because it consists of contiguous OS blocks.

Consider several things when choosing a data block size:

- *The type of database environment.* For example, is it a DSS or OLTP environment? In a data warehousing environment, where you perform many long-running queries, use a large data block size. For an OLTP system, where you have a large number of small transactions, you will benefit by using a small data block size.
- *The size of the SGA.* The database buffer size is determined by the size of the database block and the DB_BLOCK_BUFFERS set in the initialization file.

Extents

NEW TERM An *extent* is a collection of contiguous data blocks. Oracle allocates space in terms of extents. In other words, when a table, index, rollback segment, or temporary segment is created or needs more space, it is assigned a new extent. An extent can't span datafiles because it consists of contiguous data blocks.

An Oracle object such as a table or index will consist of at least one extent. Determining storage parameters for a table or index involves determining the size of its extents. It's helpful to have extents of a size that will allow them to be almost full so that a minimum amount of space is wasted. The storage parameters that can be specified include the following:

- Size of initial extent
- Size of subsequent extents
- A percentage growth factor for subsequent extents
- Maximum number of extents that can be created for the object

Segments

NEW TERM A *segment* is a chain of extents allocated for a specific database object such as a table, index, rollback segment, or temporary segment. A segment can contain noncontiguous extents and, as such, can extend across datafiles.

Four segment types can be associated with a database:

- A *data segment* contains data and is associated with tables and clusters.
- An *index segment* contains indexes that can be used to eliminate full table scans and improve the database's performance.

- A *rollback segment* contains rollback information and is used during recovery to provide read consistency and to roll back uncommitted transactions. When a transaction starts, it's allocated to a rollback segment. Rollback segments provide wraparound and are reusable. Rollback segments can be dynamically created or dropped.
- A *temporary segment* contains temporary objects. It's used during sorting of data.

Tablespaces

NEW TERM   A *tablespace* is a set of segments. A tablespace can consist of one or more datafiles, but a datafile is owned by only one tablespace. Because each segment is stored in only one tablespace, a segment can exist in one or more datafiles of the same tablespace only. Tablespaces can be of several types:

- The *system tablespace* must be available all the time and is necessary for the database to be operational. The system tablespace contains the data dictionary, stored procedures, triggers, and the system rollback segment. To avoid fragmentation of the system tablespace, place user data in individual tablespaces.
- A *data tablespace* can be used to store user data in tables and indexes. Separate a table and its associated indexes into separate tablespaces so that there's no contention. User data tablespaces don't have to be online all the time, but they should be available so that users can access the objects stored in them.

Useful Data Dictionary Tables and Views

The data dictionary contains information about the database that can be accessed by means of the various tables and views described in Table 1.1.

TABLE 1.1   USEFUL DATA DICTIONARY VIEWS

Data Dictionary View	Obtains Information About...
DBA_CATALOG	All the database tables, views, and sequences
DBA_CONSTRAINTS	Constraints on the database tables
DBA_INDEXES	All the indexes in the database
DBA_SEQUENCES	All the sequences in the database
DBA_TABLES	All the tables in the database
DBA_USERS	All the users of the database
DBA_VIEWS	All the views in the database
DBA_DATA_FILES	All the datafiles and tablespaces in the database

Data Dictionary View	Obtains Information About...
DBA_EXTENTS	All the database extents
DBA_ROLLBACK_SEGMENTS	Rollback segments
DBA_FREE_SPACE	Free space available in the database
V$SESSION	Current sessions running against the database
V$DATABASE	Database information such as database name, archivelog mode, and so forth
V$LOCK	Locking information
V$PARAMETER	Database parameters in effect
V$LOGFILE	Redo log files

To Do: Use the Data Dictionary Views to Obtain Database Information

The data dictionary of an Oracle database provides a wealth of information regarding the database. Now perform some simple exercises to query the data dictionary and gather information.

- Determine when a database is created and whether it's in archivelog mode: Frequently during database recovery, you might need to know when the database was created and whether it was running in the archivelog mode. Querying v$database can provide this information.

```
SVRMGR> select name, created, log_mode
from v$database;
NAME      CREATED    LOG_MODE
--------- ---------- ------------
ORCL      03-DEC-98  ARCHIVELOG
1 row selected.
```

- Find which files need media recovery: If the database does not start because a file needs recovery, you can query v$recover_file to determine the files that need to be recovered.

```
Svrmgr> select * from v$recover_file;
FILE#     ONLINE  ERROR              CHANGE#     TIME
--------- ------- ------------------ ---------- ----------
0 rows selected.
```

▼
- Find out information about the rollback segments: On several occasions, such as when you are performing a large export, you might want to determine whether your large rollback segments are online. This can be verified by querying dba_rollback_segs.

INPUT/OUTPUT
```
Svrmgr> select segment_name, owner,
              Tablespace_name, status
        From dba_rollback_segs;
SEGMENT_NAME               OWNER   TABLESPACE_NAME        STATUS
-------------------------  ------  --------------------   ---------
SYSTEM                     SYS     SYSTEM                 ONLINE
SYSROL                     SYS     SYSTEM                 OFFLINE
RB0                        PUBLIC  RBS                    ONLINE
RB1                        PUBLIC  RBS                    ONLINE
4 rows selected.
```

- Find the optimal setting for the rollback segments: During the tuning of a database, you might need to make sure that the optimal setting of your rollback segments is proper. This can be verified by querying v$rollstat.

INPUT/OUTPUT
```
Svrmgr> select usn, rssize, optsize, status
        From v$rollstat;

USN         RSSIZE      OPTSIZE     STATUS
----------  ----------  ----------  ----------------
        0      401408                ONLINE
        2     1220608                ONLINE
        3      401408                ONLINE
3 rows selected.
```

- Find information about the datafiles associated with the database: For purposes of backup, you might want to get a list of all your datafiles comprising the database. A simple query of dba_data_files can provide this information.

INPUT/OUTPUT
```
Svrmgr> select file_name, file_id, tablespace_name
              Status, autoextensible
        From dba_data_files;
FILE_NAME                  FILE_ID  TABLESPACE_NAME STATUS     AUT
-------------------------  -------  --------------- ---------  ---
C:\ORANT\ORCL\SYSTEM01.DBF 1 SYSTEM                 AVAILABLE  YES
C:\ORANT\ORCL\RBS01.DBF    2 RBS                    AVAILABLE  YES
C:\ORANT\ORCL\USERS01.DBF  3 USERS                  AVAILABLE  YES
C:\ORANT\ORCL\TEMP01.DBF   4 TEMP                   AVAILABLE  YES
C:\ORANT\ORCL\INDX01.DBF   5 INDX                   AVAILABLE  YES
5 rows selected.
```
▼

▼ • Find the dump destinations and the maximum dump file size: In addition to other database parameters, v$parameter can provide information about the location where the dump files and trace files for your database will be created.

```
SVRMGR> select name, value, description
        From v$parameter
        Where name like '%dump%';
NAME                      VALUE                 DESCRIPTION
------------------------  --------------------  -------------------------
background_dump_dest      c:\orant\orcl\bdump   Detached process dump dir
user_dump_dest            c:\orant\orcl\udump   User process dump directo
max_dump_file_size        10240                 Maximum size (blocks) of
                                                ➥dump file
```

▲   3 rows selected.

Summary

To successfully administer an Oracle8i database on Windows NT, not only should you be knowledgeable on Oracle8i, but you also should be familiar with the Windows NT architecture so that you can make the best out of the combination. By now, you should understand the physical, as well as logical, components that comprise Oracle8i on Windows NT.

Q&A

Q It seems that knowledge of Windows NT is essential for successfully administering Oracle8i on Windows NT. Should I take some Windows NT classes?

A It's true that the more knowledge you have about Windows NT, the better you can manipulate Oracle8i on Windows NT. However, you don't have to take Windows NT–specific training because this book discusses enough topics to make you very comfortable in the Windows NT environment. After reading this book, you shouldn't have to take any extensive Windows NT training.

Q I've worked with Oracle in the UNIX environment. Can I apply my experience in the Windows NT environment?

A You can apply much of your experience in running Oracle on other platforms. To get the most out of running Oracle8i on Windows NT, however, you need some special knowledge, which this book provides.

Workshop

The Workshop contains quiz questions and activities to help reinforce what you've learned in this hour. You can check Appendix A for the answers (but don't peek!).

Quiz

1. Can Oracle8i be used with Windows NT on ALPHA platforms?
2. What file systems does Windows NT support? Which file system provides file-level security?
3. Which Oracle background threads are required?
4. What does the control file contain?
5. Which data dictionary view can be used to determine whether a database is in archivelog mode?

Exercises

1. You've lost the control file for a database. Generate a trace file that contains the `create controlfile` statement.
2. Determine the amount of free space available in a database.

HOUR 2

Using Windows NT Tools for Oracle8i

This lesson looks at the most important but basic Windows NT tools that you can use to administer and maintain an Oracle8i database on Windows NT. Specifically, this lesson analyzes the following tools:

- Control Panel
- Event Viewer
- Windows NT Registry
- Performance Monitor
- User Manager

Windows NT Registry

Windows NT uses the concept of a Registry, which centrally stores all the hardware and software parameters. All the Oracle-specific environment variables such as ORACLE_HOME and ORACLE_SID are placed in the Registry. The Registry is fault-tolerant to operating system failures and is very robust. Information is stored in a hierarchical structure that's made up of trees, subtrees, keys, and values.

Hives are used to place the keys in different sections. Oracle records most of its information in the Windows NT Registry under the HKEY_LOCAL_MACHINE\SOFTWARE\ORACLE hive (see Figure 2.1). These entries include

- NLS_LANG
- ORACLE_HOME
- ORACLE_SID
- ORA_*sid*_WORKINGSETMAX
- ORA_*sid*_WORKINGSETMIN
- ORA_SHUTDOWN (specifies whether an *immediate* shutdown should be performed when the service or an Oracle instance is stopped from the Control Panel)
- ORA_SHUTDOWN_TIMEOUT (specifies a timeout period for an *immediate* shutdown that's indicated when the service is stopped)
- Variable declarations for use in SQL*Plus
- Product-specific variables

FIGURE 2.1

The Registry showing Oracle-specific parameters.

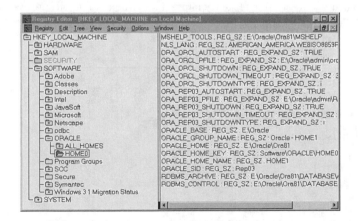

Information in the Windows NT Registry is placed under several root keys, as shown in Figure 2.2, and described in Table 2.1.

TABLE 2.1 ROOT KEYS OF THE WINDOWS NT REGISTRY

Root Key	Description
HKEY_CLASSES_ROOT	Contains entries for OLE and file associations that are used to associate file extensions with particular applications.
HKEY_CURRENT_USER	Contains settings and profiles for the current user.
HKEY_USERS	Contains information about individual user profiles.
HKEY_CURRENT_CONFIG	Contains current software configuration settings.
HKEY_LOCAL_MACHINE	Contains configuration settings about the local computer.
HKEY_DYN_DATA	Protected by Windows NT and not configurable. It contains OS kernel parameters.

2

FIGURE 2.2

The Registry hives.

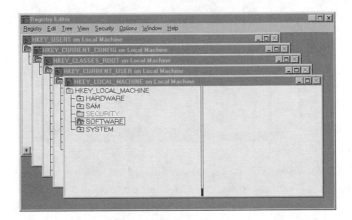

You can view and modify the Registry directly by using the Registry Editor (REGEDT32.EXE). It's recommended, however, that you not manipulate the Registry directly without fully understanding the purpose of the particular change because Registry errors can prevent an application from running or cause Windows NT to be unable to start up or run reliably.

Control Panel

The Windows NT Control Panel (see Figure 2.3) can be used to modify various system options such as

- Windows NT services
- Network configuration such as computer name, domain, network protocols, and network interface cards

- System accessories such as modems and tape drives
- Virtual memory configuration using the system applet
- Printer configuration
- Desktop configuration
- UPS (uninterruptable power supply) configuration
- Open database connectivity (ODBC) configuration

FIGURE 2.3

Control Panel icons.

Services are executable processes maintained by Windows NT. You can configure Windows NT services to start automatically, or you can start them manually. Most services are owned by the built-in user SYSTEM, but you can allow other users to own services, also. When you install Oracle and related products on Windows NT, Oracle services are created and can be manipulated through the Services dialog box. The same user should own all services associated with a particular database instance. To access Control Panel, choose Start, Settings, Control Panel.

Because an Oracle instance runs as a service in Windows NT, it can be used to start the database automatically without a user logging on. For every Oracle instance on Windows NT, there is an OracleServiceSID and an optional OracleStartSID (present only if configured for autostart) service (see Figure 2.4).

OracleServiceSID is the Oracle instance, whereas OracleStartSID automatically starts the database on server boot. If the OracleStartSID service isn't seen in Control Panel's Services tool, run the Instance Manager and edit the instance to create the missing service. The OracleStart service for a particular instance, if configured to start automatically, basically executes a file named strt*sid*.cmd in the %ORACLE_HOME%\database folder. You can modify the contents of this file and thereby perform a sequence of steps with every startup of the database.

FIGURE 2.4

Control Panel's Services tool.

The Registry entries for the Oracle services can be viewed by starting the Registry Editor and navigating to HKEY_LOCAL_MACHINE\SYSTEM\CURRENTCONTROLSET\SERVICES.

The OracleTNSListener80 service, commonly referred to as the *listener*, provides Net8 connectivity from a Net8 client to an Oracle instance. Local or remote connections to a local Oracle instance using Net8 protocols, such as TCP/IP or Named Pipes, require that a listener service be running on the Oracle host machine. While users are connected to the database, the listener service shouldn't be stopped because when a user connects to Oracle in the dedicated server mode, the user's socket connection is merely routed from the listener to the database instance, rather than released. Therefore, the listener and the database service both are using the same port. If you modify listener.ora to listen for connections to a new database, you can use the LSNRCTRL utility with the RELOAD command. Table 2.2 shows the most common services associated with an Oracle database instance.

TABLE 2.2 COMMON ORACLE SERVICES

Oracle Service	Use
OracleServiceSID*	This service must be running before the database can be started.
OracleStartSID*	This executes strt*sid*.cmd from the oracle_home\database folder. This batch file is used to start up the database.
OracleTNSListener	This Net8 listener is required if Oracle clients are required to connect to Oracle services on the machine.
OracleAgent	The Oracle intelligent agent is required if you want to configure jobs and schedule events using the Oracle Enterprise Manager.

*SID is the database instance.

By using Control Panel's Services icon, you can start, stop, pause, or continue each available Oracle service on the computer, as well as pass startup parameters to the services.

Disk Administrator

The Windows NT Disk Administrator is a GUI tool that you can use to manage disks on Windows NT systems (see Figure 2.5). You can accomplish the following tasks with this tool:

- Create and delete disk partitions.
- Manage disk volumes.
- Create and delete logical drives.
- Format disk partitions for FAT or NTFS.
- Manage raw partitions.
- Configure RAID with various configurations as described in the following sections.

To start Disk Administrator, choose Start, Programs, Administrative Tools (Common),

FIGURE 2.5

You must be a member of the administrators group to use the Disk Administrator.

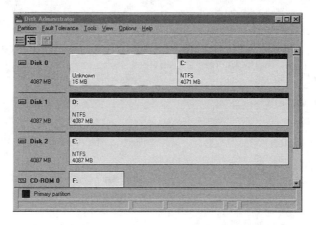

Disk Administrator, or run windisk.exe from the winnt\system32 folder.

Don't change the drive letters associated with Disk Administrator because Oracle uses entries in the Windows NT Registry that become invalid when the drive letters are changed.

Common RAID Levels in Oracle8 Installations

By using Disk Administrator, you can configure various RAID configurations. The most common configurations are as follows:

- *RAID level 0* enables high-performance, nonfault tolerance disk striping. It places multiple physical disks into one logical whole. Data operations are broken into [#ofdrives] chunks, and all disks are simultaneously accessed. It doesn't provide fault tolerance, however; when one disk fails, the whole logical volume fails and must be restored from a backup.

- In *RAID level 1*, also referred to as *disk mirroring*, every write is duplicated on another drive. This causes a performance penalty but provides fault tolerance; if the mirrored disk fails, the mirrored drive is brought online in real time. The mirror configuration is re-established after the faulted drive is replaced.

- *RAID 0+1* mixes RAID 0 and RAID 1 to provide high performance and fault tolerance. It enables mirroring of an array of striped hard disks.

- *RAID 5* provides a cost-effective alternative to disk mirroring. Multiple hard disks are combined into a striped logical volume as in RAID 1, but each drive contains parity information so that any single drive failure is tolerated. With one drive failure, the RAID 5 system allows continued access, but performance suffers.

To Do: Create a Raw Partition on Windows NT

Disk Administrator can be used to set up different disk configurations. Raw partitions can also be created using this tool. After you install Oracle on FAT or NTFS file systems, but before you create the tablespaces that belong to datafiles or put the log files on raw devices, you have to create the raw partitions on Windows NT. To do that, follow these steps:

1. Go into Disk Administrator in the Administrative Tools. If you already have free space there, single-click it.

> If you don't have free space, you have to delete a partition that you don't need anymore. To do so, select the drive that you don't want anymore, and then choose Delete from the Partition menu.

2. From the Partition menu, choose Create in the Create Primary Partition screen. Create the partition equal to the size of the file plus 1MB, and then click OK.

▼ 3. Repeat step 2 to create the new unformatted partitions for the other files.

▼ 4. From the Partition menu, choose Commit Changes Now to save the changes.

5. Each partition now is represented by a drive letter, such as E: or I:, and you can
   locate one file on each. Because the log files are I/O intensive, you might want to

▲   put them on raw partitions.

You must locate log files on raw partitions at the time of database creation. For example,

```
CREATE DATABASE CONTROLFILE REUSE LOGFILE GROUP 1 ('\\.\e:')
➥size 14M, GROUP 2 ('\\.\i:') size 14M;
```

creates a database with the log files located on raw partitions \\.\e: and \\.\i: of size
15MB. Always leave 1MB to avoid writing data to cylinder 0 of the disk.

To create data tablespaces mapped to datafiles on raw partitions, use

```
CREATE TABLESPACE DATA DATAFILE '\\.\f:' SIZE 49M;
```

This creates a 49MB tablespace on raw partition \\.\f:, with a size of 50MB. (Again,
leave 1MB to avoid cylinder 0.)

When creating a datafile that will use the raw device, make sure that the datafile is
smaller than the size of the device. For example, if you create a 100MB raw partition,
don't allocate a datafile of size 100MB. Instead, allocate a datafile of 99MB. The usual
rule of thumb is to leave 1MB unused. Following this rule ensures that you won't write
over the disk's cylinder 0.

The use of raw partitions involves a potential problem—the OS won't protect cylinder 0
of the disk if it's part of the raw partition. To prevent this, make sure that the raw partition used by Oracle doesn't start at cylinder 0. If you try to create a tablespace on a raw
partition with a size equal to the size of the raw partition, you will receive the following
error messages:

```
ORA-01119, 00000, "error in creating database file '\\.\k:' //
*Cause: Usually due to not having enough space on the device.
```

```
ORA-09200: Sfccf: error creating file OSD-04008: Writefile()
failure, unable to write to file(OS 87)
```

Event Viewer

NEW TERM The Event Viewer is a Windows NT GUI tool that allows administrators to use
system alert messages and to set up alerts to automate a reaction to those alerts
(see Figure 2.6). This tool can be used to monitor events. An *event* is an important occurrence in the system or application that needs user notification. Usually, not very critical

events are stored in the Event Viewer. Oracle has integrated with this tool and provides information such as startup/shutdown and OS audit trail in the application and the security log.

FIGURE 2.6

The system log of the Event Viewer shows system-generated events.

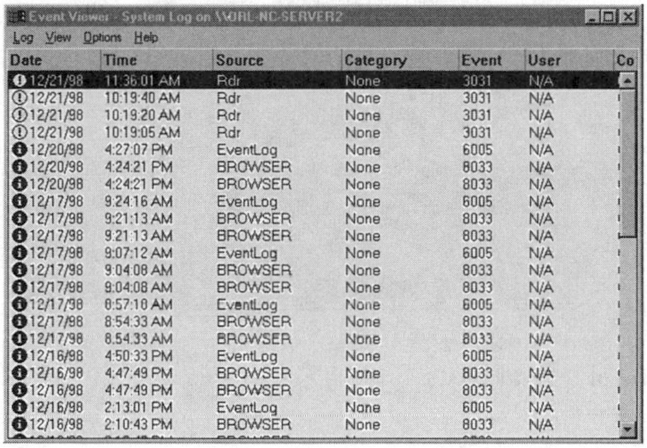

To access the Event Viewer, choose Start, Program, Administrative Tools (Common), Event Viewer, or run eventvwr.exe from the winnt\system32 folder.

> Event logging in the Event Viewer is controlled by the Eventlog service. This service can be controlled from the Services applet in the Control Panel.

Recorded Oracle8 database events include the following (see Figures 2.7 and 2.8):

- Initialization of the SGA for the active instance
- Initialization of the PGA for the background processes of the active instance

FIGURE 2.7

The application log of the Event Viewer shows application-specific events.

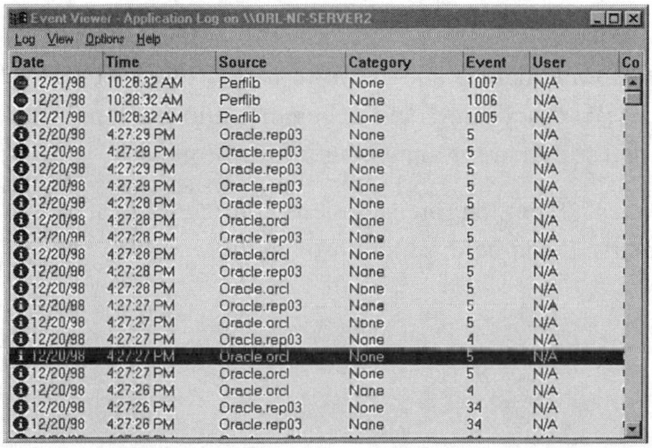

FIGURE 2.8

Event details shown by the Event Viewer.

Events can be of several types:

- Error
- Warning
- Information
- Success Audit
- Failure Audit

Event Viewer has three types of log files:

- *System*—Events generated by Windows NT services and drives are contained here, for example, the inability to load a device driver.
- *Security*—When auditing is enabled (audit policy in User Manager), the security log contains auditing information, for example, whether an unauthorized person is trying to access a file.
- *Application*—Events generated by applications such as Oracle, for example, database startup and shutdown.

You can obtain event details and get information such as the date/time of event, event identification, text description, and debugging information. Events can be filtered, rearranged, and searched for analyzing information.

The Windows NT event logging service is configured to start automatically every time the system starts. It can be disabled through the Control Panel.

The following are definitions of each column displayed in the Event Viewer window:

Date   The date on which the event occurred.

Time   The time at which the event occurred.

Source   Identifies the software that logged the event, which can be
                        an application such as Oracle or a system component.

Category   An event classification generated by the source of the
                        event. The source isn't required to classify the event.

Event   A unique number specified by the source of the event.

User   The name of the user logged on at the time of the event
                        occurrence.

Computer   The name of the computer where the event occurred.

By default, the Event Viewer displays all the events in the selected event log. It's possible
to filter events and view only events of certain characteristics. Filtering won't prevent
events from being logged. Filter settings are used only for the current Event Viewer session unless Save Settings on Exit is specified. To enable filtering, choose Filter Events
from the View menu.

You can archive an event log by using the Log menu in any of the following formats:
event log file, text file, and comma-delimited text. Log files previously stored in the
event log file format can be opened through the Log menu. When saved as text or
comma-delimited text, other applications such as spreadsheets can be used to create a
chart out of comma-delimited text. You can configure the settings for each event log to
overwrite events as needed, overwrite events older than so many days, or manually clear
events. By default, the Event Viewer displays the event logs on the local system, but it
also can be configured to view events on other Windows NT machines. The Event
Viewer provides searching and sorting capabilities to simplify event analysis.

All the three event logs are located in \winnt_root\system32\config*.evt.
When the log is saved in text or comma-delimited form, any binary data
associated with events is discarded.

To create a filter in the Event Viewer that shows Oracle-related events, follow these steps:

1. Start the Event Viewer.

2. From the Log menu, choose Application Log.

3. From the View menu, choose Filter Events.

4. In the Filter dialog box (see Figure 2.9), provide the necessary event specifications, such as the time period, event type, user, computer, and event category. Make sure that the source you specify is Oracle80.orcl.

FIGURE 2.9

Events can be filtered.

Performance Monitor

Performance Monitor is a Windows NT tool that provides detailed resource usage information through logging and charting. It also lets you save the logs from a specified time period for future analysis. The information is provided through various counters. Oracle integrated this tool to provide Oracle-specific performance counters such as the library cache hit ratio and disk utilization. You can use Performance Monitor to view the performance of processors, memory, caches, threads, and processes. Table 2.3 shows the various views that can be chosen from the View menu.

TABLE 2.3 PERFORMANCE MONITOR VIEWS

View	Use
Chart view	Displays real-time database activity.
Alert view	Notifies users when specified boundaries of performance activity are passed. In other words, minimum performance isn't being met, or maximum threshold of usage is exceeded.
Log view	Maintains performance records.
Report view	Saves performance information of specified criteria.

To access Performance Monitor, choose Start, Programs, Administrative Tools (Common), Performance Monitor, or run perfmon.exe from the \winnt\system32 folder.

Monitoring Oracle8 Objects

You can monitor the performance of an Oracle8 database instance by using the various objects provided by Performance Monitor. A selected object is associated with a counter color and is placed on the status bar at the bottom of the Performance Monitor.

To add objects to a view, follow these steps:

1. From the Edit menu, choose Add to *Object* View.

2. From the Add to *Object* dialog box (see Figure 2.10), choose the object you want to track, and click the Add button.

3. Repeat step 2 for each object that you want to track. When finished, click Done.

FIGURE 2.10

Adding objects to the charts.

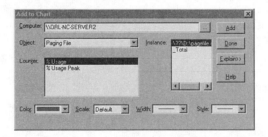

All the Oracle8 system resources that you can track are prefixed with ORACLE. These resources are defined in %ORACLE_HOME%\DBS\PERF.ORA. Table 2.4 shows the various objects and associated counters that can be tracked.

TABLE 2.4 COMMONLY USED OBJECTS IN PERFORMANCE MONITOR

Object	Counter
Oracle8 buffer cache	Phyrds/gets %
Oracle8 data dictionary cache	Getmisses/gets %
Oracle8 datafiles	Phyrds/sec
	Phywrts/sec
Oracle8 redo log buffer	Redo log space requests
Oracle8 DBWR stats1	Buffers scanned/sec
	LRU scans/sec

continues

TABLE 2.4   CONTINUED

Object	Counter
Oracle8 DBWR stats2	Timeouts/sec
	Checkpoints/sec
Oracle8 Dynamic space management	Recursive calls/sec
Oracle8 free list	Free list waits/request %
Oracle8 library cache	Reloads/pins %
Oracle8 sorts	Sorts in memory/sec
	Sorts on disk/sec

On Windows NT, the Oracle background and user processes run as threads of the main Oracle process. These threads can be monitored for several counter statistics, including

- % Privileged time
- % Processor time
- ID Process
- ID Thread
- Context switches/sec
- Priority base
- Priority current

For each process, Performance Monitor numbers its threads, starting at 0, and increments by one for each thread spawned by the process. Internally, threads are stored hexadecimally, so you need a function such as hex2dec() to convert the thread IDs to their decimal equivalent. Listing 2.1 shows how hex2dec() can be implemented. This function takes a hexidecimal value and returns a decimal value.

LISTING 2.1   IMPLEMENTING hex2dec()

```
CREATE OR REPLACE FUNCTION hex2dec (hexval in char) RETURN number IS
    cur number;
    cur_val char(1);
    cur_val_dec number;
    numdigits number;
    result number := 0;

    BEGIN
    if hexval is not null then numdigits := length(hexval);

    for cur in 1..numdigits loop
```

```
        cur_val := SUBSTR(hexval, cur, 1);
        if cur_val in ('A','B','C','D','E','F') then
            cur_val_dec := ascii(cur_val) - ascii('A') + 10;
        else
            cur_val_dec := to_number(cur_val);
        end if;
        result := (result * 16) + cur_val_dec;
    end loop;
    else result := '';
    end if;
return result;
END;
```

The following query can be useful in determining the thread IDs and other information for the background and user processes:

```
SELECT hex2dec(p.spid) "Thread ID",b.name "Background Process",
    s.username "User Name",s.osuser "OS User",s.status "STATUS",
    s.program "OS Program"
FROM v$process p, v$bgprocess b, v$session s
WHERE s.paddr = p.addr and b.paddr(+) = p.addr;
```

The query's output can be interpreted as follows:

- Thread ID value corresponds to the Thread ID counter of the Thread object.
- Background Process corresponds to the Oracle Background process.
- User Name is the name of the connected database user.
- OS User is the operating system account of the user connected to the database.
- Status displays the status of the user session.
- OS Program is the operating system executable program being executed.

The following steps can be performed after the preceding query is executed:

1. Start Oracle8's Performance Monitor.
2. From the Edit menu, choose Edit/Add to Chart.
3. In the Instance column, choose the Oracle8 thread.
4. From the Counter menu, choose ID Thread.
5. Add the thread ID of the thread and any other counters that you want to monitor.

> The thread IDs associated with user connections are valid only while the user connection is valid. After the user disconnects, the thread IDs are renumbered.

> When Performance Monitor starts, it looks at the Registry parameter
> ORACLE_SID and shows you the performance counters for only that instance.
> If you want to monitor multiple Oracle instances, you must change the set-
> ting for ORACLE_SID before starting a new Performance Monitor session.

The Oracle Performance Monitor in Windows NT shows information of only one
instance at a time. The default is set to the instance ORCL. To change the default, follow
these steps:

1. Run REGEDT32 to start the Windows NT Registry.

2. Go to HKEY_LOCAL_MACHINE on the local machine. From there, go to SYSTEM\
   CURRENTCONTROLSET\SERVICES\OracleHOME181\Performance (see Figure 2.11).

3. Change the HOSTNAME value to the instance that you want to monitor.

FIGURE 2.11

*Performance entries in
the Registry.*

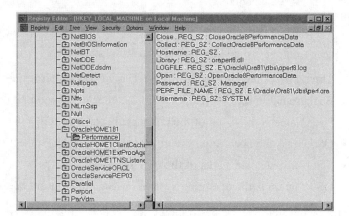

User Manager

User Manager is a GUI tool that you can use to manage security and users on a Windows
NT system (see Figure 2.12). User Manager allows you to perform several tasks, including

- Creating and managing Windows NT users
- Creating and managing local and global NT groups
- Performing OS-level auditing
- Managing passwords

FIGURE 2.12

User Manager showing the built-in accounts.

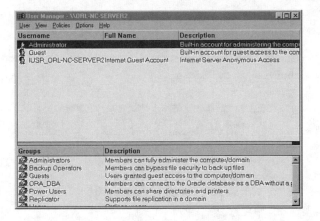

To start User Manager, choose Start, Programs, Administrative Tool (Common), User Manager, or run musrmgr.exe from the \winnt\system32 folder.

Through Windows NT's User Manager, Oracle allows the external assignment of database roles. The roles are created within Oracle but are associated with Windows NT user accounts by a Windows NT administrator outside Oracle. This strategy is limited in that it's an all-or-nothing feature; if it's used, all the roles must be externally assigned.

To Do: Create a Windows NT Account

To perform routine tasks on your Windows NT system, you need a local Windows NT account with sufficient administrative privileges. User Manager for Domains is a Windows NT tool that can be used to create Windows NT accounts.

1. Choose Start, Programs, Administrative Tools (Common), User Manager for Domains.

2. From the User menu, choose Select Domain. Type the name of the server in the dialog box, and click OK.

3. From the User menu, choose New User. In the New User dialog box (see Figure 2.13), specify the following information about the new user:

    - *Username*—The Windows NT login name for the new user. This isn't case sensitive.

    - *Full Name*—The name of the user. It's more like a description and is optional.

    - *Description*—Usually used to provide comments such as a job title.

▼ • *Password*—Any word up to 14 characters long that's associated with the user login. It's case sensitive.

• *Confirm Password*—Retype the password you provided and confirm your choice.

FIGURE 2.13

Creating a new Windows NT user.

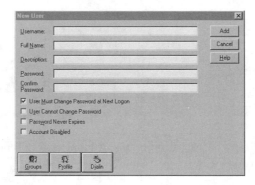

4. For the user account you're trying to create, you can select several options as needed:

   • User Must Change Password at Next Logon
   • User Cannot Change Password
   • Password Never Expires
   • Account Disabled

5. Click Add to create the user. The user creation dialog box still remains and allows you to create more user accounts.

6. After you create all the desired user accounts, click Cancel to exit the dialog box.

▲ 7. From the User menu, choose Exit to exit the User Manager for Domains tool.

To Do: Give Administrative Privileges to a Windows NT Account

By default, when a new user account is created, it becomes a member of the Users group. This group doesn't have administrative privileges. To give administrative privileges to an existing Windows NT account, follow these steps:

1. By using the local Administrative account, log on to the system.

2. Choose Start, Programs, Administrative Tools (Common), User Manager for Domains.

3. From the User menu, choose Select Domain. Type the name of the server in the dialog box, and click OK.
▼

▼   4. From the user list that appears, select the user that needs administrative privileges.

5. From the User menu, choose Properties to display the User Properties sheet.

6. Click the Groups button to display the Group Memberships dialog box (see Figure 2.14).

FIGURE 2.14

Assigning group membership to users.

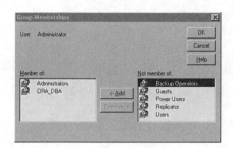

7. From the Not Member Of list, select Administrators, and then click the Add button to make the user a member of the administrators group.

8. Click OK, and then click OK again to exit the User Properties sheet.

▲   9. From the User menu, choose Exit to exit User Manager for Domains.

Windows NT Diagnostics

The graphical Windows NT Diagnostics tool, winmsd.exe, displays computer hardware and operating system information, including the following:

- Services and devices, along with their status (see Figure 2.15)
- Environment variables
- Operating system version and service pack information (see Figure 2.16)
- Network statistics
- Information about physical and virtual memory (see Figure 2.17)

FIGURE 2.15

Obtaining information about services.

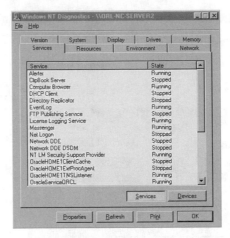

FIGURE 2.16

Obtaining version information.

FIGURE 2.17

Obtaining memory information.

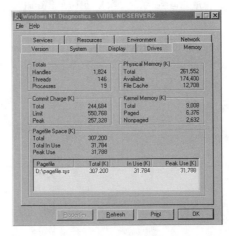

To access this tool, choose Start, Program, Administrative Tools (Common), Windows NT Diagnostics, or run winmsd.exe from the \winnt\system32 folder.

> To access diagnostics for a remote computer named ntmachine1, specify the machine name as a parameter to the winmsd command:
>
> `C:\> winmsd \\ntmachine1`

Repair Disk Utility

Windows NT provides a very important tool in the Repair Disk Utility (see Figure 2.18); it allows you to save your current system settings to an emergency repair disk that you can use to recover the operating system from catastrophic failures. The emergency repair disk contains system-dependent information and should be updated by using the Repair Disk Utility every time you make major changes to your system hardware or software configuration.

FIGURE 2.18

Using the Repair Disk Utility.

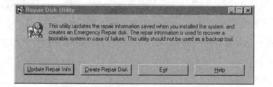

To start the Repair Disk Utility, choose Start, Programs, Administrative Tools (Common), Repair Disk, or run rdisk.exe from the \winnt\system32 folder.

You can use the Repair Disk Utility in various situations:

- To repair the Windows NT Registry
- To fix damaged system files
- To undo undesired configuration changes

> You can't use an emergency repair disk from one machine to repair another machine. The emergency repair disk is machine-dependent because it contains machine-specific information.

To Do: Create a Windows NT Repair Disk with RDISK

The importance of the emergency repair disk can't be overstressed. It can save your data from catastrophic failures such as damaged or corrupted system files. If you haven't already created an emergency repair disk during the installation of Windows NT, use the following steps to create one:

1. Choose Start, Run. Type Rdisk in the Run dialog box, and click OK.

2. To create a new emergency repair disk, place a blank formatted disk in the floppy drive, and then click Create Repair Disk. (To update an emergency repair disk, place the disk in the floppy drive, and then click Update Repair Info.)

3. When the process is complete, exit the Repair Disk Utility.

You should update the emergency repair disk after making important changes to the system.

To Do: Recover a Damaged Windows NT Configuration with the Emergency Repair Disk

You can use the emergency repair disk with the Windows NT setup disk to recover from situations such as damaged or corrupted system files, Registry damage, or a forgotten administrative password. Follow these steps:

1. Insert Windows NT setup disk #1, and reboot the system.

2. In the Welcome to Setup screen, choose the R (Repair) option.

3. Choose one of the following options, and click Continue:

   - Inspect Registry files
   - Inspect Startup Environment
   - Verify Windows NT System Files
   - Inspect Boot Sector

4. When prompted for Setup disk #3, insert the disk and press Enter.

5. When prompted for the repair disk, insert the repair disk and press Enter.

6. Depending on the problem with the system, select the components to restore. Click Continue and then press Enter.

7. Remove the repair disk from the floppy drive, and reboot the computer.

Windows NT Task Manager

Task Manager is a GUI utility that you can use to get a quick idea of your system's CPU and memory usage (see Figure 2.19). Processes and programs running on your system can be monitored and controlled by using this utility. Task Manager's most common use is to shut down hung applications. To access Task Manager, press Ctrl+Alt+Delete, or run taskmgr.exe from the \winnt\system32 folder (see Figure 2.20).

FIGURE 2.19

Obtaining process information from Task Manager.

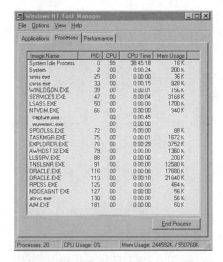

FIGURE 2.20

Obtaining performance information from Task Manager.

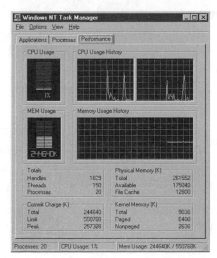

2

Don't use Task Manager to shut down an Oracle database instance because this is equivalent to a shutdown abort.

Windows NT Explorer

The Windows NT Explorer is a GUI tool that has replaced File Manager in earlier versions of Windows. It can be used for various tasks:

- Managing files and folders (directories) on your local system or on machines across the network
- Mapping drive letters to network devices
- Using file-level security on NTFS file systems
- Sharing folders with other machines
- Using folders shared by other machines

To start Explorer, choose Start, Programs, Windows NT Explorer, or run explorer.exe from \winnt\system32 folder.

Other Windows NT Tools

Windows NT provides the Add/Remove applet under the Control Panel, which you can use to install or uninstall most software on Windows NT. Add/Remove shouldn't be used to install or uninstall Oracle software, however; it can result in improper install/uninstall of Oracle because some components might not be properly removed. Use the Oracle installer to install and uninstall Oracle.

Windows NT provides two text editors, Notepad and Wordpad, that you can use to edit files.

Obtaining Help on Windows NT Networking Commands

Windows NT networking commands begin with the word net. For help on any net command, type net help followed by the command (see Figure 2.21). For example,

```
C:> net help computer
```

FIGURE 2.21

Using net help *commands.*

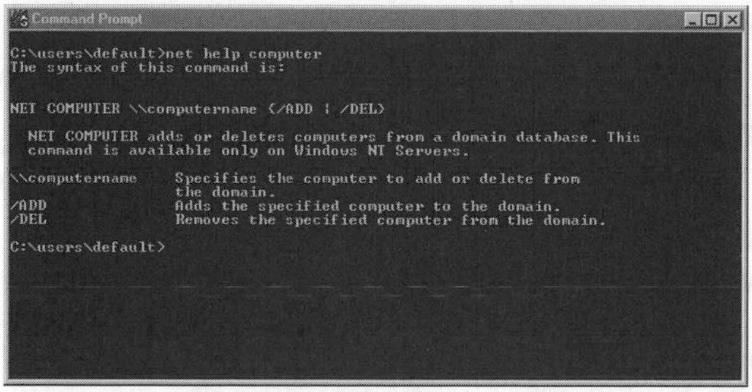

Summary

Several Windows NT tools can help you administer Oracle databases on Windows NT. This lesson looks at several useful Windows NT tools, such as the User Manager, Disk Administrator, Registry Editor, and Performance Monitor. You will be using these tools more in later chapters and will learn how you can integrate and simplify the administration of Oracle with Windows NT.

Q&A

Q Oracle also provides a Performance Monitor. How is it different from the Windows NT Performance Monitor?

A Oracle's Performance Monitor shows Oracle-specific objects. Windows NT's Performance Monitor shows Oracle objects, in addition to other operating system objects that you can use to determine overall system performance.

Q Should I make system changes by using different applets of the Control Panel, or should I use the Registry Editor?

A Don't make direct changes with the Registry Editor unless you know what you're doing. Directly changing the Registry can potentially prevent Windows NT from booting. You should use tools from the Control Panel to make such changes safely.

Workshop

The Workshop contains quiz questions and activities to help reinforce what you've learned in this hour. You can check Appendix A for the answers (but don't peek!).

Quiz

1. Which Windows NT tool can you use to start Oracle services?
2. Where is information about all the Oracle variables kept in Windows NT?
3. Which log in Event Viewer contains Oracle-related messages?
4. What tool can be used to create raw partitions?
5. What happens when the `OracleServiceORCL` service is started?

Exercises

1. Set the page file size of your system to twice the amount of physical memory.
2. Set the default `ORACLE_SID` for your Windows NT machine in the Registry.

HOUR 3

Configuring a Windows NT Server for Oracle8i

Configuration of Windows NT for Oracle8i is a step that many people don't take very seriously. Most of the time the system requirements are not very clear at the beginning of a project, and usually a lot of configuration changes are made to systems *after* the system is in production. This approach can lead to many headaches and dissatisfied users because the performance and security of the system will be jeopardized.

This hour looks at some important decisions that you have to make in order to implement a system that would be optimal for your environment:

- Choosing whether to use workgroups or domains
- Choosing a Windows NT workstation versus a Windows NT server
- Setting up trusts in Windows NT domains
- Understanding service packs
- Understanding the emergency repair process

Making the Choices

Many decisions made when installing Oracle8 on Windows NT are similar to those made when installing Oracle8 on other platforms. Several questions have to be answered:

- *What else will be running on this server in addition to Oracle8?* Non-database–related activities on the server could detract from the task of measuring the database's performance.

- *Does the database have a potential for growth?* If you anticipate that the database will grow over a period of time, you should consider scalable solutions, choose hardware vendors carefully, and concentrate on easy-to-upgrade systems.

- *Does the system use Intel or Alpha?* Intel and Alpha processors will be supported for a long time into the future. However, other factors must be considered when you're making the choice. Intel processors have the advantage in that they are extremely popular and the price-to-performance ratio keeps improving. On the other hand, the Alpha is a 64-bit RISC processor and is the fastest in the industry. Windows NT is more scalable on the Alpha.

- *Should you use more than one CPU?* Windows NT now supports up to four CPUs in a single system for most platforms and up to six CPUs on some systems. You can take advantage of Oracle8's parallel DDL (data definition language) and DML (data manipulation language) capabilities by using a machine with at least two CPUs.

- *Which file system should I use?* Performance differs very little, using FAT or NTFS. The file system must be chosen based on considerations such as the following:

Security	Because the FAT file system doesn't provide file-level security, when a user is connected to the NT server, he has full access to any FAT file. NTFS provides file-level security.
Max File Size	FAT allows a maximum file size of 4GB (16GB for Windows NT 4.0), and NTFS allows a maximum file size of 16 exabytes. (An *exabyte* is a billion gigabytes—that is, a quintillion bytes—and is equal to two to the 60th power).
Performance	Performance is better when using FAT for smaller disk volumes, and NTFS is better for disk volumes greater than 200MB.

The following recommendations can improve performance:

- Use FAT for the initial boot partition (unless you need file-level security, in which case use NTFS).
- Place the Oracle executables on FAT.
- Place system, log, and data files on NTFS.
- Raw partitions can be used for I/O bound systems.

To Do: Convert the Boot Partition from FAT to NTFS

If you plan to use file-level security, you must use the NTFS file system. Follow these steps to convert your existing boot partition from FAT to NTFS:

1. Log on as administrator.

2. From the command prompt, use the `convert` utility on the boot partition, where the c: drive is the boot partition:

   ```
   C:> convert c: /fs:ntfs
   ```

   You should receive a message indicating that the conversion isn't possible now because the operating system is using it and there is a sharing violation (see Figure 3.1).

FIGURE 3.1

A sharing violation occurs when you try to convert the boot partition to NTFS.

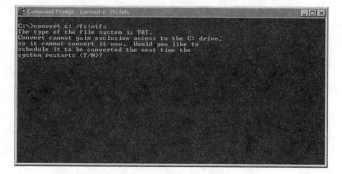

3. When prompted to schedule the conversion at the next restart of the computer, type **y** and press Enter.

4. Restart the computer. The conversion from FAT to NTFS occurs during the restart.

5. Log on again as administrator.

6. Start the Windows NT Explorer.

7. Right-click the c: drive, and choose Properties.

8. Verify that the c: drive is now on the NTFS file system.

To convert your file system from NTFS back to FAT or HPFS, you should back up the drive, reformat it, and then restore the files to the drive.

To Do: Use NTFS Compression

NTFS allows you to use file compression dynamically. This is different from ZIP files that need manual intervention. NTFS allows you to specify directories or entire drives on which you need to apply compression. The compression and decompression of files is automatic and can be achieved as follows:

1. Log on to the Windows NT machine as administrator.

2. Start the Windows NT Explorer.

3. Note the free space available on the c: drive.

4. Right-click the c: drive and select Properties.

5. Select the Compress check box and click Apply (see Figure 3.2).

FIGURE 3.2

Select the Compress check box to specify that this folder needs to be compressed.

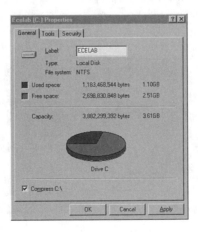

6. Select the Also Compress Subfolders check box and click OK.

7. From the View menu, choose Options.

8. On the View page, select the Display Compressed Files and Folders with Alternate Color check box and click OK (see Figure 3.3).

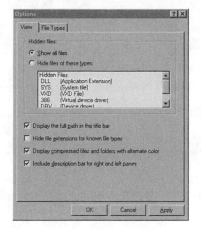

FIGURE 3.3

Set your view options so that you can see the compressed files in the Explorer.

9. Verify that the files have been compressed.

10. Note the free space now available on the c: drive.

To Do: Uncompress a Compressed Folder

NTFS compression allows easy management of files and saves space at the expense of a slight cost. The decompression process is as follows:

1. Log on to the Windows NT machine as administrator.

2. Start the Windows NT Explorer.

3. Expand the c: drive, and select the folder that needs to be uncompressed.

4. Right-click the folder and choose Properties.

5. Clear the Compress check box and click OK.

6. Select the Auto Uncompress Subfolders check box and click OK.

7. Refresh the display, and note that the files have been uncompressed. Also note the change in available free space.

To Do: Copy Files from a Compressed Folder to an Uncompressed Folder

When you copy a file, it inherits the compression attributes of the target folder. To copy a file, follow these steps:

1. Log on to the Windows NT machine as administrator.

2. Start the Windows NT Explorer.

3. Expand the c: drive, and select the folder that contains compressed files.

▼   4. Copy a file from this compressed folder to an uncompressed folder.

    5. Highlight the file in the uncompressed folder.

▲   6. Verify the compression properties of the file copied by choosing File, Properties.

The file will be uncompressed, which indicates that when you copy a file, it will inherit the compression attributes of the target folder.

To Do: Move Files from a Compressed Folder to an Uncompressed Folder

When you move a file, it retains its compression attributes from the source folder. Follow these steps to move a file:

1. Log on to the Windows NT machine as administrator.

2. Start the Windows NT Explorer.

3. Expand the c: drive, and select the folder that contains compressed files.

4. Move a file from this compressed folder to an uncompressed folder.

5. Highlight the file in the uncompressed folder.

▲ 6. Verify the compression properties of the file moved by choosing File, Properties.

The file will be compressed, which indicates that when you move a file, it will retain its compression attributes from the source folder.

To Do: Remove an NTFS Partition

The CONVERT utility can't be used to change an NTFS-formatted drive to another file system if any of the following is true:

- If Windows NT isn't installed on the NTFS partition you're trying to remove, you can use the Disk Administrator to remove the partition or run the FORMAT command from the Windows NT prompt.

- If Windows NT is installed on the NTFS partition you're trying to remove, the following steps can be taken:

    1. Place the Windows NT setup disk #1 in the floppy drive.

    2. Restart the computer.

    3. Choose Custom Installation.

    4. Press N to select a new location for the Windows NT install.

    5. When prompted for the partition to install Windows NT, select the NTFS partition you're trying to reformat, and press D to delete the partition.

    6. Continue with the setup program to re-create and format the partition as desired.

▲   7. Exit the setup.

How much memory should you have? 64MB is the bare minimum, and 128MB is the practical minimum for running Oracle8i on Windows NT. In reality, the decision regarding the amount of memory should be based on SGA size. For best performance, SGA should fit entirely into physical memory along with Windows NT; otherwise, there will be a lot of paging in the system, causing performance degradation. The SGA size depends on factors such as number of users, database size (in megabytes), and system load during peak times.

Basic Hardware Needs for Using Oracle on Windows NT

The basic hardware components you should have when running Oracle8i on Windows NT include the following:

- An uninterruptible power supply (UPS)—In case of a power outage, Windows NT can run a script file to perform an immediate database shutdown followed by the system shutdown to allow an overall clean shutdown.
- A CD-ROM drive—Oracle8 on Windows NT is available only on CD-ROM.
- A tape drive—You need one to perform backups.

Any hardware you choose for your system must be on the hardware compatibility list, which can be obtained from `http:/www.microsoft.com/hwtest` or the Windows NT Resource Kit.

To Do: Configure UPS

I hope that you are convinced already that an uninterruptible power supply is important to your overall strategy for protecting your data. The following steps make use of the UPS:

1. Physically connect the UPS to your system on an available serial port such as COM1 or COM2, and note the port you're using.

2. Choose Start, Settings, Control Panel.

3. Double-click Control Panel's UPS icon.

4. Mark the Uninterruptible Power Supply Is Installed On check box, and select the serial port to which it's connected (see Figure 3.4).

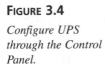

FIGURE 3.4

Configure UPS through the Control Panel.

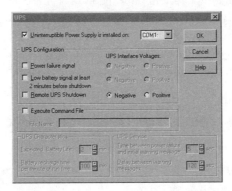

5. Refer to your UPS installation manual, and specify negative or positive UPS interface voltage, based on your particular UPS's capabilities. You should understand several options available:

   - *Power Failure Signal*—Selecting this option causes it to send a warning to Windows NT when the AC power fails. This works only if the UPS can send a positive or negative charge on the "clear to send" portion of the serial port.

   - *Low Battery Signal at Least 2 Minutes Before Shutdown*—When this option is selected, it sends a warning to Windows NT when the UPS's battery is running at lower than a threshold voltage. This works only if the UPS can send a positive or negative charge on the "data carrier detect" portion of the serial port.

   - *Remote UPS Shutdown*—When selected, this option allows a server to be shut down from another Windows NT workstation or server. This works only if the UPS can send a positive or negative charge on the "data terminal ready" portion of the serial port.

6. Specify a file to execute before system shutdown by using the Execute Command File option. This will execute the specified file that must reside in the System32 subdirectory under the Windows NT home directory.

7. Several options can be specified in the UPS characteristics portion:

   - *Expected battery life*—This option specifies the number of minutes the UPS battery is expected to function.

   - *Battery recharge time per minute of runtime*—The UPS battery recharges itself while it runs. Refer to your UPS installation manual to find out how much to specify as the amount of running time it would need for the UPS to recharge itself.

▼   8. Use the UPS service options to specify the expected behavior from the UPS:

   - *Time between power failure and initial warning message*—Specify the time delay between the detection of a power failure and when a warning message is sent to users.

   - *Delay between warning message*—Specify the time interval between consecutive transmissions of warning messages after the detection of a power failure.

▲   9. Click OK to save the settings.

Windows NT Workstation Versus Windows NT Server

3

Commercially, Windows NT is available in two packages: Windows NT Workstation and Windows NT Server. The core operating system is the same on both packages, but the capabilities are markedly different. Basically, Windows NT Server is more powerful, and its features are a superset of the capabilities you can obtain from Windows NT Workstation.

Workstation and Server have the following similarities:

- Run on multiple platforms such as Intel, DEC Alpha, RISC, and so forth.
- Support symmetric multiprocessing.
- Multitasking and multi-threading capabilities.
- Security features include mandatory logon, discretionary access control, auditing, and memory protection between processes.
- Support for MS-DOS–based, Win16-based, OS/2-based, and POSIX-compliant–based applications.
- Provide built-in networking.
- Support 4GB of RAM and 16EB of hard disk space.
- Support FAT, HPFS, NTFS, and CDFS.
- Can be used as the file server, print server, and application server.
- Can participate in Windows NT domains.

Table 3.1 lists the differences in the capabilities of the Workstation and Server software.

TABLE 3.1 COMPARING WINDOWS NT WORKSTATION AND WINDOWS NT SERVER SOFTWARE

Windows NT Workstation	Windows NT Server
Cannot act as a domain controller.	Can act as a domain controller.
Only one session for remote access.	Up to 64 sessions for remote access.
Supports only import for file replication.	Supports both import and export for file replication.
Domain logon validation is unavailable for clients.	Domain logon validation is available for clients.
Macintosh services are available.	Macintosh services are unavailable.
No disk fault tolerance.	Disk fault tolerance is available.
Uses the following services: Alerter, computer browser, Clipbook, directory replicator, event log, messenger, network DDE, RAS, stripe sets, server, volume sets, and workstation.	Uses the following services: Alerter, computer browser, Clipbook, directory replicator, event log, messenger, network DDE, RAS, stripe sets, server, volume sets, Workstation Plus, Services for Macintosh, mirroring/duplexing (RAID 1), and striping with parity (RAID 5).
Trust capabilities are available.	Trust capabilities are unavailable.
Decentralized user profiles.	Centralized user profiles.
Domain administration tools are unavailable.	Domain administration tools are available.

As far as Oracle8i is concerned, you can use either Workstation or Server unless you plan to use the Oracle Parallel Server option, in which case you have to use Windows NT Server. Performance is about the same up to 10 user connections; for a larger number of concurrent user connections, you are better off using Windows NT Server.

Workgroups and Domains

You can configure Windows NT systems in a workgroup or a domain environment. The choice of system configuration can affect the use of distributed databases and the security of the database system. Table 3.2 compares the workgroup and domain models.

TABLE 3.2 COMPARING THE WORKGROUP AND DOMAIN MODELS

Workgroup Model	Domain Model
Decentralized account administration.	Centralized account administration.
Simple design and implementation.	Design and implementation are more involved.
Doesn't require a Windows NT server machine as a domain controller.	Requires the use of a Windows NT server machine as a domain controller.
Resources can be distributed.	Resources can be distributed.
Decentralized security.	Centralized security.
Used for a limited number of workstations in close proximity.	Used for a large number of Windows NT systems that can be separated by long distances.

Workgroup Model

The workgroup model uses distributed administration because both the resources and administration in a workgroup environment are distributed throughout the network and managed by individual Windows NT machines that compose the workgroup.

The workgroup model is also referred to as a *peer-to-peer network* because every computer has its own accounts, administration, and security policies. Each machine also can share its resources, as well as access resources that other machines have shared. In other words, no one machine has control over other machines.

> In a workgroup model, each new account must be added to each machine separately.

In a workgroup environment, users must meet the following two criteria to access resources shared by other machines:

- Each user must have an account on the machine that's sharing the resource or have guest access to the resource.
- Users must be given appropriate access to the resources either directly or via a group membership.

Domain Model

A domain model provides centralized administration for accounts, resources, and security. When using a domain model, a user is authenticated by the primary domain controller (PDC) and then has access to all resources available in the domain. The user account is created only once and is maintained by the primary domain controller. However, resources can be distributed.

In a domain model, a Windows NT machine can perform one of the following functions:

- Primary domain controller (PDC)—Every domain has a machine referred to as the primary domain controller that provides domain logon validation for the domain accounts. The primary domain controller must be a Windows NT server.
- Backup domain controller (BDC)—A domain contains one or more backup domain controllers. User and security information is propagated from the primary domain controller to the backup domain controllers. If a PDC fails, BDCs have the required account information. One backup domain controller is chosen to act as the primary domain controller and starts providing domain logon validation for new connections.
- Windows NT machines—Both Windows NT workstations and servers can be part of a domain.

You can configure Windows NT systems in a variety of domain models. Four models are popular:

- The *single domain model* uses only one domain. The limitation of about 50,000 accounts per domain can become a problem for large companies, but for smaller companies, this model works very well.
- The *master domain model* uses several domains, each with its own primary domain controller. One domain acts as the central administrative unit and contains the accounts database, and the other domains act as resource domains and contain resources.
- The *multiple master domain model* uses several master domains, among which account information is distributed. This model is well suited for very large companies and makes use of the "trust" concept (discussed in the following section).
- The *complete trust model* derives its name from the use of trust between each and every domain. There is no master domain; each domain performs its own administration.

Using Trust in Windows NT Domains

NEW TERM *Trust* is an administrative and communication link that allows the sharing of account information between domains. When you use the trust concept between two domains, one domain is the *trusted* domain and the other is the *trusting* domain. Accounts reside in the trusted domain, and the resources they access are in the trusting domain. Users with accounts in trusted domains can be given access rights and permissions in any trusting domain. The physical and logical location of users isn't important as long as they have accounts in the trusted domain.

Trust relationships, when set up, aren't affected by turning off the computers.

 When representing "trust" in a diagram, the arrows point to the trusted (account) domains.

Trusts are nontransitive. For example, if domain A trusts B and domain B trusts C, domain A does not automatically trust domain C.

Using trusts makes it possible for users from one domain to be permitted to use resources in another domain, even if they don't have a user account in the resource domain. This indicates that you must be careful when setting up trusts to protect your system against unauthorized usage. User accounts and global groups also can be used in domains other than the domain where their account resides. Establishing a two-way trust between two domains is equivalent to establishing two one-way trusts.

Trust relationships are enforced by means of passthrough authentication as follows, when a user wants to log on to domain A from a Windows NT workstation in domain B:

1. The user logs on to the workstation in domain B by supplying the domain A specification in the From text box.

2. The primary domain controller in domain B can't authenticate the user and passes the user-supplied information to a server in domain A through trust.

3. The primary domain controller in domain A authenticates the user and passes the security identifier (SID) for the user to the server in domain B.

4. The user can now access the resources in domain B because domain B trusts domain A.

To Do: Promote a BDC to a PDC

To Do

Suppose you realize that the PDC crashed and, on performing some diagnostic test, you find that the hardware is bad. Replacing the hardware will take at least a couple days. You therefore need to promote a BDC to a PDC:

1. Make sure that the PDC is shut down and turned off.
2. From the BDC, start Server Manager from Windows NT Administrative Tools.
3. Select the BDC.
4. From the Computer menu, choose Promote to Primary Domain Controller.
5. Click Yes to confirm the desired change.
6. Click OK.
7. Exit the Windows NT Server Manager.

To Do: Restore the PDC When It Is Repaired

To Do

The following steps must be performed from the PDC:

1. Start the PDC computer.
2. Log on as the administrator. Because this machine was originally a PDC, you receive a warning message indicating that it can't assume the role of a PDC because another machine is acting as a PDC.
3. Click OK.
4. Start Server Manager from the Administrative Tools group.
5. Select the original PDC (this machine should be shown as being unavailable).
6. From the Computer menu, choose Demote to Backup Domain Controller.
7. Click Yes to confirm the change.
8. Select the original PDC you just demoted.
9. From the Computer menu, choose Promote to Primary Domain Controller.
10. Click Yes to confirm the change.
11. Exit the Windows NT Server Manager.

This will change the original PDC to again become the PDC while the original BDC (which had been acting as the PDC) is demoted back to BDC.

To Do: Synchronize a Backup Domain Controller with a Primary Domain Controller

The backup domain controllers should be synchronized with the primary domain controller so that the same account information exists on all domain controllers. Follow these steps from the PDC:

1. Make sure that you're logged on as the administrator.
2. Start User Manager for Domains.
3. Create a new user account.
4. Exit User Manager.
5. Start the Windows NT Server Manager from the Administrative Tools group.
6. Select the BDC.
7. From the Computer menu, choose Synchronize with Primary Domain Controller.
8. Click Yes to confirm the changes.
9. Click OK when the synchronization is complete.
10. Exit the Windows NT Server Manager.

Perform the following from the BDC to verify that synchronization is complete:

1. Log on as the new user. Successful logon indicates that the synchronization was successful.
2. Log off as the user.

An alternative way to verify that synchronization is complete is to follow these steps:

1. Log on as the administrator.
2. Start the Event Viewer from the Administrative Tools.
3. From the Log menu, choose the System log.
4. Select the most recent NETLOGON event under the Source column.
5. Double-click the event to obtain its detail.
6. Verify that the synchronization is successful.
7. Exit the Event Viewer.

3

To Do: Make a Workstation Part of an Existing Domain

Follow these steps from the Windows NT machine you want to join to the domain:

1. Log on as the administrator.
2. From the Control Panel, double-click the Network icon.
3. On the Identification page, click Change.
4. Click Domain.
5. In the Domain text box, type the domain you want to be a part of.
6. Select the Create a Computer Account In the Domain check box (see Figure 3.5).

FIGURE 3.5

Specify the domain to which the computer should belong.

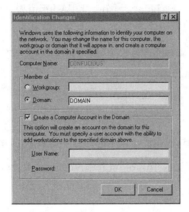

7. Supply the administrator account and password so that the transition can proceed.
8. Click OK to confirm the changes.
9. Close the Network dialog box.
10. Restart the computer.
11. In the Logon dialog box, supply the domain username and password. Also supply the domain to connect to in the From box.
12. A successful logon connects you to the domain, and all the domain resources will be available (provided you have sufficient privileges, as specified by the access control list of the resources).

Viruses are a major source of data loss on most PCs. You should minimize the data risk due to viruses by making sure that files brought to your machine are scanned and deemed virus free. Most virus sources are the result of copying files to or from floppy disks or downloading files or patches from the Internet. Make sure that you're using a tested antivirus software program, such as Norton AntiVirus from Symantec Corporation.

To Do: Install Network Protocols

▲To Do

Windows NT has built-in networking and provides four transport protocols by default: NetBeui, NWLink IPX/SPX, TCP/IP, and DLC. You can add more protocols as necessary and remove those you don't need. The protocols you install work with Oracle Net8 and allow the database to communicate with other client machines.

3

Having protocols installed that you won't be using is a waste of system resources.

Follow these steps to change the protocol bindings:

1. From the Control Panel, double-click the Network icon.

2. The Protocols page lists the currently installed protocols. Click the Add button to display the protocols available for installation. You can also add protocols from a disk (see Figure 3.6).

FIGURE 3.6

Determine the currently installed protocols.

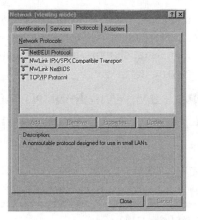

▼   3. Select the protocol you want to install and click OK.

     4. Specify the location of the Windows NT setup files and click Continue.

     5. After the protocol is installed, you return to the Network dialog box. Select the
        newly installed protocol and click the Properties button.

     6. Make any desired changes and click OK.

     7. Change the protocol bindings as desired.

▲   8. Restart the computer for the changes to take effect.

Applying Service Packs

Microsoft periodically makes service packs available to customers as a means of providing Windows NT product updates to keep the computer functionality current with the
latest features and bug fixes in the operating system. The latest service pack release for
Windows NT 3.51 is Service Pack 5, and on Windows NT 4.0 it's Service Pack 4.

> From Oracle's standpoint, when you apply Service Pack 4, some issues now
> exist that hinder the functionality of Oracle Enterprise Manager and Oracle
> Fail Safe. Microsoft and Oracle are committed to providing some hot fixes
> for these problems. Oracle doesn't certify the database against particular
> service packs, only against the operating system. In other words, you should
> be fine in applying Service Pack 4, but if you can wait for some time, you
> should apply Service Pack 3 and then apply Service Pack 4 after the hot fixes
> are available.

Service packs are cumulative and include the fixes available in earlier service packs, as
well as additional fixes. Service packs don't include just bug fixes, but also product
enhancement features, system administration tools, and drivers, all bundled for easy
download and application to the operating system.

To Do: Apply Service Pack 3 on Windows NT 4.0

You can use two methods to apply Service Pack 3. You can install it after downloading or
extract it and apply it later.

> You can download the latest service pack from Microsoft's Web site at
> http://www.microsoft.com or ftp://ftp.microsoft.com/bussys/winnt/
> winnt-public/fixes/usa/nt40.

▼ Follow these steps to install the service pack after downloading it:

1. Log on to the Windows NT machine as the administrator.

2. Download the service pack file nt4sp3_i.exe for your hardware platform to a folder on your hard disk.

3. Close all active sessions on the system.

4. Update the system emergency repair disk by running rdisk.exe with the /s option.

5. Perform a full backup of the system Registry files.

6. From the MS-DOS prompt, type the name of the self-extracting executable:

   ```
   C:> nt4sp3_I
   ```

7. Choose to create an uninstall directory when prompted.

The files are decompressed into a temporary folder specified by the environment variable %temp%, the service pack is installed, and then the decompressed files are removed from the temporary folder.

To extract the files and apply the service pack later, follow these steps:

1. Log on to the Windows NT machine as the administrator.

2. Download the service pack file nt4sp3_i.exe for your hardware platform to a folder on your hard disk.

3. Close all active sessions on the system.

4. Update the system emergency repair disk by running rdisk.exe with the /s option.

5. Perform a full backup of the system Registry files from the MS-DOS prompt.

6. Type the name of the self-extracting executable, and use the /x switch for extracting the files:

   ```
   C:> nt4sp3_I /x
   ```

7. The files are extracted. The service pack can be applied by running the update.exe executable:

   ```
   C:> update
   ```

▲ 8. Choose to create an uninstall directory when prompted.

Creating an uninstall directory requires about 60MB of free space on the drive on which Windows NT is installed. If you install new hardware or software after the application of a service pack, you should reinstall the service pack and choose to create a new uninstall directory.

To Do: Uninstall the Service Pack from Windows NT

After installing a service pack, you might find that Oracle or some other application doesn't run properly. If a particular service pack is not compatible, you might have to uninstall it and apply a lower service pack that would be compatible. Follow these steps to uninstall a service pack from a Windows NT machine:

1. Log on to the Windows NT machine as administrator.

2. Run the update.exe utility.

3. Choose the option to uninstall the service pack.

4. Restart the computer.

▲ The computer is restored to the system configuration just before the application of the service pack.

> If you have applications that use features or bug fixes from a service pack, uninstalling a service pack can adversely affect those applications.

> A service pack modifies the Security Account Manager (SAM) database in such a way that the older versions of samsrv.dll and winlogon.exe no longer recognize the database structure.

> Uninstalling a service pack doesn't return the database structure to its original state. Thus, if you uninstall a service pack and replace it with an older service pack, choose No when asked to confirm file replacement. Otherwise, you might not be able to log on to the system after the older version files replace the newer version files.

Repairing a Windows NT Installation After Applying a Service Pack

A Windows NT service pack contains a modified setup.log file you can use to recover the operating system after a software failure. If the system becomes unstable after the application of a service pack and you need to repair a problem with Windows NT by using a repair disk, you can use one of the following alternative methods:

- If you have an emergency repair disk created or updated after the application of a service pack, use that disk to perform emergency repair.

- Uninstall the service pack, and then use the emergency repair disk created or updated before the application of the service pack.

- Use the repair folder on the boot drive, and choose the option for No Emergency Repair Disk.

Basically, the emergency repair process, when successful, places the operating system in a state before service pack installation. Therefore, you have to reapply the service pack, if desired.

To Do: Perform Emergency Repair on Windows NT When RDISK Hasn't Been Run After Applying the Service Pack

You must implement an emergency repair when you want to restore your system after losing important system files. Follow these steps to perform the repair process if you have not previously run RDISK after the application of a service pack:

1. Place the emergency repair disk (pre-service pack install) in the floppy drive.

2. Modify the attributes of the setup.log as follows:

   ```
   C:> attrib -r -h -s a:\setup.log
   ```

3. Edit the setup.log file, and add the following files under the [Files.WinNt] section (Winnt represents the folder where Windows NT is installed):

   ```
   \Winnt\System32\Samsrv.dll = "samsrv.dll","30fde","\","nt40 repair
   disk", "samsrv.dll"

   \Winnt\System32\Samlib.dll = "samlib.dll","18010","\","nt40 repair
   disk", "samsrv.dll"

   \Winnt\System32\Winlogon.exe = "winlogon.exe","2d0bb","\","nt40
   repair disk", "winlogon.exe"
   ```

4. Copy samsrv.dll, samlib.dll, and winlogon.exe from the Windows NT Service Pack media to the root folder of the emergency repair disk.

5. Place the Windows NT setup disk #1 in the floppy drive, and restart the computer.

6. Select R to repair the Windows NT installation.

7. Choose Verify Windows NT System Files, and click Continue.

8. Press Esc to continue with the emergency repair process.

9. After the samsrv.dll, samlib.dll, and winlogon.exe files are replaced, exit the repair.

▼ To Do

3

▼   10. Restart the computer.

11. Log on as administrator.

These steps can be used to repair the system and security hives if the system becomes
▲   unbootable after applying a service pack.

To Do: Recover from Disaster on a Windows NT Machine with a Service Pack Installed

The following steps can be used to repair a system if you apply the service pack and the
system becomes unbootable. You've already tried to repair the system and security hives
as described earlier, or you don't have an emergency repair disk.

1. If the target file system is FAT, copy the i386 folder from the Windows NT 4.0
   CD-ROM to the hard disk. If the target file system is NTFS, copy the files to a network share.

2. Copy the samsrv.dl_, samlib.dl_, and winlogon.ex_ files from this folder to replace
   the service pack files samsrv.org, samlib.org, and winlogon.org, respectively.

3. If the file system is FAT, boot to MS-DOS, run WINNT /B from the i386 folder, and
   then choose the Upgrade option.

   If the file system is NTFS, choose a new folder for install and run WINNT32 /B.
▲   This restores the system configuration to the state before applying the service pack.

Summary

When you decide to use Oracle8i on Windows NT, you can consider several things as
part of the planning phase in order to configure Windows NT. The choices you make for
configuring Windows NT ultimately have an effect on the system's performance, security, and ease of use. It would help to have a clear understanding of the manner in which
you are planning to use the system and the type of Oracle8i environment that will be
used. You should also set up strategies to protect your system against viruses and to
recover from various scenarios such as loss of system files.

Q&A

Q Should I use NTFS compression on all Oracle8i files?

A Don't use NTFS compression for frequently used files such as redo logs and rollback segments because the maintenance of these files leads to performance problems. Other files can use NTFS compression to save space.

Q Do I have to apply service packs even if I don't see a problem with my system?

A I recommend applying service packs even if there are no obvious problems. The service packs contain important enhancements that can improve performance and fix known problems with Windows NT that you might not have yet encountered.

Workshop

The Workshop contains quiz questions and activities to help reinforce what you've learned in this hour. You can check Appendix A for the answers (but don't peek!).

Quiz

1. What do we mean by *trust* with reference to Windows NT domains?
2. Which file system provides file-level security?
3. Can you use Windows NT Workstation in a domain?

Exercises

1. What are some strategies you can use to protect your system against viruses?
2. Your server crashed. When restarting Windows NT, you get messages indicating that the Registry might be corrupt. How do you recover from this situation?

3

HOUR 4

Installing Oracle8i on Windows NT

Installing Oracle8i on Windows NT is a very simple process; however, you must understand the various alternatives available to you to configure the environment. With Oracle8i, the use of MTS (Multi-Threaded Server) is becoming quite common. You also will see how to configure MTS and become familiar with the problems associated with its use.

In this hour, you will learn the following:

- Installing Oracle8i on Windows NT
- Configuring Multi-Threaded Server
- Removing Oracle8i from Windows NT
- Configuring Legato Storage Manager
- Becoming familiar with thc starter database

System Requirements

Tables 4.1 and 4.2 describe the system requirements needed to install Oracle8i Enterprise Edition on Windows NT, whereas Table 4.3 describes the products that can be installed.

TABLE 4.1 HARDWARE REQUIREMENTS

Component	Requirements
CPU	100% IBM-compatible personal computer with a Pentium processor or higher. Multiple processors can also be used. You can also use DEC Alpha or any other system that runs Windows NT.
Memory	64MB minimum for server installation. An additional 20MB might be required to use Oracle Enterprise Manager.
Disk space	300MB of available hard disk space (typical); 35MB of available hard disk space for server installation. Additional space is needed depending on the option chosen, as follows: 1MB Oracle8 Context Cartridge, 6MB Oracle8 Spatial Cartridge, 5MB Oracle8 Parallel Server Option, 1MB Oracle8 Partitioning Option, 1MB Oracle8 Objects Option, 1MB Oracle8 Advanced Networking Option, 6MB Oracle8 Time Series Cartridge, 1MB Oracle8 Audio Data Cartridge, 1MB Oracle8 Image Cartridge, and 1MB Oracle8 Visual Information Retrieval Cartridge. Oracle8 Recovery Manager requires a media management layer such as Legato Storage Manager, which requires 32MB of RAM, 64MB available hard disk space, and a tape drive.

TABLE 4.2 SOFTWARE REQUIREMENTS

Component	Requirements
Operating system	Windows NT 4.0 Workstation or Server with Service Pack 3
Web Browser (to view online documentation)	Netscape Navigator 3.0 (or higher) or Internet Explorer 3.0 (or higher); browser should be frames- and Java-enabled
16-bit color video	
Microsoft Visual C++	Only if you plan to use the Oracle AppWizard for MS Visual C++

TABLE 4.3 PRODUCTS THAT CAN BE INSTALLED

Product	Release	Use
Assistant Common Files	8.1.5.0.0	Collection of files used by the Oracle Assistants
Java runtime environment	1.1.6.2.0	Required to run Java applications
Oracle AppWizard for Microsoft Visual C++	8.1.5.0.0	Allows developers to write applications that can make use of information stored in an Oracle database
Oracle Data Migration Assistant	8.1.5.0.0	Migrates Oracle7 databases or upgrades previous Oracle8 releases to the current Oracle8 release
Oracle Database Configuration Assistant	8.1.5.0.0	Used to create and delete Oracle databases
Oracle Documentation	8.1.5.0.0	Available in HTML and PDF format
Oracle Universal Installer	1.5.0.4.0	Used to install, update, and remove Oracle products
Oracle Intelligent Agent	8.1.5.0.0	Manages the jobs scheduled and initiated from the Oracle Enterprise Manager console
Oracle Connection Manager	8.1.5.0.0	Allows multiplexing of multiple logical client sessions to an Oracle database through a single physical transport connection
Oracle Software Packager	1.5.0.4.0	Packages software in a format that the Oracle Universal Installer can install
Oracle Home Selector	8.1.5.0.0	Edits the environment path to select a primary Oracle home directory
Oracle Installation Libraries	1.5.0.4.0	Libraries used during installation
Oracle Names	8.1.5.0.0	Naming service that helps in the setup and administration of global client/server computer networks
Net8 Assistant	8.1.5.0.0	Configures sqlnet.ora, tnsnames.ora, listener.ora, and the Oracle Names server
Net8 Client	8.1.5.0.0	Allows client connection to the database across the network

4

continues

TABLE 4.3   CONTINUED

Product	Release	Use
Net8 Server	8.1.5.0.0	Allows the network listener to accept client requests for database connections coming across the network
Oracle Advanced Networking Option Export Edition	8.1.5.0.0	Provides enhanced network security and authentication
Kerberos authentication method	8.1.5.0.0	Enables authentication with Kerberos Authentication method
RADIUS authentication method	8.1.5.0.0	Enables authentication with RADIUS-compliant devices
SecurID authentication method	8.1.5.0.0	Enables authentication with SecurID Authentication method
Named Pipes Protocol Support	8.1.5.0.0	Enables client/server communication through Named Pipes and Net8
SPX Protocol Support	8.1.5.0.0	Enables client/server communication through SPX and Net8
TCP/IP Protocol Support	8.1.5.0.0	Enables client/server communication through TCP/IP and Net8
Object Type Translator	8.1.5.0.0	Creates C-struct representations of Abstract Data Types (ADTs)
Pro*C	8.1.5.0.0	Allows you to embed SQL statements in a C/C++ program to manipulate an Oracle database
Oracle Objects for OLE	8.1.5.0.0	An OCX or ActiveX custom control with OLE in-process server that allows you to place Oracle database functionality into Windows applications
Oracle Services for Microsoft Transaction Server	8.1.5.0.0	Allows the development and deployment of COM-based application by using MTS against an Oracle database
Oracle Parallel Server Manager Server	8.1.5.0.0	Manages an Oracle Parallel Server environment
Oracle Web Publishing Assistant	8.1.5.0.0	Allows data to be queried and published via a Web page
Oracle8 Enterprise Edition	8.1.5.0.0	The Oracle database server

Product	Release	Use
Oracle Parallel Server Option	8.1.5.0.0	Allows multiple instances to share a single Oracle database
Oracle8 ConText Cartridge	8.1.5.0.0	Allows client tools to manipulate text in an Oracle database
Oracle8 Image Cartridge	8.1.5.0.0	Allows the storage, retrieval, and processing of two-dimensional, static bitmapped images
Oracle8 Objects Option	8.1.5.0.0	Allows the use of object-based concepts in an Oracle database
Oracle8 Partitioning Option	8.1.5.0.0	Allows the use of Oracle partitioning to manage tables and indexes
Oracle8 Spatial Cartridge	8.1.5.0.0	Allows the storage, retrieval, and processing of spatial data
Oracle8 Time Series Cartridge	8.1.5.0.0	Allows the storage, retrieval, and processing of timestamped data through object datatypes
Oracle8 Visual Information Retrieval Cartridge	8.1.5.0.0	Allows the storage, retrieval, and processing of images
Oracle8 Audio Data Cartridge	8.1.5.0.0	Allows the storage, retrieval, and processing of digital audio data
Oracle8 ODBC Driver	8.1.5.0.0	Supports ODBC connections from Windows NT, Windows 95, and Windows 98 clients to an Oracle8 database
Oracle8 Performance Monitor	8.1.5.0.0	Monitors local and remote database performance
Oracle8 Utilities	8.1.5.0.0	Consists of a suite of database administration tools including SQL*Loader, Export, Import, Recover Manager, OCOPY, Instance Manager, TKPROF, DBVERIFY, Migration utility, and Password utility
Oracle Call Interface	8.1.5.0.0	Application programming interface (API) that allows C/C++ programs to make calls to the Oracle database
Oracle8 Database Server-Managed Video Cartridge	8.1.5.0.0	Allows the storage, retrieval, and processing of video data

4

continues

TABLE 4.3   CONTINUED

Product	Release	Use
Oracle8 Enterprise Edition Release Notes	8.1.5.0.0	Last-minute important information about the installation and use of Oracle databases
SQL*PLUS	8.1.5.0.0	Client tool that enables the use of SQL and PL/SQL to manipulate the database
Oracle COM Cartridge	8.1.5.0.0	Allows PL/SQL developers to manipulate COM components
Pro*COBOL	8.1.5.0.0	Allows you to embed SQL statements in a COBOL program to manipulate an Oracle database
Net8 Easy Config	8.1.5.0.0	Java-based tool that allows configuration of the tnsnames.ora file and testing of the configuration

To Do: Verify Server Installation

Follow these steps to verify that the installation is successful and a starter database is created:

1. From Control Panel, double-click the Services icon and verify that the OracleServiceORCL service is started.

2. From the DOS command prompt, set the oracle_sid:

   ```
   C:> set oracle_sid = orcl
   ```

3. Start Server Manager:

   ```
   C:> svrmgrl
   ```

4. Connect as internal:

   ```
   Svrmgr> connect internal/oracle
   ```

5. Start the database:

   ```
   svrmgr> startup
   ```

6. Verify the database to which you are connected:

   ```
   Svrmgr> select * from v$database;
   ```

To Do: Take a Backup of the Registry

You should take a backup of the Registry after installing Oracle8i so that you can recover in case the Registry becomes corrupted. Follow these steps to perform a backup:

1. Start the Registry Editor from the Run dialog box:

   `C:\Windows\system32\regedt32`

2. Export the Registry by choosing Export Registry File from the Registry menu.

> The file nt.prd contains lists of all Oracle products installed on the system. You can open this file with any text editor such as Notepad.

To Do: Install Oracle8i on Windows NT

Follow these steps to install Oracle8i on Windows NT:

1. Log on to Windows NT as administrator.

2. Make sure that all the Oracle applications are stopped.

3. From the Control Panel, stop all the Oracle services.

4. Place the Oracle8 Enterprise Edition for Windows NT CD in the CD-ROM drive. The Oracle8 Enterprise Edition-Autorun dialog box appears.

> If the Install isn't set for autorun, you can start the installation process by double-clicking setup.bat from the CD-ROM.

5. Select Add/Remove Products.

6. In the Welcome dialog box (see Figure 4.1), click Next to proceed with the installation.

7. Read through the terms of the license, and select I Accept the License Terms and Export Restrictions.

8. In the File Locations dialog box (see Figure 4.2), change the location of the files in the Source section. In the Destination section, type the location where you want to install Oracle8i (the default location is c:\oracle\ora81). Click Next.

▼

FIGURE 4.1

The Welcome screen after running the Oracle Universal Installer.

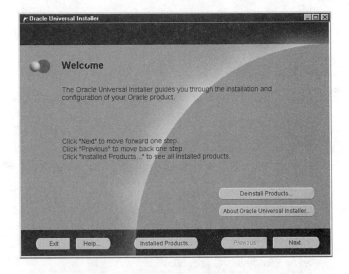

FIGURE 4.2

Specify the location of ORACLE_HOME.

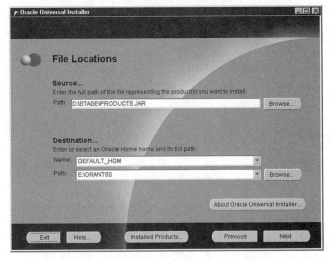

9. From the Available Products dialog box (see Figure 4.3), select the product you want to install from the following options: Oracle8 Enterprise Edition 8.1.5, Oracle8 Client 8.1.5, and Programmer 8.1.5. Click Next.

▼

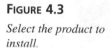

FIGURE 4.3

Select the product to install.

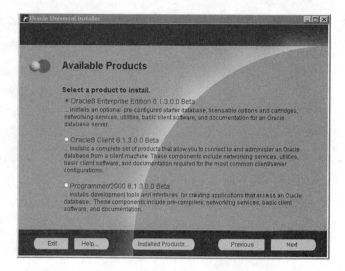

10. Select the type of installation and then click Next (see Figure 4.4):

- *Typical* installs the most common components.

- *Custom* lets you choose the components you want to install (see Figure 4.5).

- *Minimum* installs the minimum components and takes you to the Products to Be Installed dialog box (see Figure 4.6).

4

FIGURE 4.4

Choose the type of installation.

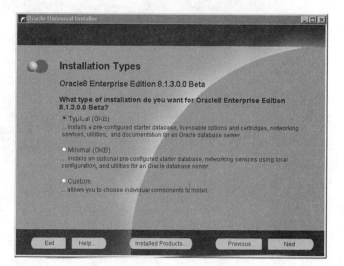

FIGURE 4.5

Choose the cartridges and options to install by using the Custom option.

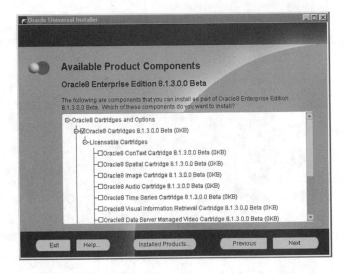

FIGURE 4.6

Use the Product Languages button to select the language in which error messages are displayed.

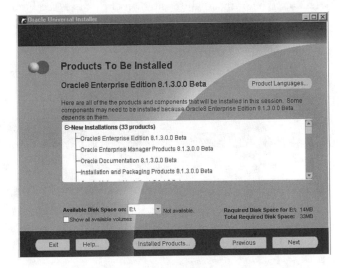

11. Select the location in which the Oracle documentation is to be installed, and click Next.

12. Select the protocol for which you want to install the Oracle Protocol support, and click Next.

13. Verify the options that you've chosen so far by using the information in the Summary dialog box (see Figure 4.7).

FIGURE 4.7

In the Summary page, verify the options you have chosen.

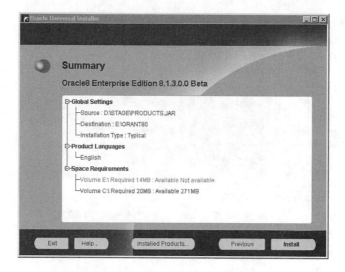

14. Click Install. Figures 4.8, 4.9, and 4.10 show the phases during the creation of the starter database.

4

FIGURE 4.8

Oracle Utilities will be set up as part of the installation.

FIGURE 4.9

Database creation phases.

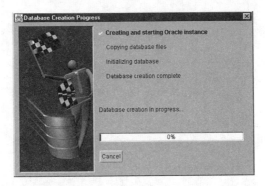

FIGURE 4.10

Verify the database creation.

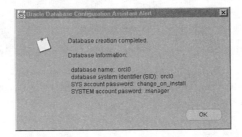

15. Configure Net8 by using the Net8 Configuration Assistant (see Figure 4.11). This is run automatically during installation. Table 4.4 lists all options configurable during installation.

TABLE 4.4 OPTIONS CONFIGURED WITH THE INSTALLATION OF ORACLE8I

Product	Automatically Configured?
Net8 network software	Automatic for server configuration files but must be done manually for client configuration files
Oracle Enterprise Manager	No, must be configured separately
Oracle cartridges	Depends on the options chosen during the installation of Oracle
Oracle8 objects	Yes
Oracle8 partitioning	Yes
Oracle8 parallel server	Depends on the options chosen during the installation of Oracle
PL/SQL external procedures	Depends on the network configuration files

▼

Product	Automatically Configured?
Oracle Services for Microsoft Transaction Server	No, must be configured separately
Oracle support for multi-threaded servers	Depends on the options chosen during the installation of Oracle
Oracle Advanced Replication support	Depends on the options chosen during the installation of Oracle

FIGURE 4.11

Verify that the Net8 and Database Configuration Assistant ran successfully.

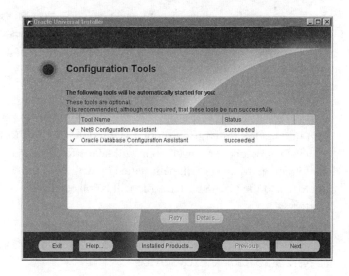

4

16. When the installation completes, click Exit to exit the Oracle Universal Installer.

17. Verify the services in the control panel for the new database (see Figure 4.12).

FIGURE 4.12

Verify the services in the Control Panel.

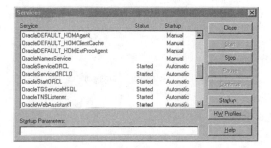

▲

If an earlier version of an Oracle database is detected on your system, you're asked whether you want to migrate the database. If you choose to migrate the database, the Oracle Data Migration Assistant starts automatically at the end of the Oracle8i installation and allows you to complete the migration process. When migrating from Oracle 7.3.x to Oracle8i, you should install the appropriate version of SQL*Net in the Oracle7 home directory before using the Oracle Data Migration Assistant.

To Do: Manually Install Legato Storage Manager

▼ To Do

Oracle8i includes a media manager from Legato called Legato Storage Manager, which interfaces with Oracle Recovery Manager to back up the databases directly to tape drives. The following steps can be used to install the Legato Storage Manager at any time after Oracle's installation:

1. Log on to Windows NT as administrator.

2. From the Control panel, stop the OracleServiceSID Oracle service.

3. From the Oracle8 Enterprise Edition for Windows NT CD-ROM, run setup.exe in the \legato directory. The installation will take a few minutes. When it's complete, Legato Storage Manager will be installed by default in the WIN32APP\NSR\BIN directory, and the ORASBT.DLL file will be placed in the WINNT\SYSTEM32 directory.

4. Double-click Control Panel's Services icon. Verify that the following services are started: Networker Backup and Recover Server, Networker Portmapper Service, and Networker Remote Exec Service.

5. Click the Environment tab.

6. From the System Variables list, select the PATH variable.

7. To the Value list, append the following line to the existing entries:

   ;c:\win32app\nsr\bin

8. Click Set.

9. Click Apply.

10. Click OK to add the Legato Storage Manager to the system path.

▲ 11. Restart the computer.

To Do: Enable/Disable Multi-Threaded Server Configuration

Before you can use shared servers in your database, you must configure multi-threaded servers. Follow these steps to enable or disable the use of shared servers for a database:

1. Log on to Windows NT as administrator.

2. Choose Start, Programs, Oracle-HOME_NAME, Oracle Enterprise Management, Database Administration Applications, Database Configuration Assistant.

3. In the Oracle Database Configuration Assistant dialog box, choose Modify a Database.

4. Provide the password for Internal when prompted, and then click Next.

5. Enable or disable Multi-Threaded Server support as desired.

6. Click Finish.

7. Choose the initialization file to use, and click OK.

8. Shut down, and then restart the database.

To Do: Configure Oracle8 Cartridge

Oracle8 provides cartridges for various features such as the use of spatial data, as well as image and audio data. The following steps show how to install the cartridges by running the scripts indicated in Table 4.5:

1. Connect to Server Manager through the internal account.

2. Start the database.

3. Run the ORDINST.SQL script:

   Svrmgr> **@%ORACLE_HOME%\ORD\ADMIN\ORDINST.SQL**

4. Run the script for the desired cartridge (see Table 4.5).

5. Exit Server Manager.

TABLE 4.5 SCRIPTS TO RUN TO INSTALL CARTRIDGES

Cartridge to Install	Script to Run
Oracle8 Audio Data Cartridge	@%ORACLE_HOME%\ORD\AUD\ADMIN\AUDINST.SQL
Oracle8 Video Cartridge	@%ORACLE_HOME%\ORD\VID\ADMIN\VIDINST.SQL
Oracle8 Image Cartridge	@%ORACLE_HOME%\ORD\IMG\ADMIN\IMGINST.SQL
Oracle8 Spatial Cartridge	@%ORACLE_HOME%\MD\ADMIN\MDINST.SQL (must be run while connected with the system account)
Oracle8 Time Series Cartridge	@%ORACLE_HOME%\ORD\TS\ADMIN\TSINST.SQL
Oracle8 Visual Information Retrieval Cartridge*	@%ORACLE_HOME%\ORD\VIR\ADMIN\VIRINST.SQL

Before configuring the Oracle8 Visual Information Retrieval Cartridge, you must configure the Oracle8 Image Cartridge.

4

To Do: Remove Oracle8i from Windows NT

Follow these steps if you need to remove Oracle8i from your Windows NT system:

1. Log on to Windows NT as administrator.

2. From Control Panel, stop all Oracle services.

3. Choose Start, Programs, Oracle Installation Products, Oracle Universal Installer.

4. In the Welcome dialog box, click the Installed Products button.

5. In the Inventory dialog box, select the components that you want to uninstall. Choose all components for a complete uninstallation.

6. Confirm the removal of the selected products.

7. Close the Inventory dialog box, and then exit the Oracle Universal Installer.

To Do: Remove the Legato Storage Manager

You might need to remove Legato Storage Manager if you plan to use another third-party media manager to interface with the Oracle Recovery Manager. Follow these steps to remove the Legato Storage Manager from your system:

1. Log on to Windows NT as administrator.

2. From Control Panel, stop the Legato Storage Manager services: Networker Backup and Recover Server, Networker Portmapper Service, and Networker Remote Exec Service.

3. Choose Start, Programs, NetWorker Group, Uninstall NetWorker.

4. Select to perform a complete or partial removal. (The complete removal option removes all database, index, and resource files.). Click OK to remove Legato Storage Manager from the system.

5. From the Windows NT Explorer, remove the ORASBT.DLL file from the c:*winnt_home*\system32 directory, where *winnt_home* is the directory in which Windows NT is installed.

Contents of the Starter Database

During Oracle8i's installation, you can choose to install the starter database. The starter database contains the following:

- User accounts

Account	Description
INTERNAL	With the password ORACLE. This isn't a true account, but an alias for the SYS account and SYSDBA privilege. It can be used for administrative tasks in addition to database startup and shutdown.
SYS	With the password CHANGE_ON_INSTALL. The *Oracle8 Enterprise Edition for NT* manual indicates that this DBA account has the following privileges: CONNECT, RESOURCE, DBA, AQ_ADMINISTRA-TOR_ROLE, AQ_USER_ROLE, DELETE_CATALOG_ROLE, EXECUTE_CATA-LOG_ROLE, EXP_FULL_DATABASE, IMP_FULL_DATABASE, RECOVERY_CATALOG_OWNER, SELECT_CATALOG_ROLE, SNMPAGENT, CTXADMIN, CTXAPP, and CTXUSER.
SYSTEM	With the password MANAGER. This account has the DBA database role.

> Upon installation, you should change the password of SYS and SYSTEM for security reasons.

User name SCOTT	With the password TIGER. This user has CONNECT and RESOURCE privileges.
User name DEMO	With the password DEMO. This user has CONNECT and RESOURCE privileges.
DBSNMP	With the password DBSNMP. This account, used as the Oracle Enterprise Manager account, has the CONNECT, RESOURCE, and SNMPAGENT database privileges.
CTXSYS	With the CTXSYS password. This account, used as the Context Administrator, has the CONNECT, RESOURCE, and DBA database privileges.

4

- Tablespaces

Tablespace	Description
System	Contains the data dictionary
User_data	Contains the application data
Temporary_data	Contains the temporary tables or indexes that are created during the execution of SQL statements that need temporary storage
Rollback_data	Contains the rollback segments

- Datafiles located in the %ORACLE_HOME%\ORADATA\ORCL directory

Datafile	Location
SYSTM01.DBF	System tablespace
USERS01.DBF	User_data tablespace
TEMP01.DBF	Temporary_data tablespace
RBS01.DBF	Rollback_data tablespace

- The INITORCL.ORA initialization file in the %ORACLE_HOME%\ORA81\ database directory
- The REDO01.LOG, REDO02.LOG, REDO03.LOG, AND REDO04.LOG redo logs in the %ORACLE_HOME%\ORADATA/ORCL directory
- The CONTROL01.CTL AND CONTROL02.CTL control files in the %ORACLE_HOME%\ORADATA\ORCL directory

Client/Server Installation

A client/server installation is the most popular configuration in use now. In a client/server configuration, an Oracle8i client application can connect to a remote Oracle8i server through Net8.

Performing a client/server installation involves several steps:

1. Verify that the network is functional. The method used to test a network depends on the network protocol in use. For example, if you're using TCP/IP, you can use the `ping` or `tracert` command to verify the network connectivity:

```
C:> ping mthakkar-pc
Pinging mthakkar-pc.us.oracle.com [130.21.45.107]
with 32 bytes of data:
Reply from 130.21.45.107: bytes=32 time<10ms TTL=128
```

```
Reply from 130.21.45.107: bytes=32 time<10ms TTL=128
Reply from 130.21.45.107: bytes=32 time<10ms TTL=128
Reply from 130.21.45.107: bytes=32 time<10ms TTL=128
```

2. Install Oracle8 and Net8 on the server (see "To Do: Install Oracle8i on Windows NT," earlier in this chapter).

3. Test a loopback connection to ensure that you can connect from a client to the server on the same machine.

4. Install the client software.

5. Create a Net8 alias by using Net8 Easy Configuration, and test the connection.

Using Multi-Threaded Server (MTS)

Several processes are involved in a multi-threaded configuration:

- *A Network listener process*—This functionality, provided by Net8, connects user processes to dispatchers or dedicated servers as requested.

- *One or more dispatcher processes*—Dispatchers are protocol-specific handlers associated with a particular instance. Now, Windows NT supports only TCP/IP dispatchers.

- *One or more shared server processes*—Shared servers satisfy the requests submitted by the dispatchers.

4

 No direct relationship exists between the number of dispatchers and shared servers.

When using multi-threaded servers, there are several enhancements to the SGA:

- Additional memory structures called *request queues* that contain the requests placed by the dispatchers

- An additional memory structure called *response queue* that is used by the shared servers to place the response to the requests

- Migration of the session information from the PGA into the SGA (this section of the SGA is known as the UGA, or *user global area*)

Connection Mechanism

The connection mechanism used with multi-threaded servers is as follows:

1. When the listener is started, it opens and establishes a communication pathway and starts listening on the listed addresses. Users communicate with Oracle through this channel. At this point, the listener is aware only of the defined services in listener.ora.

2. When an MTS-configured Oracle instance is started, each dispatcher receives its random listen address. The dispatchers call the listener by using the address specified by MTS_LISTENER_ADDRESS and give the listener the address at which the dispatcher listens for connection requests.

3. The listener adds the MTS_SERVICE and the address of the dispatcher to its list of known services.

4. The network listener process waits for incoming connection requests.

5. A user requests a connection to the database.

6. If a dedicated server process is requested, the listener creates a dedicated server process and connects the user process to it. The user communicates with Oracle through this dedicated connection.

   On the other hand, if an MTS connection is needed, the listener gives the user process the address of a dispatcher process with the lightest load.

The following steps occur only for an MTS connection:

1. The user process connects to the dispatcher, which creates a virtual circuit that it uses to communicate with the shared servers. The user process remains connected to the dispatcher throughout the life of the user process.

2. The user process issues a request, which the dispatcher places in the request queue (part of the SGA). The request queue is common to all dispatchers, but each dispatcher has its own response queue.

3. The next available shared server process picks up the request from the request queue.

4. The shared server process does all the necessary processing and returns the results to the dispatcher's response queue in the SGA.

5. The dispatcher returns the result of the processing to the appropriate user process.

The PGA of shared servers contains only stack space and process-specific variables.

Initialization Parameters for MTS

To use MTS on Windows NT, you must configure the following initialization parameters (use the sample init.ora file):

- MTS_SERVICE specifies the service name that the dispatchers will register with the listener. To request an MTS connection, a user must specify this service name in the connect string.

  If MTS_SERVICE = ORACLE_SID, connections requesting a particular SID get an available MTS connection (unless client calls request a dedicated server). If an MTS connection isn't available, a dedicated connection is made.

  If MTS_SERVICE <> ORACLE_SID, client connections can request MTS or non-MTS connections. If the requested MTS connection isn't available, they *don't* get a dedicated connection.

- MTS_SERVERS specifies the number of shared server processes to be created at instance startup. Setting MTS_SERVERS = 0 disables multi-threaded servers.

- MTS_MAX_SERVERS specifies the maximum number of shared server processes that can exist for an MTS instance. Shared servers are created automatically as needed until MTS_MAX_SERVERS are reached.

- MTS_DISPATCHERS specifies the number of dispatchers at instance startup, the protocol associated with the dispatchers, and the number of clients that can connect to a particular dispatcher.

> The initial number of dispatchers = CEIL (maximum number of concurrent sessions/connections per dispatcher).

- MTS_MAX_DISPATCHERS specifies the maximum number of dispatchers that can be created on an MTS instance.

- MTS_LISTENER_ADDRESS specifies the address on which the dispatchers will listen.

- SHARED_POOL_SIZE specifies the shared pool size. You've seen that an MTS configuration uses additional memory structures, such as request queues and response queues. Session information also is part of the UGA. You should add about 1KB for each user who will connect by using MTS.

Use the V$SESSTAT dynamic view to determine the session memory.

The following is the sample init.ora file:

```
Sample init.ora file with MTS parameters

mts_service= "YOUR_SID"
mts_listener_address="(ADDRESS=(PROTOCOL=tcp)(port=1521)
➥(host=your_machine))"
mts_dispatchers= "tcp, 1"
mts_max_dispatchers=8
mts_max_servers=10
mts_servers=6
```

 To enable multiple listeners for MTS, set MTS_MULTIPLE_LISTENERS = TRUE in the initialization file. This can help improve performance by balancing the load among the listeners.

The listener.ora file should be like the following:

```
LISTENER =
(ADDRESS_LIST =
(ADDRESS=(COMMUNITY= TCP.world)(PROTOCOL= TCP)(Host= your_machine)
➥(Port= 1521))
)

SID_LIST_LISTENER = (
SID_LIST =(SID_DESC =(SID_NAME = YOUR_SID)))
```

The tnsnames.ora for clients machine

```
YOUR_SID_TCP.world=
(DESCRIPTION =(ADDRESS=(PROTOCOL=TCP) (HOST=your_machine) (PORT=1521))
(CONNECT_DATA= (SID=YOUR_SID)(SERVER=SHARED)))
```

Common Problems with MTS

MTS configurations generally experience problems that fall into one of the following categories.

To help diagnose MTS problems, you can set events to trace the shared servers and dispatchers:

- `event='10248 trace name context forever, level 9'` gives information about dispatcher-encountered unexpected errors.
- `event = '10249 trace name context forever, level 9'` traces Multi-Threaded Server.

Connection Problems

You can check several views to verify that a particular connection is an MTS connection:

- `v$circuit` lists all the virtual circuits in the instance.
- The SERVER field of `v$session` displays SHARED or NONE if it's an MTS session.
- The Accept field in the `v$dispatcher` view determines whether the dispatchers are accepting any more connections.
- Use `v$server` to determine whether enough shared servers are available.

Check the alert log and the trace files of the dispatchers, shared servers, and PMON.

Check the listener for problems. Listener problems can result from the dispatcher not registering with it or the address used by the dispatcher to call the listener (MTS_LISTENER_ADDRESS) not matching the actual address on which the listener is listening.

Make sure that the correct listener address is being used by the client connections.

Performance Problems

Hour 17, "Managing Contention," explains how you can improve performance in a multi-threaded environment.

Summary

Oracle's Universal Installer provides a very easy and intuitive way to install Oracle8i on Windows NT. During the installation process, you can choose to install the starter database in order to test and learn Oracle's capabilities. Oracle8 on Windows NT provides the Oracle DBA with a new set of opportunities to improve database performance and efficiently use the system and network resources. The Multi-Threaded Server architecture, if used properly, can provide support for a large number of users of the complex applications and systems being built by using Windows NT as the enterprise solution. Understanding the intended purpose of the MTS architecture is valuable in determining which applications (or portions thereof) should use shared servers and which should not.

Q&A

Q I've configured Multi-Threaded Server in my database. Will all my connections be going through the shared servers?

A No. When you have multi-threaded servers configured, you can still have both dedicated as well as nondedicated connections.

Q Can I create the starter database after the installation is complete?

A Yes. The starter database can be created any time after installation by using the CREATEDB.SQL scripts.

Workshop

The Workshop contains quiz questions and activities to help reinforce what you've learned in this hour. You can check Appendix A for the answers (but don't peek!).

Quiz

1. What are the main components of a multi-threaded server environment?
2. Which file contains a list of Oracle products installed?
3. What happens to the MTS connections if `MTS_SERVICE=ORACLE_SID`?
4. What init.ora parameter can be used to disable multi-threaded servers?

Exercises

1. You have configured MTS, but all your connections are dedicated. How would you go about diagnosing the problem?
2. What can you do to improve the performance of a multi-threaded database system?

PART II
Building Databases

Hour

Hour 5

Migrating from Oracle7 to Oracle8i

All Oracle software products have version numbers of the form *A.B.C.D*, in which *A* represents the major release (such as from Oracle7 to Oracle8). The other numbers in the version represent the enhancements, bug fixes, porting changes, and other minor changes in the release.

NEW TERM An *upgrade* is usually referred to as the process of going from one Oracle release to another (the source and destination having the same major release) such as upgrading from Oracle 8.0.4 to Oracle 8.0.5. A *migration*, on the other hand refers to the process of going from one major release to another, such as migrating from Oracle7 to Oracle8i. Several times, migration is also referred to as a process of moving the database from one platform to another (such as from UNIX to Windows NT) or from a non-Oracle database to Oracle (such as MS Access or MS SQL Server to Oracle). This lesson looks at several strategies that can be used to migrate to Oracle8i:

- The MIG utility
- The Oracle Data Migration Assistant
- Export/import
- The SQL*PLUS COPY command
- Migration from Microsoft Access

Table 5.1 compares the various migration techniques.

TABLE 5.1 MIGRATION TECHNIQUES

Advantages	Disadvantages
Migration Utility or Data Migration Assistant	
Automated.	Entire database must be migrated.
Fast migration.	Must be Oracle 7.1.6 or higher.
Minimal additional space used in the system tablespace.	Fallback to Oracle7 requires restore from Oracle7 cold backup.
Export/Import	
Allows partial or full database migration.	Slow for large databases.
Database can be any Oracle7 version.	Operating system might limit the size of the export dump file.
Useful for migrating from a non-PC platform to Windows NT.	Export dump file can become very large.
Fallback to Oracle7 database is possible.	
Can also defragment the database.	
SQL*PLUS COPY or CTAS	
Allows partial or full database migration.	Slow for large databases.
Database can be any Oracle7 version.	Requires the most amount of time to perform the migration.
Useful for migrating from a non-PC platform to Windows NT.	Both source and target databases must be available.

Advantages	Disadvantages
SQL*PLUS COPY or CTAS	
Fallback to Oracle7 database is possible.	Copies only the tables and their contents. Use another approach, such as Export/Import to get all the users, stored procedures, views, and so on, into the target database.
Can also defragment the database.	

> An upgrade is usually a simple process, whereas a migration is more involved and requires more planning.

Migrating an Oracle7 database to an Oracle8i database involves the following general steps:

1. Make the choices regarding the migration process. These choices involve the following:
   - Determine the migration method you will use.
   - Determine and make sure that you have the necessary resources available.
   - Become familiar with the Oracle7 features that have become obsolete and the new Oracle8i features you're planning to use.
   - Develop a plan for testing the migrated database.
   - Decide on a backup and recovery strategy that can quickly be used to fall back to the Oracle7 database in case the migration fails.

2. Perform a test migration of an Oracle7 database.
3. Test the migrated test database, using the testing strategy developed in step 1.
4. Prepare the database for migration. This step involves taking a backup of the database, scheduling downtime for the database, and so on.
5. Migrate the database by using the strategy decided in step 1.
6. Back up the database again.
7. Tune the migrated database by using the new Oracle8i features, and tune initialization parameters as desired.
8. Migrate the applications.

5

Performing a Manual Migration with `MIG`

`MIG` is a command-line utility provided by Oracle to help during the migration process. Manual migration to Oracle 8.1.5 can be performed by using the `MIG` utility, provided the following is true:

- You are at Oracle release 7.1.3.3.6 or greater before the migration.
- The `DB_BLOCK_SIZE` is to be the same on the Oracle7 database and the migrated Oracle8 database.
- The character set is to be the same on the Oracle7 database and the migrated Oracle8 database.
- The database is not to be migrated to a different operating system.

Follow these steps before performing the migration:

1. Back up the Oracle7 database.
2. From Server Manager, create the spool file:

   Svrmgr> **spool backup.lst**

   From the spool file, you can list the files to migrate by using the following commands in Server Manager:

`select * from v$datafile;`	List of datafiles
`select * from v$logfile;`	List of redo log files
`select * from v$controlfile;`	Control files to back up

> The init.ora file to back up is located at c:\orant\database\init*SID*.ora.

3. Oracle8 binaries require about three times the amount of space needed for Oracle7 binaries. Make sure that you have enough disk space for the Oracle8 binaries.
4. Make sure that the `SYSTEM` tablespace contains enough space to contain the Oracle8 data dictionary (which might be considerably larger than the Oracle7 data dictionary). You can verify that enough space is available in the `SYSTEM` tablespace by running the `MIG` utility in check mode (as explained in the following section).
5. From Server Manager, make sure that the `SYSTEM` rollback segment isn't using the `OPTIMAL` parameter:

   ```
   Select a.usn, a.name, b.optsize
   From v$rollname a, v$rollstat b
   Where a.usn = b.usn;
   ```

If the output shows that the OPTSIZE column for the SYSTEM rollback segment has a value, you should set optimal to NULL in Server Manager:

```
Alter rollback segment system storage (optimal NULL);
```

The migration utility (MIG) can use the following parameters:

- CHECK_ONLY and NO_SPACE_CHECK are mutually exclusive and are used to check whether the system tablespace is large enough to complete the migration process.
- DBNAME specifies the name of the database to migrate.
- NEW_DBNAME specifies the new name of the database. By default, the new name of the database is DEFAULT.
- NLS_CHAR allows you to change the National Language Standard NCHAR character set used for the database.
- PFILE specifies the initialization file to use during the migration process.
- SPOOL specifies the location of the migration log file. This file should be checked for errors that may have occurred during the migration.

6. Make sure that no user or role has the name *MIGRATE*. To see whether a user has the name *MIGRATE*,

```
Select username from dba_users where username = 'MIGRATE';
```

To drop the user MIGRATE,

```
Drop user MIGRATE;
```

To check whether a role has the name *MIGRATE*,

```
Select role from dba_roles where role = 'MIGRATE';
```

To drop the role MIGRATE,

```
Drop role MIGRATE;
```

5

If you have a user or a role named MIGRATE, you should rename the user/role so that there won't be any conflict during the migration process.

7. Make sure that all the datafiles and tablespaces are online or offline normal.

8. Make sure that no datafiles need recovery. This can be verified by querying `v$recover_file` and `dba_data_files` and checking the status of the files.

9. Make sure that no in-doubt transactions exist. This can be verified by checking `dba_2pc_pending`. In-doubt transactions should be resolved by committing or rolling them back.

To Do: Check the SYSTEM Tablespace for Sufficient Space During Migration

A lot of temporary space is used during the migration process. You can't truly determine if you have enough space for a particular migration just by using `dba_free_space`. Therefore, you must do a trial migration with the parameter `check_only = y`. Follow these steps:

1. Install the Oracle8i software, if it isn't already installed. (Refer to Hour 4 for complete details of the installation of the Oracle8i software.)

2. Shut down the database if it's running.

3. Set `Oracle_sid=Your_SID`.

4. Run the MIG utility in the check mode:

   ```
   C:> mig pfile=c:\orant\database\init<SID>.ora check_only = true
   ```

   `pfile` is set to the initialization file associated with the Oracle7 database to be migrated.

To Do: Migrate an Oracle7 Database to Oracle8i by Using MIG

Before you can migrate an Oracle7 database, you need to install the Oracle8i software into a different ORACLE_HOME than the Oracle7 ORACLE_HOME. When prompted for the database you want to migrate, choose NONE. Also, choose not to create a database.

Next, follow these steps to set the Oracle7 environment variables:

1. Log on to Windows NT as administrator.

2. Run the Registry Editor (regedt32.exe).

3. Make sure that the ORACLE_HOME variable is set to Oracle7 home. `HKEY_LOCAL_MACHINE\software\oracle\Oracle_home` must be set to `c:\orant`, where `c:\orant` is the Oracle7 home.

4. Make sure that the NLS_LANG variable is set to the character set used by the Oracle7 database. `HKEY_LOCAL_MACHINE\software\oracle\nls_lang` must be set to the character set used by Oracle7 database.

5. In the Control Panel, double-click the system icon.

6. Click the Environment tab.

7. Set the PATH environment variable so that the first entry points to the Oracle7 executable (`c:\orant\bin`).

8. From the command prompt, set `oracle_sid=oracle7_sid`.

9. Connect to Server Manager as internal.

10. Shut down the database normally (or immediately).

11. Run the Oracle8i migration utility:

```
C:> mig pfile=c:\orant\database\initO7_sid.ora spool=
c:\orant\database\mig.log
```

The migration utility creates a convert file (convert.ora) that you will use later to convert the database to Oracle8i.

> From this point on, don't open the database with the Oracle7 executables; otherwise, it might become corrupted.

12. From Windows NT's Control Panel, stop the Oracle service for the Oracle7 database.

13. By using the Instance Manager (oradim), delete the Oracle service for the Oracle7 database, where *x* represents the Oracle7 major version number:

```
C:> oradim7x -delete -sid Oracle7_sid
```

5

The following steps must be performed to set the Oracle8i environment variables:

1. Run the Registry Editor (regedt32.exe).

2. Make sure that the ORACLE_HOME variable is set to Oracle8i home. `HKEY_LOCAL_MACHINE\software\oracle\Oracle_home` must be set to `c:\oracle\ora81` (where `c:\oracle\ora81` is the Oracle8i home).

3. In the Control Panel, double-click the System icon.

4. Click the Environment tab.

5. Set the PATH environment variable so that the first entry points to the Oracle8i executable (`c:\oracle\ora81\bin`).

6. Create the Oracle8 service by using the Oracle7 SID and init.ora file:

```
oradim -new -sid <Oracle7_sid> -intpwd <internal_password>-
startmode auto -pfile c:\orant\database\init<Oracle7_sid>.ora
```

▼ 7. Rename the database's control files.

8. Edit the init.ora file. Set `compatible` to `8.1.5.0.0`, and remove the init.ora parameters that have become obsolete from Oracle7 to Oracle8i.

> The following Oracle7 parameters are obsolete in Oracle8i:
>
> | | |
> |---|---|
> | CCF_IO_SIZE | OPTIMIZER_PARALLEL_PASS |
> | CHECKPOINT_PROCESS | PARALLEL_DEFAULT_MAX_SCANS |
> | GC_SAVE_ROLLBACK_LOCKS | PARALLEL_DEFAULT_SCAN_SIZE |
> | GC_SEGMENTS | SEQUENCE_CACHE_HASH_BUCKETS |
> | GC_TABLESPACES | SERIALIZABLE |
> | IO_TIMEOUT | SESSION_CACHED_CURSORS |
> | INIT_SQL_FILES | SNAPSHOT_REFRESH_INTERVAL (renamed to JOB_QUEUE_INTERVAL) |
> | IPQ_ADDRESS | SNAPSHOT_REFRESH_PROCESS (renamed to JOB_QUEUE_PROCESSES) |
> | IPQ_NET | UNLIMITED_ROLLBACK_SEGMENTS |
> | LM_DOMAINS | V733_PLANS_ENABLED |
> | LM_NON_FAULT_TOLERANT | |

9. From the MS-DOS command prompt, set `oracle_sid=Oracle7_sid`.

10. Connect to Server Manager with the internal account.

11. Start up the Oracle8i database in nomount mode.

12. Create new control files, and convert the file headers of the files to the Oracle8i format:

```
Svrmgr> alter database convert;
```

> Running ALTER DATABASE CONVERT is the point of no return. After running this command, you can't fall back to the Oracle7 database.

▼

▼ 13. Open the database and reset the logs:

Svrmgr> **alter database open resetlogs;**

14. Create the spool file that will hold the results of running the scripts in steps 15–17:

Svrmgr> **spool migscripts.log**

15. Run U0703040.sql:

Svrmgr> **@c:\oracle\ora81\rdbms\admin\U0703040.sql;**

16. Run the following only if you're using the advanced replication option:

Svrmgr> **@c:\oracle\ora81\rdbms\admin\catrep.sql**

17. Run the following only if you're using the Oracle Parallel Server option:

Svrmgr> **@c:\oracle\ora81\rdbms\admin\catparr.sql**

18. Turn off spooling:

Svrmgr> **spool out**

19. Shut down the database.

20. Back up the database.

21. Verify from the migscripts.out spool file that the scripts ran successfully. (If the scripts didn't run successfully, take care of the problem and rerun the scripts.)

▲ 22. Start up the database.

Using the Oracle Data Migration Assistant

You can use Oracle's Data Migration Assistant for the following purposes:

- Migrate Oracle7 database to Oracle8 database.
- Upgrade an earlier release of Oracle8 to a later release of Oracle8.

5

You can't use Oracle's Data Migration Assistant to upgrade an earlier release of Oracle7 to a later release of Oracle7.

You can use the Data Migration Assistant to migrate to Oracle 8.1.5, provided the following is true:

- You are at Oracle release 7.1.3.3.6 or greater before the migration.

If you are using a version lower than 7.1.3.3.6, first upgrade to Oracle 7.1.3.3.6 before using the Oracle Data Migration Assistant.

- The DB_BLOCK_SIZE is to be the same on the Oracle7 database and the migrated Oracle8 database.
- The character set is to be the same on the Oracle7 database and the migrated Oracle8 database.
- The migration is not to be performed to a different operating system.
- SQL*Net v2.x or later is installed.

Follow these steps before performing the migration:

1. Oracle8 binaries require about three times the amount of space needed for Oracle7 binaries. Make sure that you have enough disk space for the Oracle8 binaries.
2. Make sure that the SYSTEM tablespace contains enough space to contain the Oracle8 data dictionary (which might be considerably larger than the Oracle7 data dictionary). To verify that enough space is available in the SYSTEM tablespace, run the MIG utility in check mode.
3. Make sure that the SYSTEM rollback segment isn't using the OPTIMAL parameter.
4. Make sure that you have large rollback segment so that the catalog.sql and catproc.sql scripts complete successfully.
5. Make sure that no user or role has the name *MIGRATE*.
6. Make sure that no datafiles need recovery. This can be verified by querying v$recover_file and dba_data_files and checking the status of the files.
7. Make sure that there are no in-doubt transactions by checking dba_2pc_pending. In-doubt transactions should be resolved by committing or rolling them back.

To Do: Perform Migration with the Data Migration Assistant

The Data Migration Assistant provides a graphical method of migrating your Oracle7 database to Oracle8i. It's also relatively simple to use compared with the MIG utility. The following steps demonstrate how to use the Data Migration Assistant:

1. Shut down the Oracle7 database.
2. Stop all Oracle services (not just the Oracle service for the database to migrate).
3. Back up the Oracle7 database.
4. Edit the init.ora file to set compatible to 8.1.5.0.0 and to remove the init.ora parameters that have become obsolete from Oracle7 to Oracle8i.
5. Choose Start, Programs, Oracle for Windows NT, Oracle Data Migration Assistant.
6. In the Database Instance page, choose the database instance to migrate, supply the password for the internal account, and provide the location of the init.ora file.

▼ 7. In the Moving the Database page, specify (if you want) the new location for the migrated database.

8. The Backup the Database page allows you to back up the database at this time. If you haven't already backed up the database, do so now.

9. In the Character Set page, you can specify the character set to be used in the migrated database. This will be in addition to the character set in the Oracle7 database.

10. Start the migration. The migration process might take some time, depending on system memory, disk speed, CPU speed, and so on. During migration, it's quite common for the machine to appear to be hung, but in reality it's doing a lot of work.

11. When the migration is complete, you can view the Migration Report page to determine whether the migration was successful. If the migration wasn't successful, you can fall back to the backup of the Oracle7 database.

12. Edit the init.ora file, and add any new Oracle8i parameters that you plan to use.

13. Remove any old control files that might have been generated during the migration.

14. Run catrep.sql if you're running advanced replication.

▲ 15. Run catparr.sql if you're running Oracle Parallel Server.

If you opted to back up the Oracle7 database from the Data Migration Assistant, a *SID*back.bat script is created that can be used to revert back to the Oracle7 database.

5

Checking Files After Migration

After the migration process, check the files in Table 5.2 for errors.

TABLE 5.2 FILES TO CHECK FOR MIGRATION ERRORS

File	Description
Oradim73.log	Instance Manager log for Oracle7.
Oradim81.log	Instance Manager log for Oracle8.
Alert.log	Alert log.
Windows NT Event viewer	Event viewer logs.
*SID*nls.log	Check for migration of character sets.

continues

TABLE 5.2   CONTINUED

File	Description
*SID*checkspc.log	Check available space in the SYSTEM tablespace.
*SID*mig81.log	Migration log.
*SID*altdbs.log	Output of the command alter database convert.
*SID*cat8000.log	Result of running cat8000.sql.
*SID*pupbld.log	Output of running v8pupbld.
*SID*summary.log	Log containing the summary of the migration process.

Performing Migration into an Existing Directory Structure

The easiest migration process is to install the Oracle8i server in the same ORACLE_HOME as the existing Oracle7 server. This enables you to use one ORACLE_HOME and retain the Oracle7 installation. Before proceeding with the migration, you must perform a normal shutdown and take a cold backup of the Oracle7 database.

Migrating the Database During Installation

The Oracle Universal Installer can be used to migrate the Oracle7 database during the installation of Oracle8i. During the installation of Oracle8i, you can choose to install the server in the same ORACLE_HOME as the Oracle7 installation.

> The Oracle8i installation won't overwrite the files and folders from the Oracle7 installation because the files have different names.

The installer will automatically detect the existing Oracle7 version and prompt you to migrate the database at the end of the installation. You can choose the databases you want to migrate. At the end of the Oracle8i installation, the Data Migration Assistant is invoked (if you chose to perform the migration) and will guide you through the migration process. Alternatively, you can choose not to migrate during installation and perform the migration manually at a later time by using the Data Migration Assistant or the migration utility.

Performing Migration into a New Directory Structure

You should install the Oracle8i software into a new ORACLE_HOME if you're planning to remove the Oracle7 installation after a successful migration of the Oracle7 databases to Oracle8i. Before proceeding with the migration, you must perform a normal shutdown and take a cold backup of the Oracle7 database.

Migrating the Database During Installation

As discussed earlier, you can perform a migration from Oracle7 to Oracle8i during the installation of Oracle8i. If you plan to migrate to a new directory structure, you should make sure that you choose a new location for the installation of Oracle8i.

The installer will automatically detect the existing Oracle7 version and prompt you to migrate the database at the end of the installation. You can choose the databases you want to migrate. At the end of the Oracle8i installation, the Data Migration Assistant is invoked (if you chose to perform the migration) and will guide you through the migration process. Alternatively, you can choose not to migrate during installation and perform the migration manually at a later time by using the Data Migration Assistant or the migration utility.

This method will allow you to remove the Oracle7 installation after the migration is successfully completed.

Migration Through Export/Import

So far, you've seen migration by using the Data Migration Assistant and the migration utility. These are the preferred techniques for performing a migration. However, when you're migrating from a non-PC platform such as UNIX, Export/Import can be a very useful strategy. Use of Export/Import for migration basically involves taking a full database export of the source database and then importing it into Oracle8i on Windows NT.

To Do: Migrate an Oracle7 Database on UNIX to an Oracle8i Database on Windows NT by Using Export/Import

1. Shut down the Oracle7 database on UNIX in the normal mode. Don't do a shutdown immediate or shutdown abort.

```
%svrmgrl
svrmgr> connect internal
svrmgr> shutdown normal
```

▼ To Do

5

> On a Windows NT machine, you also need to shut down the Oracle7 database service from the Control Panel.

2. Take a cold backup of the database.

3. Open the database:

   %svrmgrl
   svrmgr> **connect internal**
   svrmgr> **startup restrict**

4. Take a full database export by using the Export utility or Oracle Data Manager. The following command shows how to take a full database export by using the command-line Export utility:

   ```
   exp system/manager@2:SOURCE_SID file=export.dmp log=
   export.log full=y
   ```

5. Install the Oracle8 software on the Windows NT platform and create a starter database (refer to Hour 4 for complete details on installing Oracle8i), or create a database to be used as a target database on Windows NT.

6. Transfer the file to the Windows NT machine by using FTP. You must perform the FTP transfer in binary mode; otherwise, there might be some problems in reading the export dump.

> If your Oracle7 and Oracle8i databases will coexist on the same machine, you have to make sure that the log files, data files, and control files are named differently than on the Oracle7 database. The names of the files associated with your Oracle7 database can be obtained from Server Manager. The following example shows how this can be done on Windows NT:
>
> SVRMGR> **connect internal/password@2:ORC7**
>
> SVRMGR> **spool c:\orant\database\db_files.log**
> SVRMGR> **select * from v$controlfile;**
> SVRMGR> **select name, status from v$datafile;**
> SVRMGR> **select * from v$logfile;**
> SVRMGR> **select tablespace_name from dba_tablespaces;**
> SVRMGR> **spool off**
>
> The file db_files.log lists all the files associated with the Oracle7 database.

▼   7. Make sure that the target database is running. This can be verified by using Control
        Panel's Services tool and connecting to the database from Server Manager.

     8. From the command prompt, type

        ```
        C:> set oracle_sid=Oracle8i_sid
        ```

     9. If you want to maintain the exact same structure and storage parameters for the
        tablespaces as the source database, you can perform a full import to the target data-
        base by using the export dump created in step 4. On the other hand, if you want to
        change the structure or storage parameters for the tablespaces, you can pre-create
        the tablespaces and users. After the tablespaces are pre-created with the desired
        storage setting, you can perform the full import with ignore=y:

        ```
        C:> imp81 system/manager file=export.dmp ignore=y log=
        import.log full=y
        ```

> The show=y option can be used to query the export dump for the details of
> the tablespace structure and storage parameters.

    10. View the import log file to ensure that the import was successful.

▲   11. Take a full backup of the target database.

> If you're migrating an Oracle database from Windows NT to Windows NT,
> the process is still the same.

5

To Do: Migrate an Oracle7 Database to Oracle8i by Using SQL*PLUS's COPY Command

To Do

The SQL*PLUS COPY command can be used to perform a migration similar to
export/import, but use of this technique requires that both databases be online. Follow
these steps:

     1. Install Oracle8i, if it isn't already installed (refer to Hour 4 for complete instruc-
        tions on installing Oracle8i).

     2. Create an Oracle8i database to be used as a target database.

     3. Add the required tablespaces and users to the target database.

     4. Install the required SQL*Net or Net8 software, and configure the aliases that can
▼   be used to connect to the databases.

▼

 | Oracle8i communicates only via SQL*Net version 2 or Net8.

5. Set oracle_sid=*Oracle7_sid*.

6. Connect to SQL*PLUS as the internal account.

7. Create database links from the Oracle7 database to your Oracle8i database.

8. By using the create table .. as select command (CTAS), copy the table definitions and data from Oracle7 to the Oracle8i database. Alternatively, use the SQL*PLUS COPY command to copy the tables and their contents to the Oracle8i database.

▲ 9. Add views, synonyms, stored procedures, and so on, to the target database.

Using the Oracle Migration Assistant for Microsoft Access

The Oracle Migration Assistant for Microsoft Access is an easy-to-use GUI tool you can use to migrate Access databases to Oracle8i. The wizard that's provided guides you step by step through the migration process.

To Do: Migrate a Microsoft Access Database to Oracle8i

▼ To Do

The Oracle Migration Assistant is a GUI tool that you can use to migrate a Microsoft Access database to Oracle. Most of the conversion is automatic; however, after the migration completes, verify that the data types and macros are converted without problems. The following steps show how you can perform such a migration:

1. Choose Start, Programs, Oracle for Windows NT, Oracle Migration Assistant.

2. In the Select Database dialog box, click the Add Database button and add the databases you want to migrate to Oracle. Click Next (see Figures 5.1 and 5.2).

▼

FIGURE 5.1

Access databases can be migrated using the Oracle Migration Assistant for Microsoft Access.

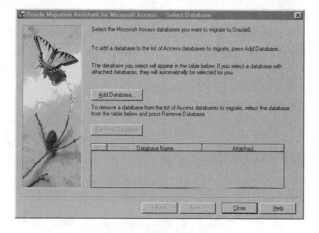

FIGURE 5.2

Choose the Access database to migrate.

An .mdb file represents a Microsoft Access database.

5

3. Customize the migration of datatypes. You can use the Customize button in this dialog box to customize the mapping of Access datatypes to Oracle datatypes. Click Next.

4. Choose the portions of the database to migrate. For example, you can choose to migrate the entire database or portions of it, such as tables, indexes, relationships, default values, and validation rules. Click Next.

5. Choose to migrate the database structure only or both the structure and the data. Click Next.

▼   6. Choose the Oracle schema and the tablespace into which you want to migrate the data. You can migrate multiple MS Access databases into the same Oracle database.

    7. Supply a valid DBA account and password to proceed with the migration. A progress bar will display the status of the migration.

    8. When migration is complete, the Oracle Microsoft Access Assistant generates a migration log and report. You should view this log and report for any error messages that occurred during the migration process.

▲

Post-Migration Steps

You might have to take several steps after a migration is complete so that the applications can use the full capabilities of the Oracle8i database:

- *Precompiler applications*—If you plan to use Oracle8i's new features, you might need to modify the application code and then recompile and relink the code. Even if you aren't going to make any changes to the application code, you should still relink the applications to the SQLLIB runtime library provided by the Oracle8i precompiler before running them against the Oracle8i database.

- *OCI applications*—You can use Oracle7 OCI applications against an Oracle8i database without making any changes. If you're using constraints in the OCI applications, however, relink the applications by using Oracle8i's OCI library (OCILIB). If you use the nondeferred mode of linking, you will receive error messages immediately after the bind and define operations, but performance will be the same as running it against Oracle7. On the other hand, if you use the deferred mode of linking, you will see the error messages later in the execution, for example during DESCRIBE, EXECUTE, or FETCH calls; performance, however, will be better than Oracle7.

- *SQL*Plus Scripts*—SQL*Plus scripts should be modified to change the compatibility from version 7 to version 8. Other than this change, the scripts should run without any problems.

Summary

Migrating an Oracle7 database to Oracle8i requires careful planning on your part. Several methods can be used to migrate, such as using the MIG utility, the Oracle Data Migration Assistant, or export/import. This hour discussed several alternatives for performing the migration. You also looked at the various migration challenges to minimize the surprises during this important task. The actual migration for your system will vary and depends on the project scope and depth. You will have to involve people from different teams and make sure that enough hardware, software, and other resources are available.

Q&A

Q Can I determine beforehand the amount of time involved in performing a migration?

A I wish we could do that, but unfortunately it's not a trivial task. The migration time will vary with your system, but you can definitely minimize it by following the suggestions discussed this hour. The extent of planning and testing of the migration depends on the number of applications used. The migration process can become involved when the system to be migrated involves different Oracle versions and other legacy systems.

Q What are some things I should check when planning the migration?

A Planning the migration is a very important step and the following checklist should help:

- Review the migration steps from the Oracle migration guide.
- List the hardware, software, and other resources you need.
- Obtain a list of any gotchas from Oracle technical support.
- Talk with peers who have performed similar migration.
- Make sure that the migration won't affect the production system.
- Inform the user community of the migration.
- Roll out the new features of the new version.

5

Workshop

The Workshop contains quiz questions and activities to help reinforce what you've learned in this hour. You can check Appendix A for the answers (but don't peek!).

Quiz

1. What alternative methods can you use to perform the migration to Oracle8i?
2. How is upgrading a database different from migrating one?
3. What are the restrictions on the use of the MIG utility to perform a migration?

Exercises

1. What are some things that you would consider for performing a smooth migration of your applications after migration to Oracle8i?

2. Estimate the amount of time it would take to migrate all your databases to Oracle8i.

HOUR 6

Creating an Oracle8i Database on Windows NT

In this lesson, you look at the various ways in which you can create an Oracle8i database on Windows NT. The following are general steps for creating a database, all of which you learn about in this lesson:

1. Create the init*SID*.ora parameter file.
2. Create an OFA-compliant directory structure.
3. Choose a method of database creation.
4. Create an Oracle service for the database.
5. Create the database, using the desired method.

Prerequisites for Creating a Database

Before you can create an Oracle database on Windows NT, you must configure the operating system. Refer to Hour 3, "Configuring a Windows NT Server for Oracle8i," for detailed analysis of the various decisions that you have to make for this purpose.

In addition to the operating system configuration, you also have to decide the manner in which the database will be used and configured. These decisions should include the following:

- *Database sizing*—Choosing the proper initialization parameters is important for obtaining an optimally tuned database system. Sizing the database files based on how the database is to be used can play an important role in choosing the initialization parameters.

- *Passwords for SYS and SYSTEM*—Change and protect these passwords. The default password for SYS is CHANGE_ON_INSTALL, and the default password for SYSTEM is MANAGER. These user accounts perform administrative tasks. The passwords of the SYS and SYSTEM users should be changed as soon as possible after database creation.

- *MTS configuration*—MTS is one option that you have for increasing the number of concurrent connections to the database. As discussed in Hour 4, "Installing Oracle8i on Windows NT," you must consider several things before using MTS in your database, such as sizing the SGA and deciding the number of shared servers and dispatchers.

- *Registry and environment variables*—The ORACLE_SID, ORACLE_HOME, and path variables should be set to the correct values so that the correct instance can be accessed.

- *An OFA-compliant directory structure*—By creating such a structure, you can more easily manage the database, and directory choices will be reflected in the initialization file parameters.

- *Backing up all existing databases*—Take a complete backup of all your existing databases to protect them against accidental modifications or deletions of existing files during the creation of the new database.

- *Mirroring control and redo log files*—These files should be mirrored because these important database components can help you recover a database. Keep at least two copies of the control file on different physical devices. The redo log files should be multiplexed, and the redo log groups should be placed on different physical devices.

- *Organizing the database contents in multiple tablespaces*—By doing so, you minimize contention. Table 6.1 shows several tablespaces (in addition to the SYSTEM tablespace) that you can use to separate database objects.

TABLE 6.1 SEPARATE DATABASE OBJECTS TO MINIMIZE CONTENTION

Tablespace	Contents
TEMP	Temporary segments
RBS	Rollback segments
APPS_DATA	Production data
APPS_IDX	Indexes

If you want to create a new database but use existing datafiles, re-create the tablespaces and reuse the files.

Choosing Initialization Parameters for Your Database

The initialization file (init*SID*.ora) provides the parameters used during database startup. Because the default initialization parameters aren't ideal for most systems, you should customize these parameters with your database environment in mind. To create an initialization file for a database instance, copy the one provided by Oracle on the distribution media, or use the init.ora file from the seed database (if installed) as a template. Table 6.2 shows some initialization parameters that should be modified.

TABLE 6.2 INITIALIZATION PARAMETERS THAT YOU SHOULD MODIFY

Parameter	Description
DB_NAME	Database identifier. If you try to mount two databases with the same name, you will get error ORA-01102: cannot mount database in EXCLUSIVE mode during the second mount.
DB_DOMAIN	The network domain where the database is created.
CONTROL_FILES	Names of the control files. If you don't change the CONTROL_FILES parameter for a new database instance, the control file of other databases can be overwritten by the new instance, making them unusable.
DB_BLOCK_SIZE	Oracle database block size in bytes.

continues

6

TABLE 6.2   CONTINUED

Parameter	Description
SHARED_POOL_SIZE	Shared pool size in bytes.
BACKGROUND_DUMP_DEST	Location of background trace files.
USER_DUMP_DEST	Location of user trace files.
DB_BLOCK_BUFFERS	Number of buffers in the database buffer cache.
COMPATIBLE	Specifies the server version that this instance is compatible with.
IFILE	Specifies another parameter file that has additional parameters used during startup.
MAX_DUMP_FILE_SIZE	Maximum size (in OS blocks) allowed for trace files.
PROCESSES	Maximum number of OS processes that can simultaneously connect to this instance.
ROLLBACK_SEGMENTS	The rollback segments allocated to this instance.
LOG_BUFFER	Size of the redo log buffer (in bytes).
LOG_ARCHIVE_START	Enables archiving if the database is in ARCHIVELOG mode.
LOG_ARCHIVE_FORMAT	Filename format to be used by default for archived logs.
LOG_ARCHIVE_DEST	Location of archived redo log files.
LICENSE_MAX_USERS	Maximum number of users that can be created in the database.
LICENSE_MAX_SESSIONS	Maximum number of concurrent sessions that can be used against the instance.

The following is a sample init.ora file:

```
db_name = PROD
db_domain = WORLD
db_files = 1020
control_files = (C:\PROD\ctl1PROD.ora, C:\PROD\ctl2PROD.ora)
db_file_multiblock_read_count = 16
db_block_buffers = 800
shared_pool_size = 12000000
log_checkpoint_interval = 4000
processes = 200
dml_locks = 200
log_buffer = 32768
sequence_cache_entries = 30
sequence_cache_hash_buckets = 23
background_dump_dest = C:\ORANT\rdbms81\trace
user_dump_dest = C:\ORANT\rdbms81\trace
db_block_size = 2048
compatible = 8.1.3.0.0
sort_area_size = 65536
```

```
log_checkpoint_timeout = 0
remote_login_passwordfile = shared
max_dump_file_size = 10240
```

Organizing Database Structures to Reduce Contention and Fragmentation

To minimize contention and fragmentation, you separate groups of objects—for example, tables with different fragmentation propensity, which indicates the expected amount of fragmentation for a particular object type. Use Table 6.3 as a guideline for separating objects.

TABLE 6.3 FRAGMENTATION PROPENSITY

Segment Type	Expected Fragmentation
Data dictionary	Zero
Rollback segments	Medium
Temporary segments	High
Application data	Low

You can help reduce disk contention by grouping objects based on their access and use:

- Segments with different backup needs
- Segments with different security needs
- Segments belonging to different projects
- Separating large segments from smaller segments
- Rollback segments
- Temporary segments
- Data segments
- Index segments

To reduce contention, these objects should be separated across different disk drives as well as tablespaces.

6

 You choose the character set during database creation. Changing the character set after the database is created requires re-creation of the database. The database character set that you choose should be the same as or a superset of all the character sets that would be used to access the database.

Setting Environment Variables

Several environment variables should be set so that the correct instance starts. Look at some important environment variables that should be set:

- ORACLE_SID can specify the default instance to connect to.

 If ORACLE_SID isn't set properly when the CREATE DATABASE statement is run, your existing data can be wiped out.

- ORACLE_HOME specifies the full pathname of the Oracle system home directory.
- PATH specifies the search path and should include the ORACLE_HOME directory.
- ORA_NLS specifies the location of the language object files. If the database is started with languages and character sets other than the database defaults, and ORA_NLS isn't set properly, they won't be recognized.

To Do: Updating ORACLE_SID in the Windows NT Registry

The default SID can be specified by setting the Registry entry ORACLE_SID. Follow these steps:

1. At the DOS command prompt, enter regedt32.
2. Select the key \HKEY_LOCAL_MACHINE\SOFTWARE\ORACLE\HOME*ID*.
3. From the Edit menu, choose Add Value.
4. Specify the following settings and then click OK:
    - In the Value name box, type ORACLE_SID.
    - For the Data Type, choose REG_SZ.
5. Type your SID in the String Editor text box (see Figure 6.1) and click OK.

 6. Exit the Registry.

FIGURE 6.1

Setting the ORACLE_SID *in the Registry.*

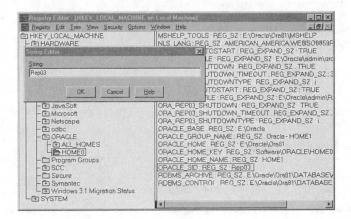

Choosing the Method for Database Creation

Several options are available for creating a database:

- *Use the Oracle installer to create a database*—This is the simplest method for database creation. It allows the creation of a seed database that you can use as a template for creating other databases.

- *Use the supplied database creation scripts*—Build_all.sql and Build_db.sql are database scripts provided with Oracle that you can modify as desired to create a database with your own schema. You can specify parameters such as MAXDATAFILES and specify multiple SYSTEM tablespace database files by using this method. After the required changes are made to the scripts, you can run the scripts to create the database.

- *Use the* CREATE DATABASE *command*—Manually run the CREATE DATABASE command to create the database (refer to the Oracle SQL reference manual for the complete syntax). This method is very flexible and allows you to specify parameters such as MAXDATAFILES and multiple SYSTEM tablespace datafiles. This method has the potential of syntax errors, however.

Using the CREATE DATABASE Command

The SQL command CREATE DATABASE can be used to create a database manually:

```
CREATE DATABASE database
    [CONTROLFILE [REUSE]]
    [LOGFILE filespec[, ...]]
    MAXLOGFILES integer
```

6

```
MAXLOGMEMBERS integer
MAXLOGHISTORY integer
DATAFILE filespec[, ...]
MAXDATAFILES integer
MAXINSTANCES integer
     ARCHIVELOG¦NOARCHIVELOG
EXCLUSIVE
CHARACTERSET charset
```

The CREATE DATABASE command has several parameters, described in Table 6.4.

TABLE 6.4   CREATE DATABASE PARAMETERS

Parameter	Description
database	Name of the database to create.
CONTROLFILE REUSE	Specifies the location of control files. This option allows the reuse of existing control files. You get an error if REUSE is omitted and control files exist.
LOGFILE	Specifies one or more redo log files. Redo log file groups containing one or more redo log file members are specified by each filespec. If filespec is omitted, two redo log file groups are created by default.
MAXLOGFILES	Specifies the maximum number of redo log file groups that can be created for this database.
MAXLOGMEMBERS	Specifies the maximum number of members for a redo log file group.
MAXLOGHISTORY	Specifies the maximum number of archived redo log files for automatic media recovery. Used with a PARALLEL SERVER option.
DATAFILE	Specifies one or more datafiles.
MAXDATAFILES	Specifies the maximum number of datafiles for this database.
MAXINSTANCES	Specifies the maximum number of instances that can simultaneously mount and open this database.
ARCHIVELOG or NOARCHIVELOG	Specifies the database mode for archive purposes. NOARCHIVELOG is the default mode.
EXCLUSIVE	Specifies exclusive mode, in which only one instance can mount the database.
CHARACTERSET	Specifies the character set used by the database to store the data. The character set for a database can't be changed without re-creating the database.

The CREATE DATABASE command does the following:

- The specified datafiles are created, and data of existing datafiles is erased.
- The specified control files are created and initialized.

- The specified redo logs are created and initialized.
- The SYSTEM tablespace and the SYSTEM rollback segment are created.
- The character set for the database is specified.

To Do: Create a Database

In this exercise, you create a database called PROD with the following specifications:

- Reuse existing control files.
- Use one datafile sized 20MB, and allow it to autoextend.
- Multiplex redo log files of size 1MB each.
- Use character set WE8ISO8859P1.

Follow these steps:

1. Create a directory called PROD:

   ```
   C:\> mkdir c:\prod
   ```

2. Copy C:\ORANT\DATABASE\INITORCL.ORA to C:\PROD\INITPROD.ORA:

   ```
   C:\> copy C:\ORANT\DATABASE\INITORCL.ORA C:\MARS\INITPROD.ORA
   ```

> If you have not created the starter database, you can use the init.ora file provided by Oracle8i. This file can be found in %ORACLE_HOME%\admin\sample\pfile\initsmpl.ora.

3. In the INITPROD.ORA file, edit the DB_NAME, CONTROL_FILES, GLOBAL_NAMES, and DB_FILES parameters to reflect the new database parameters and the location of the associated files.

4. Create the Windows NT service for the new database, using the ORADIM command. For example, from a DOS prompt, type

   ```
   C:\> oradim -NEW -SID PROD -INTPWD password -STARTMODE AUTO
           -PFILE c:\prod\initprod.ora
   ```

5. Set ORACLE_SID to PROD:

   ```
   C:\> Set ORACLE_SID=PROD
   ```

   This sets the default database that you will be connected to when you use Server Manager.

6. Use Control Panel's Services tool to start the ORACLESERVICEPROD service if it's not already started.

▼ 7. Connect to the database as internal by using Server Manager:

```
C:\> svrmgrl
C:\> connect internal/password
```

8. Start the database in the NOMOUNT state:

```
SVRMGR> STARTUP NOMOUNT PFILE=c:\prod\initprod.ora
```

9. Run the CREATE DATABASE command from Server Manager:

```
Svmgr>create database prod
  2>controlfile reuse
  3>logfile GROUP 1
  4>('C:\log1aprod.ora',
  5>'D:\log1bprod.ora') size 1M reuse,
  6>GROUP 2
  7>( 'C:\log2aprod.ora',
  8>'D:\log2bprod.ora' ) size 1M reuse
  9>datafile 'C:\prod\sys1prod.ora' size 20M ¦reuse autoextend on
 10>next 10M maxsize 200M
 11>character set WE8ISO8859P1;
```

10. Run CATALOG.SQL to generate the data dictionary:

```
SVRMGR> @%RDBMS80%\ADMIN\CATALOG.SQL
```

11. Run CATPROC.SQL to generate the objects used by PL/SQL:

```
SVRMGR> @%RDBMS80%\ADMIN\CATPROC.SQL
```

▲ 12. Run additional scripts as desired, such as CATREP.SQL for advanced
      replication.

To Do: Determine the MAX Parameters for Your Database

To Do

Now that you have created a database, you must determine the MAX parameters so you
can figure out the limitations set on the use of the database.

▼ To determine these parameters, connect to the Server Manager as internal and execute
the following:

```
SVRMGR> Alter database backup controlfile to trace
```

This command will create a SQL script that contains several database commands. You
also can identify the maximum values set for certain parameters, such as redo logfiles,
datafiles, concurrent instances that can mount the database, and so on:

```
CREATE CONTROLFILE REUSE DATABASE "PROD" NORESETLOGS NOARCHIVELOG
     MAXLOGFILES 32
     MAXLOGMEMBERS 2
     MAXDATAFILES 254
     MAXINSTANCES 1
▼    MAXLOGHISTORY 899
```

```
▼    LOGFILE
       GROUP 1 'C:\PROD\LOGPROD1.ORA'  SIZE 200K,
       GROUP 2 'C:\PROD\LOGPROD2.ORA'  SIZE 200K
     DATAFILE
       'C:\PROD\SYS1PROD.ORA',
       'C:\PROD\RBS1PROD.ORA',
       'C:\PROD\USR1PROD.ORA',
       'C:\PROD\TMP1PROD.ORA',
       'C:\PROD\INDX1PROD.ORA'
▲    ;
```

To Do: Create a Database by Using BUILD_ALL.sql

To create a database called PROD by using Build_all.sql, follow these steps:

1. Create a directory called PROD:

   ```
   C:\> mkdir c:\prod
   ```

2. Copy C:\ORANT\DATABASE\INITORCL.ORA to C:\PROD\INITPROD.ORA:

   ```
   C:\> copy C:\ORANT\DATABASE\INITORCL.ORA C:\MARS\INITPROD.ORA
   ```

3. In the INITPROD.ORA file, edit the DB_NAME, CONTROL_FILES, GLOBAL_NAMES, and DB_FILES parameters to reflect the new database parameters and the location of the associated files.

4. Create the Windows NT service for the new database by using the ORADIM command. For example, from a DOS prompt, type the following to create a new service called PROD:

   ```
   C:\> oradim -NEW -SID PROD -INTPWD password -STARTMODE AUTO
           -PFILE c:\prod\initprod.ora
   ```

   - AUTO specifies that the service is automatically started when Windows NT starts.

   - INTPWD is the password for the "internal" account.

   - The PFILE parameter provides the full pathname of init*SID*.ora.

> You might have to re-create an Oracle service for an existing database if you have problems during database startup.

6

▼   5. Set ORACLE_SID to PROD. This sets the default database that you are connected to
       when you use Server Manager:

       ```
       C:\> Set ORACLE_SID=PROD
       ```

    6. Copy the BUILD_DB.SQL script to c:\prod:

       ```
       C:\> copy c:\orant\rdbms80\admin\build_db.sql
            c:\prod\build_prod.sql
       ```

    7. Make the following changes to the Build_prod.sql script:

       - Set PFILE to the full pathname for INITPROD.ORA.

       - Change CREATE DATABASE ORACLE to CREATE DATABASE PROD.

       - Specify appropriate names for the datafiles and log files.

       - Set the Oracle home directory to C:\PROD.

    8. Use the Services icon in Control Panel to start the service ORACLESERVICEPROD if
       it's not already started.

    9. Connect to the database as "internal" by using Server Manager:

       ```
       C:\> svrmgrl
       Svrmgr> connect internal/password
       ```

   10. Start the database in the NOMOUNT state:

       ```
       SVRMGR> STARTUP NOMOUNT PFILE=c:\prod\initprod.ora
       ```

   11. Run Build_prod.sql and spool the results to build.log:

       ```
       SVRMGR> SPOOL build.log
       SVRMGR> @BUILD_PROD.SQL
       ```

       Fix the errors encountered while running Build_prod.sql, and rerun the script for
       successful completion.

   12. Run CATALOG.SQL to generate the data dictionary:

       ```
       SVRMGR> @%RDBMS80%\ADMIN\CATALOG.SQL
       ```

   13. Run CATPROC.SQL to generate the objects used by PL/SQL:

       ```
       SVRMGR> @%RDBMS80%\ADMIN\CATPROC.SQL
       ```

   14. Run additional scripts as desired, such as CATREP8M.SQL for advanced
       replication.

   15. Check build.log for errors and fix them. (See Hour 20, "Diagnosing Problems," to
▲   fix some common problems.)

Although CATEXP.SQL is called from within CATALOG.SQL, the two files aren't interdependent because no view in CATEXP.SQL depends on views defined in CATALOG.SQL.

To Do: Create a New Database with Instance Manager

You can use Instance Manager to easily create new databases:

1. Choose Start, Oracle for Windows NT, Windows NT Instance Manager. The Instance Manager starts and shows the status and startup mode of all SIDs.

2. Click the New button. In the New Instance dialog box, supply the specifications for the new instance, such as SID, internal password, and startup criteria.

3. Click the Advanced button. In the Advanced Options dialog box, supply the appropriate database name, the log file, the datafile parameters, and a character set for the new database.

To Do: Create a New Database with the Database Assistant

The Database Assistant can create new databases as follows:

1. From the Start menu, choose Programs, Oracle for Windows NT, Oracle Database Assistant.

2. Select Create a Database (see Figure 6.2) and click Next.

FIGURE 6.2

Choosing to create a database in the Database Configuration Assistant.

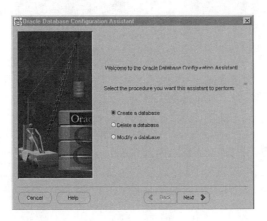

6

▼ 3. Choose the Typical (see Figure 6.3) or Custom option, and click Next. By using the Custom option, you can customize the parameters for the database that you're trying to create. You can choose to copy files from the CD or create new datafiles for the database (see Figure 6.4).

FIGURE 6.3

Choose the Typical configuration.

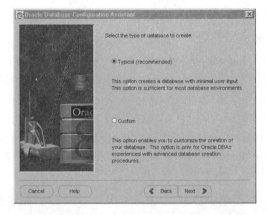

FIGURE 6.4

Files can be copied from the CD, or new files can be created for the new database.

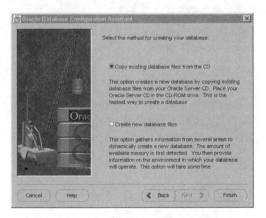

▼ 4. Choose the type of database environment (see Figure 6.5).

FIGURE 6.5

Choose the type of database environment. This will help in setting the initialization parameters.

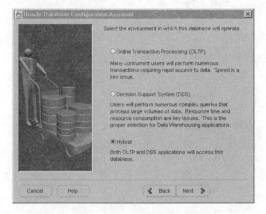

5. Choose the number of concurrent users (see Figure 6.6).

FIGURE 6.6

Choose the number of concurrent users.

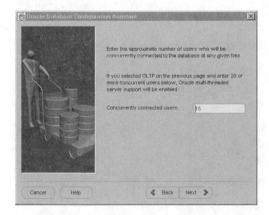

6. Select the cartridges you want for the database (see Figure 6.7).

FIGURE 6.7

Select the cartridges to install for the database.

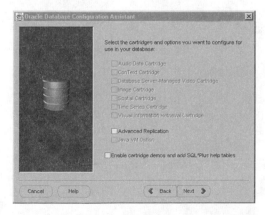

6

▼ 7. Choose to create the database now (see Figure 6.8).

FIGURE 6.8

You can choose to create the database now or save the instructions in a batch file to be executed later.

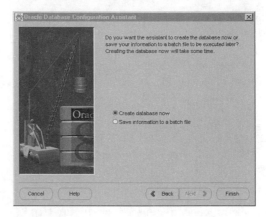

8. Choose Finish. Verify the database creation (see Figures 6.9 and 6.10)

FIGURE 6.9

The database will be created through various phases.

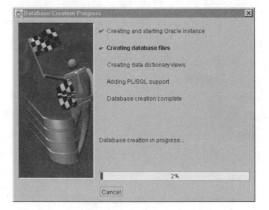

FIGURE 6.10

Verify the completion of database creation.

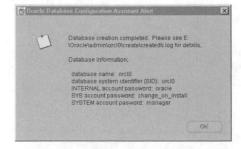

▲

Be extremely careful in making changes to the Registry parameters because improper changes can potentially prevent Windows NT from starting up.

To Do: Create an Identical Copy of the Database, but Without Data

Export and import use the view definitions in CATEXP.SQL to get the information it needs from the data dictionary. To create the export/import views, you must run catexp.sql from Server Manager while connected as SYS or the internal account. Follow these steps:

1. Take a full export of the source database with ROWS=N:

   ```
   C:\> set oracle_sid = src
   C:\> exp system/manager full=y rows=n file=sqlstmts.dmp
   ```

   This will create a full database export but without any rows. The sqlstmts.dmp file contains the SQL statements necessary to create the database objects.

2. On the destination database, run import with ROWS=N to create a database structure in the destination database that's identical to the source database:

   ```
   C:\> set oracle_sid = dest
   C:\> imp system/manager full=y rows=n file=sqlstmts.dmp
   ```

Each database has Windows NT services associated with it. These services must be started before the database can be used (see Figure 6.11). Because a running Windows NT service consumes valuable system resources, you should keep the number of services running to a minimum. Remove or disable services you don't need.

FIGURE 6.11

Disable services not needed.

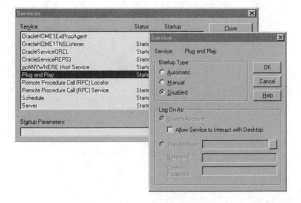

6

Table 6.5 shows various database scripts used during database creation. These scripts reside in %ORACLE_HOME%\rdbms\admin and should be run while connected as internal.

TABLE 6.5 SCRIPTS USED DURING DATABASE CREATION

Database Script	Use
Catalog.sql	Creates the data dictionary views
Catproc.sql	Creates PL/SQL objects
Catexp.sql	Creates dictionary views used by export/import
Utlxplan.sql	Objects that allow the use of the explain plan feature

To Do: Add Tablespaces and Rollback Segments to Your Database

▼ To Do

After you create a simple database, you might want to add more tablespaces and rollback segments to it. In the PROD database, create a tablespace called USER_DATA and a rollback segment called rb1 in tablespace RBS. Follow these steps:

1. Use Control Panel's Services tool to start the ORACLESERVICEPROD service if it's not already started.

2. Connect to the database as "internal" by using Server Manager:

```
c:\> set oracle_sid = prod
c:\> svrmgrl
svrmgr> connect internal/password
```

3. Open the database:

```
SVRMGR> STARTUP PFILE=c:\prod\initprod.ora
```

4. Create the USER_DATA tablespace by using the CREATE TABLESPACE command:

```
SVRMGR> create tablespace USER_DATA datafile
'd:\prod\tmp1prod.ora' SIZE 10M
storage (initial 1M next 1M);
```

5. Create the rollback segment rb1 by using the CREATE ROLLBACK SEGMENT command:

```
SVRMGR> create rollback segment rb1 tablespace rbs
Storage ( initial 1M next 1M
Minextents 2 maxextents 256);
```

6. Bring the rollback segment rb1 online:

▲
```
SVRMGR> alter rollback segment rb1 online;
```

Deleting a Database

The safest and easiest way to remove a database is to use the Database Configuration Assistant (see Figure 6.12). Alternatively, you can remove a database manually, which requires deleting all the database files and removing the Windows NT service for the database by using the ORADIM utility.

FIGURE 6.12

The Database Configuration Assistant.

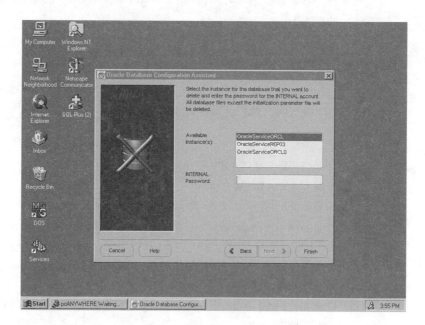

Summary

Creating an Oracle database on Windows NT isn't a difficult task. It can be accomplished by using various tools, such as the Instance Manager and Database Assistant, or even manually using scripts provided by Oracle. However, it's important to create a properly sized database to prevent administrative headaches in the future. Also consider separating objects with similar characteristics to minimize contention in the database.

6

Q&A

Q What will happen if I use control files from another database for my new database?

A This shouldn't be done because it has the potential of making the original database unusable.

Q What do you recommend for setting the init.ora parameters?

A No magic values exist for the init.ora parameters. The ideal values depend on factors such as the type of activities that will be performed against the database,
amount of data, number of concurrent users, and so on. You must choose values
after thorough understanding of your system and then fine-tune the performance.
The lessons in Part V, "Tuning and Troubleshooting the Databases," discuss this in
more detail.

Workshop

The Workshop contains quiz questions and activities to help reinforce what you've
learned in this hour. You can check Appendix A for the answers (but don't peek!).

Quiz

1. What script can be used to manually create a database?
2. How can you group objects to reduce disk contention?
3. What's the purpose of catalog.sql and catproc.sql scripts?
4. Changing which parameters will require the database to be re-created?

Exercises

1. Move your PROD database from machine A to machine B.
2. Consider some of the things necessary to size the database for your data
    warehousing system.

HOUR 7

Converting a SQL Server Database to Oracle8i with the Migration Workbench

Oracle is well established in the Windows NT market, and companies have been requesting an easy-to-use tool that will help them to migrate their existing Microsoft SQL Server databases and applications to Oracle8i.

SQL Server and Oracle have notable differences in architecture, client/server communication methods, data load methods, data retrieval methods, and data storage concepts. Other differences are as follows:

- The SQL language of SQL Server and Oracle8i also varies slightly, even though both versions are ANSI compliant. MS SQL Server uses Transact-SQL, whereas Oracle uses PL/SQL.

- Administrative tasks such as managing multiple databases are different.
- SQL Server is stream based and uses one cursor per connection. Oracle, on the other hand, is connection based and can use multiple cursors per connection.
- SQL Server automatically puts result sets in streams that are returned to the client. In Oracle, a cursor variable is returned to the client. This cursor variable is a handle to the SGA resident cursor and allows the client to fetch as much data as needed.
- SQL Server uses page-level locking, whereas Oracle uses row-level locking.

SQL Server and Oracle also have several similarities in that they're both relational databases and therefore share the following features:

- Schema objects such as tables and views
- Data types
- Support of logical transactions
- Support of triggers and stored procedures
- Support of referential integrity
- Support of check constraint
- Access to system catalog using SQL
- Server-based security

There are several methods for migrating data from MS SQL Server to Oracle:

- You can write a program that connects to both SQL Server and Oracle8i databases, retrieves from the source database, performs conversion/translation, and then inserts into the target database.
- You can use a gateway that performs a distributed query to transfer the database.
- You can use flat files for data transfer. MS SQL Server provides a tool, the Bulk Copy Program (BCP), that can be used to unload the data into flat files. This flat file can be loaded into Oracle by using Oracle's SQL*Loader utility.
- You can use Oracle's GUI Migration Workbench.

This lesson focuses on using the Migration Workbench.

Working with the Migration Workbench

Oracle's Migration Workbench is a tool, available free with Oracle Server, that you can use to easily migrate non-Oracle data and applications to Oracle. Without the Migration Workbench, you have to run multiple scripts to unload and load the data dictionary and convert application files. The current release of the Migration Workbench, V1.0.4.0.0, allows the conversion of SQL Server 6.5. Future releases will provide support for converting other databases. You can use the Workbench Software Development Kit (WSDK) to provide support for the databases.

Users can define a migration project to specify the various database and application components to be migrated. After the migration project is defined, users can use various wizards to invoke the migration process.

The Workbench can be used to manage multiple migration projects. Each migration project has its own repository to store migration information. The repository can be queried to obtain information such as object dependencies, which can help you understand the effect a change in one object can have on other objects.

The current version of the Migration Workbench doesn't support the migration of individual users or schema objects.

Errors that occur during the migration are logged in the log window. Also, three log files are created that record all the successful CREATE and ALTER statements, the equivalent DROP and ALTER statements, and all the SQL statements that are not executed. By default, the log files are placed in %ORACLE_HOME%\mwb\log.

You can set the location of the log files by using the Log File Directory setting on the Logging page of the Options dialog box.

By default, the following steps are taken during the migration:

1. Create the users.
2. Create the tables.
3. Load the data into the table.
4. Create the table constraints.

7

To Do: Delete the SYSLOGS Table

SQL Server databases have the SYSLOGS table, which contains redo information. Because this table isn't necessary in Oracle, you must delete it from the migration. Follow these steps:

1. By using Server Manager, log on to the database as the owner of the Oracle Migration Workbench Repository.

2. Execute the following SQL statement:

```
SQL> delete from MTG_SOURCE_LOAD
  2> where SOURCE_SYS_TABLE = 'syslogs';
```

Understanding the Workbench GUI

The Workbench GUI simplifies the migration process. You invoke the New Project Wizard to create a new project that describes the source and target databases. This wizard shows information in three panes:

- The *Navigator pane* navigates between the various database components in a hierarchical format. It consists of two tabs: source model (displays the application system being migrated) and Oracle model (displays the source model after it's mapped to Oracle).

- The *Property pane* displays the properties of the database component currently chosen in the Navigator pane.

- The *Logging pane* logs the actions taken during the migration.

All Migration Workbench components are written in Java and can be run on any platform that has a Java runtime environment (JRE) and ODBC support. The Migration Workbench uses JDBC/ODBC to read data from the SQL Server database and JDBC/OCI8 to load data into the Oracle database. Because SQL Server and Oracle are relational databases, they share similar objects, as shown in Table 7.1.

TABLE 7.1   ANALOGOUS COMPONENTS IN ORACLE8I AND MICROSOFT SQL SERVER 6.X

Oracle8i	MS SQL Server 6.x
Database	Database
Schema	Database and database owner (DBO)
Tablespace	Database
User	User
Role	Group
Table	Table

Oracle8i	MS SQL Server 6.x
Cluster	N/A
N/A	Temp tables
Column-level check constraint	Column-level check constraint
Column default	Column default
Unique constraint	IDENTITY property of column
Primary key constraint	Primary key constraint
Foreign key constraint	Foreign key constraint
Index	Index
PL/SQL procedure	Transact-SQL procedure
PL/SQL function	Transact-SQL function
Packages	N/A
Before triggers	Rules
After triggers	Triggers
Synonyms	N/A
Number column with associated IDENTITY property of column sequence and trigger[1]	
Snapshot	N/A
DATE[2]	DATETIME
BLOB	BINARY
View	View

1   When a new row is inserted, the trigger queries the sequence for the next value and inserts it into the column.

2   Milliseconds aren't supported by the DATE data type. Therefore, columns with the DATE data type can't be used as a primary key.

The Migration Workbench has several key features:

- Migrates a complete application system that includes the database schema, users, stored procedures, views, triggers, and embedded SQL
- Migrates multiple SQL Server databases to a single Oracle8i database
- Automatically maps the reserved words between SQL Server and Oracle8i
- Generates ANSI-compliant names, which allows the schemas to be quoted before generation
- Simplifies the migration task with its GUI interface
- Customizes storage parameters before generation
- Analyzes dependencies among the components being migrated

7

- Specifies the type of information displayed in the log that's generated during migration and which indicates the actions taken during the migration
- Allows migration to be performed in one step or broken down into several stages, such as loading the SQL Server model, mapping, generating, and moving the data
- Can launch the workbench from the Oracle Enterprise Manager (OEM)
- Protects the Workbench repository and the migration projects
- Supports the use of Oracle gateways for bulk data transfer
- Supports unloading and loading of projects using eXtensible Markup Language (XML) files
- Provides an extensive debugging facility

You can use the Migration Workbench to migrate a SQL Server database to an Oracle7 database if none of the source tables contain multiple text or binary data:

- Map TEXT to VARCHAR2 (if the text is less than 4,000 characters) or LONG (if the text is more than 4,000 characters).
- Map IMAGE, BINARY, and VARBINARY to LONG RAW.

There can be only one LONG or LONG RAW column in an Oracle database. Therefore, the source tables can't have more than one of the preceding datatypes in the same table.

Non-Oracle data types are mapped to Oracle data types that encapsulate types with similar characteristics. You can view and modify data type mappings by using the Options dialog box (choose Tools, Options). These changes affect all columns, and the source model must be remapped before the changes take effect.

Preserving Schema Objects

SQL Server is case sensitive, whereas Oracle is not. Thus, you might encounter problems when trying to migrate SQL Server objects such as TEST and test, because they would map to the same Oracle object. You should therefore use quoted names for the objects when they're migrated to Oracle. For example, "TEST" and "test" would be treated as two separate objects.

Another point to note is the usage of reserved words as names. For example, DATE is a reserved word in Oracle but not in SQL Server. As a result, the migration won't be successful for the SQL Server objects that use Oracle reserved words.

Choose object names in SQL Server that are unique by case. The object names also shouldn't use Oracle reserved words.

Installing the Oracle Migration Workbench

Oracle Migration Workbench can be installed on a Windows NT 4.0 or Windows 95/98 machine. Before installation, however, check the network hardware and software, and make sure that you can access an Oracle 8.0.5 database or higher from this machine.

You can't install two Oracle versions in the same Oracle home directory if they are of the same major release.

Hardware requirements for the Windows NT/95/98 clients to use Oracle Migration Workbench include the following:

- Intel 80486 or higher processor
- 64MB RAM minimum
- VGA video (recommended SVGA)
- CD-ROM drive
- Free hard disk space 180MB (for documentation, Migration Workbench repository, and so on)

Oracle Migration Workbench cannot be installed into a nondefault Oracle home because it depends on Oracle's JDBC driver, which in turn depends on the Oracle Net8 client. The Oracle Net8 client can't be installed in a nondefault Oracle home.

7

To Do: Install the Migration Workbench

The following steps can be performed to install the Migration Workbench on Windows NT. The steps assume that you are installing from the CD-ROM.

1. Log on to Windows NT as a member of the administrators group.

2. Stop all Oracle applications.

3. From the Control Panel, stop all the Oracle services.

4. Insert the Oracle Migration Workbench for Windows NT/95 CD in the CD-ROM. The Oracle installer should automatically start (otherwise, use Windows Explorer to go to the CD-ROM drive, and double-click setup.exe).

5. In the Oracle Installation Settings dialog box, specify the following (see Figure 7.1):

    • *Company name*—Name of your company.

FIGURE 7.1

Specify the Oracle home location during installation.

    • *Oracle home name*—Choose any 1–16 characters (only alphanumeric characters and underscores allowed) to specify the long name for the Oracle home. The default is DEFAULT_HOME.

    • *Oracle home location*—Specify the subdirectory under which the Oracle products are to be installed.

    • *Oracle home language*—The only language available is English.

6. Click OK.

7. The Select Installation Options dialog box appears with the following options (see Figure 7.2):

    • *Oracle Migration Workbench Software and Repository Install* installs the Oracle Migration Workbench software and creates the Oracle Migration Workbench repository. It doesn't install the Oracle Migration Assistant for Microsoft Access.

FIGURE 7.2

Choose whether you want to install the migration software, repository, or both.

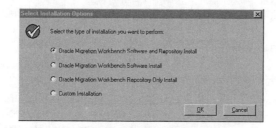

- *Oracle Migration Workbench Software Install* installs the Oracle Migration Workbench software only. It doesn't install the Oracle Migration Assistant for Microsoft Access.

- *Oracle Migration Workbench Repository Only Install* installs the Oracle Migration Workbench Repository only.

- *Custom Installation* lets you customize and choose the products that you want to install.

Select the installation option, and click OK.

8. A progress bar indicates the progress of the installation. When the installation completes, exit the installer.

Oracle Migration Workbench File Locations

By default, when the Oracle Migration Workbench is installed, the files for the software are located in %ORACLE_HOME%\mwb under several subdirectories:

Admin	SQL scripts necessary to create the Oracle Migration Workbench Repository
Bin	The Java runtime environment and command-line interfaces used to launch the Migration Workbench
Classes	Images for the Migration Workbench and the online HTML help files
Doc	Online guide for the Migration Workbench
Lib	Java and property files

7

Creating the Oracle Migration Workbench Repository

The Oracle Migration Workbench Repository is a set of database tables that the Migration Workbench requires in order to perform a migration to Oracle. A user named MIGRATE is created during the installation.

 Installation of the Oracle Migration Workbench Repository requires the SYS-TEM user password for the database where the Oracle Migration Workbench Repository is to be created. If you want to install the Oracle Migration Workbench Repository in a database on a remote machine, the TNS alias for the database should be set up in tnsnames.ora.

If you don't install the Oracle Migration Workbench Repository during installation of the Migration Workbench, you can create it later:

- By running the Oracle installer and choosing the Oracle Migration Workbench Repository Only option
- By executing the script mwbrinst.bat in the %ORACLE_HOME%\mwb\admin directory

The mwbrinst.bat script can be executed as follows (Table 7.2 lists more useful scripts that you can use with the Migration Workbench):

```
%ORACLE_HOME%\mwb\admin\mwbrinst username password service
```

where *username* is the database schema that will own the Migration Workbench Repository, *password* is the password of the username that will own the repository, and *service* is the TNS alias of the database that will contain the repository.

 Migration Workbench's logon dialog box doesn't allow the use of the entire connect string in the username box. The following DDL commands aren't currently handled by the converter:

CREATE INDEX	DROP VIEW
DROP INDEX	GRANT
CREATE VIEW	DROP PROCEDURE

TABLE 7.2 USEFUL SCRIPTS ASSOCIATED WITH THE ORACLE MIGRATION WORKBENCH

SQL Script	Use
%ORACLE_HOME%\mwb\bin\mwb.bat	Launch the Oracle Migration Workbench.
%ORACLE_HOME%\mwb\admin\mwbcre.sql	Create additional migration repositories.
%ORACLE_HOME%\mwb\bin\mwbrinst.bat	Create a new migration repository.

To Do: Change the Storage Options for All Oracle Tables

The Migration Workbench provides the flexibility to change the storage parameters for all objects as part of the migration process. The following steps demonstrate how you can specify the storage parameters for all tables:

1. Start the Migration Workbench.
2. Click the Oracle Model tab in the Navigator panel.
3. Highlight the table's container.
4. In the Properties pane, go to the Creation Options tab and make the desired changes.
5. Click Apply.

To Do: Change the Storage Options for a Particular Oracle Table

The Migration Workbench also provides the flexibility to change the storage parameters for the objects for a specific table as part of the migration process. The following steps show how you can specify the parameters:

1. Start the Migration Workbench.
2. Click the Oracle Model tab in the Navigator panel.
3. Expand the table's container.
4. Highlight the desired table.
5. In the Properties pane, go to the Creation Options tab and make the desired changes.
6. Click Apply.

7

To Do: Change the Password of a User Being Migrated

Through the Migration Workbench, you can change the passwords of the users being migrated. Follow these steps:

1. Start the Migration Workbench.

2. Click the Oracle Model tab in the Navigator panel.

3. Expand the user's container.

4. Highlight the desired user.

5. In the Properties pane, go to the General tab and change the password.

6. Click Apply.

If you receive the following error during the migration of a SQL Server database, you have a user in the target Oracle database that's the same as a user being migrated from the SQL Server database:

```
Failed to create a user: java.sql sql exception: ora-01017
invalid username/password' logon denied
```

To fix this problem, change the password of the username being migrated to be the same as the password of the Oracle username.

User-defined types are migrated to their base types.

Oracle Migration Workbench Parser Issues

You should be aware of several issues regarding the parser used to perform the migration—issues that might prevent some views and triggers from being migrated:

- If the parser can't perform name resolution, it places * in the package definition.

- ORDER BY clauses fail on aliased columns because those columns are generally quoted. Therefore, the alias should be quoted even when used in the ORDER BY clause:

```
Select total=sum(cost) from orders order by total;
```

This clause parses to the following Oracle statement:

```
Select sum(cost) "total" from orders order by total;
```

The current version of the Migration Workbench parses and generates all stored procedures at the same time. Individual stored procedures can't be migrated.

ALL_OBJECTS in Oracle contains object information that's equivalent to the SYSOBJECTS table in SQL Server.

- Creation of views, triggers, and packages sometimes fails because the dependencies of these objects are stored by the Oracle Migration Workbench but aren't used by the Workbench during creation of these objects. As a result, the objects are created in the wrong order. This problem can be resolved by rerunning the Migration wizard.

- Temporary table creation can result in errors, which are recorded in the log window.

- SQL statements such as EXEC ("exec_string") are treated as dynamic SQL and sent to an EXEC_SQL PL/SQL stored procedure for execution. Other statements, such as EXEC (exec_string), are converted to PL/SQL procedure calls.

- LIKE clauses can be used in SQL statements if they don't use regular expressions as in UNIX.

- LOAD and DUMP commands result in parser errors.

- Most SQL Server DDL commands are ignored, and warnings are written to the log window.

- An extra argument of type REF CURSOR is added for result sets and dynasets. REF CURSOR can be manipulated by PL/SQL and Oracle JDBC. The Oracle ODBC driver doesn't support REF CURSORs, which means that the client application code must be changed to handle REF CURSOR. Some third-party vendors, such as Intersolv ODBC driver for Oracle, support REF CURSORs, so no change is required in the application code. For example, the Oracle Migration Workbench parses the following MS SQL Server stored procedure:

```
CREATE PROCEDURE bytitles
AS
Select title_id from titles
GO
```

7

And generates the following Oracle package and stored procedure:

```
PACKAGE BYTITLESpkg AS
TYPE RECTYPE IS RECORD (
    Title_id       titles.title_id%TYPE
);
TYPE RCTYPE IS REF CURSOR RETURN REC1;
END;

PROCEDURE         bytitles(
RC1    IN OUT bytitlespkg.rctype)
AS
O_selcnt    INTEGER;
O_error    INTEGER;
O_rowcnt    INTEGER;
O_sqlstatus    INTEGER;
O_errmsg    VARCHAR2(255);
BEGIN
    OPEN RC1 FOR
    SELECT title_id FROM titles;
END bytitles;
```

Migrating DATETIME Data Types

In Microsoft SQL Server, the DATETIME datatype stores data and time values to a precision of 1/300 of a second. The DATE type in Oracle stores data and time values to a precision of 1 second. Many applications use the DATETIME values as unique IDs. Others, however, don't use DATETIME values for uniqueness but still require a precision higher than 1 second. Several strategies can be used to convert the SQL Server DATETIME values to Oracle:

- The DBMS_UTILITY package has a function (GET_TIME) that returns the time in 1/100th of a second. You can replace the DATETIME data type with a combination of DATE and NUMBER column, in which the NUMBER column is inserted with values returned by DBMS_UTILITY.GET_TIME.

- Pre-create the SQL Server table with an additional integer column as follows. The integer column will contain only NULLs in SQL Server:

```
CREATE TABLE test_table
(column1    datetime    not null,
column2    int        null,
column3    varchar(20)    null)
```

this will be migrated to Oracle as follows,

```
CREATE TABLE test_table
(column1    date         not null,
column2    number      null,
column3    varchar2(20)    null)
```

Also, create a sequence on the number column that starts at 1 and increments by 1:

```
CREATE SEQUENCE datetime_seq
```

Error Handling Within Stored Procedures

In SQL Server, when a SQL statement is executed, control is passed to the next statement irrespective of any error generated by the preceding statement. The developer must check for errors. On the other hand, the Oracle PL/SQL checks for errors generated by a SQL statement before proceeding to the next statement. If the SQL statement generates an error, control is passed to an exception handler. As a result, you don't have to perform error checking for each SQL statement. If you want the Oracle procedure resulting from the migration to behave the same way as a SQL Server procedure, wherein control is passed to the next statement irrespective of any errors, you should enclose each SQL statement in a PL/SQL block and perform all error handling for the SQL statement in that block.

> An Oracle PL/SQL block ideally has only one exception block that handles all the exceptions.

For example, in the following SQL Server stored procedure, if the first `select` statement doesn't bring any data, the value of @x is *undefined*, and you have to handle the exception:

```
Begin
    ......
    select @x = column1 from table1 where column2 = 'XYZ'
    select @y = column1 from table2 where column2 = @x
    ......
end
```

The same procedure in Oracle PL/SQL will raise a `NO_DATA_FOUND` exception under the same conditions.

7

RAISERROR Statement

The SQL Server RAISERROR statement passes the error code and message to the client and continues further with the stored procedure but doesn't return to the calling routine. On the other hand, the Oracle RAISE_APPLICATION_ERROR statement returns to the calling routine. SQL Server's RAISERROR must be followed by a RETURN statement so that after conversion it will behave the same as the Oracle RAISE_APPLICATION_ERROR statement.

Customized Error Messages

SQL Server allows you to use system procedures to add customized error messages to a system table. I don't recommend using this feature, however, because no Oracle equivalent exists. Instead, you should use a user-defined error messages table and write routines to insert and retrieve user-defined messages from this table.

Migrating Individual SQL Statements

When you are using individual SQL statements in SQL Server, you should try to follow the ANSI-standard SQL whenever possible because this will make the conversion to Oracle very easy.

> Usually, developers use database-specific SQL constructs for performance enhancements and simplicity of writing code.

The following examples indicate how you can manually intervene to convert SQL Server–specific constructs to Oracle8i.

- SQL Server construct: DELETE

```
DELETE titles
FROM publishers, titles
WHERE publishers.pub_id = titles.pub_id
AND publishers.pub_name = 'Macmillan Computer Publishing'

ORACLE8i equivalent:

DELETE
FROM titles
WHERE pub_id IN
(SELECT pub_id
FROM publishers
WHERE pub_name = 'Macmillan Computer Publishing')
```

- MS SQL Server construct: UPDATE

```
UPDATE titles
SET price = price + royaltyper/100
FROM titles, titleauthor
WHERE titles.title_id = titleauthor.title_id

Oracle8i equivalent:

UPDATE titles t
SET price = (SELECT (t.price + ta.royaltyper/100)
             FROM titleauthor ta
             WHERE ta.title_id = t.title_id)
```

ANSI-standard SQL statements are automatically converted from SQL Server to Oracle.

Handling Logical Transactions

Transactions are explicit in SQL Server, whereas in Oracle they are implicit. In SQL Server, by default, an individual SQL statement isn't part of a logical transaction. Therefore, an individual SQL statement is committed on completion. To make a SQL statement part of a logical transaction, the SQL statement must be placed in a logical transaction that begins with BEGIN TRANSACTION (or BEGIN TRAN). The logical transaction ends with a corresponding COMMIT TRANSACTION (COMMIT TRAN) or ROLLBACK TRANSACTION (ROLLBACK TRAN) statement.

In Oracle, transactions follow the ANSI standard, which means that the transactions are implicit. Therefore, an individual SQL statement will be part of a logical transaction that ends with a COMMIT or ROLLBACK. When an individual SQL statement ends, it's not committed to the database. When a COMMIT statement is run, all statements that are part of the logical transaction are committed.

The differences in the transaction model between SQL Server and Oracle affect the coding of applications. For client/server applications, you can simplify the migration from SQL Server to Oracle by making the transaction-handling constructs part of the client procedures instead of the server procedures. In other words, avoid using BEGIN TRAN, COMMIT TRAN, and ROLLBACK TRAN statements in the server procedures. As a result, the stored procedures will be portable and the migration will be simplified because they will be independent of the transaction models.

7

Migrating Temporary Tables

SQL Server uses temporary tables for several situations:

- Simplify coding.
- Improve the performance of multitable joins.
- Consolidate data for decision support systems.
- Simulate cursors when processing data coming from multiple tables.
- Perform UNION operations.

Temporary tables allow a query to be broken down into different queries so that the result of one query can be stored in a temporary table and used by another query. The temporary tables can be joined with other database tables. Such SQL Server codes that use temporary tables can be converted to Oracle code by using multitable joins.

> The parallel query option can be used to improve the performance of multitable join queries.

Perform UNION Operations

In SQL Server, multitable joins are very inefficient. Therefore, developers sometimes use temporary tables to avoid their use. However, because Oracle8i performs multitable joins more efficiently than SQL Server, you should use UNION operations whenever possible. The following example shows how this is achieved:

In Microsoft SQL Server:

```
INSERT #EMP_EXP
SELECT emp.emp_id,
       Emp.start_date,
       Emp.end_date
FROM   emp, dept
WHERE emp.emp_id = dept.emp_id
AND       dept.dept_name = 'CONSULTING'
AND         emp.start_date BETWEEN @start_date AND @end_date

INSERT INTO #EMP_EXP
VALUES (10001, getdate(), NULL)
```

In Oracle8i:

```
SELECT emp.emp_id,
       Emp.start_date,
       Emp.end_date
FROM   emp, dept
```

```
WHERE emp.emp_id = dept.emp_id
AND       dept.dept_name = 'CONSULTING'
AND        emp.start_date BETWEEN I_start_date AND I_end_date
UNION
SELECT 10001, SYSDATE, NULL
FROM dual
```

Eliminate Joins While Requerying Multiple Tables

In SQL Server, you often use temporary tables to store summary data. Later, you can query these from just one table (temporary table), rather than access multiple tables each time.

In MS SQL Server:

```
INSERT #EMP_EXP_DEPT
SELECT emp.emp_id,
       Emp.start_date,
       Emp.end_date
FROM  emp, dept
WHERE emp.emp_id = dept.emp_id
AND       dept.dept_name in ('CONSULTING', 'DEVELOPMENT')
```

Later in the procedure, if you want to obtain the same information, you have to query the temporary table #EMP_EXP_DEPT:

```
SELECT * FROM #EMP_EXP_DEPT
```

In Oracle8i:

```
SELECT emp.emp_id,
       Emp.start_date,
       Emp.end_date
FROM  emp, dept
WHERE emp.emp_id = dept.emp_id
AND       dept.dept_name in ('CONSULTING', 'DEVELOPMENT')
```

Later in the procedure, if you want to obtain the same information, you have to perform this query again.

Simulating Cursors

SQL Server uses temporary tables to simulate cursors, but such cursors aren't supported in Oracle. You must manually intervene and modify such procedures to implement cursors and achieve efficient code.

In MS SQL Server:

```
SELECT * INTO #EMP_CONSULT
FROM employee
WHERE employee.dept in (5,10,12)
```

7

```
SELECT @cnt = @@rowcount
WHILE @cnt > 0
BEGIN
    SELECT @emp_id = emp_id, @name = name, @sal = salary
    FROM #EMP_CONSULT
    WHERE emp_id = (SELECT MAX(emp_id) FROM #EMP_CONSULT)
        /* Process the row */
    DELETE FROM #EMP_CONSULT WHERE emp_id = @emp_id
    SELECT @cnt = @cnt -1
END
```

In Oracle8i:

```
FOR emp_record IN
(SELECT emp_id, name, salary FROM employee WHERE dept in (5,10,12))

LOOP
    /* Process the row */
END LOOP
```

Summary

More and more companies are migrating their SQL Server databases to Oracle, a process that can be simplified by using the Oracle Migration Workbench. Currently, the Migration Workbench has several issues that you must be aware of, as discussed in this hour. Parser issues should be understood, and the migration of procedures might require manual intervention to optimize the code after it is migrated to Oracle.

Q&A

Q Are there plans to allow selective migration of users and objects in the future releases?

A Yes.

Q Can the Migration Workbench be used to migrate from Sybase to Oracle8i?

A Although Sybase is similar to SQL Server, the current release of the Migration Workbench doesn't allow the migration of Sybase to Oracle8i. Plans exist for future releases to be more generic, allowing migration from various sources.

Workshop

The Workshop contains quiz questions and activities to help reinforce what you've learned in this hour. You can check Appendix A for the answers (but don't peek!).

Quiz

1. What methods are available to you for migrating from SQL Server to Oracle8i?

2. What script can you use to create the Oracle Migration Workbench Repository?

3. Where is the redo information contained in SQL Server?

4. How do you convert DATETIME values from SQL Server to Oracle8i?

Exercises

1. Suppose that you want to migrate only tables belonging to your schema from a SQL Server database to Oracle8i. How would you go about doing this?

2. SQL Server uses page-level locking, whereas Oracle uses row-level locking. How can you use the Oracle8i locking features in the applications you plan to migrate from MS SQL Server?

7

HOUR **8**

Integrating and Administering Oracle8i on Windows NT

In this lesson, you consider various strategies that can help you integrate Oracle8i with Windows NT. You also look at several basic administrative tasks that you will be performing daily.

A three-tier architecture can be used so that the Oracle database resides on one server, applications reside on another server, and clients can access the application server, which in turn can communicate with the database server. All these machines can be part of different domains that have established trust relationships.

You can use client/server architecture to allow clients from Windows NT workstations, Windows 95, or network computers to connect to the Oracle server by using TCP/IP or SPX/IPX networking. The SQL*NET layer allows clients even on UNIX machines to connect to the Oracle database on Windows NT, as long as the same protocol is used. You can follow various strategies to simplify the administration of an Oracle database.

OS Authentication

Oracle on Windows NT supports OS authentication. This is achieved by linking Oracle accounts with Windows NT user accounts so that when users successfully log on to Windows NT, they can use the Oracle database without supplying a username and password again. In other words, the users aren't authenticated by Oracle again. Oracle user accounts are created as OPS$*nt_user_accounts* and are identified externally.

The following results are obtained while using OS authentication with Oracle8 and different Windows NT models:

- In a single-domain model and proper Windows NT/Oracle setup, the operating system can authenticate any domain user if domain logon is successful.

- In two-domain master-resource and master-master domain models with proper Windows NT/Oracle setup, the operating system can authenticate any domain user, provided the user logs on successfully into one of the Windows NT domains.

- OS authentication doesn't depend on who's logged on to the Windows NT server on which the database resides because the Oracle services and Windows NT security accounts database operate independently of the user now logged on.

- In a workgroup model, when users log on locally to their Windows NT machines and not to a domain, the operating system can authenticate them if the same username/password combination is defined locally on the client and server machines. The operating system also can authenticate client users if they map a drive to the Oracle server machine using the username and password of a local server account that's valid to both Windows NT and Oracle.

Creating DBA Accounts Authenticated by Windows NT

On UNIX platforms, you can connect as INTERNAL without supplying the password. In Oracle7, you also can set the Registry entry DBA_AUTHORIZATION to BYPASS to get the same result. However, Oracle8 doesn't support this Registry entry.

8

In Oracle8, you can use a local or domain account that's authenticated by Windows NT as follows:

1. Create a local group named ORA_DBA or ORA_*sid*_DBA by using the Windows NT User Manager (replace *sid* with the instance name).

2. Assign the Windows NT accounts for each administrator to the ORA_DBA or ORA_*sid*_DBA group. These accounts now can connect by using the INTERNAL logon or the SYS...AS SYSDBA logon, without supplying the password.

For Windows NT authentication, ensure that the SQLNET.ORA file contains the following line:

```
SQLNET.AUTHENTICATION_SERVICES = (NTS)
```

To Do: Connect as INTERNAL Without a Password

To connect as INTERNAL without a password, follow these steps:

1. Create one of the following new local Windows NT user groups:

   ORA_DBA   SYSDBA database privileges applicable to all SIDs.
                       ORA_DBA is automatically created during installation.

   ORA_*sid*_DBA   SYSDBA database privileges applicable to the specified
                       SID.

2. Add a Windows NT operating system local or domain user to that group.

The following steps allow you to log on to a local computer or a Windows NT domain. Then you are automatically validated as an authorized DBA with access to the Oracle8 database without a password.

1. Create a local or domain Windows NT user account.

2. In the init.ora file, set the parameter REMOTE_LOGIN_PASSWORDFILE to NONE.

> REMOTE_LOGIN_PASSWORDFILE can also be set to SHARED, but the recommendation is to set it to NONE so that you can get trusted authenticated connections.

3. In the sqlnet.ora file, set the following:
   ```
   SQLNET.AUTHENTICATION_SERVICES = (NTS)
   ```

4. Start the User Manager application.

5. From the User menu, choose New Local Group.

▼

6. In the New Local Group dialog box, enter ORA_*SID*_DBA or ORA_DBA in the Group Name field.

7. Click Add.

8. In the Add Users and Groups dialog box, select an appropriate Windows NT local or domain user from the Names field, and click Add.

9. Click OK to add your selection to the Members list of the New Local Group dialog box.

10. Click OK.

11. Exit User Manager.

12. Shut down the database:

    SVRMGR> **SHUTDOWN**

13. Restart the database:

    SVRMGR> **STARTUP**

14. Test your configuration by connecting to the database with the INTERNAL account:

▲   SVRMGR> **CONNECT INTERNAL**

To Do: Perform Operating System Authentication for a Nonprivileged Database User

When you use operating system authentication for nonprivileged database users, you are leaving all the authentication for that user to Windows NT. If this user is local, he logs into his local Windows NT machine and can access an Oracle8 database on that machine. On the other hand, if this user is a domain user, after he is authenticated by the domain, he will have access to all domain resources, including Oracle8 databases. The following example uses user account MEGH:

1. In the init.ora file, add

    REMOTE_LOGIN_PASSWORD = NONE

    The value of OS_AUTHENT_PREFIX is a prefix to local or domain usernames that are attempting to connect to the server. When a connection to the database is attempted, the prefixed username is compared with the Oracle username in the database. OS_AUTHENT_PREFIX = " ", for example, indicates that there's no prefix.
▼   Table 8.1 shows the effect of using OS_AUTHENT_PREFIX with various users.

▼

TABLE 8.1   RESULTS OF USING VARIOUS VALUES FOR OS_AUTHENT_PREFIX

User Type	Result
	OS_AUTHENT_PREFIX = ABC
Local user MEGH	ABCMEGH is compared with the database account.
User MEGH in domain ORLANDO	ABCORLANDO\MEGH is compared with the database account.
	OS_AUTHENT_PREFIX = " "
Local user MEGH	MEGH is compared with the database account.
User MEGH in domain ORLANDO	ORLANDO\MEGH is compared with the database account.
	OS_AUTHENT_PREFIX Is Unspecified
Local user MEGH	OPS$MEGH is compared with the database account.
User MEGH in domain ORLANDO	OPS$ORLANDO\MEGH is compared with the database account.

> OS_AUTHENT_PREFIX values are case sensitive.

2. Start User Manager.

3. Create a Windows NT local or domain username for MEGH.

4. In the sqlnet.ora file, set

   SQLNET.AUTHENTICATION_SERVICES = (NTS)

5. Set oracle_sid to the correct database instance:

   C:\> **set oracle_sid = prod**

6. Start Server Manager:

   C:\> **SVRMGRL**

7. Connect to the database with the INTERNAL account:

▼   SVRMGR> **CONNECT INTERNAL/PASSWORD**

▼　　　8. Create an operating system–authenticated database user account. If you are authenticating a local user account, use

```
SVRMGR> CREATE USER MEGH IDENTIFIED EXTERNALLY
➥DEFAULT TABLESPACE USER_DATA TEMPORARY TABLESPACE
➥TEMP_DATA;
```

If you are authenticating a domain user account, use

```
SVRMGR> CREATE USER "ORLANDO\MEGH" IDENTIFIED
                         EXTERNALLY;
```

9. Grant the appropriate roles to the database account. For a local username, use

```
SVRMGR> GRANT RESOURCE TO MEGH;
SVRMGR> GRANT CONNECT TO MEGH;
```

If domain username, use

```
SVRMGR> GRANT RESOURCE TO "ORLANDO\MEGH";
SVRMGR> GRANT CONNECT TO "ORLANDO\MEGH";
```

10. Shut down the database:

```
SVRMGR> SHUTDOWN
```

11. Restart the database:

▲　　　　```
SVRMGR> STARTUP
```

# Optimal Flexible Architecture (OFA) on Windows NT

OFA provides a structured method for installing Oracle databases and applications to simplify the maintenance. OFA on Windows NT allows easy maintenance for Oracle databases and requires separating database files from Oracle software files. It's also recommended that you separate database files across devices for improving performance and database recovery.

## Why Use an OFA-Compliant Database?

Using an OFA-compliant database has several advantages:

- Ease of database management.
- Easier control over database growth.
- Better diagnosis of performance problems.
- Easier management of database files.
- Minimizes disk contention by separating administrative files, binary files, and database files.
```

- Better fault tolerance.
- Simplifies testing of new applications.
- Simplifies database upgrades.
- Uses consistent naming conventions for the database files so that the files can be distinguished easily from files belonging to other databases and also from nondatabase files.
- Categorizes and separates files into independent subdirectories so that the operations on files in the same category don't affect files in another category.
- Easy to distinguish between the contents of different tablespaces. This minimizes the fragmentation of tablespace free space and disk contention by balancing the load.

Windows NT Administration Standards

You should adopt some standards for your Windows NT user and group management so that the administration can be simplified. The following guidelines are recommended for Windows NT:

1. Create a Windows NT user account called ORACLE to install and administer all databases. Grant the Windows NT administrator privilege to this operating account.

2. Create a LOCAL Windows NT group called ORAadmin. To this group, add the ORACLE account and the personal accounts of all Windows NT users who will be administering Oracle/Windows NT databases. Assign Windows NT file permissions for all Oracle-related files to the ORAadmin group.

3. Create a top-level directory called ORADATA on each drive that will contain Oracle database files.

4. Create a top-level directory called ORADBA on a drive with sufficient disk space to hold all RDBMS administrative scripts for the entire Windows NT server machine.

5. Store Oracle-related files for secure databases on NTFS volumes instead of FAT volumes to take advantage of operating system file protections.

6. Separate database servers from file servers for optimal performance.

7. Configure the database server machine with the following parameters:

   - Balance foreground and background applications.
   - Optimize memory for network applications rather than file services.

Oracle/Windows NT Installation Standards

The Windows NT user account ORACLE should be used for database server operations only. Install Oracle/Windows NT software on any drive in a top-level directory called ORANT.

Oracle/Windows NT Database Creation Standards

By using proper standards during database creation, you can simplify the administration of Oracle databases. The following guidelines are recommended:

1. Create the following subdirectories below the ORADBA directory: ADMIN, LOCAL, and PATCH.

2. For each database on a Windows NT server, create a directory called ORADBA\ADMIN*sidname*, where *sidname* is the name of the database SID to be created.

3. Under each SID-specific directory, create the following directories: ARCH, BDUMP, EXP, LOGBOOK, PFILE, SCRIPTS, and UDUMP.

4. Copy the default INIT.ORA file from the correct subdirectory of the ORANT software to the PFILE subdirectory of the correct SID-specific directory.

5. Change the following initialization parameters to point to SID-specific sub-directories: `BACKGROUND_DUMP_DEST`, `USER_DUMP_DEST`, and `LOG_ARCHIVE_DEST`.

6. Set the `REMOTE_LOGIN_PASSWORDFILE` parameter to `EXCLUSIVE` to support the use of SYSDBA and SYSOPER privileges.

7. Create a subdirectory called ORADATA*sidname* on each drive to hold database-related files for an instance.

8. Create two or more control files on two separate physical drives.

9. Restrict all filenames to 8.3 notation.

> Existing OFA rules can be used for segment separation, database filenames, tablespace names, and so on.

The following shows a sample OFA-compliant directory tree structure:

```
DISK_1 : \WINNT
         Windows NT base code
```

```
DISK_2: \ORANT
        Oracle 32-bit base code
        \database
            \strt<sid>.cmd
            Script to autostart Oracle instance
DISK_3 :\ORACLE_BASE
        The default oracle_base is c:\oracle
\ORACLE_HOME1
    1st Oracle home
\BIN
Oracle Binaries
\NETWORK
Oracle Net8 files
\ORADATA
Oracle database configuration files
\DB_NAME1
Configuration files for database#1
\CONTROL01.CTL
1st control file
\SYSTEM01.DBF
System tablespace datafile
                                        \RBS01.DBF
        Rollback segment tablespace datafile
                                        \INDX01.DBF
                Index tablespace datafile
                                        \TEMP01.DBF
                Temporary tablespace datafile
                                        \USERS01.DBF
                User tablespace datafile
\OEMREP01.DBF
Oracle Enterprise manager datafiles
\REDO0101.LOG
Redo log group #1, member one
                                        \REDO0201.LOG
                Redo log group #2, member one
                                        \REDO0301.LOG
                Redo log group #3, member one
                                        \REDO0401.LOG
                Redo log group #4, member one
DB_NAME2
                                        \CTL \DBF \LOG
                Configuration files for 2nd database
                    \ADMIN
        Administrative files
                                    \DB_NAME1
    \ADHOC
    Adhoc SQL admin scripts
                                    \ADUMP
                Archive log dump destination
    \ARCH
    Archive redo logs
```

```
                                                \BDUMP
                     Background dump destination
                                                \CDUMP
                     Core dump destination
                                                \CREATE
                     Database creation scripts
\EXP
Export dump files
\PFILE
Initialization parameter file
                                                \UDUMP
                     User dump destination
\DB_NAME2
Files for 2nd database
        \ . . .
\ORACLE_HOME2
2nd Oracle home

                               \ . . .

\ORACLE_HOME3
3rd Oracle home
\ . . .


DISK_4: \ORADATA
Oracle database configuration files
\<sid>
Instance specific files
\CONTROL02.CTL
2nd control file
\REDO0102.LOG
Redo log group #1, member two
                                                       \REDO0202.LOG
                     Redo log group #2, member two
                                                       \REDO0302.LOG
                     Redo log group #3, member two
                                                       \REDO0402.LOG
                     Redo log group #4, member two
```

Configuring Automatic Shutdown

When Windows NT shuts down, it stops all services, including Oracle services, which is equivalent to a SHUTDOWN ABORT. Beginning with Oracle 8.0.3, you can use special Registry parameters to provide a cleaner shutdown. When the service for an instance is stopped, the scripts ORASHUT.BAT (which starts Server Manager) and ORASHUT.SQL (which performs a shutdown immediate) are executed when the ORA_SHUTDOWN Registry entry is set to TRUE. In Oracle8, there are several Registry parameters that can help you shut down an Oracle database when you shut down the Oracle service for that database.

To Do: Configure Your Database for Automatic Shutdown

One way in which you can simplify the administration of your Oracle databases is to automate database shutdown. You can use several Registry parameters for this purpose. Follow these steps:

1. Execute REGEDT32 to start the Registry Editor.

2. Go down the following tree:

```
    HKey_local_machine
            Software
oracle
```

and set one of the following parameters to TRUE:

ORA_SHUTDOWN	Allows the shutdown of the selected Oracle8 database. Any database in the current Oracle home can be shut down by using this parameter.
ORA_*SID*_SHUTDOWN	Allows the shutdown of the Oracle8 database identified by the SID value.

> The number of Oracle homes that you have on your machine determines the location of these parameters. If you have only one Oracle home, these parameters are in HKEY_LOCAL_MACHINE\SOFTWARE\ORACLE\HOME0. For multiple Oracle homes, they are in HKEY_LOCAL_MACHINE\SOFTWARE\ORACLE\HOME*ID*.

3. The following Registry parameters can be optionally set:

ORA_*SID*_SHUTDOWNTYPE	Indicates the database shutdown mode: A (abort), I (immediate, the default), or N (normal).
ORA_*SID*_SHUTDOWN_TIMEOUT	Indicates the maximum time to wait before the service stops.

Test your settings by using Control Panel's Services tool and stopping the OracleServiceSID service. This will automatically start Instance Manager and shut down the database as specified by the ORA_SID_SHUTDOWNTYPE entry.

Encrypting Database Passwords

To encrypt database passwords so that they aren't sent over the network "in clear," set the following parameters:

- Set the database initialization parameter DBLINK_ENCRYPT_LOGIN to TRUE for the Oracle instance, and restart the instance.
- Set the environment variable ORA_ENCRYPT_LOGIN to TRUE for each user that connects to Oracle.

Automating Database Startups

Because Oracle runs on Windows NT as a service, it can be automated to start when Windows NT is booted. This can be achieved by

- Creating the OracleStartsid service (by using Instance Manager)
- Setting it to start automatically (by using Control Panel)

To Do: Autostart an Oracle Database Instance and Perform Other Tasks Before Instance Startup

To simplify administration of Oracle databases, automate the startup procedures. The Registry contains several parameters that you can use for this purpose. The following steps show an example of how you can automate the execution of certain instructions as part of the startup procedure:

1. Execute REGEDT32 to start the Registry Editor.

2. Go down the following tree:

```
HKey_local_machine
    software
        microsoft
            WindowsNT
                current version
                    winlogon
```

3. In the WINLOGON item, edit the SYSTEM entry and append a command line that points to a startup command file such as c:\prod\startins.cmd.

Commands in the SYSTEM entry should be separated by commas.

4. By using an editor such as Notepad, create a file startins.cmd in the prod directory, as follows. This file will be used to start the database instance.

```
net start OracleServicePROD
        SET ORACLE_SID=PROD
        svrmgr30 @c:\PROD\startdb.sql
```

5. Again by using an editor such as Notepad, create a file startdb.sql in the prod directory, as follows. This file will be used to start up the database.

```
connect internal/Your_Password
        startup
        exit
```

> If you change the password for the internal account, you should change the password in the startdb.sql script, also.

6. Make sure that in Control Panel's Services tool, the OracleServicePROD service is set to start manually. This is necessary because the services will be started per the Registry entry set in step 3.

Now, when Windows NT is booted, the services are started as specified in the SYSTEM Registry entry, which in turn executes the batch scripts. These batch scripts can contain other commands that can be used for debugging purposes.

Troubleshooting Tips When the Database Doesn't Autostart

Suppose you've configured your database to start automatically by using the OracleStart service and find that it doesn't start the database. The following checklist can help you diagnose where the problem exists and fix it:

- Use Control Panel's Services tool to verify that the OracleStart service exists. If this service exists, go to the next item in the checklist. Otherwise, create the service as follows:

  1. Start the Windows NT Instance Manager.

  2. Select the instance and choose the Edit option.

  3. In the Instance Startup Mode section, choose Automatic and verify that the path of the initialization file is correct.

  4. Click OK and supply your internal password.

- Verify that the service is set to start automatically. If it's not set for automatic startup, make it automatic.
- When the `OracleStartsid` service runs, it executes the strt*SID*.cmd file in the oracle_home\database directory. Verify that this file can run successfully when executed as a standalone by following these steps:
  1. From the Run dialog box, execute C:\%oracle_home%\database\strtsid.cmd.
  2. Check the log file (%oracle_home%\rdbms81\oradim81.log) generated from this execution for errors, and fix the errors.

  If this file runs successfully as a standalone, go to the next item in the checklist; otherwise, open the strtsid.cmd file in Notepad, and verify that the internal password is correct and the path of initialization file is correct. If these entries are valid, the file might contain some hidden characters, so you should re-create the strtsid.cmd file by using an editor. This file should contain the instance startup command.

- If your oracle_home\database\strt*sid*.cmd file works when executed standalone but not through the `OracleStartsid` service, you will have to re-create this service as follows:
  1. Start the Windows NT Instance Manager.
  2. Select the instance and choose the Edit option.
  3. In the Instance Startup Mode section, choose Manual.
  4. Click OK and supply your internal password.
  5. Delete the oracle_home\database\strt*sid*.cmd file.
  6. Select the instance again and choose the Edit option.
  7. In the Instance Startup Mode section, choose Automatic.
  8. Verify that the path of the initialization file is correct.
  9. Click OK and supply your internal password.

These steps should take care of the database autostart problem.

Using 16-Bit Applications on Windows NT

When running 16-bit applications on Windows NT, you can configure them to run in a shared Windows NT virtual DOS machine (NTVDM) or in their own memory spaces, thereby creating multiple NTVDMs. Each Win-16 based application runs in either its own NTVDM or a shared NTVDM. Only one NTVDM can allow shared 16-bit applications.

Using multiple NTVDMs comes with these advantages:

- Problems with one Win-16 based application don't affect the other applications.
- When running in separate NTVDMs, a busy 16-bit application doesn't prevent other applications from continuing with what they're doing.
- On multiprocessor machines, you can achieve multitasking and multiprocessing of 16-bit applications.

Using multiple NTVDMs also has its disadvantages:

- Running 16-bit–based applications in their separate memory space introduces additional overhead.
- 16-bit applications that don't follow the OLE and DDE specifications can't be guaranteed to interoperate with applications in separate NTVDMs.

Troubleshooting 16-Bit Applications Under Windows NT

Many 16-bit applications have been tested to run fine on Windows NT. However, you might encounter instances when a 16-bit application doesn't run as desired. The most common problems when running 16-bit applications are usually due to incompatibility with Windows NT. Use the following guidelines to troubleshoot such behavior:

- If possible, verify that the 16-bit applications work properly on Windows 3.0 and 3.1. If the application requires Windows 3.0 and 3.1 to be running in 386 enhanced mode, the application might have problems on the DEC ALPHA or MIPS version of Windows NT.
- Some MS-DOS applications write directly to the hardware. These won't run under Windows NT because Windows NT doesn't allow direct access to the hardware.
- Some 16-bit applications require that a default printer be selected. Check Control Panel to make sure that a default printer has been selected.
- If the application requires a virtual device driver (VxD), it might not run properly under Windows NT because these drivers write directly to the hardware.
- Verify that any dynamic link libraries (DLLs) used by the application are both current and can be located by the application.
- Remove unnecessary device drivers.
- If you've added new hardware, check for interrupt conflicts.
- Try using standard device drivers such as standard VGA.
- If the application uses Java, use 256-color minimum.
- Use a clean copy of autoexec.nt and config.nt files.

Running a 16-Bit Application in Its Own NTVDM

Running a 16-bit application in its own NTVDM is advantageous because it won't be affected by problems in other 16-bit applications. In other words, if one 16-bit application crashes, it won't cause 16-bit applications in other NTVDMs to also crash. There are several ways in which you can achieve this result.

From the Command Prompt

The `start` command can be used to specify that you want to run a particular 16-bit application in its own NTVDM:

```
C:\> start /separate [path]application
```

From the Start Menu

Follow these steps:

1. From the Start menu, choose Run.

2. In the Run dialog box, enter the full path and the name of the application, and select the Run in Separate Memory Space check box.

> If the Run in Separate Memory Space check box is grayed out, the application isn't 16-bit.

By Using File Associations

You can use file associations to start an application in its own NTVDM when it's opening a document with which it's associated. Follow these steps:

1. Start the Windows NT Explorer.

2. From the View menu, choose Folder Options.

3. On the File Types page, select the application and then click the Edit button.

4. Double-click Open.

5. Edit Application Used to Perform Action as follows:

```
Cmd /c start /separate path application_executable %1
```

Setting Up an Application as a Windows NT Service

You can use the INSTSRV.exe and SRVANY.exe utilities from the Windows NT Registry to set up an application as a Windows NT service. Running an application as a service has several benefits:

- Applications can be started and shut down independent of user logon or logoff. As a result, you don't have to start or shut down the application for each user logon or logoff.
- It allows automation of applications without user intervention.
- It allows applications to run and perform tasks by using a different account from the user currently logged on.

The following steps can be used to give you a good start:

1. Create a new Windows NT service, using the INSTSRV.exe command from the Windows NT Resource Kit, where *service* is the service you want to create:

   ```
   C:>INSTSRV service c:\SRVANY.exe
   ```

2. By using Control Panel's Services tool, configure your new service to start manually or automatically.

3. In the Startup dialog box, define the host account for the service. This will be the account used by the service to log on to the operating system and perform its tasks. If you have to interact with the screen or the keyboard, you must choose the local system account and click the Allow Service to Interact with Desktop option. Otherwise, you can choose any valid Windows NT account.

Because the local system account doesn't support network access, you can't log on to a remote database.

4. Configure the Registry for this new service by using REGEDT32.exe and providing the application parameters under HKEY_LOCAL_MACHINE\SYSTEM\CurrentControlSet\Services*service*.

Using Windows NT Scheduler

Scheduling commands on Windows NT requires the use of the Scheduler service. This service can be controlled through Control Panel's Services tool. By default, the Scheduler service runs under the system account, so you have to make sure that this account has the appropriate directory permissions. However, just like any other service, you can run Scheduler under any other account.

To invoke the Windows NT Scheduler, run the at command from the MS-DOS prompt. You can obtain help on the at command by running

```
C:> at ?
```

This command results in the following output:

OUTPUT

```
AT [\\computername] [ [id] [/DELETE] ¦ /DELETE [/YES]]
AT [\\computername] time [/INTERACTIVE]
      [ /EVERY:date[,...] ¦ /NEXT:date[,...]] "command"
```

\\computername	Specifies a remote computer. Commands are scheduled on the local computer if this parameter is omitted.
id	Is an identification number assigned to a scheduled command.
/delete	Cancels a scheduled command. If it is omitted, all the scheduled commands on the computer are canceled.
/yes	Used with cancel all jobs command when no further confirmation is desired.
time	Specifies the time when command is to run.
/interactive	Allows the job to interact with the desktop of the user who is logged on at the time the job runs.
/every:date[,...]	Runs the command on each specified day(s) of the week or month. If date is omitted, the current day of the month is assumed.
/next:date[,...]	Runs the specified command on the next occurrence of the day (for example, next Thursday). If date is omitted, the current day of the month is assumed.
"command"	Is the Windows NT command or batch program to be run.

To Do: Schedule Commands in Windows NT

Use the Windows NT AT command-line scheduler to schedule a batch file, c:\batch\run-batch.cmd, to run every weekday at 10 p.m., and append the output to c:\batch\out.log and the errors to c:\batch\err.log. The following command run from the MS-DOS prompt will accomplish this task:

```
C:> at 10:00pm /every:M,T,W,Th,F " c:\batch\runbatch.cmd"
➥1>> c:\batch\out.log 2>> c:\batch\err.log
```

You can verify the schedule:

INPUT/ OUTPUT

```
C:> at
Status   ID   Day        Time        Command Line
-        4    Each M T   10:00 PM    c:\batch\runbatch
              W Th F                 .cmd 1>>
                                     c:\batch\out.
                                     log 2>> c:\
                                     batch\err.log
```

▲

After you install the Windows NT Resource Kit, you can use its GUI scheduler.

Using Instance Manager (ORADIM)

You can use ORADIM (Oracle's graphical Instance Manager) and the Oracle Database Configuration Assistant to manage databases (refer to Hour 6, "Creating an Oracle Database on Windows NT," for a discussion of Oracle Database Configuration Assistant). Although they perform similar tasks, there are differences, as shown in Table 8.2.

TABLE 8.2   COMPARING ORADIM AND THE ORACLE DATABASE CONFIGURATION ASSISTANT

Oracle Instance Manager	Oracle Database Configuration Assistant
Can be used to create, modify, delete, start, and stop Oracle instances	Can't be used to start and stop Oracle instances
Can't be used to delete any associated database files	Can be used to create and delete databases and their associated instances and services
Can be used to modify instance parameters such as instance name, password, startup, and shutdown modes	Can't be used to modify an instance
Creates the following: instance, service, and password file	Creates the following: database, instance, service, and password file

When you use Instance Manager (ORADIM.exe), all operations are recorded in the ORADIM.LOG log file, which is opened in %ORACLE_BASE%\%ORA-CLE_HOME%\DATABASE or the directory specified by the ORA_CWD Registry parameter. Instance Manager is part of the Oracle Enterprise Manager.

Before you can work with a database, you have to make sure that its associated instance is started. The instance also must be stopped after shutting down the database. You can use Instance Manager to start and stop the instance and the database.

You must first log on to Instance Manager by using an account with administrative privileges.

If you get error ORA-1031 during logon, the password you supplied isn't correct. If you get error ORA-9352 during database startup, the OracleServiceSID Windows NT service isn't running.

Instance Manager allows you to perform several actions:

- Start the database instance.
- Stop the database instance.
- Query the status of the database.
- Change the initialization parameters.
- Manage startup configurations.
- Monitor database access sessions.
- Rename an Oracle instance.
- Delete an Oracle instance.

In Instance Manager, you can use the Status page to query and change the status of the chosen database. To start and stop the database, choose the appropriate option and then click the Apply button. Table 8.3 shows the various options available.

TABLE 8.3 THE VARIOUS DATABASE STARTUP AND SHUTDOWN OPTIONS

Option	Use
Instance Started	Also referred to as NOMOUNT state; can be used to create a database but not open it.
Database Mounted	Also referred to as MOUNT state; can be used during database recovery and while performing database maintenance.
Database Open	Opens the database and makes it available for access by everyone.
Shutdown	Shuts down the database in one of three ways:
	Normal prevents new users from accessing the database but allows existing users to finish their work. When the existing users disconnect, the database is shut down.
	Immediate rolls back any open transactions and disconnects existing users. No new connections are allowed.
	Abort disconnects existing users and shuts down the instance. Because it doesn't roll back existing transactions, instance recovery is needed during the next startup.

8

> To obtain options associated with Instance Manager and their descriptions, execute the following from the command prompt:
>
> `C:\> ORADIM -?`

To Do: Create an Instance Called TEST

Use the command-line Instance Manager to create this instance:

From the command prompt, execute the following:

```
C:\> ORADIM -NEW -SID TEST -INTPWD PASSWORD -STARTMODE
     AUTO -PFILE C:\ORACLE\ADMIN\TEST\PFILE\INITTEST.ORA
```

In this command,

- NEW indicates that you intend to create a new database instance.
- SID specifies the name of the instance to create. Instead of this parameter, you can specify -SRVC *SERVICE_NAME* to indicate the name of the service to create.
- INTPWD INTERNAL_PWD specifies the password for the INTERNAL account.
- STARTMODE AUTO¦MANUAL indicates whether to start the instance automatically or manually at startup. MANUAL is the default.
- PFILE *PATHNAME* indicates the location of the parameter file.

To Do: Start an Instance with Instance Manager

From the command prompt, execute the following:

```
C:\> ORADIM -STARTUP -SID TEST -STARTTYPE SRVC -PFILE
           C:\ORACLE\ADMIN\TEST\PFILE\INITTEST.ORA
```

where

- STARTUP indicates that you want to start up an existing instance.
- SID is the name of the instance to start up.
- STARTTYPE SRVC¦INST indicates whether you want to start the service, the instance, or both.

To Do: Stop an Oracle Instance with Instance Manager

From the command prompt, execute the following:

```
C:\> ORADIM -SHUTDOWN -SID TEST -SHUTTYPE SRVC INST
     SHUTMODE I
```

where

- SHUTDOWN indicates that you want to shut down the database instance.

- SID indicates the instance to shut down.

- SHUTTYPE SRVC¦INST indicates whether you want to start the service, the instance, or both.

- SHUTMODE A¦I¦N indicates the shutdown mode. A is Abort, I is Immediate, and N is normal (the default).

To Do: Change the Name of the TEST Instance to PROD

From the command prompt, you can execute the following:

```
C:\> ORADIM -EDIT -SID TEST -NEWSID PROD -INTPWD PASSWORD
     -STARTMODE AUTO -PFILE C:\ORACLE\ADMIN\LYNX\PFILE\INIT.ORA
```

where

- EDIT indicates that you want to modify an instance.

- SID is the instance to modify.

- NEWSID is an optional parameter that indicates the instance's new name.

- INTPWD PASSWORD is the password for the INTERNAL account.

- STARTMODE AUTO¦MANUAL indicates whether to start the instance automatically or manually (the default) at startup.

- PFILE PATHNAME indicates the location of the parameter file.

To Do: Delete the PROD Instance

From the command prompt, execute the following:

```
C:\> ORADIM -DELETE -SID PROD -SRVC ORACLESERVICEPROD
```

In this command,

- DELETE indicates that you want to delete an Oracle instance.

- SID indicates the instance to delete. You also can specify the service to delete by using - SVRC SRVC service_to_delete.

Summary

This lesson outlines several key strategies you can implement on Windows NT to integrate operating system and database administration and ultimately gain an efficient overall system. Setting up operating system authentication and creating an OFA-compliant database are explained. You also saw how to use Instance Manager for various database management tasks.

8

Q&A

Q Can I integrate the Windows NT groups into the scheme of OS authentication?

A Yes. You can integrate the Windows NT groups with the Oracle roles similarly to the integration of Windows NT users with Oracle users.

Q Can I have OS authentication set up for some Windows NT accounts but not for others?

A Yes. You can set up authentication for some users; users who don't match according to OS_AUTHENT_PREFIX will have to explicitly log on to the database.

Workshop

The Workshop contains quiz questions and activities to help reinforce what you've learned in this hour. You can check Appendix A for the answers (but don't peek!).

Quiz

1. What parameters must be set to encrypt database passwords?
2. What is the advantage of running a 16-bit application in its own VDM?
3. How can you set up a Windows NT application as a service?

Exercises

1. Set up OS authentication to the ORCL database for all the users in your Engineers Windows NT group.
2. You try to start up the ORCL database but get ORA-9352. How would you resolve this error?

PART III
Working with Oracle Utilities

Hour

Hour 9

Using Oracle Utilities

You can populate an Oracle database with information from various sources. Oracle provides several utilities to facilitate the loading and unloading of data from the database.

This lesson describes the three utilities that Oracle provides for moving and manipulating data:

- SQL*Loader loads data from a flat file into an Oracle database. Information in the flat file can come from various sources, such as other Oracle databases, non-Oracle databases, and spreadsheets.

- The Export utility backs up the entire database, entire schema, or specified tables into a proprietary binary file that only the Import utility can read. It allows you to use incremental exports, which are useful for large databases.

- The Import utility restores data backed up with the Export utility.

Using SQL*Loader

Oracle's SQL*Loader loads ASCII data from various sources, including spreadsheets, mainframes, or other databases. You can then use SQL*Loader to load the text file into the database. You also can manipulate the data before it's loaded into the database.

Working with SQL*Loader's Files

SQL*Loader uses several files to perform a data load. SQL*Loader's operation is controlled by the Data Definition Language (DDL) in its control file, which you can also use to manipulate data before it's loaded into the database. SQL*Loader provides a direct path option that can speed up the data load process.

SQL*Loader's Control File

SQL*Loader's control file contains the necessary DDL to indicate the location of the input files, log file, and the bad file. It can also include data mappings. The DDL used in the control file basically consists of reserved words that specify, among other things,

- The name and format of the datafiles
- The character set
- The datatypes of the data being loaded

Table 9.1 lists the reserved words used by the control file. Some reserved words are required, and others are optional. The control file isn't case sensitive.

TABLE 9.1 RESERVED WORDS USED IN THE CONTROL FILE

AND	DATA	FORMAT
APPEND	DATE	GENERATED
BADFILE	DECIMAL	GRAPHIC
BDDN	DEFAULTIF	INDON
BEGINDATA	DISCARDDN	INDEXES
BLANKS	DISCARDFILE	INFILE
BLOCKSIZE	DISCARDMAX	INSERT
BY	DISCARDS	INTEGER
CHAR	DOUBLE	INTO
CONCATENATE	ENCLOSED	LAST
CONSTANT	EXTERNAL	LOAD
CONTINUE_LOAD	FIELDS	LOG
CONTINUEIF	FIXED	MAX
COUNT	FLOAT	NEXT

9

NO	RECLEN	TABLE
NULLCOLS	RECNUM	TERMINATED
NULLIF	RECORD	THIS
OPTIONALLY	REPLACE	TRAILING
OPTIONS	RESUME	UNLOAD
PARALLEL	SEQUENCE	VARCHAR
PART	SKIP	VARGRAPHIC
PIECED	SORTNUM	VARIABLE
POSITION	SQL/DS	YES
PRESERVE	STREAM	ZONED
RAW	SYSDATE	WORKDDM

The control file specifies the type of data load:

- INSERT requires that the table not have any data; otherwise, it returns an error.
- APPEND adds rows to the table (which might already have data).
- REPLACE replaces the table's current data with the new data. It uses the SQL DELETE command and allows the referential integrity constraints to be maintained.
- TRUNCATE replaces the table's current data with the new data. Referential integrity constraints on the table should be disabled.

SQL*Loader's Datafile

The datafile, also referred to as the *input file*, contains the data to be loaded. Every line in this file is treated as a physical record to be loaded. If you're loading the data into a table with many columns, several physical records can compose the row (a logical record). Data records can be one of two formats:

- *Fixed* requires that a data column be of the same size for all the logical records and that the columns be delimited by position and length.
- *Variable* requires that each column be delimited in one of two ways: terminated by a character such as a comma or period (as in cat, dog) or enclosed by a special character, such as quotation marks before and after the column (as in "Florida","California").

SQL*Loader's Log File

The log file contains detailed information about any messages and errors that occur during the SQL*Loader run.

SQL*Loader's Bad File

SQL*Loader's bad file contains records that were loaded unsuccessfully into the target table. Records might not be loaded for several reasons:

- They have an invalid format.
- They have data that violate referential integrity constraints.
- They are an incompatible datatype with the target table.

SQL*Loader's Discard File

The discard file contains the records discarded during the SQL*Loader run because they didn't meet the conditional DDL statements specified in the control file.

Performing a Data Load

You can perform a data load by using one of two methods: a conventional data load or a direct path data load. Conventional data load uses SQL*Loader as a normal background process, which competes with other processes for system resources. Direct path load can bypass the SQL engine and allow processing to be faster. Direct path load, however, has certain restrictions that can preclude its use.

Performing a Conventional Data Load

Conventional load is the default way to load data. It uses the SGA buffer cache and INSERT statements with a bind-array buffer for processing data during the load. The user ID specified in the control file must have insert privileges on the target table. (If the REPLACE option is used, the user ID should have delete and insert privileges.)

A conventional data load can be used in any of the following situations:

- When the target table is clustered.
- When the load is being performed over SQL*Net.
- When SQL functions are being performed on the data.
- When the loading is performed on a table that can't be locked for the entire duration of the load. In other words, other activities (such as inserts and updates) are occurring on the target table during the load.

Performing a Direct Path Load

A SQL*Loader direct path (DIRECT=TRUE) can improve the performance of a data load:

```
C:\> sqlldr scott/tiger control=countries.ctl DIRECT=TRUE
```

Direct path load doesn't use an INSERT statement, but instead formats the data in the Oracle data block configuration and loads it directly into the database file. The user ID specified in the control file must have insert privileges on the target table. (If the REPLACE option is used, the user ID should have delete and insert privileges.)

Using a direct path load comes with certain restrictions:

- Clustered tables can't be loaded.
- Loaded tables can't have active transaction on them.
- The control file shouldn't contain SQL functions.
- SELECT statements can't be issued against the table during the load if it contains indexes.
- Referential integrity constraints are disabled during the load but re-enabled after the load.
- Default column values aren't used

If an index is placed in the direct load state after a direct path load, you must drop and re-create the index to make it usable.

You can use several options to further improve the performance of a direct-path load operation:

- UNRECOVERABLE prevents the generation of redo during the data load (if the target table has indexes, the index change will generate redo).

If you use the UNRECOVERABLE option, take a backup of the tablespace immediately after the data load is complete.

- SORTED INDEXES improves performance if the target table has an index and the data is presorted in the order of the index.
- PARALLEL allows you to run multiple parallel SQL*Loader sessions.
- PIECED and READBUFFERS can be used to load long datatypes.

To Do: Load a Table with Variable-Length Data

Suppose you're trying to load the countries table in the schema scott. The countries table has the following definition:

```
(country_code     number(2) NOT NULL,
country     varchar2(30))
```

The control file contains the data, which is separated by commas. The following steps show how to create a control file that also contains the data to be loaded:

1. By using any text editor such as Notepad, create a control file with the following contents, and save it as countries.ctl:

    ```
    LOAD DATA
    INFILE *
    INTO TABLE countries
    FIELDS TERMINATED BY ',' OPTIONALLY ENCLOSED BY '"'
    (country_code, country)
    BEGINDATA
         91,"INDIA"
         44,"ENGLAND"
         61,"AUSTRALIA"
         07,"RUSSIA"
         33,"FRANCE"
         49,"GERMANY"
    ```

2. From the MS-DOS prompt, invoke SQL*Loader and perform the data load:

    ```
    C:\> sqlldr userid=scott/tiger control=countries.ctl
            log=countries.log
    ```

To Do: Load a Database Sequence into a Table by Using a Fixed Position

The data is in fixed position. The target table positional_seq_tab is in the schema scott and has the following definition:

```
(seq_num NUMBER,
 column1 NUMBER,
 column2 NUMBER,
 column3 CHAR(10) );
```

The following steps show how you can load a table by using fixed positional data:

1. Connect to Server Manager with the scott schema:

    ```
    SvrmgrL> connect scott/tiger
    ```

2. Create the sequence:

    ```
    Svrmgr> CREATE SEQUENCE test_seq
        2    START WITH 1
        3    INCREMENT BY 1;
    ```

3. By using any text editor, create a control file with the following contents, and save it as seq.ctl:

```
LOAD DATA
INFILE *
INTO TABLE positional_seq_tab
(seq_num "test_seq.nextval"
 column1 POSITION(1:5),
 column2 POSITION(6:10),
 column3 POSITION(11:20)
)
BEGINDATA
    1111122222AAAAA
    2222233333BBBBB
3333344444CCCCC
4444455555DDDDD
```

9

4. From the MS-DOS prompt, load the data by using SQL*Loader:

```
C:\> sqlldr userid=scott/tiger control=seq.ctl log=seq.log
```

5. Verify that the data was loaded properly:

```
Svrmgr> SELECT * FROM positional_seq_table;
SEQ_NUMBER COLUMN1   COLUMN2   COLUMN3
11111                22222     AAAAA
22222                33333     BBBBB
33333                44444     CCCCC
44444                55555     DDDDD
```

To Do: Load the Name of the User Executing SQL*Loader with Comma-Delimited Columns

The data fields are comma-delimited. The target table user_delimited_tab is in the schema scott and has the following definition:

```
(uname   CHAR(20),
 column1 NUMBER,
 column2 NUMBER,
 column3 CHAR(10) );
```

In this example, the comma-delimited fields will cause SQL*Loader to expect the username in the datafile. The username, however, will depend on the user who's now executing the data load and doesn't exist in the datafile. Therefore, the control file should be created so that the username is the last field. You also use the TRAILING NULLCOLS clause to indicate that null or nonexistent information might be in the trailing columns. Follow these steps:

1. By using any text editor, create a control file with the following contents and save it as uname.ctl:

```
LOAD DATA
INFILE *
INTO TABLE scott.user_delimited_tab
FIELDS TERMINATED BY ","
TRAILING NULLCOLS
(column1 ,
 column2 ,
 column3 ,
 uname "USER")
BEGINDATA
    11111,22222,AAAAA
    22222,33333,BBBBB
 33333,44444,CCCCC
 44444,55555,DDDDD
```

2. From the MS-DOS prompt, load the data by using SQL*Loader and the schema scott:

```
C:\> sqlldr userid=scott/tiger control=uname.ctl log=uname.log
```

From the MS-DOS prompt, load the data by using SQL*Loader and the schema john:

```
C:\> sqlldr userid=john/john control=uname.ctl log=uname.log
```

John should have the permissions to insert into the table scott.user_delimited_tab.

3. Verify that the data was loaded properly

```
Svrmgr> SELECT * FROM scott.user_delimited_tab;
UNAME     COLUMN1     COLUMN2     COLUMN3
SCOTT     11111       22222       AAAAA
SCOTT     22222       33333       BBBBB
SCOTT     33333       44444       CCCCC
SCOTT     44444       55555       DDDDD
JOHN      11111       22222       AAAAA
JOHN      22222       33333       BBBBB
JOHN      33333       44444       CCCCC
JOHN      44444       55555       DDDDD
```

Improving SQL*Loader Performance

Sometimes SQL*Loader performance might not be as expected. Try the following suggestions to improve the performance of data loads:

- Remove the indexes on the target table before the data load, load the table, and then re-create the indexes. This reduces the amount of rollback and redo information generated during the load.
- Set the ROWS parameter and perform commits less frequently:

```
C:> sqlldr username/password file=file1.dat rows=500
```

This will require that you use large rollback segments during the load.

- Schedule the data load during periods of the least database activity.
- Use fixed format for loading data whenever possible.
- When using variable format for the data load, use the RECLEN parameter and specify the maximum possible logical record size so that SQL*Loader can preallocate the buffer and improve performance:

```
C:> sqlldr username/password file=file1.dat reclen=500
```

- Tune the database to minimize I/O contention.
- Set the bind array size (BINDSIZE) parameter as high as possible:

```
BINDSIZE = (maximum row size in bytes)*(number_of_rows)
```

- Use the UNRECOVERABLE clause to reduce the amount of redo generated. This clause can be used during creation of a table or index:

```
Create index ix on tb(col) unrecoverable;
```

- If the target table has an index and the data is presorted in the order of the index, you can use the SORTED INDEXES clause:

```
C:> sqlldr username/password file=file1.dat sorted_indexes
```

Use of SORTED INDEXES requires that the table be empty before the data load.

> If the SORTED INDEXES clause is used and the data isn't presorted, the indexes will be left in DIRECT LOAD state after the load.

- Use multiple SQL*Loader sessions and load the target table in parallel by using the PARALLEL clause:

```
C:> sqlldr username/password file=file1.dat parallel
```

- If possible, use a direct path load.

Introducing the Export/Import Utilities

Oracle provides the Export/Import utility combination for data transfer. Export generates an Oracle proprietary file that contains the necessary data and information to perform the data transfer. The dump file generated from export can be read only by the Import utility.

The export dump file is in a binary format; it's not editable, but you can use a text editor to view portions of this file. The dump file contains data, as well as all the DDL commands to re-create the data dictionary. Editing the export dump file will lose some binary information, making the file unusable.

For the most part, export dump files aren't specific to a version of Oracle. Dump files also aren't OS-specific; as a result, you can use Export/Import to transfer data between databases on different platforms.

> When transferring dump files across different platforms, transfer them in binary format, not ASCII.

Export/Import can be used to move information as follows:

- Between databases on the same version of Oracle
- Between databases on different versions of Oracle
- Between databases on different operating system platforms
- From one schema to another schema
- From one tablespace to another tablespace
- The entire database

Exports can be performed at three levels of data collection:

- *Incremental export* backs up data that has changed since the last incremental backup.
- *Cumulative export* backs up data that has changed since the last cumulative backup. It can be used to condense incremental backups.
- *Complete export* backs up the entire database.

Suppose you're using the following export strategy every evening:

Sunday	Complete export
Monday	Incremental export
Tuesday	Incremental export

Wednesday	Incremental export
Thursday	Cumulative export
Friday	Incremental export
Saturday	Incremental export

This strategy takes a complete export every Sunday (longest), incremental exports (fastest and shortest) daily, and cumulative exports on Thursdays.

If recovery is needed on Tuesday (before the Tuesday incremental export), you apply the following:

- Full export from Sunday
- Incremental export from Monday

If recovery is needed on Thursday (before the Thursday cumulative export), you apply the following:

- Full export from Sunday
- Incremental export from Monday
- Incremental export from Tuesday
- Incremental export from Wednesday

If recovery is needed on Friday (before the Friday incremental export), you apply the following:

- Full export from Sunday
- Cumulative export from Thursday

Tables 9.2 and 9.3 show the order in which objects are exported and imported.

TABLE 9.2 ORDER OF EXPORTING OBJECTS

Table Mode	User Mode	Full Database Mode
For each table listed in the TABLES parameter, the following are exported in the order specified:	For each user listed in the OWNER parameter, the following are exported in the order specified:	For database objects except those owned by SYS, the following are exported in the order specified:
—Table definitions	—Snapshots	—Tablespace definitions
—Table data	—Snapshot logs	—Profiles
—Table constraints	—Job queues	—User definitions
—Owner's table grants[1]	—Refresh groups and children	—Roles

continues

TABLE 9.2   CONTINUED

Table Mode	User Mode	Full Database Mode
—Owner's table indexes[2]	—Database links	—System privilege grants
—Analyze tables	—Sequence numbers	—Role grants
—Column comments	—Cluster definitions	—Default roles
—Audit	Then, for each table that the user owns:	—Tablespace quotas
—Table referential integrity constraints	—Table definitions	—Resource costs
—Table triggers	—Table constraints	—Rollback segment
	—Owner table grants	—Table data definitions
	—Owner table indexes[3]	—Database links
	—Analyze table	—Sequence numbers
	—Column comments	—All snapshots
	—Audit	—All snapshot logs
	—Private synonyms	—All job queues
	—User views	—All refresh groups and children
	—User stored procedures, packages, and functions	—All cluster definitions
	—Analyze cluster	—Table definitions
	—Referential integrity constraints	—Table data
	—Trigger	—Table constraints
		—Table grants
		—Table indexes
		—Analyze tables
		—Column comments
		—Audit
		—Referential integrity constraints
		—All synonyms
		—All views
		—All stored procedures, packages, and functions
		—All triggers
		—Analyze cluster
		—Default and system auditing

1   *Owner's grants for the specified tables are exported.*

2   *Owner's indexes for the specified tables are exported.*

3   *Only indexes on the user's tables are exported.*

TABLE 9.3 ORDER OF IMPORTING OBJECTS

Table Mode	User Mode	Full Database Mode
For each table listed in the TABLES parammeter, the following are imported in the order specified:	For each user listed in the OWNER parammeter, the following are imported in the order specified:	For database objects except those owned by SYS, the following are imported in the order specified:
—Table definitions[1]	—Snapshots	—Tablespace definitions
—Table data	—Snapshot logs	—Profiles
—Table constraints	—Job queues	—User definitions[5]
—Owner's table grants[2]	—Refresh groups and children	—Roles
—Owner's table indexes[3]	—Database links	—System privilege grants
—Analyze tables	—Sequence numbers	—Role grants
—Column comments	—Cluster definitions	—Default roles
—Audit	Then, for each table the user owns:	—Tablespace quotas
—Table referential integrity constraints	—Table definitions	—Resource costs
—Table triggers	—Table data	—Rollback segment definitions
	—Table constraints	—Database links
	—Owner table grants	—Sequence numbers[6]
	—Owner table indexes[3, 4]	—All snapshots
	—Analyze table	—All snapshot logs
	—Column comments	—All job queues
	—Audit	—All refresh groups and children
	—Private synonyms	—All cluster definitions
	—User views	—Table definitions[1]
	—User-stored procedures, packages, and functions	—Table data
	—Analyze cluster	—Table constraints
	—Referential integrity constraints	—Table grants
	—Trigger	—Table indexes
	—Postable actions	

continues

9

TABLE 9.3   CONTINUED

Table Mode	User Mode	Full Database Mode
		—Analyze tables
		—Column comments
		—Audit
		—Referential integrity constraints
		—All synonyms
		—All views
		—All stored procedures, packages, and functions
		—All triggers
		—Analyze cluster
		—Default and system auditing

1   *Comments and audit options are included with the table definitions.*

2   *Owner's grants for the specified tables are imported.*

3   *Owner's indexes for the specified tables are imported.*

4   *Only indexes on the user's tables are imported.*

5   *During import, user definitions are created by using the CREATE USER command. If you're importing from an export file that was created with a previous version of export, the user isn't automatically granted the CREATE SESSION privilege.*

6   *Before importing to an existing database, you should drop the sequences because they won't be set to the value captured in the export file.*

Oracle Export and Import Parameters

Oracle's Export utility generates a binary file as output that can be read only by Oracle's Import utility. Several parameters are common to both utilities, whereas others are unique.

The following parameters are available when you use Oracle's Export utility:

- BUFFER specifies the size in bytes of the data buffer used for the export run:

   Buffer size = maximum row size*num rows in array

   It must be as large as the longest row of data to be exported, or Export will generate an error. The larger the buffer, the faster the export.

- If COMPRESS is set to Y, segments in multiple extents are compressed into one initial extent. Otherwise, it keeps them in multiple extents.

- CONSISTENT specifies whether Export will use the SET TRANSACTION READ ONLY setting to ensure a read-consistent export. CONSISTENT isn't valid for an incremental export.

- CONSTRAINTS specifies whether constraints should be exported.

- DIRECT allows you to perform a direct path export faster than a conventional export because it bypasses the SQL command-processing layer. It can be used to reduce contention for resources with other user processes.

- FEEDBACK specifies whether export should provide a progress meter in terms of dots per specified number of rows exported.

- FILE specifies the name of the file to contain the export.

- When you have the EXP_FULL_DATABASE role, you can perform a full export of the database by setting the FULL parameter to Y. It can't be used with the TABLES and OWNERS parameters.

- GRANTS specifies whether object grants should be exported.

- HELP displays a help message with the export parameters.

- INCTYPE specifies the type of incremental export. Valid values are COMPLETE, CUMULATIVE, and INCREMENTAL.

- INDEXES specifies whether indexes should be exported.

- LOG specifies the name of the file to which information and error messages during export should be written.

- OWNER specifies a list of users whose objects need to be exported. Using OWNER without the TABLES parameter signifies a user mode export. OWNER can't be used with the FULL=Y parameter.

- PARFILE specifies the full path of the parameter file that supplies the export parameters. If a directory isn't specified, the file is expected in the current directory.

- RECORD specifies whether you want to record an incremental or cumulative export in the database tables SYS.INCVID, SYS.INCFIL, and SYS.INCEXP.

- RECORDLENGTH specifies the length of the file record in bytes. Use this parameter if the import will be performed on a different OS platform from the export platform.

- ROWS specifies whether the data rows of the table are to be exported.

- STATISTICS specifies the type of optimizer statistics to generate when the data is imported. Valid values are NONE, ESTIMATE, and COMPUTE.

- TABLES specifies a list of tables to export. Use of this parameter indicates a table mode export. It can't be used with the FULL=Y parameter.

- USERID specifies the username and password of the user to perform the export.

9

The following parameters are available when you use Oracle's Import utility:

- BUFFER specifies the size in bytes of the data buffer used for the import run:

  Buffer size = maximum row size*num rows in array

  It must be as large as the longest row of data to be imported; otherwise, Import generates an error. The larger the buffer, the faster the import.

- COMMIT specifies whether Import should commit after each array insert. By default, a commit takes place after each object is loaded.

- DESTROY specifies whether existing datafiles should be reused.

> If you've precreated the tablespace for the database, leave DESTROY=N; otherwise, the precreated tablespaces will be lost.

- FEEDBACK specifies whether Import should provide a progress meter in dots per specified number of rows imported.

- FILE specifies the name of the file to be imported.

- FROMUSER specifies a list of usernames whose objects are to be imported. If TOUSER clause isn't specified, the specified objects are imported into the FROMUSER schema. If the specified user doesn't exist in the target database, the objects are imported into the schema of the importer. If the TABLES parameter isn't used, this parameter signifies a user mode export. It can't be used with the FULL=Y parameter.

- When you have the IMP_FULL_DATABASE role, you can perform a full import of the database by setting the FULL parameter to Y. FULL can't be used with the TABLES and FROMUSER parameters.

- GRANTS specifies whether object grants should be imported.

- HELP displays a help message with the import parameters.

- IGNORE specifies how object creation errors are to be handled during the import. If IGNORE=Y, object creation errors are ignored; for tables, IGNORE=Y causes rows to be imported into existing tables. If IGNORE=N, object creation errors are displayed, and then import proceeds to the next object.

- INCTYPE specifies the type of incremental import. Valid values are SYSTEM and RESTORE.

- INDEXES specifies whether indexes should be imported.

- INDEXFILE specifies a file to be used to write the index creation statements that are part of the export file. It also places the associated table and cluster creation statements as comments. You can edit and use this file as a regular SQL script. It doesn't import any database objects.
- LOG specifies the name of the file to which information and error messages during import should be written.
- RECORDLENGTH specifies the length of the file record in bytes. Use this parameter if the export file is coming from a different OS platform to the import platform.
- ROWS specifies whether the data rows of the table are to be imported.
- TABLES specifies a list of tables to import. Use of this parameter indicates a table mode import. It can't be used with the FULL=Y parameter.
- TOUSER specifies a list of usernames to whose schema the data will be imported. You must have the IMP_FULL_DATABASE role to use TOUSER. This parameter can be used to import to a user different from the original owner.
- USERID specifies the username and password of the user to perform the import.

Optimizing Database Exports

Follow these guidelines to optimize your exports:

- Minimize I/O contention by placing the export dump file on a disk separate from the disk containing the datafiles.
- Break the export into smaller exports, and then run each export in parallel.
- Export only the information needed during recovery. For example, don't export indexes if they can be easily re-created. If roles, profiles, and security information don't change after the initial setup, you don't need to export them every time.
- Export to a high-speed disk rather than to a tape.
- Determine whether incremental and cumulative exports will be really useful. Suppose that many changes are happening in the database and that about 80% or more must be backed up every time. In this case, you're better off using a full database export and thereby dealing with only one file instead of many files.
- Use a large buffer size. The BUFFER parameter determines the number of rows in the array to be exported. The larger the buffer size, the better the performance. The setting for BUFFER is influenced by the amount of memory on your system; be careful not to introduce paging (by setting it too high).
- Don't back up read-only tablespaces. Also, make sure that the read-only tablespace wasn't read-write during the last export and has switched to read-only since that time.

- Schedule the export during periods of the least database activity.
- Make sure that the frequency of performing an export is proper. In other words, if not much activity is going on in the database, you're better off exporting less frequently.

Optimizing Database Imports

You can take several actions to optimize a database import:

- Use a large buffer size. The BUFFER parameter determines the number of rows in the array to be inserted by the import. The larger the buffer size, the better the performance. The setting for BUFFER is influenced by the amount of memory on your system, so be careful not to introduce paging (by setting it too high).
- Don't use COMMIT=Y. When COMMIT=N, the commit takes place after each object load instead of each array insert. This improves performance but requires that you use large rollback segments.
- Use a large rollback segment, and offline other rollback segments to ensure that the import uses a large rollback segment. Using a large rollback segment and about 20 extents minimizes dynamic space management.
- Take a backup and disable archiving. Putting the database in NOARCHIVELOG mode is a good idea because import generates a lot of redo that doesn't need to be recorded. A backup also should be taken at this point because you aren't planning to use ARCHIVELOG mode.
- Use large online redo logs and reduce the checkpoint frequency. This can be done by increasing the value of the LOG_CHECKPOINT_INTERVAL parameter. This will help in conserving system resources.
- Pre-create the tables without the indexes and constraints, load the data, and then create the indexes and constraints. Use the INDEXFILE parameter to help in index creation.
- Minimize I/O contention by placing the export file on a disk other than the datafiles.
- Schedule the import during periods of the least database activity.
- Import from a disk rather than directly from a tape.
- Use a large value for the SORT_AREA_SIZE parameter to speed up the index creation process.

Working with Export Views

Export views are created by CATEXP.SQL script. The Export utility uses these internal views to organize the data that will be sent to the export dump file.

Export views aren't the same across Oracle versions and are changed to reflect the changes in the data dictionary between the different Oracle versions. When you run an export executable from one version of Oracle against a different-version database, you might encounter export errors due to version-related changes in the export views. The following steps indicate what should be done when you encounter such a situation.

When exporting to an older version database, follow these steps:

1. Run the older catexp.sql on the source database.
2. Create the export dump file by using the older export executable.
3. Import to the target database by using the older import executable.
4. Run the newer catexp.sql on the source database to update its export views.

When exporting to a newer version database, follow these steps:

1. Run the newer catexp.sql on the source database.
2. Create the export dump file by using the newer export executable.
3. Import to the target database by using the newer import executable.
4. Run the older catexp.sql on the source database to update its export views.

Export/Import and Sequences

When you export sequences (during a FULL export), you can potentially lose sequence numbers if one of the following occurs:

- Users are accessing the sequence while the export is running.
- Cached sequences are used. Export will get the current value from the data dictionary; cached numbers are skipped.

If you have a table column that's updated with sequences, the result after an export/import depends on how the column is updated:

- If both conditions are false, the values should come back exactly as they now exist.
- If you use a front-end application to insert rows into the table and the application accesses the sequence, the column values that exist in the dump file are used during the import without reaccessing the sequence.

- If an INSERT trigger populates the columns by using sequence.nextval and the trigger is enabled during the import, the insert during import will fire the trigger, and the sequence will be accessed. This might result in sequence numbers different from the original sequence numbers.

To Do: Perform a Full Database Export with a Parameter File

The following steps use a parameter file to perform full database export:

1. By using a text editor such as Notepad, create the c:\backups\exp_param file with the following contents:

```
Userid=system/manager
Full=y
File=c:\exports\full_export.dmp
Log=c:\exports\full_export.log
Buffer=50000000
```

2. Set the ORACLE_SID environment variable to point to the correct database:

```
C:\> set ORACLE_SID=ORCL
```

3. From the MS-DOS prompt, perform the export by using the exp_param.txt parameter file:

```
C:\> exp parfile=c:\backups\exp_param
```

▲ You should get the message that the export completely successfully.

To Do: Perform a Full Database Import with a Parameter File

The following steps use a parameter file to perform a full database import:

1. By using a text editor such as Notepad, create the file c:\backups\imp_param with the following contents:

```
Userid=system/manager
File=c:\exports\full_export.dmp
Log=c:\exports\full_import.log
Buffer=50000000
```

2. Set the ORACLE_SID environment variable to point to the correct database:

```
C:\> set ORACLE_SID=ORCL
```

3. From the MS-DOS prompt, perform the import by using the imp_param parameter file:

```
C:\> imp parfile=c:\backups\imp_param
```

▲ You should receive the message that the import completed successfully.

Summary

Export/Import and SQL*Loader are valuable utilities provided by Oracle for the purpose of populating the database. Export and Import work together—the Export utility can send database definitions and data into an export dump file that is read by the Import utility. On the other hand, SQL*Loader can be used to load data derived from other non-Oracle sources into Oracle databases. This lesson also looks at several strategies you can use to optimize the performance of these utilities.

9

Q&A

Q Can I edit the export dump file and manipulate the data before loading it into the database?

A Don't edit the export dump file—you can potentially corrupt the export dump file, making it unusable.

Q I've taken exports from an Oracle database on UNIX. Can I import it into an Oracle database on Windows NT?

A Yes. Just make sure that the file is transferred in binary format.

Workshop

The Workshop contains quiz questions and activities to help reinforce what you've learned in this hour. You can check Appendix A for the answers (but don't peek!).

Quiz

1. What Oracle utility can you use to load an ASCII text file obtained from a Sybase database into an Oracle database?

2. What restrictions are involved in using direct path load?

3. Can you lose sequence numbers as part of database exports?

Exercises

1. Create a SQL*Loader control file that can be used to merge the firstname and lastname fields. Load the combined result into a name field.

2. The import of your database is very slow. What are some ways in which you can increase the performance?

HOUR 10

Managing Oracle8i with the Oracle Enterprise Manager

Oracle provides the Oracle Enterprise Manager (OEM) as an integrated and comprehensive systems management platform for managing databases and networks by combining a graphical console, agent processes, database management applications, performance tuning, diagnostic applications, and common services. OEM version 2.x uses a three-tier distributed architecture to provide scalability and Java architecture to make it portable. OEM version 2.x has several characteristics:

- It allows you to administer, diagnose, and tune multiple databases.
- It provides an integrated job and event system that you can use to schedule jobs on multiple nodes.
- It can be used to monitor objects and events such as database and node failures throughout the network from one centralized location.
- It uses Oracle Management Server (OMS) to achieve load balancing and failover.

- It can use shared repositories.
- It provides Web-enabled console and database applications.
- It allows the integration of third-party tools.

In this hour, you will understand how to use OEM to perform different tasks such as the following:

- Start and stop your Oracle databases.
- Tune your Oracle databases.
- Manage storage.
- Understand the interaction of the various OEM components.

Introducing OEM Components

 As of the writing of this chapter, OEM 2.0 was not available in production version, and therefore some of the steps in this chapter might differ in the final release.

Table 10.1 shows the various database applications provided by OEM.

TABLE 10.1 OEM DATABASE APPLICATIONS AND THEIR USE

OEM Application	Use
Instance Manager[1]	Manages database instances and initialization parameters
Storage Manager[1]	Manages datafiles, rollback segments, and other storage parameters
Security Manager[1]	Manages users, roles, privileges, and profiles
Schema Manager[1]	Manages schema objects such as tables, indexes, views, clusters, synonyms, and sequences
Software Manager[2]	Manages the process of distributing software
Backup Manager[2]	Performs database backups and recovery and creates scripts that can be used to take backups
Replication Manager	Manages the replication environment
SQL Worksheet[2]	Executes SQL queries and DML
Data Manager[2]	Performs database export/import and data loads

1 Java-based application
2 Win32-based application

In addition to the database applications in Table 10.1, OEM provides two optional packs containing various applications used for database tuning (the tuning pack) and diagnostic purposes (the diagnostic pack).

The OEM environment uses a three-tier architecture to increase scalability and availability. It also allows multiple types of clients, such as browser-based or OEM version 1 applications or version 2 applications. OEM v2.x consists of the following major components:

- OEM console
- OEM repository
- Communication daemon
- Intelligent agents
- Common services
- Application Programming Interface (API)
- Oracle Management Server
- Integrated applications

10

OEM Console

The console is the graphical user interface (GUI) that provides windows for various views of the system. The OEM console can be browser-based, and there's only one console per client machine.

The console includes menus, toolbars, and palettes that simplify administrative tasks. It enables the launching of integrated applications and third-party applications. You can customize the console as desired.

The console consists of several components:

- *Navigator window* is a tree view of all objects in the system and their relationships.
- *Map window* can be used to customize the system views.
- *Job window* interfaces to the Job Scheduling system.
- *Event Management* interfaces to the Event Management system.

OEM Repository

The repository is a set of tables in your schema that contains information such as jobs and event status, discovery cache, tasks performed, and messages from the notification queue in the communication daemon. You can place the repository in any Oracle database in the system.

When a user logs in to OEM, a connection to the repository is established. You can install a repository on any database accessible from the console and move it to another Oracle database.

OEM v2.x makes it possible to merge multiple repositories into one shared repository. OEM v2.x also allows the use of domains that equate to a database repository schema—an administrator created in one domain can't log in to another domain, and data can't be shared between domains.

> At any given time, a user is connected to only one repository.

Communication Daemon

OEM uses a multi-threaded process to manage console communication activities. The communication daemon performs several tasks:

- It communicates with agents and nodes for job scheduling.
- It communicates with agents and nodes for event monitoring.
- It periodically queues and retries failed jobs.
- It is used during service discovery.
- It periodically contacts the nodes to make sure that they are alive.

Intelligent Agents

The intelligent agents are domainless intelligent processes that run on remote nodes and service requests from multiple domains. Intelligent agents perform the following functions:

- They accept jobs or events from the console or third-party applications.
- They cancel jobs or events as directed.
- They run jobs, collect the results, and queue them for the communication daemon.
- They handle SNMP requests, if supported on the agent's platform.

Common Services

All OEM components share several services:

- *Job service*—This service enables the scheduling of jobs on remote sites by specifying the task to perform, the start time, and the frequency of execution. Each job has an owner and associated privileges. By default, the creator of a job is the owner, and anyone with full permission can change the job owner. When a job is created, it can be submitted for execution, saved in the library, or both.

To use the Job Scheduling system, the intelligent agent should be installed and configured. The intelligent agent should run on every database server against which jobs will be scheduled to run.

The Job menu has an option (Create Like) you can use to create a new job that performs the same tasks as the highlighted job.

- *Security services*—These services manage administrative privileges for nodes and services in the system. A list of administrators that should be notified when an event occurs can be maintained by the security services.

- *Event services*—An event comprises *tests* (a condition that must be checked). You can use event services to monitor events at remote sites, alert administrators when a problem is detected, and optionally fix the problem according to a prespecified criteria. An alert can be one of several levels of severity: clear, warning, critical, or unknown. All events have an owner and permissions. By default, the creator of an event is the owner, and anyone with full permission can change the event owner. Users can have various types of access on events: none, view, modify, and full. You can use an event library to store events. When an event is created, it can be registered, saved in the library, or both. An event log is provided that logs instance changes and assignment changes.

The Event menu also has the option Create Like, which you can use to create an event exactly the same as the highlighted event.

10

You can use the job and event management systems together to establish a reactive management system.

- *Discovery service*—This service is used to maintain an up-to-date view of the nodes and services being managed.

Application Programming Interface (API)

OEM provides an API that enables third-party applications to integrate the console with the common services. You can use third-party applications to analyze the data gathered by the Oracle Expert and other OEM performance-tuning tools. Integration can occur at the console level or the agent level.

Communication among the various OEM components occurs as follows:

- *Console and the communication daemon*—The console sends various job and event requests to the communication daemon. The communication daemon in turn sends the status of these jobs and events back to the console. Authentication requests for users that log on to the console are also sent to the communication daemon. The communication daemon also sends information such as service discovery, which can be used to populate the console's navigator trees.

- *Communication daemon and common services*—The communication daemon sends the jobs and events requests to the job or event services. User authentication requests are sent to the security services. The common services send job, event, authentication, and service discovery information back to the communication daemon.

- *Communication daemon and intelligent agents*—Intelligent agents running on remote nodes communicate the result of reports and various status messages for the jobs and events to the communication daemon.

- *Common services and the repository*—The job and event service writes information about jobs and events to the repository via OMS.

Examples of Client Files Required by OEM

Look at the contents of the client and server files so that you can become familiar with what to expect in these files. Cross-check the contents as suggested in the text following each file listing so that OEM can function properly with the correct configuration.

SQLNET.ORA Client File

```
AUTOMATIC_IPC=OFF
trace_level_server=off
TRACE_LEVEL_CLIENT=16
trace_file_client=client.trc
trace_directory_client=c:\oracle81\network\trace
SQLNET.EXPIRE_TIME=0
NAMES.DEFAULT_DOMAIN=world
NAME.DEFAULT_ZONE=world
```

In this sqlnet.ora file, the default domain and default zones are set to world. Therefore, you should ensure that the service names in TNSNAMES.ORA should have world tagged to them.

TNSNAMES.ORA Client File

10

```
#Agent Addresses
test_agent.world=(description=
        (address=
            (community=tcp.world)
            (protocol=tcp)
            (host=machine1)
            (port=1521)
        )
    )
#Database Addresses
test.world=(description=
        (address_list=
            (address=
                (community=tcp.world)
                (protocol=tcp)
                (host=machine1)
                (port=1729)
            )
        )
        (connect_data=
            (sid=test)
            (global_name=test.world)
        )
    )
```

The agent port (1521) should match that of the port in the snmp.ora file. The listener port (1729) should match that of the port in the listener.ora file.

The database and SID name is test. The domain world must match the sqlnet.ora file. The port numbers used in this file should be valid TCP/IP port numbers and should not be used by other services.

TOPOLOGY.ORA Client File

```
# Services of node: test.world
test_agent.world = (oracle_agent, machine1)
testlsnr.world = (oracle_listener, machine1)
test.world = (oracle_database, machine1, testlsnr.world)
#
```

The agent name should match the agent name in TNSNAMES.ORA. The listener name should match the listener name in LISTENER.ORA. The database name should match the one in TNSNAMES.ORA.

SQLNET.ORA Server File

```
AUTOMATIC_IPC=OFF
trace_level_server=off
TRACE_LEVEL_CLIENT=off
SQLNET.EXPIRE_TIME=0
NAMES.DEFAULT_DOMAIN=world
NAME.DEFAULT_ZONE=world
```

TNSNAMES.ORA Server File

```
#Database Addresses
test.world=(description=
      (address_list=
          (address=
              (community=tcp.world)
              (protocol=tcp)
              (host=machine1)
              (port=1729)
          )
      )
      (connect_data=
              (sid=test)
              (global_name=test.world)
      )
   )
```

LISTENER.ORA Server File

```
testlsnr=
    (address_list=
        (address=
            (protocol=ipc)
            (key=test.world)
        )
```

```
        (address=
            (protocol=ipc)
            (key=test)
        )
        (address=
            (community=tcp.world)
            (protocol=tcp)
            (host=machine1)
            (port=1729)
        )
    )
startup_wait_time_testlsnr=0
connect_timeout_testlsnr=10
trace_level_testlsnr=off
sid_list_testlsnr=
    (sid_list=
        (sid_desc=
            (sid_name=test)
            (oracle_home= c:\oracle81)
        )
    )
```

10

The port number (1729) must match the one in the TNSNAMES.ORA on the client and server machines.

SNMP.ORA Server File

```
snmp.visibleservices=(test,testlsnr)
snmp.index.test=1
snmp.index.testlsnr=2
snmp.sid.test=test
dbsnmp.address=(description=
            (address=
                (community=tcp.world)
                (protocol=tcp)
                (host=machine1)
                (port=1526)
            )
        )
```

The dbsnmp.address must exactly match the agent address in the TNSNAMES.ORA file on the client machine.

Using the Database Applications

OEM provides several database applications you can use to simplify the task of adminis-trating multiple databases. Some applications are Java based, whereas others are Win32 based. The database applications can be run in two modes:

- *From the console, using OMS*—This approach enables you to run the application in a browser and allows the application to support multiple databases in the navigator. The disadvantage of this approach is that you must specify Enterprise Manager v2 framework and it must be running. Also, it manages only those databases that are discovered.

- *From the command line, using* `oemapp tool_name oms_machine_name`—This approach works just like v1.x and doesn't require the setup of Enterprise Manager v2 framework. It doesn't run in a browser and uses only one database in the navigator. Also, no OMS functionality such as jobs and events is available.

> When a database application uses OMS, the communication to the repository occurs through the OMS.

To Do: Manage OMS

OMS is managed by using the OEMCtrl utility, as shown in Figure 10.1. To start OMS, use the following command:

`OEMCtrl START OMS`

To shut down OMS, use this command:

`OMSCtrl STOP OMS emsuperuser/empassword@domain`

To check the status of OMS, use

`OEMCtrl STATUS OMS emsuperuser/empassword@domain`

The default Enterprise Manager superuser is SYSMAN, with the password `oem_temporary_password`.

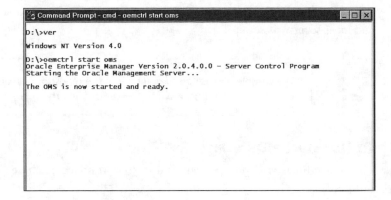

FIGURE 10.1

Managing OMS.

To Do: Set Preferred Credentials

You should set up preferred credentials for users to avoid retyping the service name, service type, and username for each database, listener, or node that users intend to access. The Preferred Credentials tabbed page (see Figure 10.2) shows the list of databases, listeners, and nodes in the network. To access this dialog box, follow these steps:

1. From the console menu bar, choose System, Preferences.

2. On the Preferences tabbed page, populate the Username, Password, Confirm, and Role fields for any account.

3. Click OK.

FIGURE 10.2

Setting preferred credentials.

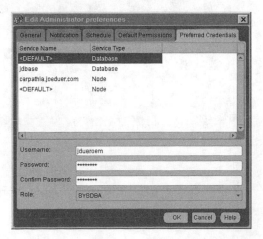

Starting and Shutting Down a Database

You can use the OEM console to start or shut down an Oracle database after the remote and local security is set up.

> The console allows you to manipulate the repository in various ways, but it can't be used to shut down the server running the repository.

To Do: Start a Database

The Oracle Enterprise Manager can be used to start up the database (see Figure 10.3) as follows:

1. Start up and log on to the Oracle Enterprise Manager.

2. Select the database object to be started from the database folder.

3. Specify the correct username and password for this host when prompted (if preferred credentials are set up, this isn't required).

4. On the General page of the Database property sheet, select the Startup mode.

5. Specify the location of the init.ora file.

6. Click Apply.

FIGURE 10.3

Starting a database.

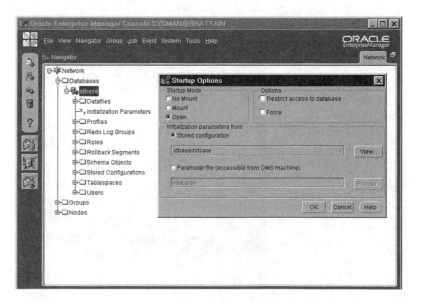

To Do: Shut Down a Database

The Oracle Enterprise Manager can be used to shut down the database (see Figure 10.4) as follows:

1. Start up and log on to the Oracle Enterprise Manager.

2. Select the database object to be stopped.

3. Specify the correct username and password for this host when prompted (if preferred credentials are set up, this isn't required).

4. On the General page of the Database property sheet, select the Shutdown mode.

5. Click the Shutdown button.

FIGURE 10.4

Shutting down a database.

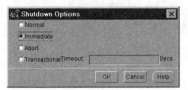

Using Storage Manager to Manage Database Storage

Administrative tasks associated with managing database storage such as managing tablespaces, rollback segments, and adding and renaming datafiles can be performed by using the Storage Manager.

To Do: Create a Datafile Similar to an Existing Datafile

Storage Manager can be used to quickly create a new datafile by using an existing datafile as a template (see Figure 10.5). Follow these steps:

1. Launch Storage Manager from the OEM console or as a standalone, and connect to a database. If you choose to launch it as a standalone, type `oemapp storage` at the command prompt.

2. From the tree on the left, select a datafile in the Datafiles folder.

3. Choose Objects, Create Like.

4. The Create Datafile property sheet appears, with all parameters except the new datafile name set. Provide an appropriate name to the new datafile.

5. Click Apply.

10

FIGURE 10.5

Creating a datafile like another existing datafile.

To Do: Create a Tablespace

▼ To Do

Storage Manager provides a graphical means for creating tablespaces (see Figure 10.6), as demonstrated by the following steps:

1. Launch Storage Manager from the Oracle Enterprise Manager console or as a standalone, and connect to a database. If you're launching it as a standalone, type `oemapp storage` at the command prompt.

2. Choose Object, Create.

3. Choose Tablespace.

4. On the General page of the Create Tablespace property sheet, specify the details of the new tablespace to be created:

Name	Specify the name of the tablespace (maximum 30 characters long).
Status	Choose the tablespace's status, such as online or offline.

   The datafiles belonging to the tablespace are listed. You can add, remove, or edit datafiles belonging to the tablespace.

5. On the Extents page, specify the default storage parameters of all objects belonging to this tablespace. Click the Override Default Values check box to allow the editing of all the following storage parameters:

▼

▼	Initial Size	Specify the size of the object's first extent. Specification can be KB or MB.
	Next Extent	Specify the size of the next extent allocated to the object. Specification can bc KB or MB.
	Minimum Size	Specify the minimum size allocated to the object. Specification can be KB or MB.
	Minimum Extents	Minimum number of extents that can be allocated to the object.
	Maximum Extents	Maximum number of extents that can be allocated to the object. You can specify a value or unlimited extents.

6. Click Apply.

FIGURE 10.6

Creating a tablespace.

▲

To Do: Drop a Tablespace

Storage Manager makes it very easy to drop a tablespaces (see Figure 10.7). Follow these steps:

1. Launch Storage Manager from the Oracle Enterprise Manager console or as a standalone, and connect to a database.

2. From thc tablespace list, select the tablespace to drop.

3. Choose Objects, Remove.

▼ 4. Confirm the removal of the tablespace.

FigURE **10.7**

Removing a table-space.

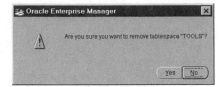

Performing Advanced Management Tasks

Identifying and reducing resource contention is an ongoing task DBAs must perform. Tuning isn't a science; it takes much experience and understanding of the environment (database, applications, system configuration, and so on) to obtain a system that performs as desired. OEM provides various predefined charts to help you monitor the usage of different resources that can contribute to contention. The following system resources have been found to be the source of contention for most systems:

- *CPU*—When a process executes on the server, it needs a CPU time slice to complete its task. It's very important to identify CPU-intensive tasks in your system.
- *Disk access*—A disk access occurs when a process needs data and the data isn't found in the database buffer cache. You should identify and minimize the amount and frequency of disk activity because it's very time-consuming.
- *Memory*—Insufficient memory on the system leads to performance degradation due to paging.

Using the Performance Pack

OEM provides the Performance Pack, which is a combination of the tuning and diagnostic packs, as a value-added component. The Performance Pack consists of various tools (see Table 10.2) that you can use to monitor and tune the performance of a database using statistics gathered over a period of time.

TABLE 10.2   FUNCTIONS PERFORMED BY THE PERFORMANCE PACK'S VARIOUS COMPONENTS

Performance Pack Component	Use
Performance Manager	Uses predefined and customized charts to display tuning statistics on resource contention.
Oracle TopSessions[1]	Displays the top sessions based on any criteria that you specify, such as CPU usage and disk I/O.

Performance Pack Component	Use
Oracle Expert	Collects and analyzes performance tuning data based on predefined rules. It also provides tuning recommendations and generates scripts that can be used to implement the tuning recommendations.
Oracle Trace	Collects performance data based on events and generates data the Oracle Expert can use.
Oracle Lock Manager	Displays blocked and waiting sessions.
Tablespace Viewer	Displays the space used by each datafile.

1   *Before running TopSessions for Oracle8, create the supporting tables by running $ORACLE_HOME/sysman/smptsi80.sql.*

10

Tuning a system's performance should be a preventive action based on trends detected through the analysis of data gathered over a period of time by using tools such as those provided by the Performance Pack. Use the Performance Pack launch palette or the Tools, Performance Pack option of the OEM console to launch the performance-monitoring applications.

To Do: Use the Oracle TopSessions Application

To Do ▼

For this exercise, use TopSessions to display the top 10 sessions accessing the ORCL database. The information is to be sorted by the CPU Used by This Session user statistic and updated automatically every minute. Follow these steps:

1. Start up, and log on to the Oracle Enterprise Manager.

2. Select the ORCL database from the Navigator window.

3. Launch the Oracle TopSessions application from the OEM toolbar.

4. Specify the criteria for the sessions in the Sort page of the Options property sheet:

    • Select User in the Statistics Filter list box.

    • Select CPU Used by This Session in the Sort Statistics list box.

5. Specify the refresh type and interval in the Refresh page of the Options property sheet:

    • Choose Automatic Refresh.

    • Set the Refresh Interval to 60, and reset the Minutes and Hours text boxes to 00.

6. Specify the number of sessions to display in the Count page of the Options property sheet. Click the Display Top *N* Sessions button and change the count to 10.

▲   7. Click OK.

To Do: Use Oracle Performance Manager to Monitor a Database's Performance

To Do

Monitor the Disk Access, Resource Contention, and Memory Utilization tools to determine the performance of the ORCL database. Follow these steps:

1. Start up, and log on to the Oracle Enterprise Manager.

2. Select the ORCL database from the Navigator window.

3. Launch the Oracle Performance Manager application from the OEM toolbar.

4. Choose Charts, Define Window.

5. Provide a unique name for the window.

6. From the list of available charts, choose the chart you want, and click the << button.

7. Repeat step 6 for all charts needed to monitor the performance of the database.

8. Click OK.

Oracle Performance Manager Charts

Oracle Performance Manager provides several categories of predefined charts described in Table 10.3. The predefined charts can be accessed from Performance Manager's Display menu.

TABLE 10.3 PREDEFINED CHARTS OF THE ORACLE PERFORMANCE MANAGER

Category	Charts Included in the Category
Contention	Circuit, Dispatcher, Free List Hit %, Latch, Lock, Queue, Redo Allocation Hit %, Rollback NoWait Hit %, and Shared Server
Database_Instance	Process, Session, System Statistics, Table Access, Tablespace, Tablespace Free Space, #Users Active, #Users Waiting for Locks, and #Users Running
I/O	Load Buffer Gets Rate, Network Bytes Rate, Redo Statistics Rate, Sort Rows Rate, Table Scan Rows Rate, and Throughput Rate
Overview	#Users Active, #Users Logged On, #Users Running, #Users Waiting, Buffer Cache Hit, Data Dictionary Cache Hit, File I/O Rate, Rollback NoWait Hit %, System I/O Rate, and Throughput
User-defined	Charts created by the user

The overview charts provided by Oracle Performance Manager are a set of predefined charts that give a good overall picture of the system performance. Table 10.4 lists the charts included in this category.

TABLE 10.4 CHARTS INCLUDED IN THE OVERVIEW CATEGORY

Chart	Use
Number of users active	Obtains its information from v$session and shows the number of users actively using the database instance
Number of users logged on	Obtains its information from v$license and shows the number of users concurrently logged on, whether or not any activity is occurring
Number of users running	Obtains its information from v$session_wait and shows the number of users concurrently logged on and performing a transaction
Number of users waiting	Obtains its information from v$session_wait and shows the number of users now waiting
Buffer cache hit %	Obtains its information from v$sysstat and displays the buffer cache hit %
Data Dictionary cache hit	Obtains its information from v$rowcache and displays the data dictionary cache hit
File I/O	Obtains its information from v$dbfile and shows the amount of read and write occurring against each file in the database
Rollback NoWait Hit %	Obtains its information from v$rollstat and shows the hits and misses occurring for online rollback segments
System I/O rate	Obtains its information from v$sysstat and shows the I/O statistics, including buffer gets, block changes, and physical reads per second for the database instance
Throughput rate	Obtains its information from v$sysstat and shows the number of user calls and transactions per second for the instance

To Do: Create Your Own Charts

You should create your own charts if the predefined charts don't provide the information you're trying to obtain. Follow these steps to create a chart:

1. Start up, and log on to the Oracle Enterprise Manager.
2. Select the ORCL database from the Navigator window.
3. Launch the Oracle Performance Manager application.

▼   4. Choose Charts, Define Charts.

5. Specify a name for the new chart.

6. In the SQL Statement text box, specify the SQL statement that will gather the statistics to display in the chart.

7. Click the Execute button.

8. Verify the results in the Results field to make sure that the SQL statement returns the desired information.

9. On the Display Options page, enter the required information for each variable you want to display, and click the Add button.

10. Click the Apply button and then click OK.

▲   11. Save the chart in the repository by choosing File, Save Chart.

Summary

Oracle Enterprise Manager provides a comprehensive set of tools for managing Oracle databases. In addition to database applications, OEM provides the performance pack that can be used to tune Oracle databases. OEM uses a repository to store information such as jobs and event status, discovery cache, tasks performed, and messages from the notification queue in the communication daemon.

Q&A

Q Can OEM 1.x be used with Oracle8i?

A No. You must use at least OEM 2.0.

Q Can I connect to more than one repository simultaneously?

A No. You can connect to only one repository at a time.

Workshop

The Workshop contains quiz questions and activities to help reinforce what you've learned in this hour. You can check Appendix A for the answers (but don't peek!).

Quiz

1. Which files are used by OEM?

2. What does Oracle TopSessions provide?

3. What are the main OEM components?

Exercises

1. All reports generated against your Oracle database are very slow. What OEM applications can you use to diagnose the problem?

2. How can you configure your OEM environment so that you can manage all your databases from one central location?

10

HOUR 11

Using the Replication Manager

Oracle provides the advanced replication option as a way to transmit changes made to a group of objects in one instance to be applied to the corresponding objects in another instance. It's very popular for distributed database systems and uses a store-and-forward mechanism for transmitting the changes across database instances. In this hour, you will

- Understand the various replication configurations
- Use Replication Manager to set up a multimaster replication environment
- Understand how to resolve conflicts that can arise during replication
- Resolve common errors that occur during replication

As of this writing, OEM 2.0 was not available in production version; therefore, some of the steps in this chapter might differ in the final release.

Understanding Replication

Replication provides several benefits:

- It's a high-availability solution in which the source and destination databases can be used simultaneously.

- Changes are propagated from server to server. Hence, different applications can connect to different instances, and the changes are eventually propagated between the instances. Figure 11.1 shows the various components involved when using replication.

FIGURE 11.1

Replication components.

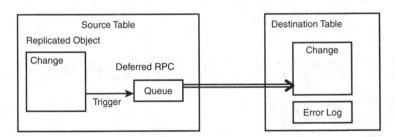

- Ease of configuring and monitoring a replication environment can be increased by the use of the GUI Replication Manager.

- Flexible configurations meet your specifications, ranging from basic publish-and-subscribe replication to update-anywhere models.

- Replication is fully integrated with Oracle and provides high performance and compatibility with other Oracle features.

Replication isn't ideal for use with a high-transactional OLTP systems due to
the amount of data changes that can occur in such systems. These changes
can cause performance problems during replication.

Replication Configurations

Oracle8i provides several types of replication models and supports full-table replication and table subsets. Replication can be symmetric or asymmetric, as shown in Table 11.1.

TABLE 11.1 COMPARING SYNCHRONOUS AND ASYNCHRONOUS REPLICATION

Symmetric Replication	Asymmetric Replication
Performs the desired transactions immediately	Defers the execution of the transactions to a later time
Provides poor performance because all sites are updated at the same time	Better performance
Uses two-phase commit	Doesn't have to use a special technique for committing transactions
Conflicts don't occur	Conflicts can occur
Data is up-to-date on both sites	Sites might be working with out-of-date data
Lower data availability	Higher data availability

Several replication configurations are popular. The choice of a particular configuration is based on the specific business need that should be satisfied:

- *N-way replication or multiple-master replication*—This configuration uses multiple-master sites and a push-push configuration (see Figure 11.2). Replication occurs for the entire contents of tables at all sites. Database triggers are defined on each table, and deferred Remote Procedure Calls (RPCs) are used to replicate row changes to each site. No single point of failure exists for block propagation between replicated sites. Periodically, you should execute the `difference` procedure (check for differences between tables regarding columns, contents, and so forth) and `rectify` procedure (synchronize the tables) to make sure that the tables on replicated sites are synchronized with each other. Full table replication occurs between the master sites.

11

FIGURE **11.2**

Multimaster configuration.

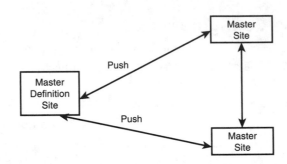

- *Updateable snapshots*—Updateable snapshots use a pull-pull configuration (see Figure 11.3). Each snapshot communicates with only one master site, regardless of the number of master sites. A snapshot refresh pulls changes from the master site. Multiple snapshots can be refreshed from masters on demand. Database triggers are defined on each table, and deferred RPCs are used to replicate row changes to each site. This configuration supports replication of subsets of tables. Replication occurs between an updateable master table and a snapshot table that can also be updated.

FIGURE **11.3**

An updateable snap-shot configuration.

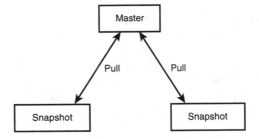

- *Hybrid configuration*—This configuration combines multimaster and updateable snapshots (see Figure 11.4). Both full-table replication and table subset replication are supported in the same system. A hybrid configuration combines a snapshot and multiple master configuration.

FIGURE 11.4

Hybrid configuration.

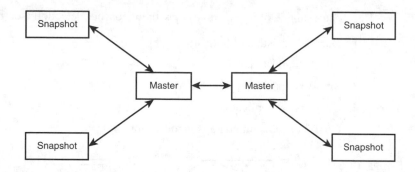

Data Distribution Methods

The methods for data distribution depend on the ownership of data and the availability needed. These methods include the following:

- *Basic techniques*—Basic techniques such as primary site ownership try to avoid conflicts at the expense of some performance degradation. Primary site ownership allows only one site to update the data in a table; therefore, it becomes the owner of that table. Primary site ownership technique can result in conflicts if you allow various sites to own different partitions in the same table. You can use horizontal or vertical partitioning, but the primary site ownership technique, in general, is slightly slower than other advanced techniques discussed next.

- *Advanced techniques*—Several advanced techniques can be used with replication, including dynamic ownership and shared ownership. Both techniques are a little complex to implement but are efficient. It's also possible to have conflicts when using these methods.

In a dynamic ownership model, the state of the data determines the ownership site. Data control is ordered; the site that owns the data can update the data, and only the rows with a given status can be updated. Each site updates the status to the next state and pushes ownership to the next site.

A shared ownership model allows multiple sites to update the same data. This configuration can result in update conflicts. Therefore, some method must be used to detect and resolve conflicts so that eventually all the replicated data converges to a consistent state at all sites.

Here's an example of update conflict without conflict detection (see Figure 11.5):

1. Data is consistent at both sites.

2. Site A is updated.

3. Site B is updated.

4. Changes are replicated.

5. Conflict occurs and data is inconsistent.

FIGURE 11.5

*Update conflict
without detection.*

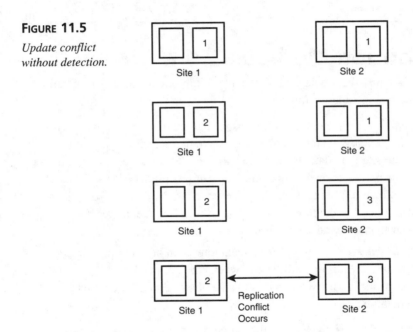

When update conflict detection is used, row-level replication is used to propagate before-image values of modified rows with the changed values. Before a change is applied to remote replicas, the before-image value is compared with the current value at the destination. If the values are different, Oracle signals that a conflict has occurred and calls a user-specified stored procedure to resolve the conflict.

Here's an example of update conflict with conflict detection (see Figure 11.6):

1. Data is consistent at both sites.

2. Site A is updated.

3. Site B is updated.

4. Changes are replicated with before-image values.

5. Values are compared and found to be different. Conflict is detected.

FIGURE 11.6

Update conflict with detection.

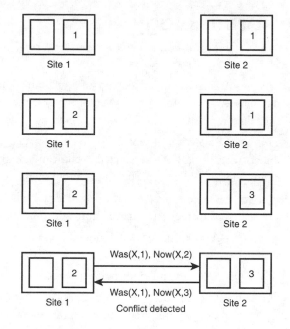

Conflict detected

Conflict Resolution

You've already seen how conflicts can occur in a replicated environment. Conflicts must be detected and resolved to keep the data consistent in a distributed environment. You can use several conflict resolution methods, including the following:

- Timestamps require that the servers at all the sites have the same time zone. If the replicated environment involves distributed systems that span time zones, you should use some standard time such as GMT on all sites. Suppose that the replicated configuration allows multiple sites such as HQ and satellite offices to update customers' addresses. The timestamp method allows a replicated change to update the current value only if the replicated change has a more recent timestamp.

- The additive method adds the delta value (difference) of replicated changes to the current value. Suppose that you have an orders table that can be used to add new customer orders from two sites. An order_count is maintained for each customer. Every time an order is added, the order_count is incremented by 1; it's decremented by 1 every time an order is cancelled. Update conflicts for the order_count are resolved by adding the delta value of the replicated change to the current value.

11

Replication Terminology

New Term You must understand some common terms used with replication:

- *Replicated object*—A database object copied and maintained at multiple sites in a distributed database environment. Any replica of the object can be updated, and the updated changes are replicated to all the other copies.

- *Replicated group*—A collection of replicated objects updated as a single unit. The replicated objects that are part of a replicated group can belong to different schemas, but a replicated object can't belong to more than one replicated group.

- *Deferred transaction remote procedure call*—A deferred transaction is basically a set of RPCs executed as a single transaction at the destination site.

- *Replication catalog*—A set of tables that contain all the necessary information to maintain a replicated environment.

- *Job queue*—PL/SQL code scheduled for periodic execution.

- *Replication facility*—A set of packages, such as `DBMS_REPCAT` and `DBMS_DEFER_SYS`, that use deferred transactions, replication catalog, and job queue to maintain data consistency in a replicated environment.

- *Master definition site*—At this site, replicated schemata and replicated objects are defined. Replicated object groups are created at this site.

- *Master site*—This site contains replicated schemata and replicated objects that are identical to the master definition site.

- *Snapshot site*—This site contains a replicated schema name that's identical to a master site, a subset of the replicated objects, and updateable snapshots of the replicated tables at the master site.

- *Quiesce*—The process of suspending replication at all sites so that a DDL change can be made to a replicated object.

The following tables make up the deferred transaction queue:

- `deftran` contains one record for each transaction.

- `defcall` contains the remote procedure calls.

- `deftrandest` contains the list of destinations for each deferred transaction.

- `defcalldest` contains the list of destinations for each remote procedure call.

Changes can be replicated from one site to another by using row-level or procedure-level replication. When using row-level replication, the entire row is forwarded to all other master sites, regardless of the number of columns changed. On the other hand, when using procedure-level replication, the data is updated through a procedure and is replicated to all other master sites by using the same procedure and the same arguments. Row-level and procedure-level replication are compared in Table 11.2.

TABLE 11.2   ROW-LEVEL VERSUS PROCEDURE-LEVEL REPLICATION

Row-Level Replication	Procedure-Level Replication
Uses a direct interface	Uses a wrapper-interface
Simple to use because Oracle writes the underlying code, which includes the following: $RT—Replication trigger $TP—Trigger package $RP—Replication package $RR—Replication resolution	You must write the code in order to implement the process
Can't be customized	You can customize the procedures and control what gets propagated
Automatic conflict detection	Conflict detection isn't automatic; you must write the code
Can use built-in conflict resolution routines	Can't use built-in conflict resolution routines
Much data is propagated between sites	The wrapper uses the same procedure and arguments to propagate the changes

11

Deferred transactions are employed when you use row-level or procedure-level replication. In a replicated environment, transaction consistency is maintained by applying the calls associated with a transaction in the same order in which they originally occur.

The replication catalog contains several important views:

- `repcatalog` contains information about asynchronous administration requests.
- `repddl` shows DDL changes that have to be applied.
- `repobject` contains information about the replicated objects.
- `repgroup` contains information about the replicated groups.
- `repprop` contains propagation about the replicated objects.

- `repsite` contains information about the replication groups and the master sites.
- `repkey_columns` contains the primary key columns for a table that uses row-level replication.

 Every table involved in replication must have a primary key. If a replicated table doesn't have a primary key, it must use the `repkey_columns` specified.

Several views can be queried to find information about the following jobs:

- `DBA_JOBS`—For information about all the jobs submitted to the database. Also see Table 11.3 for some useful procedures that are part of this package.
- `USER_JOBS`—For information about all the jobs submitted by a particular user only.
- `DBA_JOBS_RUNNING`—For information about all the jobs now running.

TABLE 11.3   THE DBMS_JOB PACKAGE TO MAINTAIN JOBS

DBMS_JOB *Procedure*	*Use*
SUBMIT	Submits a job to the job queue. Periodically, a background process wakes up and executes a procedure you specify. The interval for executing the procedure can also be specified.
CHANGE	Changes the job characteristics, such as the procedure to execute, the date of the next execution, or the execution interval.
NEXT_DATE	Changes the date of the next execution for a job.
INTERVAL	Changes the execution interval for a job.
REMOVE	Removes a job from the job queue.
BROKEN	Specifies that a job is broken or has been fixed and can be re-executed.
WHAT	Changes the procedure to execute for a job.
RUN	Sets NEXT_DATE to SYSDATE and forces the job to execute immediately.

Manipulating Jobs in the `job_queue`

You can run the following queries from Server Manager at the master site. (See Table 11.4 for some useful data dictionary views that can be used with the replication components.) In addition, Table 11.5 indicates some useful initialization parameters that are used with replication.

- Query the jobs in the `job_queue`:

```
SELECT job, what, broken
FROM dba_jobs;

JOB   WHAT                                                          BROKEN
----  -----------------------------------------------------------  ------
      dbms_repcat.do_deferred_repcat_admin('"SALES"', FALSE);   N
      dbms_repcat.do_deferred_repcat_admin('"SALES"', FALSE);   N
      sys.dbms_defer_sys.execute(destination=>'ORLANDO.WORLD');  N
      sys.dbms_defer_sys.execute(destination=>'CHICAGO.WORLD');  N
```

- Determine the number of sessions holding job queue locks:

```
SELECT sid, type, id1, id2
FROM v$lock
WHERE type = 'JQ';

SID  TYPE      ID1   ID2
---  --------  ----  ----
8    JQ        0     12910
```

In this output, `ID2` indicates the job number that's running and holding the `JQ` lock. `ID1` is always `0` from job queue locks.

- Run job 12910 immediately:

```
EXEC DBMS_JOB.RUN(12910);
```

- Remove job 12910 from the job queue:

```
EXEC DBMS_JOB.REMOVE(12910);
```

TABLE 11.4 REPLICATION COMPONENTS AND THE DATA DICTIONARY

Component	Use	Relevant Dictionary Tables and Packages
Job queue	Execute jobs automatically	DBA_JOBS, DBA_JOBS_RUNNING, DBMS_JOBS
Replication catalog	Performs DDL and other administrative tasks	DBA_REPCAT, DBA_REPGROUP, DBA_REPOBJECT, DBMS_REPCAT_ADMIN
RPC queue	Performs DML and other RPC tasks	DEFTRAN, DEFCALL, DEFERROR, DBMS_DEFER, DBMS_DEFER_SYS

11

TABLE 11.5   INITIALIZATION PARAMETERS USED WITH REPLICATION

Initialization Parameter	Use
compatible	This must be set to at least 8.1.5.0.
job_queue_processes	The number of job queue processes that can be started.
job_queue_interval	The time interval for execution of jobs.
shared_pool_size	Makes the size large enough to hold the replication packages and PL/SQL code.
distributed_transactions	The number of distributed transactions that can be run concurrently.
global_names	Must be set to TRUE.
open_links	The number of links that individual users can have open at one time.

Alternatives for Replicating Data

Replication lets you maintain multiple copies of data at different sites in a distributed environment. It also allows the different sites to run autonomously in the event of failure of other sites. You can use several strategies to achieve data replication in a distributed environment:

- *Export/Import*—This asynchronous method requires you to manually re-export the object so that the changes can be replicated. It also requires that an entire table be replicated.
- *Create Table as Select*—This asynchronous method requires that the table not exist before its creation. In other words, because this method will create a new table, you should drop any table replicas that already exist at the destination site.
- *SQL*PLUS COPY Command*—This asynchronous method has to be executed on demand.
- *Database Trigger*—This synchronous method requires that the database and the network be highly available.
- *Snapshot*—This asynchronous method allows the replication of an entire table of a subset of the table content.

Replication Accounts

You must set up two special accounts for the administration of a replication environment:

- *SYS Surrogate User*—Some activities must be performed under the SYS account and require access to the remote nodes, but this account doesn't need all the privileges associated with the SYS account. Therefore, you need to create a SYS surrogate user that acts as the user SYS and is used to perform DDL changes. Execute the following commands from Server Manager to create the SYS surrogate user:

```
CREATE USER syssur IDENTIFIED BY syssur;
EXECUTE DBMS_REPCAT_AUTH.GRANT_SURROGATE_REPCAT(syssur)
```

  These create a user named syssur that acts as a SYS surrogate.

- *Replication Administrator*—The replication administrator controls the replication environment. All replication commands are executed while you're connected as the replication administrator. You can allow replication administrators to administer any objects or only the objects they own. The following commands can be executed from Server Manager to achieve both types of replication administrator.

  To create a global replication administrator, use these commands:

```
Svrmgrl> CREATE USER global_rep IDENTIFIED BY global;
Svrmgrl> EXECUTE dbms_repcat_admin.grant_admin_any_repgroup
      2> ('global_rep');
```

  To create a specific group administrator, use these commands:

```
Svrmgrl> CREATE USER specific_rep IDENTIFIED BY specific;
Svrmgrl> EXECUTE dbms_repcat_admin.grant_admin_repgroup
      2> ('specific_rep');
```

In addition to creating special user accounts, you must create several database links:

- One public database link:

```
target_database_name USING 'SQL*Net alias';
```

- Two private database links. One private link is for the SYS surrogate user:

```
target_database CONNECT TO surrogate_user
IDENTIFIED BY surrogate_user_password;
```

  The other is for the replication administrator:

```
target_database CONNECT TO rep_admin_user
IDENTIFIED BY rep_admin_user_password;
```

11

In Windows NT, a separate thread named SNP0 wakes up periodically as specified by job_queue_interval and executes snapshot refresh for all snapshots scheduled for a refresh. In a busy system with many snapshots, you can create additional snapshot processes (SNP1, SNP2, and so on) by setting job_queue_processes.

Replication Manager Features

Replication Manager is a GUI tool that administrators can use to perform replication-related activities. Replication activities can be performed with master groups, snapshot groups, and standalone snapshots. You can run Replication Manager as a standalone application or launch it from the Oracle Enterprise Manager, as shown in Figure 11.7.

FIGURE 11.7

The Replication Manager and Setup Wizard, launched from Enterprise Manager.

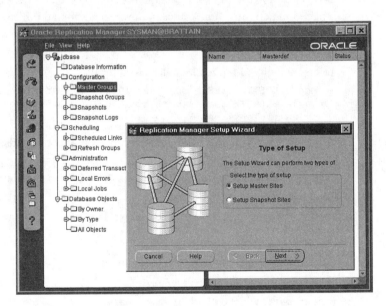

Replication Manager can be run against Oracle 7.3 and higher.

Replication Manager has several useful features that simplify administration and troubleshooting of a replication environment:

- Wizards are provided to configure replication.
- It can be used to create repgroups and supporting objects.
- It can be used to replicate to multiple sites by setting up multimaster configuration, including account, schema, and link creation.
- It can perform snapshot replication by setting up snapshot configuration, including account, schema, and link creation.
- It provides a single point for remote administration of replication.
- It can create snapshots and snapshot groups.
- Snapshot refresh intervals can be scheduled.
- It uses async or sync propagation mode.
- It provides several built-in routines for conflict resolution: latest timestamp, unique, site priority, and user-defined.
- It can be used to view and apply admin requests.
- It can be used to view deferred transaction queues at each site and reschedule or force immediate execution.
- It troubleshoots errors that occur in a replication environment.
- Drag-and-drop functionality is available for master groups and snapshots.
- Extensive online help is available.

11

To Do: Use Replication Manager to Create a Multimaster Replication Environment

To Do

The following steps should be performed on the machine that you want to be the master definition site:

1. Launch Replication Manager.

   When Replication Manager is launched, the Setup Wizard is automatically started and gives you the option of creating a master definition site or a snapshot site.

2. Choose Setup Master Site, and click Next.

3. Identify the database you want to use as the master definition site by choosing Add.

4. In the New Master Site window, provide a SQL*Net connect string for the site and the password for the system account.

5. Click OK.

▼   6. In the Select Master Sites dialog box, the database you identified as the master def-
            inition site is displayed. All replication-related objects (tables, views, and so on)
            are placed in the master definition site.

        7. Click Next.

        8. **NEW TERM** In the Default Admin/Propagator/Receiver dialog box, specify the
            administrator and the propagator for this site. The *propagator* refers to
            the account that is used to perform the replication.

> Usually, the Replication Administrator and propagator are the same user,
> but you might want to make them different for security reasons.

        9. If the user already exists, specify the administrator's password. Otherwise, the wiz-
            ard will prompt you to specify the schema that will contain replication objects.

> The wizard creates schemas with the same name and password at all master
> sites.

        10. Click Next.

        11. In the Defaults for Scheduled Links dialog box, specify the default propagation
            characteristics for all master sites. Specifications include next date, interval, paral-
            lel propagation and number of parallel processes, and whether the replication
            should stop on an error.

        12. Specify the default purge schedule for the deferred transaction queue.

        13. If desired, you can customize the settings for individual master sites. Otherwise,
            each site will have the same

            • Replication administrators, propagators, and receivers

            • Database link specifications

            • Scheduled propagation and purge settings

        14. After customization of the master sites, click Next.

        15. In the final dialog box, you can check the Record a Script check box to enable the
            wizard to generate a script of the replication management API calls used to build
            the system.

        16. Click Finish.

        17. Verify all the settings you've chosen, and click OK. The master site is created and
▲   displayed in Replication Manager.

To Do: Create Master Groups at the Master Definition Site

Master groups are created at the master definition site and can be used to specify the unit of replication as shown here:

1. Launch Replication Manager.

2. Double-click the Database Connections folder.

3. Double-click the master definition site from the list of sites available.

4. At the logon dialog box, provide the administrator password, and click Connect.

5. Double-click the Configuration folder under the chosen master definition site.

6. Highlight the Master Groups folder, and click Create.

7. Specify a name for the new master group.

8. Expand the Database Objects folder. Drag the objects (such as tables and views) that you want to be part of the master group, and drop them into the group.

9. In the Support for Group dialog box, specify generation of row replication support, min communications, and resumption of replication activity. Select the check box to generate support for row replication but deselect Resume Replication Activity.

10. Click OK.

> You will resume replication activity after all the master sites are added and the errors during generation of replication API calls are resolved.

11. Expand the master group, and verify that all objects generated from the generate replication support API call are valid.

To Do: Add a Master Site to a Master Group

A master site can be added to a master group so that you can specify the sites to which the changes are propagated. The Replication Manager can simplify this task as shown in the following steps:

1. Launch Replication Manager.

2. Expand the Database Connections folder, the master definition site, the Configuration folder, and the Master Groups folder.

3. Right-click the master group to which you want to add the master site, and choose Properties.

4. On the Destination page, click the Add button.

11

▼   5. The Add Destination to Group dialog box displays all the master sites for which a
          database link already exists. Choose the database link desired, and click Add to add
          the master site to the master group.

          In this dialog box, you also can choose the propagation mode and whether row
          data is to be copied. If the object is very large, deselect the Copy Row Data check
          box, and copy the object by using Export/Import.

▲   6. Click OK.

To Do: Create a New Database Connection

A new database connection can be made from the Replication Manager as demonstrated
in the following steps:

1. Launch Replication Manager.

2. Right-click the Database Connections folder.

3. In the Create DB Connection dialog box, specify the administrator password and
   the SQL*Net alias to the master site.

To Do: Resume Replication Activity

After you have made the configuration changes, the replication activity can be resumed:

1. Launch Replication Manager.

2. Right-click the master group at the master definition site, and choose Properties.

3. On the Operations page, click the Resume Replication button.

The requests generated from resuming the replication activity can be viewed under the
Admin Requests folder.

To Do: Remove a Multimaster Replica

When you no longer want to propagate changes to a particular master site, you should
remove the master site as shown here:

1. Launch Replication Manager.

2. To remove the master site, right-click it and choose Delete.

3. Click OK to confirm the deletion. You are prompted to remove the master group
   from the master definition site.

4. Right-click the master group in the master definition site.

5. Choose the Properties option.

▼   6. In the Properties dialog box, select the Destination tab.

▼   7. Click the master site that you used to remove the master group in steps 2, 3, and 4.

      8. Click Remove.

▲   9. Click OK to confirm.

Common Problems with Replication

Most of the problems that occur in a replication environment are caused by incorrect configuration. This section looks at some common problems that you might encounter when using replication and also at how you might go about resolving them.

Changes Aren't Being Pushed

Usually, this is a problem with the execution of the job for some reason. Verify the following:

- `job_queue_processes > 0`
- `job_queue_interval > 0`
- Check `DBA_JOBS` for failure of `EXECUTE` jobs.
- Check the SNP trace files for errors.

Replication Is Hanging

Check the following based on the symptom evidenced during the hang:

- Make sure that there isn't a long-running transaction on the table that may have locked the rows of the table.
- Check for deferred transaction errors by querying `DEFERROR`.

You Get an ORA-1403 Error

The error 01403, 00000, "no data found" indicates that a conflict was encountered. Check the DEFERROR table for further details of the type of conflict and take necessary actions to recover from this conflict (such as deleting a row or updating the row to a default value).

You Get an ORA-1017 Error

If you get the error `01017, 00000, "invalid username/password; logon denied"`, verify the context of the schema under which the execution is occurring.

11

An ORA-6550 Error Occurs, Indicating That DBMS_DEFER Must Be Declared

If you get the error `06550, 00000, "line %s, column %s:\n%s"`, verify that execute permission has been granted at both sites, to both REPADMIN and the replicated schema user. Also, check the accompanying PL/SQL error.

You Get an ORA-942 Error

If you get the error `00942, 00000, "table or view does not exist"`, verify whether the replicated table has a foreign key constraint. If a foreign key is used, the referenced table must be replicated first.

You Can't Drop a Repobject or Repschema

Query the DEFTRAN table for DMLs that are waiting to be pushed. These DMLs have to be deleted from the DEFTRAN table by executing `DBMS_DEFER_SYS.DELETE_TRAN`.

You Must Remove Entries in the Job Queue

You might have to remove entries from the job queue in order to eliminate jobs that are in an inconsistent state. You can use `DBMS_JOB.REMOVE` for this purpose. For example, the following command would remove the job with `job_id = 4`:

```
Svrmgrl> dbms_job.remove(4)
```

You Must Delete Entries in the deferror Table

Use `DBMS_DEFER_SYS.DELETE_ERROR`.

You Connect Through a Remote Database Link and Get ORA-2085

Make sure that GLOBAL_NAMES is set to TRUE in the init.ora file.

ORA-06550 and PLS-00302 Occur When You Are Trying to Create a Master Replication Group

Make sure that the REPADMIN has execute privileges on DBMS_REPCAT.

Summary

As a result of today's global environment, organizations have data distributed all over the world, and they need the information to be exchanged in a timely and reliable manner. The Oracle Replication feature is widely used to manage such distributed databases and also provide redundancy in order to protect the data.

Oracle Replication Manager is a GUI tool that can be used to build and manage replicated schema. It can be used to set up various replication configurations and display information that is easy to understand.

Q&A

Q Can I use replication to achieve a 24×7 database system?

A No. Replication can result in conflicts that might have to resolved, so you cannot use replication on its own to achieve a 24×7 database system. You should use other techniques such as Oracle Parallel, uninterruptible power supply (UPS), and mirroring of your devices.

Q Can I customize the conflict resolution procedures?

A Yes. You can customize the conflict resolution procedures. After you make changes to these procedures, however, the configuration might no longer be supported by Oracle.

Workshop

The Workshop contains quiz questions and activities to help reinforce what you've learned in this hour.

Quiz

1. Why is replication not ideal for OLTP environments?

2. What are some methods for conflict resolution?

3. Where are replicated object groups created?

Exercises

1. Set up an updateable snapshot configuration using the Replication Manager.

2. Compare replication with other methods that can be used for a reliable backup strategy.

11

HOUR 12

Managing Objects

For most corporations, relational databases have been the database of choice since their advent more than a decade ago. In a client/server environment, a third-generation language (3GL) such as C++ is used to write applications that access the data stored in the RDBMS. Relational databases can easily store application data; however, there's a problem when you try to capture the application data. Also, most relational databases require complex queries when the type of information that's stored can't be represented by the basic datatypes. As a result, developers usually place the application logic in the front-end applications. Because of the explosion and widespread use of the Internet, databases now must be able to store and manipulate complex data such as hypertext, image, and audio data, in addition to traditional scalar data.

Corporations are under increasing pressure to build efficient and cost-effective database systems that can quickly react to changing market conditions and customer requirements. This can be achieved by applications that closely match business models and processes. For example, manufacturers need assembly lines that can quickly and easily adapt to change in market conditions and customer demands.

An object-relational DBMS such as Oracle8i stores not only the data but also the logic. Oracle8i uses objects to capture the attributes and functionality of the entity being represented. By using objects, Oracle8i can handle such complex needs and at the same time retain the scalability, robustness, and ease of use found in relational databases. Also, the current application base mostly comprises relational database applications. Therefore, there should be a simple and easy process to mix the object technology with relational technology.

In addition to Oracle8i, other object-relational databases include IBM's DB2 and Sybase System 10.

By using the Oracle8i objects option, you can create and manipulate object types, in addition to the built-in types provided by Oracle. Real-world entities can be modeled, along with the operations that can be performed on those entities.

Oracle8i features such as client-side caching of objects and single round-trip retrieval of related objects improve the performance of object-based applications. The performance gain is essentially due to reduced network traffic.

You can convert traditional relational database applications to object-relational database applications so that they can use object modeling and other high-performance multimedia capabilities provided by object-relational databases. Later in this chapter, the section "Case Study: Purchase Order System" describes how such a conversion from a relational model to an object-based model can be made.

Objects in Oracle8i

Oracle8i provides several key features you can use for the object-relational paradigm. Oracle8i extends the type system to include this collection of objects:

- The OBJECT type allows the implementation of structured objects.
- The REF type allows objects to be referenced.
- The LOB type allows the use of large unstructured objects.

- The TABLE type allows the use of unordered collections of objects.
- The VARRAY type (variable-size array) allows the use of ordered collections of objects.

SQL DDL and DML have been extended to facilitate the creation, retrieval, and modification of objects and collections.

Working with Object Types

Oracle8i allows you to model real-world entities by using an *object type*, a user-defined type that allows you to define an object's attributes and methods. Table 12.1 compares standard database tables and object types.

TABLE 12.1 COMPARING DATABASE TABLES AND OBJECT TYPES

Oracle8i Table	Oracle 8i Object Type
Stores data	Doesn't store data
Can't be used as a template	Can be used as a template for creating objects
Can contain complex data	Can't contain data
Can't contain procedural	Can contain procedural code code
Can't have a body	Can have a body that's separate from the specification
DML privilege must be granted to users or roles	EXECUTE privilege must be granted to users or roles

The use of object types provides several benefits:

- It standardizes applications and promotes easy data transfer between applications.
- Methods can be defined and reused, so development of applications can be fast and efficient.
- Object types make it easy to model real-world entities.

Consider a large corporation that consists of many divisions. Each division has its own information systems department. Suppose that the human resources department creates an application and decides to use employee_id with the datatype number(5). The consulting department, on the other hand, uses applications that define employee_id with the datatype varchar2(10). These nonstandard data definitions can lead to problems when the applications decide to share data. You can create object types used as standards throughout the corporation and thereby simplify such cross-department application sharing.

12

Object types have the following features:

- One or more attribute—An *attribute* represents a characteristic of the entity being defined. Object attributes can be represented by using various datatypes, such as scalar (number, char), collection (nested table or variable-size array), REF (reference to an instance of object type), LOB (large object), or others.

- Zero or more methods—You can use methods to specify the actions that can be performed on the entity being represented. Object methods can be written in PL/SQL or in a 3GL such as C++ or Java. Objects have several methods associated with them, such as `constructor` (instantiates and creates object instances) and `destructor` (cleans out the object when the object is removed from the system).

- You can use object types to define a column's datatype.

- Instances of object types are stored and manipulated by using SQL and DML extensions.

- Database features such as indexes and triggers are also available to object types.

The following example demonstrates the creation of object types through the CREATE TYPE command (refer to the *Oracle SQL Language* manual for the complete syntax of the CREATE TYPE statement). Consider a publishing company such as Macmillan Computer Publishing. It keeps track of the books published by using various tables. Such a database system can use the following object-based approach:

1. Create an object type, `author_type`, that represents author information such as last_name, first_name, royaltyper, city, state, and zip:

```
SQL> CREATE OR REPLACE TYPE author_type as object (
        Last_name       varchar2(20),
        First_name      varchar2(20),
        Royaltyper      number,
        City            varchar2(10),
        State           varchar2(2),
        Zip             varchar2(5));
SQL> /
```

2. Use the SQL*PLUS DESC command to find out the details about object types:

```
SQL> desc author_type

NAME                        NULL?      TYPE
-------------------------   -------    --------------
LAST_NAME                              VARCHAR2(20)
FIRST_NAME                             VARCHAR2(20)
ROYALTYPER                             NUMBER
CITY                                   VARCHAR2(10)
STATE                                  VARCHAR2(2)
ZIP                                    VARCHAR2(5)
```

You can use this object type just like any standard datatype such as number or char.

3. Create a new type, book_type, by using the author_type object type:

```
SQL> CREATE OR REPLACE TYPE book_type as object (
     ISBN           varchar2(20),
     title_name     varchar2(30),
     author         author_type,
     category       varchar2(10),
     price          number(5));
SQL> /
```

4. Verify the creation of the type:

```
SQL> desc book_type

NAME                    NULL?    TYPE
--------------------    -------  --------------
ISBN                             VARCHAR2(20)
TITLE_NAME                       VARCHAR2(30)
AUTHOR                           AUTHOR_TYPE
CATEGORY                         VARCHAR2(10)
PRICE                            NUMBER(5)
```

5. Create a book_sales table by using the book_type datatype:

```
SQL> CREATE TABLE book_sales (
     Order_id      integer,
     Customer_id   integer,
     Book          book_type,
     Quantity      number(10));
SQL> /
```

6. Insert a row into the book_sales table:

```
SQL> insert into book_sales
     Values(111111,999999,
     Book_type('0-123-45678-9','Oracle8i demystified',
     Author_type('Thakkar','Megh',20,'Orlando','FL','12345'),
     'Software',50),25);
```

7. To reference an element within an object type, you must prefix the element with the object type. For example, you want to find the price of the book with the order_id of 111111:

```
SQL> SELECT order_id, x.book.price
     FROM   book_sales x
     WHERE  order_id = '111111';

order_id     book.price
----------   ----------
111111          50
```

12

Object References

Objects can be uniquely identified and located using object references. A unique identifier is generated by Oracle for every object stored in a reference table.

Using REFs in Columns

A column of a table or an attribute of an object type can be declared as a REF type. A column defined with the REF type can contain references to objects of the declared object type, regardless of the object table in which the object is stored.

> It's possible to scope a REF type column. When a REF column is scoped, it contains references only to objects from a specified object table.

REFs vary from foreign key columns in several aspects:

- REFs provide navigational access to the referenced object. An object reference or REF is a direct pointer to the referenced row, whereas a foreign key is a data value that can be used to join to the referenced table.

- Currently, a REF can reference only a table of abstract datatypes (ADT).

- It's possible to have "dangling" references, so the reference value can refer to nonexistent objects.

In the following example, the ACCOUNTS table references the CUSTOMERS table:

1. Create an object type customer_type for customers:

```
SQL> CREATE OR REPLACE TYPE customer_type AS OBJECT
     (cust_no          CHAR(5),
      cust_lastname    varchar2(10),
      cust_firstname   varchar2(10));
SQL> /
```

2. Create the customers table by using customer_type:

```
SQL> CREATE TABLE customers OF customer_type;
```

3. Create the accounts table to reference the customers:

```
SQL> CREATE TABLE ACCOUNTS as (
     ACCTNO number,
     ACCTYPE char(4),
     BALANCE number,
     CUST ref CUSTOMERS
     );
```

You can reference only objects stored in an object table.

Using the REF Operator

The REF operator can be used to obtain a reference to an object in an object table. The following example shows how to insert a record into an object table and obtain a reference to it at the same time:

1. Create a type cust_type for the customers:

```
SQL> CREATE OR REPLACE TYPE cust_type as object (
     Lastname      varchar2(20),
     Firstname     varchar2(20));
SQL> /
```

2. Create a table by using the type:

```
SQL> Create table customers (
     Cust_id       integer,
     cust_detail   cust_type);
```

3. Declare a variable as a reference to the customers table:

```
DECLARE reftojohn REF customers;
```

4. Insert a record into the customers table. The following transaction inserts a record into the customers table and returns a reference to the record in the reftojohn variable:

```
BEGIN
    INSERT INTO customers custref
    VALUES (11111, cust_detail('John','Doe'))
    RETURNING REF(custref) INTO reftojohn;
END;
```

You can use the reference to an object in several ways:

- Improve performance by pinning the object in the cache.
- Use the Oracle Call Interface (OCI) to manipulate the object.
- The SELECT or UPDATE statement can use the object reference in its predicate.

The object reference can serve as a pointer to the object and simplify access and manipulation of the object.

12

DEREF Operator

The DEREF operator does the opposite of the REF operator and can be used to obtain the object by means of its reference. The following example uses the reference reftojohn to update a column in the accounts table:

```
UPDATE accounts
SET cust_info = DEREF(reftojohn)
WHERE acct_id = 12345;
```

Using Collections

NEW TERM   A *collection* is an ordered group of elements of the same datatype. Collections have the following characteristics:

- A unique subscript determines the position of elements in the collection.
- Collections can have only one dimension and must be integer indexed. Other than this, they are similar to an array.
- Collections can be used as attributes of object types.

Oracle8i provides two types or collections:

- *Nested tables* are unbounded and don't retain the order in which elements are added to the collection.
- *Variable-size arrays*, also referred to as VARRAYs, are bounded and retain the order in which elements are added to the collection.

To Do: Use Nested Tables in Oracle8i

You can use nested tables efficiently to represent relationships between objects where one object has one or more columns that can contain multiple occurrences of the other object. The following steps create a nested table, projects, to represent each project involving many employees:

1. Create an object type emp_type for the employees:

```
SQL> CREATE OR REPLACE TYPE emp_type AS OBJECT
     (emp_id          integer,
      emp_lastname    varchar2(20),
      emp_firstname   varchar2(20),
      emp_position    varchar2(20));
```

2. NEW TERM   Create an object table called employees (an *object table* is a database table defined using an object type only):

```
SQL> CREATE OR REPLACE TYPE employees
     AS TABLE OF emp_type;
```

▼ 3. Verify the details of the object table:

```
SQL> desc employees

    Employees TABLE OF EMP_TYPE

    NAME                        NULL?    TYPE
    --------------------        -------  -------------
    EMP_ID                               INTEGER
    EMP_LASTNAME                         VARCHAR2(20)
    EMP_FIRSTNAME                        VARCHAR2(20)
    EMP_POSITION                         VARCHAR2(20)
```

4. Create a nested table projects by using the object table employees:

```
SQL> CREATE TABLE projects(
    Project_id      number(5),
    Project_name    varchar2(20),
    Proj_emps       employees)
    Nested table proj_emps store as employees_table;
```

5. Verify that the nested table has been created:

```
SQL> desc projects

    NAME                        NULL?    TYPE
    --------------------        -------  -------------
    PROJECT_ID                           NUMBER(5),
    PROJECT_NAME                         VARCHAR2(20),
    PROJ_EMPS                            EMPLOYEES
```

6. Insert two records into the nested table:

```
SQL> insert into projects
    Values (11111,'Venus',
            Employees(
                Emp_type(123,'Thakkar','Megh','Manager'),
                Emp_type(456,'Smith','Bruce','Engineer')));

SQL> insert into projects
    Values (22222,'Jupiter',
            Employees(
                Emp_type(123,'Thakkar','Megh','Manager'),
                Emp_type(789,'Doe','John','Architect')));
```

12

7. Query the projects table (nested table) to obtain the names of employees working in project Venus. This can be achieved by using the THE function:

```
SQL> select emp_list.emp_lastname, emp_list.emp_firstname
    From THE
    (select proj_emps from projects
    where project_name = 'Venus') emp_list;
```

▲

To Do: Use a VARRAY in Oracle8i

VARRAYs can commonly be used to represent relationships between objects where an uncertain number of occurrences of one object can be used in columns of another object. The following steps create a table, customers, by using a VARRAY called accounts because the number of accounts that a customer can have isn't fixed for each customer:

1. Create an object type account_type:

```
SQL> CREATE TYPE account_type as OBJECT
     (account_no    INTEGER,
     account_type    CHAR(2),
     balance         NUMBER(10));
```

2. Create a VARRAY for accounts by using the object type account_type:

```
SQL> CREATE TYPE account_array AS VARRAY(10) OF account_type;
```

3. Create an object type customer_type:

```
SQL> CREATE TYPE customer_type AS OBJECT
     (cust_no        CHAR(5),
     accounts        account_array);
```

4. Create a customers table by using the object type customer_type:

```
SQL> CREATE TABLE customers OF customer_type;
```

5. Insert the following into the object table customers:

```
SQL> INSERT INTO customers
     VALUES (88888,
        account_array(
          account_type(55,'C',2300),
              account_type(99,'S', 20000)));
```

▲

As you can see, VARRAY is essentially a PL/SQL table housed in a column. It provides the capability for a repeating group to be contained in a row. Such repeating groups can be useful for applications in which you take sets of readings and always process them as a group, never individually. A VARRAY type has a fixed number of entries and is placed in-line with the rest of the row. Retrieval of the components of an object type can be done by their names. However, retrieving information from a VARRAY requires the use of PL/SQL of OCI.

> It's easier to populate a VARRAY than it is to query information from it.

To Do: Retrieve Information from a VARRAY

The following example demonstrates the use of PL/SQL to retrieve information from a VARRAY:

1. Create a VARRAY that stores dimensions of various items:

```
SQL> CREATE or REPLACE TYPE dimension_t AS VARRAY(3) of NUMBER;
```

2. Create an items table that uses the VARRAY:

```
SQL> CREATE TABLE inventory
     (itemno        integer,
     item_desc     varchar2(30),
     dimensions    dimension_t,
     price         number
     primary key   (itemno));
```

3. Insert values into the tables:

```
SQL> insert into inventory
     Values (123, 'Bookshelf', dimension_t(6,4,2),125);

SQL> insert into inventory
     Values (124, 'Refrigerator', dimension_t(12,5,7),600);
```

4. Write a PL/SQL block to retrieve the dimensions of item 123:

```
Declare
     Isize dimension_t;
Begin
     Select dimensions into isize
     From  inventory
     Where itemno = 123;
     Dbms_output.putline('Item is ' ||
                          To_char(isize(1)) || '*'
                          To_char(isize(2)) || '*'
                          To_char(isize(3)));
End;
/
```

Case Study: Purchase Order System

Consider an example of a purchase order system to understand how to convert a relational model to an object-relational model.

The purchase order system contains several important entities. Customers place orders for items in the inventory. The system can be represented by a relational model consisting of several tables:

12

- `customers` contains customer-specific information such as address and phone number, which doesn't depend on the order (if any) that the customer places.
- `orders` contains information specific to an order placed by a customer.
- `line_items` contains details of each order.
- `inventory` contains information about the various items that can be purchased.

The following DDL statements can be used to create the tables:

```
SQL> Create table customers (
     custno          number,
     custname        varchar2(50),
     address1        varchar2(100),
     address2        varchar2(100),
     city            varchar2(40),
     state           char(2),
     zip             varchar2(10),
     phone1          varchar2(20),
     phone2          varchar2(20),
     primary key     (custno));

SQL> create table orders (
     pono            number,
     custno          number references customers(custno),
     orderdate       date,
     shiptoaddress1  varchar2(100),
     shiptoaddress2  varchar2(100),
     shiptocity      varchar2(40),
     shiptostate     char(2),
     shiptozip       varchar2(10),
     primary  key    (pono));

SQL> create table inventory (
     itemno          number,
     itemdesc        varchar2(100),
     price           number,
     primary  key    (itemno));

SQL> create table line_items (
     lineitemno      number,
     pono            number references    purchase_order(pono),
     itemno          number references    inventory(itemno),
     quantity        number,
     primary key     (pono,lineitemno));
```

You can write applications by using a 3GL such as C++ to access information from this database. To receive any meaningful report from this database, however, you must write queries that perform multitable joins. An object-based approach can significantly improve the performance. The same database can use objects; the corresponding DDL statements are as follows:

```
SQL> create type item_t as object (
     itemno          number,
     itemdesc        varchar2(100),
     price           number);

SQL> create type address_t as object (
     address1        varchar2(100),
     address2        varchar2(100),
     city            varchar2(40),
     state           char(2),
     zip             varchar2(10));

SQL> create type phone_t as varray(10) of varchar2(20);

SQL> create type line_item_t as object (
     lineitemno      number,
     itemref         ref  item_t,
     quantity        number);

SQL> create type line_item_list_t as table of  line_item_t;

SQL> create or replace type purchase_order_t as object (
     pono            number,
     custref         ref customers_t,
     orderdate       date,
     line_item_list  line_item_list_t,
     shipto_addr     address_t);

SQL> create type po_reflist_t as table of REF purchase_order_t;

SQL> create or replace type customer_t as object (
     custno          number,
     custname        varchar2(50),
     address         address_t,
     phone_list      phone_t,
     po_list         po_reflist_t);
```

12

Working with Object Views

An object view allows you to map relational data to structured data and thereby retrofit object types and collection types into a relational database system. Object views have the following features:

- They contain objects in their rows.

- An identifier is associated with each object. Usually, the primary key of the base tables serves as the identifier.

- Object views are updatable. Instead-of triggers can be defined for views that are inherently nonupdatable.

Use of object views can provide several benefits:

- A gradual migration path from relational systems to object-based systems
- Coexistence of relational and object-oriented applications because you can still access the base tables directly
- Improved performance by giving you the choice of using the best available strategies for manipulating data

To Do: Create and Use an Object View

▼ To Do

Object views can represent a gradual migration from relational systems to object-based systems. The following steps show how an object view can be built on top of a relational table and how you can manipulate the objects that comprise the object view:

1. Be sure to have a base relational table to work with. This example uses the employees table:

   ```
   SQL> desc employees
   ```

NAME	NULL?	TYPE
EMPID		NUMBER(5)
LAST_NAME		VARCHAR2(20)
FIRST_NAME		VARCHAR2(20)
DEPTID		NUMBER(3)
SALARY		NUMBER(7,2)
JOB		VARCHAR2(10)
CITY		VARCHAR2(10)
STATE		VARCHAR2(2)
ZIP		VARCHAR2(5)

2. Define an object type that will represent the objects in the object view:

   ```
   SQL> CREATE TYPE emp_t as OBJECT (
        EMPNO     NUMBER(5),
        LNAME     VARCHAR2(20),
        FNAME     VARCHAR2(20),
        DEPTNO    REF department,
        SALARY    NUMBER(7,2),
        JOB       VARCHAR2(10),
        CITY      VARCHAR2(10),
        STATE     VARCHAR2(2),
        ZIP       VARCHAR2(5));
   ```

▼

▼ 3. Create an object view, and specify how the object identifiers are constructed, based on some attributes of the underlying data:

```sql
SQL> CREATE VIEW employees_ov OF emp_t
     WITH OBJECT OID (empno)
     AS
     SELECT e.empid, e.last_name, e.first_name, NULL,
            e.salary,e.job,e.city,e.state,e.zip
     FROM   employees e;
```

You can insert data into the employees table directly or through the employees_ov view.

4. Insert the following into the object view:

```sql
SQL> Insert into employees_ov
  2> Values (emp_t(12345,'Thakkar','Komal',12,120000.00,
  3> 'Manager','Orlando','FL','32817');
```

▲

Object views behave like an object table and allow you to uniquely identify the object instances it contains. The WITH OID clause specifies how unique object IDs (OIDs) are generated.

In most cases, the unique OID is based on the base table's primary key.

You can use the MAKE_REF operator to convert a foreign key in a relation to a REF attribute in an object view. The number of columns specified in the MAKE_REF operator should be the same as the number of attributes used in the WITH OID clause of the object view you're referencing. Suppose that the departments table has an object view departments_ov created on it. The CAST expression can be used to take the results of a subquery and build a nested table out of it.

Create an object view based on the departments table:

```sql
SQL> CREATE VIEW departments_ov OF dept_t
     WITH OBJECT OID (deptid)
     AS
     SELECT deptid, dept_name
       CAST(MULTISET(SELECT e.empid, e.last_name, e.first_name, NULL,
                     e.salary,e.job,e.city,e.state,e.zip
              FROM   employees e
              WHERE e.deptid = d.deptid)
              AS EmployeeSet)
     FROM departments d
```

12

Create an object view, based on the `employees` table, that makes a reference to the `departments_ov` object view:

```
SQL> CREATE VIEW employees_ov OF emp_t
     WITH OBJECT OID (empno)
     AS
     SELECT e.empid, e.last_name, e.first_name,
        MAKE_REF(departments_ov, e.deptid),
        e.salary,e.job,e.city,e.state,e.zip
     FROM    employees e;
```

Using Object Methods

 A *method* is basically a PL/SQL procedure or function associated with an object. Oracle8i supports different methods:

- *Constructor*—A constructor method, automatically created for each object, enables you to perform initialization and other DML with that object. The constructor for an object has the same name as the object, and the attributes of an object become the parameters for its constructor. For example, in the following `insert` statement, `book_type` and `author_type` are the constructor methods:

```
SQL> insert into book_sales
     Values(111111,999999,
     Book_type('0-123-45678-9','Oracle8i demystified',
     Author_type('Thakkar','Megh',20,'Orlando','FL','12345'),
     'Software',50),25);
```

- *Member*—A member method is a stored procedure associated with an object type. You can create member methods by using PL/SQL. They also can be external functions created by using a 3GL such as C++. Before using a member method, you must associate methods with an object. Association of methods with object types can be done by using the CREATE TYPE or ALTER TYPE statement.

To Do: Use Member Methods to Calculate the Value of the Books in Stock

Member methods can simplify access to objects, as demonstrated in the following example. The following steps allow you to use PL/SQL procedures to manipulate object attributes that have been encapsulated in the object:

1. Create an object type with member methods to calculate the value of books in stock:

```
SQL> CREATE OR REPLACE TYPE book_type as object (
     ISBN          varchar2(20),
     title_name    varchar2(30),
     author        author_type,
```

```
category        varchar2(10),
price           number(5),
quantity        number(5),
member function book_value return number,
PRAGMA RESTRICT_REFERENCES(book_value, WNDS,WNPS));
```

In this example, PRAGMA RESTRICT_REFERENCES is a compiler directive that indicates the restrictions on the specified attribute. Table 12.2 explains the various restrictions.

TABLE 12.2 UNDERSTANDING THE RESTRICTIONS PLACED ON ATTRIBUTES

Value	Interpretation
WNDS	Write no database state.
WNPS	Write no package state.
RNDS	Read no database state.
RNPS	Read no package state.

2. Verify the methods associated with an object by using the DESC command:

```
SQL> desc book_type

     NAME                      NULL?    TYPE
     ----------------------    -------  --------------
     ISBN                               VARCHAR2(20)
     TITLE_NAME                         VARCHAR2(30)
     AUTHOR                             AUTHOR_TYPE
     CATEGORY                           VARCHAR2(10)
     PRICE                              NUMBER(5)
     QUANTITY                           NUMBER(5)

     METHOD
     ---------------
     MEMBER FUNCTION BOOK_VALUE RETURNS NUMBER
```

3. Create the PL/SQL code to define the body of the member method:

```
SQL> CREATE or REPLACE TYPE BODY book_type AS
     Member function book_value
     Return number IS
     Begin
         Return self.price * self.quantity;
     End book_value;
     End;
/

Type body created.
```

▼   4. Use the member method in a PL/SQL program:

```
Declare
Book_type1 book_type := book_type('0-123-45678-9','Oracle8I
 demystified', Author_type('Thakkar','Megh',20,'Orlando','FL',
 '12345'),
 'Software',50,25);

 Book_type2 book_type := book_type('0-123-12345-9','C++
 demystified', Author_type('Thakkar','Megh',20,'Orlando',
 'FL','12345'),
 'Software',30,60);

 begin
     dbms_output.put_line('Book value for book_type1 is :'¦¦
          to_char(book_type1.book_value));
     dbms_output.put_line('Book value for book_type2 is :'¦¦
          to_char(book_type2.book_value));
 end;
 /
```

▲
```
Book value for book_type1 is :1250
Book value for book_type2 is :1800
```

Summary

With the explosive growth of the Internet, the demands on the type of data stored in the database and the type of data processing have increased tremendously. We need efficient and cost-effective ways of data management. Oracle8i provides object features such as object types and methods that allow you to hide the data's complexity and store the logic of data manipulation in the database.

This lesson also focuses on the various object features provided by Oracle8i and analyzed the manner in which a relational database model can be converted into an object-based model.

Q&A

Q Does Oracle8i provide all the object-oriented features?

A No. Oracle8i is still object based because it uses the *concept* of objects. It doesn't include features such as inheritance and polymorphism and therefore isn't truly object oriented.

Q Can I have both objects and relational data in the same database?

A Yes. In fact, the object views discussed in this lesson are examples of objects based on relational tables.

Workshop

The Workshop contains quiz questions and activities to help reinforce what you've learned in this hour. You can check Appendix A for the answers (but don't peek!).

Quiz

1. What is a method?
2. What are the benefits of using object views?
3. What are the benefits of using object types?

Exercises

1. Write a PL/SQL object method to determine the average salary of all the employees living in Boston, Massachusetts.
2. What would you consider when choosing between nested tables and VARRAYs for your object model?

12

PART IV
Protecting Your Database

Hour

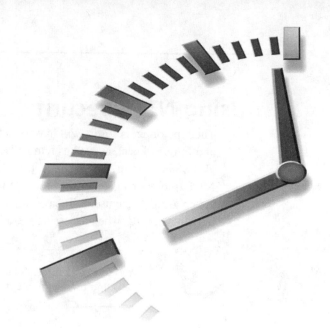

HOUR 13

Securing an Oracle8i Database on Windows NT

To achieve file-level security in Windows NT, use the NTFS (New Technology File System) file system. This hour covers the following topics:

- NTFS security
- Database roles
- System and object privileges
- Application context and fine-grained access control

As of this writing, OEM 2.0 was not available in production version. Therefore, some of the steps in this chapter might differ in the final release.

Using NTFS Security

The type of access users will have on a file is determined by the permissions set on files and folders. Local, as well as remote, access to files and folders is affected by the set NTFS permissions. For example, if you create a shared folder from within the Windows NT Explorer and give a user FULL CONTROL permissions, but the NTFS permissions are set up as READ, the user will have full access to the folder when accessing it locally, but only READ access when accessing the folder remotely.

> You can audit successful and unsuccessful access to files and folders by selecting the auditing options from the User Manager's Policies/Audit menu.

Understand that user and group permissions are cumulative, whereas file and folder permissions aren't. For example,

- If user X is granted permission to read a file but is a member of group Y, which is granted permission to read and write the same file, the effective permission user X will have is to read and write the file.

- User X is granted the CHANGE permission on a folder but only READ permission on a file in the folder. User X effectively can only read the file, even though he has permission to CHANGE in the directory containing the file.

- If user X has NOACCESS on a file, but the group that he belongs to has been granted READ permission on the file, NOACCESS overrides all other permissions. The user, in effect, will have NOACCESS on the file.

> NOACCESS overrides all other access.

In summary, when users try to access a resource, user permissions are determined as follows (Table 13.1 shows how the NTFS permissions are used):

- User and group permissions are cumulative unless one permission is NO ACCESS, in which case, the cumulative is NO ACCESS.

- If permissions aren't granted explicitly, the default is to deny access.

By default, the creator of a file or folder is the owner of that file or folder. The creator can give another user or group the right to take ownership, but to become the owner, the user would have to exercise the right and take owner-ship.

Administrators can always take ownership of a file or directory. If a member of the Administrators group takes ownership of a file, the entire Administrators group becomes the owner. Therefore, any user who's a member of the Administrators group effectively becomes the owner of that file.

TABLE 13.1   NTFS SECURITY

Permission	R	X	W	D	P	O
No access						
List (directory only)	×	×				
Read	×	×				
Add (directory only)		×	×			
Add and read (directory only)	×	×	×			
Change	×	×	×	×		
Full control	×	×	×	×	×	×
Special access	(1)	(1)	(1)	(1)	(1)	(1)

In Table 13.1, special access allows the tasks determined by the particular privilege granted:

- R allows users to read or display data, attributes, owners, and permissions.
- X allows users to run or execute the file or files in the directory.
- W allows users to modify the file or files in the directory or change the attributes.
- D allows users to delete the file or directory.
- P allows users to change the permissions on the file or files in the directory.
- O allows users to take ownership of the file or directory.

To change the permissions on a file or directory, you must meet one of the following conditions:

- You have full access control on the file or directory.
- You have the Change Permission permission.
- You are the owner or you've taken ownership of the file or directory.

13

Logon Security

Windows NT has a mandatory logon that provides several security benefits:

- During mandatory logon, access to user mode programs is suspended. As a result, a hacker who's trying to steal valuable logon/password information can't use Trojan horses.

- Two or more users can share the same computer and have different user profiles.

- This mandatory logon can authenticate users, and a security identifier is attached to the user process throughout the life of the user connection. The security identifier contains important information such as access permissions granted to the user.

If you change a user's access permissions on a particular resource, the changes take effect only when the user logs out and logs back in. This is due to the security identifier being attached to the user process on logon and being regenerated only when the user logs on again to Windows NT.

Access to objects in Windows NT is controlled by means of an Access Control List (ACL). Entries in the ACL are called Access Control Entries (ACE). The security identifier, also referred to as the *access token*, is checked against an object's ACL to determine the actions the user can take on a particular object.

An ACL associated with an object is checked only when the object is initially opened. Subsequent changes to the ACL take effect only when the object is reopened.

To Do: Change Access Permission on a Directory

For this example, the c: drive is on an NTFS partition. You want to remove the permissions from the group Everyone and grant the user `utest` Read permission on the directory. The following assumes that you've already created the user `utest`:

1. In the Windows NT Explorer, create c:\test and highlight it.

2. Choose File, Properties.

3. On the Security page, click the Permissions button.

4. In the Directory Permissions dialog box, select the group Everyone and click Remove (see Figure 13.1).

FIGURE 13.1

Determine the permissions assigned to the various users and groups.

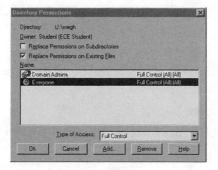

5. Click Add.

6. Click the Show Users button to list all the users in the Add Users and Groups dialog box (see Figure 13.2).

FIGURE 13.2

Obtain a list of users that can be assigned permissions.

7. Select the user `utest` and give the Read permission to that user.

8. Click Add.

9. Click OK three times to exit all the dialog boxes.

13

To Do: Enable File and Directory Auditing

For this example, you enable file and directory auditing for an unsuccessful attempt to take ownership of the c:\test directory. It's assumed that the c: drive is on NTFS partition. Follow these steps:

1. Choose Start, Programs, Administrative tools, User Manager.
2. Choose Policies, Audit.
3. Select Audit These Events.
4. Select the File and Object Access check box so that you can audit failures (see Figure 13.3).

FIGURE 13.3

Choose the auditing policy.

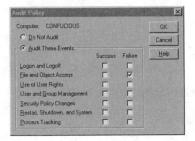

5. Click OK.
6. Start the Windows NT Explorer.
7. Select c:\test.
8. Choose File, Properties.
9. On the Security page, click Auditing (see Figure 13.4).

FIGURE 13.4

Choose the auditing for particular directories.

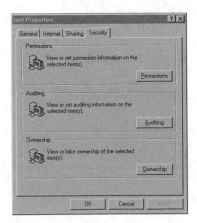

▼   10. Click Add in the Directory Auditing dialog box.

   11. In the Add Users and Groups dialog box, select Everyone for the names list (see Figure 13.5).

FIGURE 13.5

Enable auditing for the desired users and groups.

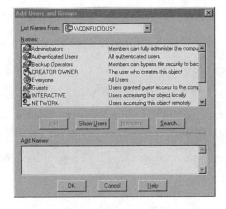

   12. Click OK.

   13. Select the Failure check box for the Take Ownership event.

   14. Click OK.

▲   15. Close the windows and exit Explorer.

To Do: Copy and Move Files and Folders in NTFS Partitions

This exercise assumes that the c: and d: drives are NTFS. First, you must be set up for the exercise. Follow these steps:

   1. Log on as the administrator.

   2. Create directories c:\test1, c:\test2, c:\test3, and c:\test4.

   3. In the Windows NT Explorer, highlight c:\test1.

   4. Choose File, Properties.

   5. On the Security page, click the Permissions button.

   6. In the Directory Permissions dialog box, choose the group Everyone and click Remove.

   7. Click Add.

   8. Select the Users group and give it the Read permission.

   9. Click Add.

▼   10. Click OK three times to close all the dialog boxes.

13

▼   11. Repeat steps 3–10 for directories c:\test2 and c:\test3.

Now, to see the effect of copying a folder to the same NTFS partition, follow these steps:

1. Copy c:\test1 to c:\test4\test1.

2. Find the permissions associated with c:\test4\test1 by choosing File, Properties.

To see the effect of copying a folder to a different NTFS partition, follow these steps:

1. Copy c:\test1 to d:\test1.

2. Find the permissions associated with d:\test1.

When a file or folder is copied within the same NTFS partition or copied to a different NTFS partition, it inherits the permissions of the folder into which it was copied.

To see the effect of moving a folder in the same NTFS partition, follow these steps:

1. Move c:\test2 to c:\test4\test2.

2. Find the permissions associated with c:\test4\test2.

When a file or folder is moved within the same NTFS partition, it retains its original permissions.

To see the effect of moving a folder to a different NTFS partition, follow these steps:

1. Move c:\test3 to d:\test3.

2. Find the permissions associated with d:\test3.

When a file or folder is moved to a different NTFS partition, it inherits the permissions
▲   of the folder into which it was copied.

Database Security

Oracle8i provides various security mechanisms to control data access. These security features include user logons, passwords, privileges, auditing, and fine-grained access control. These features can be manipulated by using the Security Manager (see Figure 13.6).

FIGURE 13.6

Oracle's Security Manager interface.

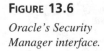

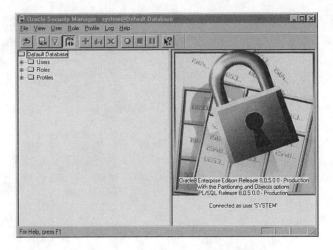

FIGURE 13.6

Oracle's Security Manager interface.

Database Users

Before you can access any information in the database, you must log on to the database with a valid username and password. (The database username is different from the operating system username that you use to log on to Windows NT.) Usernames can be created by using SQL or by using the GUI Oracle Security Manager (part of the Oracle Enterprise Manager). Figures 13.7 through 13.10 show the various options that you can use during user management. Refer to Hour 8, "Integrating and Administering Oracle8i on Windows NT," for a refresher on how to use operating system authentication so that you don't have to remember two usernames and passwords.

FIGURE 13.7

The Oracle Security Manager's General page for users.

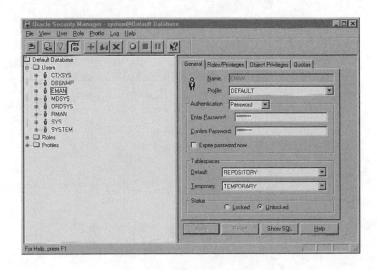

13

FIGURE 13.8

The Oracle Security Manager's Roles/Privileges page for users.

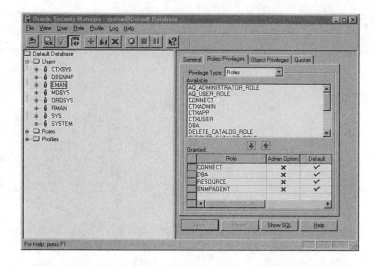

FIGURE 13.9

The Oracle Security Manager's Object Privileges page for users.

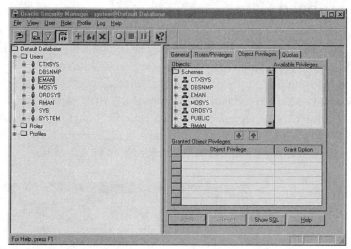

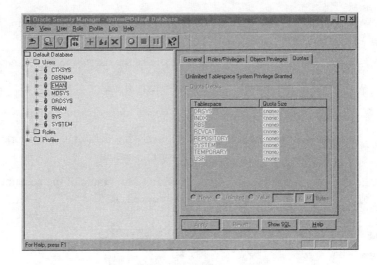

FIGURE 13.10

The Oracle Security Manager's Quotas page for users.

Oracle usernames aren't case sensitive.

Oracle creates several users automatically on database creation with the CREATE DATA-BASE command:

- The SYS account, with the password change_on_install, can be used to manage the database. It also owns the data dictionary.

- The SYSTEM account, with the password manager, can be used to administer the database and create database objects.

- The SCOTT account, with the password tiger, owns several sample objects that you can use to perform testing and run sample queries while learning to use Oracle.

To Do: Create a Database User with the Security Manager

You can use the Security Manager to graphically manage users. The following steps show how to create a user:

1. Start Oracle's Security Manager from the Oracle Enterprise Manager group (choose Start, Programs, Oracle Enterprise Manager, Security Manager).

2. Choose User, Create User.

To Do

13

▼   3. On the General page of the Create User dialog box, shown in Figure 13.11, do the following:

Name	Specify the username for the new account.
Profile	Specify the user profile to use.
Authentication	Specify and confirm the password.
Tablespaces	Specify the default and temporary tablespace to use for this account.
Status	Specify the status of the account to be locked or unlocked.

FIGURE 13.11

Creating a new user.

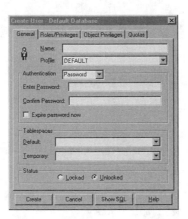

4. On the Roles/Privileges page, specify the roles and system privileges assigned to this user.

5. On the Object Privileges page, specify the object privileges assigned to this user.

6. **NEW TERM** You can use *quotas* to restrict the amount of space and resources that a user can use. On the Quotas page, specify the user quotas.

▲   7. Click Create to create the user.

> Use the Show SQL button to display the SQL that would be used to create the user. By looking at this SQL, you can understand how Oracle optimizes SQL that it generates behind the scenes and gain valuable insight into the internals of Oracle.

> If a user account is locked and the user tries to access the account, the user will receive the error ORA-28000, `The account is locked`. To unlock a locked account, select the username from the Users folder in the Oracle Security Manager, and change its status to unlocked on the General page.

To Do: Drop a Username by Using Security Manager

Oracle Security Manager can be used to drop users, as shown in the following steps:

1. In Security Manager, expand the Users folder in the appropriate database.
2. Highlight the user to be dropped.
3. Choose User, Drop User.
4. Confirm the operation to drop the user.

Password Management

Oracle8i conveniently allows you to manage and protect user passwords. The passwords are globally managed by using the Password page of the user profile. Here, you can specify

- Password expiration
- A password history to prevent users from choosing the same password
- Enforcement of password complexity to determine whether the password can be easily guessed
- Account lockup after a certain number of unsuccessful attempts

> The number of unsuccessful attempts after which the account locks up shouldn't be set too low. Otherwise, you might receive many calls from users who tend to forget their password easily and frequently lock their account.

13

System Privileges

System privileges specify the tasks users can perform in the database. You can assign a large number of system privileges to database users; Figure 13.12 lists some of these privileges. However, you must understand the implications of the various system privileges very well before you assign them to a user.

FIGURE 13.12

Assigning privileges to users.

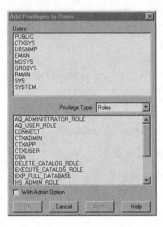

To Do: Grant System Privileges to a User

With the Security Manager, you can grant privileges to users easily, as follows:

1. In Security Manager, expand the Users folder in the appropriate database.

2. Highlight the particular user.

3. On the Roles/Privileges page, select System Privileges from the Privilege Type drop-down box.

4. Choose the desired system privilege from the Available list box.

5. Click the down arrow, and verify that the chosen system privilege appears in the Granted list.

6. Repeat steps 4 and 5 for each system privilege to be granted to the user.

7. Click the Apply button.

8. Expand the Users folder in the tree pane.

9. Expand the folder for the user whose privileges you're trying to verify.

10. Expand the System Privileges Granted folder to verify the system privileges granted.

> When granted to a user with the Admin option, a system privilege gives the user the ability to grant the privilege to other users.

To Do: Revoke a User's System Privileges

You can revoke user privileges by using the Security Manager, as follows:

1. In Security Manager, expand the Users folder in the appropriate database.

2. Highlight the particular user.

3. On the Roles/Privileges page, select System Privileges from the Privilege Type drop-down box.

4. Choose the system privilege to remove from the Granted list.

5. Click the up arrow, and verify that the chosen system privilege appears in the Available list box.

6. Repeat steps 4 and 5 for each system privilege to be revoked from the user.

7. Click the Apply button.

8. Expand the Users folder in the tree pane.

9. Expand the folder for the user whose privileges you're trying to verify.

10. Expand the System Privileges Granted folder to verify that the system privileges are revoked.

> You can grant or revoke system privileges within Security Manager by also choosing User, Add Privileges to a User.

Object Privileges

Object privileges can be used to control a user's access on various database objects such as tables, views, procedures, and synonyms. For example, you can use object privileges to specify whether a user can SELECT, INSERT, UPDATE, or DELETE from a table, execute a procedure, or access a view.

To Do: Grant Object Privileges to a User

Use the Security Manager to easily assign object privileges to users:

1. In Security Manager, expand the Users folder in the appropriate database.

2. Highlight the particular user.

3. On the Object Privileges page, select the schema that contains the object from the Objects list.

4. Expand the object on which you want to grant the privilege, such as the Tables folder.

13

▼   5. Scroll down the list of objects, and select the particular object.

6. From the Available Privileges list box, select the object privilege you want to assign.

7. Click the down arrow, and verify that the chosen privilege appears in the Granted Object Privileges list.

8. Repeat steps 3–7 for each object privilege to be granted to the user.

9. Click the Create button.

10. Expand the Users folder in the tree pane.

11. Expand the folder for the user whose privileges you're trying to verify.

12. Expand the Object Privileges Granted folder to verify that the object privileges are
▲   granted.

To Do: Revoke a User's Object Privileges

To revoke object privileges from users, use the Security Manager as follows:

1. In the Oracle Security Manager, expand the Users folder in the appropriate database.

2. Highlight the particular user.

3. On the Object Privileges page, select the schema that contains the object from the Objects list.

4. Expand the object on which you want to revoke the privilege, such as the Tables folder.

5. Scroll down the list of objects, and select the particular object.

6. From the Granted Object Privileges list, select the object privilege you want to revoke.

7. Click the up arrow, and verify that the chosen object privilege appears in the Available Privileges list.

8. Repeat steps 5–8 for each object privilege to be revoked from the user.

9. Click the Create button.

10. Expand the Users folder in the tree pane.

11. Expand the folder for the user whose privileges you're trying to verify.

12. Expand the Object Privileges Granted folder to verify that the object privileges are
▲   revoked.

Roles

Because Oracle8i provides many privileges, the task of assigning user privileges can become very tedious if you do so to individual users. Roles enable you to group privileges based on user functionality. In other words, suppose that in your system you have users who perform various functions, such as clerks, managers, and developers. Each "role" requires a certain set of privileges in the database so that the role can successfully perform the task. Database roles are a way by which you can group the privileges and then assign the role (instead of individual privileges) to the users. Figures 13.13 through 13.15 show how easily you can manage and manipulate the roles.

FIGURE 13.13

Oracle Security Manager's General page for roles.

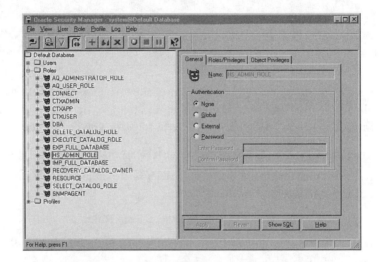

FIGURE 13.14

Oracle Security Manager's Roles/Privileges page for roles.

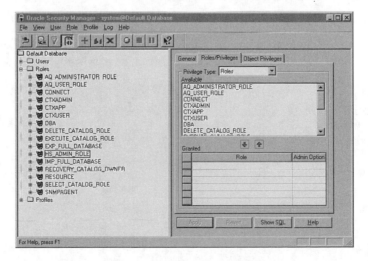

13

Figure 13.15

Oracle Security Manager's Object Privileges page for roles.

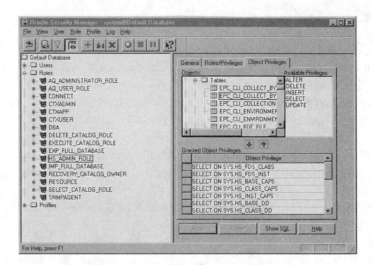

Oracle creates several roles during installation, such as the DBA role that, when granted, allows the user to perform database administrator–type functions in the database. You can immediately start using these predefined roles, or you can create new roles.

To Do: Create a New Role with Security Manager

Roles simplify the management of privileges. To create database roles by using the Security Manager, follow these steps:

1. In Security Manager, choose Role, Create Role.

2. On the General page of the Create Role dialog box, specify the following (see Figure 13.16):

Name	The name given to the role
Authentication	The type of authentication. Also, provide and confirm the password.

Figure 13.16

Creating a new role.

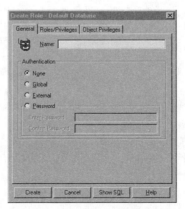

3. On the Roles/Privileges page, specify the roles and system privileges assigned to this role.

4. On the Object Privileges page, specify the object privileges assigned to this role.

5. Click Create to create the role.

To Do: Drop a Role with Security Manager

When you no longer need a particular role in the database, you should remove the role to simplify database management. Follow these steps:

1. In Security Manager, expand the Roles folder in the appropriate database.

2. Highlight the role to be dropped.

3. Choose Role, Drop Role.

4. Confirm the operation to drop the role.

To Do: Grant a Role to a User

After a role is created, you should assign it to users rather than individually assign privileges. Use the Security Manager and follow these steps to assign a role:

1. In Security Manager, expand the Users folder in the appropriate database.

2. Highlight the particular user.

3. On the Roles/Privileges page, select Roles from the Privilege Type drop-down list.

4. Choose the desired role from the Available list.

5. Click the down arrow, and verify that the selected role appears in the Granted list (see Figure 13.17).

FIGURE 13.17

Assigning roles to users.

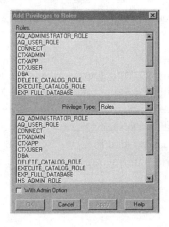

13

▼   6. Repeat steps 4 and 5 for each role to be granted to the user.

7. Click the Apply button.

8. Expand the Users folder in the tree pane.

9. Expand the folder for the user whose roles you're trying to verify.

▲ 10. Expand the Roles Granted folder to verify the roles granted to the user.

When granted to a user with the Admin option, a role gives that user the ability to grant the role to other users and to alter or drop the role.

To Do: Revoke a User's Role

You can use Security Manager to remove roles from a user, as follows:

1. In Security Manager, expand the Users folder in the appropriate database.

2. Highlight the particular user.

3. On the Roles/Privileges page, select Roles from the Privilege Type drop-down list.

4. Select the role to remove from the Granted list.

5. Click the up arrow, and verify that the chosen role appears in the Available list.

6. Repeat steps 4 and 5 for each role to be revoked from the user.

7. Click the Apply button.

8. Expand the Users folder in the tree pane.

9. Expand the folder for the user whose privileges you're trying to verify.

▲ 10. Expand the Roles Granted folder to verify that the roles are revoked.

Profiles

NEW TERM   Oracle8i lets you restrict the system resources a user can access, by using *profiles*. You can manage profiles through Oracle's Security Manager (see Figures 13.18 and 13.19). Profiles can be used to restrict resources such as CPU time, connect time, idle time, the number of concurrent sessions per user, the size of private SGA, and the number of database blocks that can be read in a call. Setting limitations on the use of system resources can help you control runaway processes in the system.

FIGURE 13.18

Oracle Security Manager's General page for profiles.

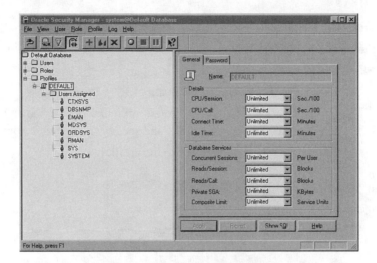

FIGURE 13.19

Oracle Security Manager's Password page for profiles.

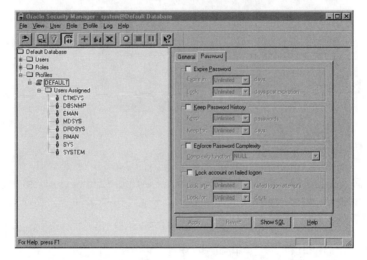

13

During the installation of Oracle, a DEFAULT profile with unlimited resource usage is created. This default profile is assigned to all newly created users unless specified otherwise.

To Do: Create a New Profile with Security Manager

To create additional profiles (other than the default profile) through Security Manager, follow these steps:

1. In Security Manager, choose Profile, Create Profile.
2. On the General page of the Create Profile dialog box, shown in Figure 13.20, provide a name for the new profile, and specify the system resource restrictions.
3. Click the Create button to create the profile.

FIGURE **13.20**

Creating profiles.

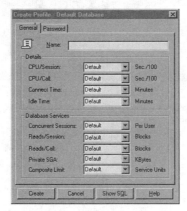

To Do: Drop a Profile

System requirements can change as the database is used, and you might want to drop some profiles and create some new ones. To use the Security Manager to drop profiles no longer needed, follow these steps:

1. In Security Manager, expand the Profiles folder in the appropriate database.
2. Highlight the profile to be dropped.
3. Choose Profile, Drop Profile.
4. Confirm the operation to drop the profile.

To Do: Assign a Profile to an Existing User

After a profile is created, you can assign it to particular users so that you can restrict their resource utilization. Follow these steps:

1. In Security Manager, expand the Users folder in the appropriate database.
2. Highlight the particular user.
3. Choose User, Alter User.

▼ 4. On the General page, select the profile to associate with the user (see Figure 13.21).

5. Click the Apply button.

FIGURE 13.21

Assigning profiles.

▲

 A profile can be associated with a user during the creation of the user.

Securing Applications with Views

You can use views as a way to control access to the information stored in the database.

Suppose that you have an employees table containing information about all employees. However, you want employees to have access to information that pertains only to them. To achieve this, a simple view can be created as follows:

```
Create view employees_v as
    Select * from employees
    Where emp_name = USER
```

As another example, you want a user to have access to only records modified by that user. Assume that the table to be accessed has a modified_by field that identifies the user making changes to the record. The following view can be used:

```
Create view orders_v as
    Select * from orders
    Where modified_by = USER
```

13

Several problems are associated with the use of views for providing security:

- They aren't very flexible. For example, you might want to give different privileges to various users based on their authority: An employee can view only his records, a manager can view the records of all employees in her department, and an HR manager can view the records of all company employees. Essentially, you have to create different views to satisfy all these requirements—a very costly solution because of the cost of managing the large number of views and associated synonyms. You could, however, create a complex view that encompasses all the scenarios, but this view will perform very poorly.

- You can have security implemented at runtime. In other words, the nature and extent of access to an object can be related to the time of the day, the IP address of the machine, and the task that currently can be performed by the application.

- Experienced and knowledgeable users might be able to access the information directly from the base table and bypass the views altogether.

Using Application Contexts and Fine-Grained Access Control

You can provide a much more robust security environment for the database by using application contexts and fine-grained access control.

Using Application Contexts

 Application contexts—a new database object type in Oracle8i—enable you to cache session information securely. Application contexts can be created by using the following syntax:

```
CREATE OR REPLACE CONTEXT namespace using package;
```

You can retrieve attribute values of the context by using the new SQL function SYS_CONTEXT:

```
SYS_CONTEXT(namespace,attribute);
```

Oracle uses a "primitive" context to store certain information for a session, such as the username, session ID, and IP address. The namespace reserved by Oracle for storing primitive contexts is called USERENV. For example, the following can be used to obtain the username:

```
SYS_CONTEXT('userenv','username');
```

A nonprimitive context should be set by the designated procedure through the DBMS_SES-SION.SET_CONTEXT procedure, as follows:

DBMS_SESSION.SET_CONTEXT(*namespace*,*attribute*,*value*);

Attributes stored by a context have several useful features:

- Attributes are transient and, when set or reset, are valid for the entire duration of the user session.

- Attribute values are stored in the private memory of the session.

- SYS_CONTEXT() is treated as a bind variable during the execution of the query. Therefore, it provides good performance.

- Each application can have its own context.

- The context can be set only by the designated procedure. Thus, security can be achieved.

- You can control data access by using the state information that has been stored securely.

Using Fine-Grained Access Control (FGAC)

 NEW TERM The *fine-grained access control* feature of Oracle8i allows you to define policies on tables and views. These user-defined policies dynamically generate predicates on operations performed on these table and views that have the policy set on them.

> You can set multiple policies on a table or view.

The DBMS_RLS package contains the necessary interfaces to manage policies:

add_policy(*object_schema*, *object_name*, *policy_name*,
policy_function_schema, *policy_function*, *statement_type*, *update_check*,
enable);

drop_policy(*object_schema*, *object_name*, *policy_name*);

enable_policy(*object_schema*, *object_name*, *policy_name*, *enable*);

refresh_policy(*object_schema*, *object_name*, *policy_name*);

The policy function is defined using the following syntax:

FUNCTION *policy_function*(*schema_name* VARCHAR2, *object_name*
        VARCHAR2) RETURN VARCHAR2;

13

Whenever a query accesses the object (table or view) that's protected by a policy, Oracle invokes the policy function. The policy function dynamically generates the predicate (a WHERE clause) that's attached to the query. The predicate is generated by using the application context or some other policy-specified condition.

You can apply a different policy for SELECT, INSERT, UPDATE, and DELETE on a table or view.

Use policies only where it makes sense. They shouldn't be used as an alternative to using constraints. (Constraints are discussed in Hour 1, "Understanding the Architecture of Windows NT and Oracle8i.")

Fine-grained access control provides several benefits:

- *Security*—The policies set for an object can't be bypassed, irrespective of how the object is accessed.
- *Flexibility*—Predicates are generated dynamically, based on the application's state, and thus can serve diverse requirements.
- *Transparency*—The security rules can be changed for the object by changing the associated policies and without requiring any change to the applications accessing the object.
- *Scalable*—If queries are written, they're automatically optimized and the execution plan is sharable.

To Do: Use FGAC to Select from a Table

For this example, you use fine-grained access control to select from the projects table so that an employee can view only projects belonging to him. The projects table has the following description:

```
(proj_id    number(5),
 proj_desc  varchar2(30),
 proj_lead  number(6))
```

The employees table has the following description:

```
(emp_id    number(6),
 emp_name  varchar2(20))
```

▼ Suppose that you want employees to be able to view only those projects that they lead. Follow these steps:

1. Connect to Server Manager as internal.

2. Create the application context:
```
create or replace context proj_ctx
using sec_admin.pj_ctx;
```

3. Create the trusted package:
```
Create or replace package sec_admin.pj_ctx as
   Procedure set_emp_number;
End pj_ctx;
```

4. Create the package body:
```
CREATE PACKAGE BODY pj_ctx IS
  PROCEDURE set_emp_number IS
    empnum NUMBER;
    BEGIN
      select emp_id into empnum
      from employees
      where emp_name = sys_context('userenv', 'session_user');
      dbms_session.set_context('proj_ctx', 'proj_lead', empnum);
    END set_emp_number;
  END pj_ctx;
```

5. Grant permissions to everyone to execute the package:
```
GRANT EXECUTE ON pj_ctx TO PUBLIC;
```

6. Create the policy function:
```
CREATE PACKAGE sec_admin.proj_security AS
    FUNCTION empnum_sec(owner VARCHAR2, object_name VARCHAR2)
    RETURN VARCHAR2;
    END proj_security;
```

7. Create the package body for the policy function:
```
CREATE PACKAGE BODY proj_security IS
    FUNCTION empnum_sec(owner VARCHAR2, object_name VARCHAR2)
    RETURN VARCHAR2 IS
    BEGIN
        RETURN ('proj_lead =
            sys_context("proj_ctx",  "emp_id")');
        END empnum_sec;
    END proj_security;
```

8. Add the new policy to the projects table:
```
execute DBMS_RLS.ADD_POLICY('apps','projects', 'proj_policy',
'sec_admin', 'proj_security.empnum_sec');
```

▼

13

▼   With this policy added to the projects table, whenever an employee tries to access the
    table, the predicate `'where proj_lead = sys_context("proj_ctx", "emp_id")'` is
▲   added to the query, thereby controlling access to the projects in the table.

Summary

The information placed in databases can be very sensitive. It also is shared by various
users with different levels of authority. You must implement security in your system so
that unauthorized users cannot have access to sensitive information.

In addition to physical security for the system, you should use the various features provided by the operating system and the database to protect the data. Windows NT provides the NTFS file system, which allows file-level security. Oracle also enables you to
create roles and profiles to manage users and resource usage. Oracle8i allows you to use
application context and fine-grained access control to dynamically control security at
runtime.

Q&A

**Q If I don't use NTFS security, can I still use all Oracle-provided database-level
   security?**

A Yes, you can still use the Oracle-provided security features such as roles, users,
   password, fine-grained access control, views, and so on, in the same manner.

Q Can I combine the auditing of Windows NT with that of Oracle?

A No. Unfortunately, they audit different objects. The result of auditing is also stored
   in different places and cannot be combined.

Workshop

The Workshop contains quiz questions and activities to help reinforce what you've
learned in this hour.

Quiz

1. What are the benefits of using fine-grained access control?
2. If user John is given NO_ACCESS on a file, but the group Engineers is given READ
   access to the same file and John is a member of the Engineers group, what is the
   effective right that John has on the file?
3. When is the ACL associated with an object checked?

Exercises

1. What are the disadvantages of using views for the purpose of database security?

2. Make a checklist of all the things you can do to implement security in your database system.

13

HOUR 14

Performing Backups

To develop an optimal backup and recovery strategy, you must understand the application, system, and database environments under consideration. Likewise, a complete picture of the business processes and the interaction between the system and the applications in use is essential. You must consider the anticipated future growth of the system, application, and data needs as well. All the relevant documentation for planned strategies in the production system (in case the current system is still in development or testing) must be collected. The following checklist will help you understand the requirements of a backup and recovery strategy:

- What line of business is the application used for?
- Is the application an online transaction processing (OLTP) system or decision support system (DSS)?
- What's the interaction between this application and other applications in the system: batch communication or online connection?
- What's the system configuration of the machine in use?
- How many databases are involved?

- Do all the databases have the same or varying backup, availability, and recovery requirements?
- Are the databases distributed or replicated?
- What backup tools, media managers, and other utilities are available for you to use?
- What's the mode of the databases—archivelog or noarchivelog?

In this lesson, you will learn how to do the following:

- Determine the right backup strategy for your environment.
- Use a standby database.
- Use a database in archivelog mode.
- Take hot and cold backups of an Oracle8i database on Windows NT.

Types of Failure

When choosing a backup strategy, you must consider the different types of failures that can occur in your environment and how you plan to protect the data against these failures. It will definitely help to have an uninterrupted power supply (UPS) and mirror the disks and most important database files. Despite all the precautions you take, some type of failure will still occur in the system.

The following types of failures can occur:

- *Instance failure* is usually the result of an operating system error, a hardware error, or an Oracle exception (or some other software-related error). Most often, a simple restart of the database instance helps recover from an instance failure. Keep in mind that instance failures can potentially corrupt the database.
- *Media failure* is usually the result of a disk drive failure, bad disk blocks, or damaged or deleted database files. Recovery from a media failure is more involved and makes use of your backups.
- *Application/user failure* refers to the loss of data that can occur when the user or application accidentally drops a row or table. You have to use your backup or a valid export to recover from user failures.

Backup Strategies

NEW TERM   Because large systems usually have large databases, the main goal of a backup strategy for such databases should be to reduce the mean time to backup (MTTB). *Mean time to backup* is the average time required to back up a database so that if recovery is needed, all the required components are available. The backup strategy should be such that it allows the recovery strategy to meet its requirements.

MTTB doesn't require that the entire backup be done in one session. In fact, minimizing MTTB can be achieved by minimizing the MTTB each session. You can reduce MTTB in the following ways:

- Reduce the amount of data that needs to be backed up regularly.
- Increase the rate at which data is backed up each time.

Increasing the Rate of Backup

Follow these guidelines to speed up the backup process:

- Back up to disk instead of tape.
- Back up in parallel. Backup time can be reduced by simultaneously copying the data to multiple devices.
- Use backup devices with high capacity.
- Make sure that the backup devices are connected locally to the machine and aren't over the network.
- If the backup is too large to be completed in the backup time window, consider logically splitting the backup over several nights (backup windows).

Reducing the Amount of Data to Back Up

To determine the amount of data to back up regularly, you must be familiar with the database design so that you can identify the components to be backed up and the frequency of backup. The following guidelines can be useful:

- Because read-only tablespaces should contain unchanging data, their objects should be backed up only once. Be very careful in verifying that the read-only tablespace isn't switched between read-only and read-write—in other words, the tablespace should be read-only at the time of backup and shouldn't have switched to read-write and back to read-only after the previous backup.

14

You can also determine whether your system contains tables you can partition as read-only. Such partitions can be backed up only once. Suppose that
you have an orders tables that maintains orders made by customers all year
round. However, at the end of each month the old orders aren't changed but
are maintained only for report generation. In this case, if you are in the
month of December, you can place data in the months of January–November
in read-only partitions (so that they don't have to be backed up daily).

- Lookup tables are usually static and don't change often. These tables can be
  backed up less frequently.
- Indexes can be re-created quickly with parallel index creation.
- In data warehouses, temporary tablespaces can be quite large and don't have to be
  backed up.
- In a data warehouse application, reloading and resummarizing the fact data can be
  faster than restoring and recovering the database. Summarized data should be
  backed up to a certain point in time. Thus, if you have to recover the database, the
  database can be restored to the point of the last complete backup, the fact table
  reloaded up to the point of failure, and the summary data regenerated. This
  minimizes the amount of data backed up daily.
- Oracle8 allows you to take incremental backups, which back up only changed
  blocks.

Table 14.1 describes several common high-availability techniques. You can use these
techniques to recover the database quickly in the case of a failure.

TABLE 14.1   HIGH-AVAILABILITY TECHNIQUES

Technique	Advantages	Disadvantages
Using Export/Import and SQL*Loader to perform object-level recovery	Fast recovery.	Object dependencies must be understood and considered.
Hardware redundancy (failover provided by another node)	Redundancy eliminates data loss.	No scalability; also expensive to implement.

Technique	Advantages	Disadvantages
Oracle standby database (redo logs of the primary database are maintained on the standby database, which is used in case the primary node fails)	Provides failover, fast recovery, simple implementation; works with all data types.	Rarely completely updated; data loss is possible; standby database doesn't share workload with the production database; can't be used for point-in-time recovery.
Oracle symmetric replication (uses Oracle's replication feature)	No data loss.	Uses transactions, so recovery is slow; use of two-phase commit can cause problems in maintaining database consistency.
Oracle Fail Safe	Simple setup; can use independent workloads on the nodes during normal conditions.	Now supports only two-node clusters; low scalability.
Oracle Parallel Server	No data loss; fast failover; high scalability; balances load among nodes.	Tuning can be difficult; depends on proper application design.
Customized store-and-forward (uses advanced queuing or trigger-based asynchronous replication)	No data loss; fast recovery.	Complex implementation.

Using Standby Databases

NEW TERM   Standby databases, also referred to as *hot databases*, were introduced in Oracle v7.3.3. A *standby database* is essentially one that's almost up-to-date with another database so that if the primary database crashes and can't be used, the standby database can be quickly opened to continue servicing the client applications.

14

In terms of sharing workload, the standby database is essentially idle. However, it's always in recovery mode because a cold backup of the production database is applied to it, and then the archive logs generated while the production database is running are applied to the standby database.

> Standby databases don't eliminate the necessity for normal backups because point-in-time recovery can't be performed by using standby databases.
>
> In other words, suppose you want to recover an accidentally dropped table. This table will be dropped from the standby database, also. If you have hot backups, you can perform recovery to the point when the table was dropped, export the table, and import it into the production database.

To Do: Create a Standby Database

You can use standby databases to improve the reliability and fault tolerance of your Oracle databases. The following steps demonstrate how you can create a standby database:

1. Place the production database in the archivelog mode (if it's not already in archivelog mode).

2. Take a backup (cold or hot) of the production database.

3. Create a control file for the standby database by executing the following Server Manager command at the production database:

   ```
   Svrmgr> alter database
         2> create standby controlfile as 'control.std';
   ```

   This creates a standby control file in the Oracle_home directory.

4. Open the production database (if it's not already open), and then archive the current redo log file group of the production database by forcing a log switch:

   ```
   Svrmgr> alter system archive log current;
   ```

5. Transfer the following files to the system that will be used as the standby database:

   - The files from the backup taken in step 2

   - The standby control file generated in step 3

   - The archive log generated in step 4

6. Create an initialization file for the standby database. The initialization parameters for the standby database must be identical to those of the production database because in case of a failover, the standby should provide the same functions provided by the production database.

To Do: Keep the Standby Database Synchronized with the Production Database

To Do ▼

After you copy the necessary files from the production database to the standby database, you have to keep the standby up-to-date with the changes in the production database so that it can easily be brought online and made functional if the production database becomes unavailable. Follow these steps:

1. `Startup nomount` the standby database by executing the following from the Server Manager prompt:

   `Svrmgr> `**`startup nomount;`**

2. Mount the standby database in standby exclusive mode:

   `Svrmgr> `**`alter database mount standby database;`**

3. Recover the standby database by applying the archived redo logs received from the production database:

   `Svrmgr> `**`recover from location standby database until cancel;`**

   The `from location` clause in this command isn't required if the archive logs are available in `LOG_ARCHIVE_DEST`.

4. Apply the archive logs as prompted by Oracle, and then cancel the recovery if the specified archive log isn't available.

Using unrecoverable data loads and no-logging features on the production database's tables and indexes won't generate redo and won't appear in the archived logs. Therefore, the standby database won't know of the changes, and the target objects will be marked as corrupt. You must use Export/Import or some other method of loading the data into the target objects.

If you add a datafile to the production database, you should add a copy of the datafile to the standby database before applying the redo log generated while the file was added. The new file will be added to the control file of the standby database, and the recovery will proceed as normal.

A datafile dropped from the production database will also be dropped from the standby database when the redo log is applied to the standby.

Performing an incomplete recovery of the production database and opening it with the `resetlogs` option will invalidate the standby database.

▲

14

To Do: Activate the Standby Database

The standby database is mounted and is in the recovery mode. Follow these steps to activate the standby database:

1. Apply all the archived and unarchived redo logs from the production database to the standby database.

2. Activate the standby database:

   ```
   Svrmgr> alter database activate standby database;
   ```

To Do: Find the Database's Current Mode

When recovering a database from a media failure, the recovery process depends on the mode in which the database is running. The backup strategy and overall database maintenance also is determined by whether the database is running in archivelog mode. Follow these steps to determine the current mode of your database:

1. Start Server Manager and connect as internal:

   ```
   C:\> svrmgrl
   Svrmgr> connect internal
   ```

2. Check the LOG_MODE column of the v$database view:

   ```
   Svrmgr> select name, log_mode from v$database;
   ```

   The output of this query might look like this:

   ```
   NAME        LOG_MODE
   ----        --------
   TEST        NOARCHIVELOG
   ```

   This shows that the TEST database isn't in archivelog mode.

Performing Cold and Hot Backups

Oracle provides several strategies for you to implement a reliable and efficient backup and restore procedure. Despite the strategy you use to protect your data, it's very important that you thoroughly test your procedure so that no surprises occur during a recovery of the database. You should also understand the advantages and disadvantages of the various methods.

Finding the Location of External Files

You can use several data dictionary views to obtain the location of the external files so that they can be backed up. The following Server Manager queries can be useful:

- Obtain all the datafiles associated with the database:

  ```
  Svrmgr> select name from v$datafile;

  NAME
  - - - - - - - - - - - - -
  c:\orant\database\test\systest.ora
  c:\orant\database\test\rbs1test.ora
  c:\orant\database\test\rbs2test.ora
  c:\orant\database\test\usr1test.ora
  c:\orant\database\test\usr2test.ora
  c:\orant\database\test\tmptest.ora
  ```

- Obtain the redo logs associated with the database:

  ```
  Svrmgr> select member from v$logfile;

  MEMBER
  - - - - - - - - - - - - - - -
  c:\orant\database\test\redo1atest.ora
  c:\orant\database\test\redo2atest.ora
  d:\orant\database\test\redo1btest.ora
  d:\orant\database\test\redo2btest.ora
  ```

- Obtain the location of the control files:

  ```
  Svrmgr> select name from v$controlfile;

  NAME
  - - - - - - - - - - - - - - - -
  c:\orant\database\test\control01.ctl
  d:\orant\database\test\control02.ctl
  e:\orant\database\test\control03.ctl
  ```

- Obtain information of archive redo logs by using v$loghist. The v$loghist view
  shows the sequence number of the archive redo log and the time it was generated:

  ```
  Svrmgr> select sequence#, first_time from v$loghist;

  SEQUENCE#, FIRST_TIME
  - - - - - - - - - - - - - - - - - - - -
  50     12/23/98     09:41:25
  49     12/22/98     19:23:48
  48     12/22/98     16:19:36
  47     12/22/98     11:51:25
  46     12/21/98     21:38:05
  45     12/21/98     10:22:20
  44     12/21/98     05:33:34
  ```

14

Using Cold Backups

Cold backups are the simplest type of Oracle backups. Taking a cold backup of an Oracle database involves shutting down the database and backing up all the relevant database files, including

- Datafiles
- Control files
- Redo logs
- Archived redo logs
- Initialization files

> You must do a shut down `normal` on the database before you take a cold backup. Otherwise, the backup may become corrupt and therefore useless. After the database instance is shut down, you can use a Windows NT utility or third-party tool to take a backup of the database file.

Using a cold backup has several advantages:

- Fast and easy backups
- Fast and easy restores
- Simple implementation

There are several disadvantages, also:

- The database has to be shut down.
- The cold backup can't be used to perform point-in-time recovery.

The script `cbackup.cmd` can be used to perform all the steps necessary for a cold backup:

```
REM cbackup.cmd
REM Author: Megh Thakkar
REM  Script to perform cold backup of an Oracle database
REM  on a Windows NT system
REM  We will use the sample ORCL database
REM The script assumes that the database is up and running
REM  Set the ORACLE_SID to the database to back up
set ORACLE_SID=ORCL
REM Create the backup directory
mkdir c:\backup
REM Set the path to the backup directory
set O_BACKDIR=c:\backup
REM Create a script to shut down the database and start up in
```

```
REM restricted mode
echo connect system/manager; > db_restrict.sql
echo shutdown immediate; >> db_restrict.sql
echo startup restrict pfile=
➥%ORACLE_HOME%\database\init%ORACLE_SID%.ora ; >> db_restrict.sql
echo exit >> db_restrict.sql
REM Create a script to shut down the database
echo connect system/manager; > db_shut.sql
echo shutdown immediate; >> db_shut.sql
echo exit >> db_shut.sql
REM Create a script to start up the database
echo connect system/manager; > db_start.sql
echo startup pfile=%ORACLE_HOME%\database\init%ORACLE_SID%.ora ;
➥>> db_start.sql
echo exit >> db_start.sql
REM Execute db_restrict.sql to shut down the database and start up
REM in the restricted mode
Svrmgrl system/manager @db_restrict.sql
REM Create a SQL*PLUS script to create a batch file to take cold backup
Echo Creating cold.sql to perform cold backup
Echo set heading off; > %O_BACKDIR%\cold.sql
Echo set feedback off; >> %O_BACKDIR%\cold.sql
Echo spool %O_BACKDIR%\cold.cmd; >> %O_BACKDIR%\cold.sql
Echo select 'copy '^¦^¦name^¦^¦' %O_BACKDIR% from v$controlfile;
➥>>%O_BACKDIR%\cold.sql
Echo select 'copy '^¦^¦member^¦^¦' %O_BACKDIR% from v$logfile;
➥>>%O_BACKDIR%\cold.sql
Echo select 'copy '^¦^¦file_name^¦^¦' %O_BACKDIR% from dba_data_files;
➥>>%O_BACKDIR%\cold.sql
Echo spool off; >>%O_BACKDIR%\cold.sql
Echo exit; >>%O_BACKDIR%\cold.sql
REM
REM Run the SQL*PLUS script cold.sql to generate cold.cmd
REM
Sqlplus system/manager @%O_BACKDIR%\cold.sql
REM
REM Shut down the database by executing db_shut.sql
REM
Svrmgrl system/manager @%O_BACKDIR%\db_shut.sql
REM
REM Run cold.cmd to perform the cold backup
REM
Call %O_BACKDIR%\cold.cmd
REM
REM Start up the database
REM
Svrmgrl @db_start.sql
REM
REM End of cold backup
REM
Echo Cold backup is complete
```

14

Performing Hot Backups of Oracle on Windows NT

NEW TERM   *Hot backups* refer to the process of backing up a database while it's open and in use. You can make a hot backup of a database if the database is in archivelog mode. Mission-critical applications that require a database to be operational 24 hours, 7 days a week (24×7) should use hot backups for point-in-time recovery (when needed).

Hot backups have the following advantages:

- The database can be open while backup is going on.
- Hot backups can be used to perform point-in-time recovery.

The following are the disadvantages of hot backups:

- They require a complex implementation.
- You can't use operating system utilities to copy open files; therefore, you have to use OCOPY.exe (an executable program provided by Oracle that allows you to copy open files to disk).
- Testing isn't easy because the database is usually up.

Hot backups incur overhead in CPU, I/O, and overall system performance. Therefore, you should make sure that hot backups are scheduled during periods of the least database activity.

> Archived logs and init.ora files are closed during a hot backup, so they can be copied by using Windows NT's copy command.

Determine the archive logs that must be backed up:

1. Connect to Server Manager as system/manager.
2. Find the oldest online log sequence number by issuing the following:

```
Svrmgr> archive log list
Database log mode            ARCHIVELOG
Automatic archival           ENABLED
Archive destination          c:\archives
Oldest online log sequence   48
Next log sequence to archive 50
Current log sequence         50
```

All the archive logs starting from the oldest online log sequence (in this example, 48) should be part of the online backup. The following steps indicate how you can take a hot backup of your database:

1. Copy the init.ora file to the backup directory.

2. Place a tablespace in begin backup mode.

3. Use OCOPY to copy the tablespace, and then place the tablespace in end backup mode.

> OCOPY can't be used to copy an open file to tape.

4. Perform steps 2 and 3 for each tablespace in the database.

> Use dba_tablespaces and v$datafile to determine the tablespaces and datafiles in the database.

5. Obtain the current log sequence number by executing archive log list in Server Manager. This indicates the last redo log that should be part of the hot backup.

6. Force a log switch so that all redo logs will be archived:

   Svrmgr> **alter system switch logfile;**

7. Take a backup of the control file.

8. Using the Windows NT command-line copy command, copy the archive logs from LOG_ARCHIVE_DEST.

The hbackup.cmd script can be used to perform all the steps necessary for a hot backup:

```
REM hbackup.cmd
REM Author: Megh Thakkar
REM  Script to perform hot backup of an Oracle database
REM  on a Windows NT system
REM  We will use the sample ORCL database
REM The database should be up and running
REM  Set the ORACLE_SID to the database to back up
set ORACLE_SID=ORCL
REM Create the backup directory
mkdir c:\backup
```

14

```
REM Set the path to the backup directory
set O_BACKDIR=c:\backup
REM Back up the initialization file
echo Backing up the init.ora file
copy %ORACLE_HOME%\database\init%ORACLE_SID%.ora c:\backup
REM
REM Create a SQL*PLUS script to obtain the minimum log sequence
REM number
REM
Echo set heading off; >%O_BACKDIR%\minlog.sql
Echo set feedback off; >>%O_BACKDIR%\minlog.sql
Echo spool %O_BACKDIR%\minlog.cmd; >>%O_BACKDIR%\minlog.sql
Echo select 'set minlog_value='^¦^¦min(sequence#) from v$log where
➥UPPER(status) = UPPER('INACTIVE'); >>%O_BACKDIR%\minlog.sql
Echo spool off; >>%O_BACKDIR%\minlog.sql
Echo select 'exit;' from dual; >>%O_BACKDIR%\minlog.sql
Echo exit; >>%O_BACKDIR%\minlog.sql
REM
REM Run the SQL*PLUS script minlog.sql to create minlog.cmd
REM
Sqlplus system/manager @%O_BACKDIR%\minlog.sql
REM
REM Run minlog.cmd to set minlog_value
REM
Call %O_BACKDIR%\minlog.cmd
REM
REM Create a SQL*PLUS script that can be used to generate a script
REM to back up the datafiles
REM
Echo set heading off; >%O_BACKDIR%\tblspc1.sql
Echo set feedback off; >>%O_BACKDIR%\tblspc1.sql
Echo spool %O_BACKDIR%\tblspc2.sql; >>%O_BACKDIR%\tblspc1.sql
Echo select 'connect system/manager;' from dual;
➥>>%O_BACKDIR%\tblspc1.sql
Echo select 'alter tablespace '^¦^¦tablespace_name^¦^¦'
➥begin backup;'^¦^¦ '>>%O_BACKDIR%\tblspc1.sql
Echo '^¦^¦ 'host start /wait ocopy '^¦^¦ file_name^¦^¦ '
➥%O_BACKDIR%; '^¦^¦' >>%O_BACKDIR%\tblspc1.sql
Echo '^¦^¦' alter tablespace '^¦^¦ tablespace_name^¦^¦'
➥end backup;' from dba_data_files; >>%O_BACKDIR%\tblspc1.sql
Echo spool off; >>%O_BACKDIR%\tblspc1.sql
Echo select 'exit;' from dual; >>%O_BACKDIR%\tblspc1.sql
Echo exit; >>%O_BACKDIR%\tblspc1.sql
REM
REM Run the SQL*PLUS script tblspc1.sql to create tblspc2.sql
REM
Sqlplus system/manager @%O_BACKDIR%\tblspc1.sql
REM
REM Run tblspc2.sql from server manager to back up the datafiles
REM
svrmgrl system/manager @%O_BACKDIR%\tblspc2.sql
```

```
REM
REM Create a SQL*PLUS script to obtain the maximum log sequence
REM number
REM
Echo set heading off; >%O_BACKDIR%\maxlog.sql
Echo set feedback off; >>%O_BACKDIR%\maxlog.sql
Echo spool %O_BACKDIR%\maxlog.cmd; >>%O_BACKDIR%\maxlog.sql
Echo select 'set maxlog_value='^¦^¦max(sequence#) from v$log where
➥UPPER(status) = UPPER('CURRENT'); >>%O_BACKDIR%\maxlog.sql
Echo spool off; >>%O_BACKDIR%\maxlog.sql
Echo select 'exit;' from dual; >>%O_BACKDIR%\maxlog.sql
Echo exit; >>%O_BACKDIR%\maxlog.sql
REM
REM Run the SQL*PLUS script maxlog.sql to create maxlog.cmd
REM
Sqlplus system/manager @%O_BACKDIR%\maxlog.sql
REM
REM Run maxlog.cmd to set maxlog_value
REM
Call %O_BACKDIR%\maxlog.cmd
REM
REM Create a SQL*PLUS script that can be used to generate a script
REM to back up the controlfile
REM
Echo set heading off; >%O_BACKDIR%\control1.sql
Echo set feedback off; >>%O_BACKDIR%\control1.sql
Echo spool %O_BACKDIR%\control2.sql; >>%O_BACKDIR%\control1.sql
Echo select 'connect system/manager;' from dual;
➥>>%O_BACKDIR%\control1.sql
Echo select 'alter database backup controlfile to trace ' from dual;
➥>>%O_BACKDIR%\control1.sql
Echo spool off; >>%O_BACKDIR%\tblspc1.sql
Echo select 'exit;' from dual; >>%O_BACKDIR%\tblspc1.sql
Echo exit; >>%O_BACKDIR%\tblspc1.sql
REM
REM Run the SQL*PLUS script control1.sql to create control2.sql
REM
Sqlplus system/manager @%O_BACKDIR%\control1.sql
REM
REM Run control2.sql from server manager to back up the controlfile
REM
svrmgrl system/manager @%O_BACKDIR%\control2.sql
REM
REM Create a SQL*PLUS script that can be used to generate a batch
REM file to copy the archive logs
REM
Echo set heading off; >%O_BACKDIR%\archive.sql
Echo set feedback off; >>%O_BACKDIR%\archive.sql
Echo spool %O_BACKDIR%\archive.cmd; >>%O_BACKDIR%\archive.sql
Echo select 'copy '^¦^¦archive_name^¦^¦' %O_BACKDIR% from
```

14

```
➥v$log_history where sequence# between %minlog_value% and
➥%maxlog_value%+1; >>%O_BACKDIR%\archive.sql
Echo spool off; >>%O_BACKDIR%\archive.sql
Echo select 'exit;' from dual; >>%O_BACKDIR%\archive.sql
Echo exit; >>%O_BACKDIR%\archive.sql
REM
REM Run the SQL*PLUS script archive.sql to create archive.cmd
REM
Sqlplus system/manager @%O_BACKDIR%\archive.sql
REM
REM Run archive.cmd to copy the archive logs
REM
Call %O_BACKDIR%\archive.cmd
REM
REM End of hot backup
REM
Echo End of hot backup
```

Archivelog Versus Noarchivelog Mode

The Oracle database redo logs record all transactions going on in the database. The LGWR background thread writes to these redo logs in a circular fashion. It writes from one redo log to the other until it comes to the end of the group; then it starts writing from the first redo log. In noarchivelog mode, the first redo log is written when the end of the circle is reached. Therefore, the only recovery option for a database in noarchivelog mode is to use a cold backup.

On the other hand, in archivelog mode, when the redo log fills up, the ARCH background thread reads the full redo log and writes its contents to the archived redo log. This enables you to use hot backups and perform point-in-time recovery.

In archivelog mode, if the archive log destination becomes full, database activity comes to a halt. You will have to free up space so that the archiver can finish archiving the redo log and database activity can continue. Usually, a trace file is generated in background_dump_destination to indicate that the archiver is having problems.

To Do: Stop the Archiving of a Database

In some situations, you might want to stop the archiving of a database. Usually, a database shouldn't be in archivelog mode when you're trying to perform maintenance operations that generate numerous archive logs that don't have to be archived. You might want to place the database in archivelog mode for the duration of such maintenance operations and place it back in archivelog mode when the operation completes.

▲ To Do

▼ If you stop archiving a database, instance failure can still occur. In case of a media failure, however, you have to restore the database from the last cold backup and can't recover to the point of failure.

Follow these steps to stop archiving a database:

1. Start Server Manager and connect with the internal account:

```
C:\ svrmgrl
Svrmgr> connect internal
```

2. Shut down the database (normal or immediate):

```
Svrmgr> shutdown immediate;
```

3. Mount the database in exclusive mode:

```
Svrmgr> startup mount exclusive;
```

4. Enable noarchivelog mode for the database:

```
Svrmgr> alter database noarchivelog;
```

5. Open the database:

```
svrmgr> alter database open;
```

6. Verify that the database is in noarchivelog mode by checking the LOG_MODE column from v$database:

▲
```
Svrmgr> select * from v$database;
```

To Do: Start Archiving for a Database

By default, a database is placed in noarchivelog mode after it's created. As a result, the database can't perform point-in-time recovery in case of media failure. To protect the database from a media failure, you must place the database in the archivelog mode.

> When a database is placed in archivelog mode, it will stay in that mode until it's placed in noarchivelog mode.

To place the database in archivelog mode, follow these steps:

▼ 1. Edit the initSID.ora file by adding the following parameters:

14

▼

Parameter	Description	Value
Log_archive_start	When set to TRUE, automatic archiving of filled redo logs is enabled for the database.	TRUE
Log_archive_dest	Specifies the directory where the database archive log files should be written. This directory requires a lot of free space; if the the archive destination is full, all database activities could halt.	%ORACLE_HOME%\
Log_archive_format	Specifies the format of the archived redo log filenames. Use %s to denote the sequence number of the archive logs.	"%sTEST.arc"

2. Start Server Manager, and connect with the internal account:

   ```
   C:\ svrmgrl
   Svrmgr> connect internal
   ```

3. Shut down the database (normal or immediate):

   ```
   Svrmgr> shutdown immediate;
   ```

4. Mount the database in exclusive mode:

   ```
   Svrmgr> startup mount exclusive;
   ```

5. Enable archivelog mode for the database:

▼

   ```
   Svrmgr> alter database archivelog;
   ```

▼ 6. Open the database:

`svrmgr>` **`alter database open;`**

7. Shut down the database again (normal or immediate):

`Svrmgr>` **`shutdown immediate;`**

8. Perform a cold backup of the database. The archive logs will be useful only when applied to a cold backup of the database taken after the database is placed in archivelog mode.

9. Start up the database:

`Svrmgr>` **`startup;`**

10. Verify that the database is in archivelog mode by checking the LOG_MODE column from `v$database`:

▲ `Svrmgr>` **`select * from v$database;`**

Using Export/Import as a Backup Strategy

Cold and hot backups are often referred to as *physical backups* because they back up physical database files. Using Export/Import to back up a database is referred to as *logical backup* because it backs up database objects such as tables.

Logical backups have several advantages:

- They can perform object or row recovery. For example, if someone accidentally deletes a row or drops an object, it's difficult to recover the lost data by using a physical backup. Using an export in this situation is usually faster.

- Often when you're upgrading your database to a major release, you will find that it's faster to export and import the database for a backup and then perform the upgrade.

- When you are migrating and moving across platforms, exporting the source database and then importing it to the target platform is usually very fast.

- The database can be up and running.

> Export/Import isn't a substitute for cold/hot backups. Hot backups can be used to protect against media failure, whereas Export/Import can be used to protect against user or application errors.

14

In most database environments, you can identify tables that don't change very often. Oracle8 provides the ability to take incremental exports that back up only those tables that have changed since the last full or incremental export backup. Using incremental backups can reduce the space and time needed for a database export. However, when using incremental backups, you have to keep handy all the exports since the last complete database export.

Summary

Using a sound backup strategy is crucial for the protection of valuable data. This lesson analyzes the various alternative ways you can implement the best backup strategy for your environment. The database must be run in archivelog mode if you want to take hot backups of the database. It's important to take frequent backups of the database and to test the backup against sample recovery scenarios so that you aren't surprised in the event of database failure.

Q&A

Q Can I use Export/Import in lieu of a cold backup for my database?

A No. Export/Import can be used in addition to, but not instead of, a cold backup. Cold and hot backups are used for achieving recovery to the time of failure, whereas Export/Import can't be used for this purpose.

Q If money isn't an issue, which backup strategy would you suggest for maximizing the protection of my data?

A You should use RAID 0+1 (disk mirroring) as a way to achieve high fault tolerance. Also, you should mirror your most important files and take backups more frequently.

Workshop

The Workshop contains quiz questions and activities to help reinforce what you've learned in this lesson.

Quiz

1. Can a cold backup be used to perform incomplete recovery?
2. How do you copy open files on Windows NT?
3. Can you use a standby database for other applications?
4. Which data dictionary view can be used to obtain the location of control files?

Exercises

1. Write a script to perform hot backups of all the databases on your server at the same time.

2. You have a 24×7 database environment. Determine the best backup strategy for your system.

3. Implement a standby database for the ORCL database.

14

HOUR 15

Performing Database Recovery

When a database has to be recovered, you should choose a recovery strategy after considering factors such as the following:

- The nature of the database failure
- The tolerable downtime of the database
- The backup strategy in place
- The cost of different recovery strategies

In this lesson, you will learn the following:

- The general steps required to recover a database
- How to recover the database in various situations
- How to re-create a control file when all control files are lost
- How to perform database recovery based on the type, time, and extent of failure

Understanding Mean Time to Recovery

NEW TERM   *Mean time to recovery* (MTTR) is an important factor in the recovery of systems that need high availability. MTTR for a database depends on the database size, complexity of the system, database structure, and application structure.

Follow these guidelines to minimize MTTR:

- Use partitioning techniques to reduce the effect of a failure on the overall system.
- Design the database so that the components are small and autonomous. Recovery will be fast. Also, recovery of one component won't affect the rest of the system.
- Make sure that the backup is easily accessible. The recovery process can be expedited as soon as you have valid backups.
- Verify that the backups are valid by testing them against dummy recovery scenarios.
- Familiarize yourself with the recovery procedures for the various scenarios so that you will be comfortable when a situation does arise.

You can follow these general steps while recovering a database:

1. Detect the failure. Usually, it's not difficult to realize that the database has a problem—the database or the application accessing the database might display error messages. (Table 15.1 shows solutions for some common errors indicating that the database needs recovery.) However, database failures don't always prevent database usage. For example, you might have a corrupt control file, but normal database operations would continue until an operation is performed that accesses the control file.

TABLE 15.1 DATABASE ERRORS INDICATING THAT RECOVERY MIGHT BE NECESSARY

Oracle Error (ORA-XXX)	Error Interpretation	Solution
00205, 00000, "error in identifying controlfile, check alert log for more info"	The control file of the specified name and size couldn't be found by the system.	Verify that all control files are present and accessible.
00280, 00000, "change %s for thread %s is in sequence #%s"	Specifies the redo log file required.	This error is usually accompanied by other errors. Make the specified redo log file available.

Oracle Error (ORA-XXX)	Error Interpretation	Solution
00312, 00000, "online log %s thread %s: '%s'"	Specifies the redo log file required.	This error is usually accompanied by other errors. Make the specified redo log file available.
00314, 00000, "log %s of thread %s, expected sequence# %s doesn't match %s"	Indicates that the online log is corrupted or is an old version.	Provide the correct version of redo logs, or reset the logs.
00376, 00000, "file %s cannot be read at this time"	Indicates that the specified file is unreadable.	Check the status of the specified file by looking at v$databafile. You might have to restore the file or bring it online.
00604, 00000, "error occurred at recursive SQL level %s"	Indicates that an error occurred while processing a recursive SQL statement (usually performed when accessing the data dictionary).	This error is usually accompanied by other errors. Refer to accompanying errors for further details.
01110, 00000, "data file %s: '%s'"	Reports a filename that's having a problem.	Refer to accompanying errors for further details.
01116, 00000, "error in opening database file %s"	The specified file isn't accessible.	Check the status of the specified file by looking at v$databafile. You might have to restore the file or bring it online.
01157, 00000, "cannot identify data file %s - file not found"	The specified file can't be accessed.	Make the file available to the database, and then open the database or do an ALTER SYSTEM CHECK DATAFILES.

continues

TABLE 15.1   CONTINUED

Oracle Error (ORA-XXX)	Error Interpretation	Solution
01194, 00000, "file %s needs more recovery to be consistent"	The file wasn't closed cleanly. Indicates that an incomplete recovery session was started, but an insufficient number of logs was applied. As a result, the file isn't consistent with the the rest of the database.	Recover this file to a a time when it wasn't being updated, apply more logs until the file is consistent, or restore the file from an older backup and repeat the recovery.

2. Determine the extent and type of failure. This is an important consideration in deciding the strategy that you will use to recover the database. In large systems, this task can take a long time.

3. Determine the database components that need recovery. The recovery strategy depends on the database components that need recovery.

4. Determine interdependencies between the components that need recovery. For example, when a table is lost, you also lose the associated indexes. Recovering a table doesn't automatically rebuild the indexes. Therefore, be aware of the database structure so that you can decide what other objects need recovery as a result of recovering a particular database component.

5. Determine the location and type of backup. The MTTR will depend highly on the ease of accessing the backup.

6. Restore the backup. This involves restoring the physical files from disk or tape and placing them at a location where the database can access them. Several factors affect the restore time:

   - File location (disk or tape)
   - File size
   - File format (raw, export, blocks, or extracts)
   - Feasibility of using parallel restore

7. Recover the database, apply redo logs (if database is in archivelog mode), and resync all database components.

Determining the Extent and Type of Failure

As mentioned earlier, the choice of recovery strategy depends on the extent and type of failure. The following checklist will help you in this process:

- Which activity resulted in the failure: power outage, upgrade (OS, database, hardware), routine maintenance (OS, hardware, network, database)?
- How was the failure detected: performing database operations, the database went down, error messages returned by the database or the application, at startup, at shutdown, database parameters changed?
- Is the database up or down? If it's down, how did it go down: shutdown abort, crash, normal shutdown?
- Are there any operating system errors?
- Do the event viewer logs show any errors?
- Does the alert log show any errors?
- Are any trace files generated?
- Is this an Oracle Parallel Server configuration?
- Is this is an Oracle Fail Safe configuration?
- What steps were performed after the failure?
- Is the backup strategy in place?
- Are the backups tested?
- Is the database is in archivelog mode? Are all archive logs available?
- Are there mirrored online redo logs?
- Are there mirrored control files?
- Did you have a recent full database export?
- Can you mount and open the database?
- What are the system availability requirements?
- What's the database size?
- Can you can easily re-create the data?

Database Recovery: Case Studies

The procedure to recover a database depends on the type of tablespace that's lost—such as rollback, user, index, or read-only tablespace.

A Datafile in the User or Index Tablespace Is Lost

When a datafile in the user or index tablespace is lost, the recovery procedure depends on the type of backup: cold or hot.

To Do: Recover with a Cold Backup

If you have a cold backup and are in noarchivelog mode, the datafile recovery will be complete if the redo to be applied is within the range of your online redo logs. Follow these steps to recover from the loss:

1. Shut down the database.

2. Restore the lost datafile from the backup.

3. Startup mount the database:

   Svrmgr> **STARTUP MOUNT;**

4. Determine all your online redo log files, their respective sequence, and their first change numbers with the following query:

   Svrmgr> **SELECT X.GROUP#, MEMBER, SEQUENCE#, FIRST_CHANGE#**
         2> FROM V$LOG X, V$LOGILE Y
         3> WHERE X.GROUP# = Y.GROUP#;

5. Determine the CHANGE# of the file to be recovered:

   Svrmgr> **SELECT FILE#, CHANGE#**
         2> FROM V$RECOVER_FILE;

> You can recover the datafile if the CHANGE# obtained is greater than the minimum FIRST_CHANGE# of your online redo logs.

6. Recover the datafile by using the online redo logs:

   Svrmgr> **RECOVER DATAFILE '*full_path_of_datafile*'**

   Supply the files that you're prompted for during the recovery until you receive the message Media Recovery complete.

7. Open the database:

▲ Svrmgr> **ALTER DATABASE OPEN**

To Do: Recover with a Hot Backup

▼To Do

If you have a hot backup and are in archivelog mode, datafile recovery will be complete if the redo to be applied is within the range of your online logs. Follow these steps:

1. Shut down the database.

2. Restore the lost datafile from the backup.

3. Startup mount the database:

   ```
   Svrmgr> STARTUP MOUNT;
   ```

4. Determine all your online redo log files, their respective sequence, and their first change numbers with the following query:

   ```
   Svrmgr> SELECT X.GROUP#, MEMBER, SEQUENCE#, FIRST_CHANGE#
        2> FROM V$LOG X, V$LOGILE Y
        3> WHERE X.GROUP# = Y.GROUP#;
   ```

5. Determine the CHANGE# of the file to be recovered:

   ```
   Svrmgr> SELECT FILE#, CHANGE#
        2> FROM V$RECOVER_FILE;
   ```

> You can recover the datafile if the CHANGE# obtained is greater than the minimum FIRST_CHANGE# of your online redo logs. Otherwise, the file can't be completely recovered, and you have two choices:
>
> - If you can easily re-create the data since the last cold backup, you can restore the last cold backup and recover the database until that point.
> - If the data can't be easily re-created, you have to re-create the tablespace as described in the following To Do section.

6. Recover the datafile by using the archived and online redo logs:

   ```
   Svrmgr> RECOVER DATAFILE 'full_path_of_datafile'
   ```

   Supply the files that you're prompted for during the recovery until you receive the message Media Recovery complete.

7. Open the database:

   ```
   Svrmgr> ALTER DATABASE OPEN
   ```

To Do: Recover with Missing Redo Data

If redo data is missing, the recovery won't be complete. You have to re-create the table-space and load the data by using a database export or SQL*Loader. You also have to re-create the indexes after the tablespace is re-created. Follow these steps:

1. Shut down the database.

2. Startup mount the database:

   Svrmgr> **Startup mount**

3. Offline drop the datafile:

   Svrmgr> **ALTER DATABASE DATAFILE** *'fullpath of datafile'*
           2> OFFLINE DROP;

4. Open the database:

   Svrmgr> **ALTER DATABASE OPEN;**

5. Drop the user tablespace:

   Svrmgr> **DROP TABLESPACE** *tablespace_name* **INCLUDING CONTENTS;**

6. Re-create the tablespace and the tablespace objects.

Recovering from a Lost Datafile in a Read-Only Tablespace

Recovery of a read-only tablespace is simple because the datafile isn't modified. You can simply restore the datafile from its last backup to its original location. There's no need to perform media recovery.

> Before recovering a read-only tablespace, make sure that the tablespace was read-only at the time of the last backup *and* it hasn't been changed to read-write since that time.

Recovering from a Lost Datafile in a Rollback Tablespace

When you lose rollback segments, the recovery steps are very involved, and the procedure depends on the database state at the time of failure detection.

> Recovering from the loss of rollback segments is a critical procedure and should be performed with the help of Oracle Support Services. Active transactions can be lost while the recovery is being performed.

15

The Database Is Down

While trying to startup the database, you get the ORA-1157 and ORA-1110 Oracle errors and other operating system errors. You also find out that the tablespace having problems has rollback segments. Depending on how the database was shut down, you can take the appropriate actions.

The Database Was Cleanly Shut Down

Check the last shutdown entry in the alert log to verify that the database shutdown was normal or immediate. The following log entry indicates that the shutdown was clean:

```
'alter database dismount
completed: alter database dismount"
```

This might be followed by an attempt that you made to startup, resulting in the ORA errors and also a subsequent SHUTDOWN ABORT by Oracle. The following steps can be used to recover from this situation:

1. In the init*sid*.ora file, modify the ROLLBACK_SEGMENTS parameter by removing all the rollback segments belonging to the damaged tablespace. If you aren't sure which rollback segments are part of the damaged tablespace, comment out the ROLLBACK_SEGMENTS parameter by placing a # at the beginning of its line.

2. Mount the database in restricted mode:

   Svrmgr> **STARTUP RESTRICT MOUNT**

3. Offline drop the lost datafile:

   Svrmgr> **ALTER DATABASE DATAFILE '*full_path_of_datafile*'**
           2> OFFLINE DROP;

4. Open the database:

   Svrmgr> **ALTER DATABASE OPEN**

   If you get error codes ORA-604, ORA-376, and ORA-1110, shut down the database and continue to step 5; otherwise, skip to step 6 after the statement is processed.

5. Perform this step only if step 4 resulted in errors. Edit the init*sid*.ora file as follows:

- Comment out the ROLLBACK_SEGMENTS parameter.
- Add the following line:

  _Corrupted_rollback_segments = (*rollback1*,...,*rollbackN*)

where (*rollback1*,...,*rollbackN*) is the list of rollback segments that originally appeared in the ROLLBACK_SEGMENTS parameter.

> Use undocumented (underscore) parameters with extreme caution and with the help from Oracle Support Services because there's a potential of database corruption, which could require a database rebuild.

Now, startup the database in restricted mode:

Svrmgr> **startup restrict mount**

6. Drop the damaged rollback tablespace:

Svrmgr> **drop tablespace *tablespace_name* including contents;**

7. Re-create the rollback tablespace with all its rollback segments.

8. Bring the rollback segments online.

9. Make the database available for general use:

Svrmgr> **alter system disable restricted session;**

10. Shut down the database.

11. Edit the init*sid*.ora file as follows:

- Uncomment the ROLLBACK_SEGMENTS parameter.
- If you had to perform step 5, remove the following line:

  _Corrupted_rollback_segments = (*rollback1*, ...,*rollbackN*)

12. Startup the database.

The Database Wasn't Cleanly Shut Down

This scenario results when the database crashed or was shutdown aborted. In this case, the datafile can't be dropped because there might be active transactions. Follow these steps to recover from this situation:

1. Restore the lost datafile from a backup.

2. Mount the database.

3. Bring the file online if it's not already online:

```
Svrmgr> SELECT FILE#, NAME, STATUS FROM V$DATAFILE;
```

If the file is offline:

```
Svrmgr> ALTER DATABASE DATAFILE 'full_path_of_datafile'
    2> ONLINE;
```

4. Determine all your online redo log files, their respective sequence, and their first change numbers with the following query:

```
Svrmgr> SELECT X.GROUP#, MEMBER, SEQUENCE#, FIRST_CHANGE#
    2> FROM V$LOG X, V$LOGILE Y
    3> WHERE X.GROUP# = Y.GROUP#;
```

5. Determine the CHANGE# of the file to be recovered:

```
Svrmgr> SELECT FILE#, CHANGE#
    2> FROM V$RECOVER_FILE;
```

 You can recover the datafile if the CHANGE# obtained is greater than the minimum FIRST_CHANGE# of your online redo logs, by proceeding with step 6. Otherwise, you have two options:

- Restore from a full database backup. This can result in data loss.
- Force the database to open in an inconsistent state. This would require a database rebuild.

6. Recover the datafile by using the online redo logs:

```
Svrmgr> RECOVER DATAFILE 'full_path_of_the_datafile'
```

Supply the files that you're prompted for during the recovery until you receive the message Media Recovery complete.

7. Open the database:

```
Svrmgr> ALTER DATABASE OPEN
```

Forcing a Database to Open in an Inconsistent State

The following steps should be taken as the last resort when you have no export, insufficient backup, and the rollback segment corruption/loss is unrecoverable:

1. Shut down the database.
2. Take a full database cold backup.

3. Edit the init*sid*.ora file as follows:

- Add the following lines:

```
_allow_resetlogs_corruption = true
_corrupted_rollback_segments = list_of_all_rollback_segments
```

- Comment out the `rollback_segments` parameter.

4. Startup mount the database.

5. Perform an incomplete database recovery:

Svrmgr> **RECOVER DATABASE UNTIL CANCEL;**

6. When prompted for the file, type **CANCEL**.

7. Open the database by resetting the logs:

Svrmgr> **ALTER DATABASE OPEN RESETLOGS;**

This results in a database that's potentially in an inconsistent state. You should take a full database export at this time and use that export for rebuilding the database.

The Database Is Up and Running

If the loss of a datafile in the rollback tablespace is detected while the database is up and running, *don't shut down the database.* You might want to create additional rollback segments in a different tablespace so that you can continue working with the database while recovery is being performed.

If the database is in archivelog mode, follow these steps to perform a quick recovery:

1. Offline the lost datafile:

   ALTER DATABASE DATAFILE *'full_path_of_datafile'* OFFLINE;

2. Restore the datafile from a backup.

3. Apply media recovery on the datafile:

   RECOVER DATAFILE *'full_path_of_datafile'*;

4. Bring back the datafile online:

   ALTER DATABASE DATAFILE *'full_path_of_datafile'* ONLINE;

The following steps can be taken to recover the database whether it is in archivelog mode or not but is not so quick in comparison to the preceding method:

1. Offline all the rollback segments in the tablespace to which the datafile belongs:

   `Svrmgr> ALTER ROLLBACK SEGMENT rollback_segment OFFLINE;`

   This statement should be repeated for all rollback segments in the affected tablespace.

2. By using the following query, verify that the rollback segments are offline:

   ```
   Svrmgr> SELECT SEGMENT_NAME, STATUS
        2> FROM DBA_ROLLBACK_SEGS
        3> WHERE TABLESPACE_NAME = 'tablespace_name';
   ```

   If this query is successful, skip to step 6; otherwise, continue with step 3.

3. If step 2 indicates that you have active transactions in the rollback segments, run the following query to determine the active transactions:

   ```
   Svrmgr> SELECT SEGMENT_NAME, XACTS ACTIVE_TX, V.STATUS
        2> FROM V$ROLLSTAT V, DBA_ROLLBACK_SEGS
        3> WHERE TABLESPACE_NAME = 'tablespace_name' AND
        4> SEGMENT_ID = USN;
   ```

   Check the ACTIVE_TX column for the rollback segments that have the status of PENDING_OFFLINE. Segments with a value of zero will soon go offline; a non-zero value, however, indicates that you have active transactions that have to be committed or rolled back.

4. By using the following query, identify the users who have transactions assigned to the rollback segments being considered:

   ```
   Svrmgr> SELECT S.SID, S.SERIAL#, S.USERNAME, R.NAME "ROLLBACK"
        2> FROM V$SESSION S, V$TRANSACTION T, V$ROLLNAME R
        3> WHERE R.NAME IN
        4> ('pending_rollback1', ... 'pending_rollbackN');
   ```

5. Inform these users to commit or rollback their transactions or kill their sessions by executing the following:

   `Svrmgr> ALTER SYSTEM KILL SESSION 'sid, serial#';`

6. Drop all the offline rollback segments:

   `Svrmgr> DROP ROLLBACK SEGMENT rollback_segment;`

7. Drop the tablespace, including contents.

8. Re-create the rollback tablespace.

9. Re-create the rollback segments, and bring them online.

Recovering from the Loss of System Tablespace

If a datafile from the system tablespace is lost, your recovery options rely heavily on the availability of a good backup. In the absence of a good backup, you could be faced with the undesirable alternative of rebuilding the database with possible data loss.

To Do: Recover with a Cold Backup

▼ To Do

There might be occasions when the system tablespace is lost and the only backup available is the cold backup. The following steps can be used to recover from this situation:

1. Shut down the database.

2. Restore the lost datafile from the backup.

3. Startup mount the database:

   ```
   Svrmgr> STARTUP MOUNT;
   ```

4. Determine all your online redo log files, their respective sequence, and their first change numbers with the following query:

   ```
   Svrmgr> SELECT X.GROUP#, MEMBER, SEQUENCE#, FIRST_CHANGE#
        2> FROM V$LOG X, V$LOGILE Y
        3> WHERE X.GROUP# = Y.GROUP#;
   ```

5. Determine the CHANGE# of the file to be recovered:

   ```
   Svrmgr> SELECT FILE#, CHANGE#
        2> FROM V$RECOVER_FILE;
   ```

> You can recover the datafile if the CHANGE# obtained is greater than the minimum FIRST_CHANGE# of your online redo logs. Otherwise, the file can't be completely recovered, and you have two choices:
>
> - If you can easily re-create the data since the last cold backup, you can restore the last cold backup and recover the database till that point.
> - If the data can't be easily re-created, you will have to re-create the tablespace as described earlier in the section "To Do: Recover with Missing Redo Data."

6. Recover the datafile by using the online redo logs:

   ```
   RECOVER DATAFILE 'full_path_of_the_datafile'
   ```

   Supply the files that you're prompted for during the recovery until you receive the message Media Recovery complete.

7. Open the database:

   ```
   ALTER DATABASE OPEN
   ```

15

To Do: Recover with a Hot Backup

To Do ▼

In situations where the system tablespace is lost and you have a hot backup that can be used to recover, the following steps can be used:

1. Shut down the database.

2. Restore the lost datafile from the backup.

3. Startup mount the database:

   Svrmgr> **STARTUP MOUNT;**

4. Determine all your online redo log files, their respective sequence, and their first change numbers by using the following query:

   ```
   Svrmgr> SELECT X.GROUP#, MEMBER, SEQUENCE#, FIRST_CHANGE#
        2> FROM V$LOG X, V$LOGILE Y
        3> WHERE X.GROUP# = Y.GROUP#;
   ```

5. Recover the datafile by using the archived and online redo logs:

   Svrmgr> **RECOVER DATAFILE '*full_path_of_datafile*'**

   Supply the files that you're prompted for during the recovery until you receive the message Media Recovery complete.

6. Open the database:

   Svrmgr> **ALTER DATABASE OPEN**

The following parameters can have a very harmful effect on the database. Use them with caution and with the help of Oracle Support Services:

- _allow_resetlogs_corruption, when set to TRUE, allows the opening of the database with the resetlogs option, even if some hot backups require more redo applied or the datafiles are out of sync for some other reason:

  ALTER DATABASE OPEN RESETLOGS;

- _corrupted_rollback_segments is used in situations when a database doesn't start because of corrupt rollback segments. By listing the rollback segments in this parameter, you can force the database to be open without using these rollback segments. It prevents the rollback of active transactions in the specified corrupted rollback segments.

- _offline_rollback_segments prevents the rollback of active transactions in the listed offline rollback segments.

Recovering from the Loss of a Control File

A problem with a control file usually isn't detected while the database is up and running, unless you're changing the database structure and the control file is accessed. A damaged or lost control file is identified by ORA-205, error in identifying control file '%s', along with an operating system–level error during database startup.

To Do: Recover with a Mirrored Control File

If you have mirrored copies of the control file, you can use the good copies to recover. Follow these steps:

1. Shut down the database (if it's running).

2. Fix any hardware problems (disk or controller) that could have caused the problem with the control file.

3. Copy a good copy of the control file to a good disk.

4. Edit the CONTROL_FILES parameter in init*sid*.ora to reflect the new location of the control file.

5. Start up the database.

To Do: Recover Without a Mirrored Control File

Follow these steps to recover if all the control files are lost or you don't have a control file that accurately reflects the database structure:

1. Shut down the database (if it's running).

2. Startup mount the database.

3. Generate a trace file containing the statement that can be used to create the control file:

   Svrmgr> **alter database backup controlfile to trace;**

   This command creates a trace file in USER_DUMP_DEST. Listing 15.1 shows an example of such a trace file.

LISTING 15.1   SAMPLE CONTROL FILE CREATION SCRIPT

```
# The following commands will create a new control file and use it
# to open the database.
# Data used by the recovery manager will be lost. Additional logs may
# be required for media recovery of offline datafiles. Use this
# only if the current version of all online logs is available.
STARTUP NOMOUNT
CREATE CONTROLFILE REUSE DATABASE "ORCL0" NORESETLOGS NOARCHIVELOG
    MAXLOGFILES 32
```

15

```
▼        MAXLOGMEMBERS 2
         MAXDATAFILES 254
         MAXINSTANCES 1
         MAXLOGHISTORY 226
LOGFILE
  GROUP 1 'E:\ORACLE\ORADATA\ORCL0\REDO01.LOG'  SIZE 1M,
  GROUP 2 'E:\ORACLE\ORADATA\ORCL0\REDO02.LOG'  SIZE 1M
DATAFILE
  'E:\ORACLE\ORADATA\ORCL0\SYSTEM01.DBF',
  'E:\ORACLE\ORADATA\ORCL0\RBS01.DBF',
  'E:\ORACLE\ORADATA\ORCL0\USERS01.DBF',
  'E:\ORACLE\ORADATA\ORCL0\TEMP01.DBF',
  'E:\ORACLE\ORADATA\ORCL0\INDX01.DBF',
  'E:\ORACLE\ORADATA\ORCL0\OEMREP01.DBF'
CHARACTER SET WE8ISO8859P1
;
# Recovery is required if any datafiles are restored backups
# or if the last shutdown was not normal or immediate.
RECOVER DATABASE
# Database can now be opened normally.
ALTER DATABASE OPEN;
# No tempfile entries found to add.
#
```

4. Edit this trace file as follows, and then save it:

   - Remove the header information.

   - Make any changes desired (such as MAXLOGFILES and MAXDATAFILES).

5. Perform a shutdown normal of the database.

6. Take a cold backup of the database.

7. Execute the script saved in step 4 to create a new control file:

   Svrmgr> **@create_controlfile.sql**

8. Open the database:

   Svrmgr> **Alter database open;**

9. Perform a shutdown normal of the database.

10. Take a full database backup.

If the damaged control file(s) prevents you from mounting the database, you can execute the CREATE CONTROLFILE statement with the database in the NOMOUNT state and create a new control file. Media recovery can then be performed, and the database opened. For

▼ example,

▼   1. Startup nomount.

     2. Create the control file:

```
Svrmgr> Create Controlfile reuse database "TEST"
     2> noresetlogs noarchivelog
Maxlogfiles  100
     Maxlogmembers  3
     Maxdatafiles  500
     Maxinstances   8
     Maxloghistory  500
   Logfile
     Group 1 'c:\orant\database\test\log1test.ora' size 5M,
     Group 2 'c:\orant\database\test\log2test.ora' size 5M,
     Group 3 'c:\orant\database\test\log3test.ora' size 5M,
   Datafile
     'c:\orant\database\test\systest.ora' size 80M,
     'c:\orant\database\test\data1test.ora' size 20M,
     'c:\orant\database\test\data2test.ora' size 20M;
```

     3. Perform media recovery on the database:

```
Svrmgr> Recover database;
```

     4. Open the database:

▲   `Svrmgr> alter database open;`

Summary

In case of a database failure, you should first understand the type and extent of failure before you start performing any recovery. You should also be familiar with the backup strategy in place so that you can choose the best recovery approach.

This lesson looks at various scenarios of database failures from which you might have to recover. When a database failure occurs, don't panic—instead, gather all the pertinent information, and follow the guidelines you've learned this hour. It always helps to have tested your backups before a failure. You also should have information about your database's physical and logical structures recorded at an easily accessible location.

Q&A

Q If I have neither a good cold backup nor a good export, can I recover from a database failure?

A Yes. It depends first on the type and extent of damage. Even in the worst case, alternatives can be used to force a database open, after which you can take a full database export. Also, you can contact Oracle Support Services, which can use tools such as the Data Unloader (DUL) to extract data from a corrupt database.

Q **Some recovery procedures use underscore parameters. How can I get a list of these parameters?**

A The underscore parameters are hidden parameters and shouldn't be used without the help of Oracle Support Services. If you want a list of these parameters, query `X$KSPPI`.

Workshop

The Workshop contains quiz questions and activities to help reinforce what you've learned in this hour. You can check Appendix A for the answers (but don't peek!).

Quiz

1. How can you reduce MTTR?
2. Your control files are damaged, and the database instance doesn't mount. What do you do?
3. If you lose a datafile that contains the index tablespace, what's the quickest way to recover from this?
4. A read-only tablespace is lost, and you don't have valid archive logs. What do you do?

Exercises

1. You get `ORA-205` when you try to start the database. Recover from this situation.
2. You get `ORA-376` when you try to start the database. Recover from this situation.

Hour 16

Using Recovery Manager (RMAN)

Previous lessons stress the importance of a good backup strategy. Oracle8i provides you with Recovery Manager (RMAN), an excellent tool for performing backups and recovery on a database system. It simplifies and automates a number of tasks associated with a backup strategy.

For Oracle8i databases, RMAN replaces the Enterprise Backup Utility (EBU) available for Oracle7 databases.

With RMAN, you can perform various backups and recover a database under various scenarios. RMAN has two interfaces: command-line (RMAN) and GUI (OEM's Backup Manager). This lesson focuses on the command-line interface accessed through the RMAN utility. We will discuss the following:

- Understanding the RMAN components
- Using RMAN to perform backups
- Using RMAN to recover from a variety of scenarios
- Using RMAN to perform point-in-time recovery

 The following terminology must be understood in reference to Recovery Manager:

- *Whole backup*—A backup of all datafiles and the control file.
- *Full backup*—A nonincremental backup of one or more datafiles.
- *Incremental backup*—A backup of datafiles that include only the blocks that have changed since the last incremental backup. A level 0 incremental backup will back up all the blocks.
- *Operating system–level backup*—A backup of files made by using operating system utilities.
- *Closed backup*—Backing up a complete database or part of it with the database closed.
- *Open backup*—Backing up a complete database or a part of it with the database open. Don't confuse an open backup with a hot backup: Open backups allow you to back up particular objects, whereas hot backups copy the redo log files to archive log files.

Introducing RMAN

RMAN has several important features:

- It can be used to perform incremental backups (up to four levels: level 0 and levels 1–4). Level 0 is a complete backup and isn't considered a true incremental backup.
- During a backup and restore, RMAN detects corrupt blocks and reports them in the alert log, trace file, and other data dictionary views such as v$backup_corruption and v$copy_corruption.
- It can be used to back up archived redo logs.

- RMAN manages load balancing while performing backups, restores, and recoveries across clustered nodes of an Oracle Parallel Server.

- It provides several performance enhancements, such as automatic parallelization of backup, restore, and recovery operations; a limit to the number of reads per file; multiplexing of file backups; and not generating extra redo during backups.

- RMAN allows the limiting of the backup piece size, which enables easy backup of very large databases.

- RMAN allows you to perform online backups without putting the tablespaces in hot backup mode.

16

> You can also write and use backup and restore scripts with RMAN to automate or repeat the backup and restore process. Some sample scripts are discussed later in this chapter.

Understanding RMAN Components

Recovery Manager consists of four main components (see Figure 16.1). In the figure, the RMAN executable is in the middle of the figure and the arrows show the channels.

- RMAN executable (`rman`)
- Target database
- Recovery catalog or the database's control file
- Channel

FIGURE 16.1

RMAN components.

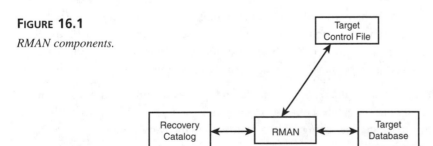

Each component plays an important role in the overall RMAN strategy.

RMAN Executable

The RMAN executable is a PRO*C application that translates RMAN commands into a sequence of PL/SQL calls:

- `dbms_backup_restore` performs backup and restore operations on the target database.
- `dbms_rcvman` queries the recovery catalog or the database's control file for the information to perform the backup/restore operations.
- `dbms_rcvcat`, if a recovery catalog is used, updates the recovery catalog.

Target Database

This is the database on which the desired backup, restore, and recovery operations are to be performed.

Recovery Catalog

NEW TERM   The *recovery catalog* is a repository of information stored in an Oracle database—a set of tables, views, indexes, and packages created and maintained under a schema known as the *recovery catalog owner*. It includes the following information:

- Physical schema of the target database
- Backup sets and pieces
- Copies of datafiles
- Archived redo logs
- Reusable stored scripts

You can use RMAN with or without a recovery catalog. A recovery catalog is usually stored in a database separate from the database being backed up and consists of all the information regarding a backup, such as backup structure, backup history of the database it backs up, and any other pertinent information that can be used to recover the database.

Recovery Manager updates the recovery catalog and queries the information in it while performing certain operations. If the recovery catalog isn't used, RMAN queries the control file of the target database. Using RMAN without the recovery catalog has several disadvantages:

- If all the control files are lost, you have to first recover the control files.
- Point-in-time recovery is very difficult.
- Stored scripts can't be used.
- Restore operations are slow.

Channel

Channels are allocated to initiate an Oracle server process that's used for backup/restore/recovery operations of the target database. The type of channel allocated determines the type of media used, such as disk or SBT_TAPE. By using channels, you can limit the backup piece size, read rate, and degree of parallelization.

Starting RMAN: Two Scenarios

16

You can start RMAN in several ways, depending on how it's configured.

If RMAN isn't using a recovery catalog, and user megh has SYSDBA role, follow these steps:

1. Set the oracle_sid to the target database prod:

   C:> **set oracle_sid=prod**

2. Start RMAN without the catalog:

   C:> **rman81 nocatalog**

3. Connect to the target database:

   RMAN> **connect megh/megh target**

> Alternatively, you can combine steps 2 and 3:
>
> C:> **rman81 target megh/megh nocatalog**

If RMAN is using a recovery catalog stored in database rcat and user megh has SYSDBA role, follow these steps:

1. Set the oracle_sid to the target database prod:

   C:> **set oracle_sid=prod**

2. Start RMAN and connect to the recovery catalog:

   C:> **rman81 rcvcat rman/rman@rcat**

3. Connect to the target database:

   RMAN> **connect megh/megh target**

> Alternatively, you can combine steps 2 and 3:
>
> C:> **rman target megh/megh@prod rcvcat rman/rman@rcat**
>
> where prod is the TNS alias of the target database.

Using RMAN for Backups

By using RMAN, you can take a backup of a closed or open database. A closed database should be mounted. If you're taking a backup of an open database, don't place the tablespaces in hot backup mode. Figure 16.2 shows how you can perform backups of a database using RMAN. Different server processes are used during this task, and files can be backed up in parallel.

FIGURE 16.2

Using RMAN for backups.

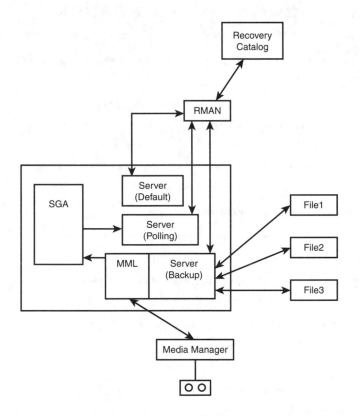

 When taking a backup of an open database with RMA, don't issue the `alter tablespace begin backup` command because RMAN will automatically do it.

Whether a database is open or closed, you can used RMAN to back up a whole database or part of it, including the tablespace, datafile, control file, and archived redo logs. You can use RMAN to perform two types of backups.

File Copy Backup

NEW TERM A *file copy* is like an operating system backup and is an image copy of the file. It can be written only to a disk and can contain only one file as input.

You can use a file copy as part of an incremental backup strategy, but it can be only level 0. The biggest advantage a file copy has is that it can be used immediately without having to be restored.

The following example shows how you can perform a file copy. Type the following at the RMAN prompt:

```
Run {
    Allocate channel dk1 type disk;
    Copy
        Level 0
        Datafile 1 to 'c:\backups\data1prod.ora';
}
```

The following example shows how to parallelize file copy operations (you have to allocate multiple channels to achieve this):

```
Run {
    Allocate channel dk1 type disk;
    Allocate channel dk2 type disk;
    Allocate channel dk3 type disk;
    Allocate channel dk4 type disk;
    Allocate channel dk5 type disk;
    Allocate channel dk6 type disk;
Copy
    Datafile 1 to 'c:\backups\data1prod.ora',
    Datafile 2 to 'c:\backups\data1prod.ora',
    Datafile 3 to 'c:\backups\data1prod.ora',
    Datafile 4 to 'd:\backups\data1prod.ora',
    Datafile 5 to 'd:\backups\data1prod.ora',
    Datafile 6 to 'd:\backups\data1prod.ora';
        Sql 'alter system archive log current';
}
```

RMAN executes its commands serially.

16

Backup Sets

 A *backup set* is a logical set consisting of one or more physical files called *backup pieces*. Backup sets can be of two types:

- Datafile backup sets, which can include datafiles and control files
- Archive log backup sets, which can include only archive logs and can be only full backups

You can write a backup set to a disk or an sbt_tape. Restoring the datafiles from the backup set is required before performing a database recovery. The following example shows how to obtain a backup set:

```
Run {
    Allocate channel tp1 type 'SBT_TAPE';
    Backup
        Format 'c:\backups\df_%t_%s_%p'
        (database);
}
```

To perform parallelization of obtaining backup sets, you can allocate multiple channels and specifying files per set, as follows:

```
Run{
    Allocate channel tp1 type 'SBT_TAPE';
    Allocate channel tp2 type 'SBT_TAPE';
    Allocate channel tp3 type 'SBT_TAPE';
    Allocate channel tp4 type 'SBT_TAPE';
    Backup
        Filesperset 4
        Format 'c:\backups\df_%t_%s_%p'
        (database);
        sql 'alter system archive log current';
}
```

 The format specification (see Table 16.1) in the preceding examples is used to determine the output filename.

TABLE 16.1   USING VARIABLES IN FORMATTING FILENAMES

Substitution Variable	Use
%d	The name of the database
%p	The number of the backup piece within the backup set
%s	The number of the backup set

Substitution Variable	Use
%t	The timestamp
%u	A value comprising the backup set number and its time of creation

Usually, a backup set consists of only one backup piece unless the piece size is limited by the user. In the following example, there will be only one backup piece if the output is less than 2GB; otherwise, there will be more than one backup piece. Also, each backup piece will have blocks from four files multiplexed together.

```
Run {
    Allocate channel tp1 type 'SBT_TAPE';
    Set limit channel tp1 kbytes 2097152;
    Backup
        Filesperset 5
        Format 'c:\backups\df_%t_%s_%p'
        (tablespace user_data1);
}
```

The following example shows how to obtain an archive log backup set:

```
Run {
    Allocate channel tp1 type 'SBT_TAPE';
    Backup
        Filesperset 20
        Format 'c:\backups\al_%t_%s_%p'
        (archivelog all delete input);
}
```

Understanding Incremental and Cumulative Backups

Incremental backups can reduce the amount of backup that must be taken. An incremental backup copies only Oracle blocks that have changed since a previous incremental backup. Incremental backups are always in reference to a level 0 backup set or a level 0 file copy.

Incremental backups are noncumulative. An incremental backup at level *N* (where *N* is greater than 0) backs up all Oracle blocks that have changed since the last incremental backup at a level less than or equal to *N*.

16

Cumulative backups take longer and are larger than incremental backups. A cumulative backup of level N contains all the Oracle blocks changed since a prior backup at a level less than N.

In performing a database recovery, a cumulative backup of level N supersedes all incremental backups of the same level. Therefore, you require only one incremental backup of any particular level to perform recovery.

Using RMAN for Restores

RMAN can restore or extract an original file from a backup set. You can restore any logical unit of a database. Using RMAN's `restore` command, you can restore a database, tablespace, datafile, control file, or archive log file.

 A file copy backup doesn't require a restore of files. Archive logs are automatically restored by RMAN as necessary during recovery, or you can restore them manually.

The database's state determines how much of a restore you can do:

- If a database instance is in NOMOUNT state, the control file can be restored.
- If a database instance is mounted, the whole database or the system tablespace can be restored.
- If the database is open, the offline tablespace or datafile can be restored.

When performing a restore, Recovery Manager queries the recovery catalog (or the target database's control file) and takes the following into consideration to determine which available backups are optimal for the current scenario:

- Is point-in-time recovery desired?
- What type of channel is allocated: disk or SBT_TAPE?
- Is a file copy available?
- What backup set levels are available?
- Is backup incremental or cumulative?

To Do: Restore a Whole Database and Control File

To Do ▼

If you are moving a database from one machine to another machine, you might need to restore the entire database and the associated control files. RMAN can be used to perform this task as demonstrated here:

1. Set `oracle_sid` to the target database `prod`:

   ```
   C:> set oracle_sid=prod
   ```

2. Connect to Server Manager as internal:

   ```
   C:> svrmgrl
   Svrmgr> connect internal
   ```

3. Shut down the database:

   ```
   Svrmgr> shutdown immediate
   ```

4. Startup nomount the database instance:

   ```
   Svrmgr> startup nomount
   ```

5. Exit Server Manager:

   ```
   Svrmgr> exit
   ```

6. Connect to the recovery catalog and the target database by using RMAN from the command prompt:

   ```
   C:> rman target internal/oracle@prod rcvcat rman/rman@rcat
   ```

7. Perform the restore of the database and control file:

   ```
   RMAN> run {
        Allocate channel tp1 type 'SBT_TAPE';
        Allocate channel dk1 type disk;
        Restore controlfile to 'c:\prod\ctr1prod.ctl';
        Replicate controlfile from 'c:\prod\ctr1prod.ctl';
        Sql 'alter database mount';
        Restore (database);
        }
   ```

▲ If the restored database backup is consistent, you can open the database without recovery; otherwise, you have to apply redo and perform database recovery.

Restoring to Perform Point-In-Time Recovery

Point-in-time recovery is necessary to recover the database to a specific time before an error. Point-in-time recovery requires the use of an `until` clause that specifies up to what event you need to recover. The event to recover can be

- A specific time
- A log sequence number
- An SCN (system change number)

16

To Do: Restore a Database and Control File to a Point in Time

The following steps restore a whole database and a control file in preparation for a point-in-time recovery for 4:20 p.m., January 20, 1999:

1. Set `oracle_sid` to the target database **prod**:

   ```
   C:> set oracle_sid=prod
   ```

2. Connect to Server Manager as internal:

   ```
   C:> svrmgrl
   Svrmgr> connect internal
   ```

3. Shut down the database:

   ```
   Svrmgr> shutdown immediate
   ```

4. Startup nomount the database instance:

   ```
   Svrmgr> startup nomount
   ```

5. Exit Server Manager:

   ```
   Svrmgr> exit
   ```

6. Connect to the recovery catalog and the target database from the command prompt:

   ```
   C:> rman target internal/oracle@prod rcvcat rman/rman@rcat
   ```

7. Perform the restore of the database and control file:

   ```
   RMAN> run {
           Set until time '1999/01/20 16:20:00';
           Allocate channel tp1 type 'SBT_TAPE';
           Allocate channel dk1 type disk;
           Restore controlfile to 'c:\prod\ctr1prod.ctl';
           Replicate controlfile from 'c:\prod\ctr1prod.ctl';
           Sql 'alter database mount';
           Restore (database);
           #recover database
           }
   ```

In this example, the `recover database` command is commented out, but you should try to perform database recovery with the same command.

Performing Recovery Using RMAN

RMAN can perform two types of database recovery:

- A complete recovery of a database is performed by applying all the changes (including those in the online redo logs) made to the database because the restored backup is applied to the database.

- An incomplete database recovery is performed by stopping a database recovery before applying all the changes made to the database. Although the database recovery is incomplete, all the files are recovered to the same point in time and are consistent.

To Do: Use RMAN to Perform Tablespace Recovery

You can recover a tablespace while the database is open. Suppose that you need to recover tablespaces user_data1 and user_data2, and the database is open. Follow these steps:

1. Connect to the recovery catalog and the target database:

   ```
   C:> rman target internal/oracle@prod rcvcat rman/rman@rcat
   ```

2. Restore the tablespace and perform recovery. The tablespace should be placed offline during the restore and recovery process:

   ```
   RMAN> run {
         Allocate channel tp1 type 'SBT_TAPE';
         Allocate channel tp2 type 'SBT_TAPE';
         Sql 'alter tablespace user_data1 offline immediate';
         Sql 'alter tablespace user_data2 offline immediate';
         Restore tablespace user_data1;
         Restore tablespace user_data2;
         Recover tablespace user_data1;
         Recover tablespace user_data2;
         Sql 'alter tablespace user_data1 offline immediate';
         Sql 'alter tablespace user_data2 offline immediate';
         }
   ```

To Do: Create a Script to Parallelize the Recovery of Four Tablespaces

The script you create will recover the user_data1, user_data2, user_data3, and user_data4 tablespaces. You execute the stored script to perform the recovery operation. Follow these steps:

1. Connect to the recovery catalog and the target database through RMAN:

   ```
   C:> rman target internal/oracle@prod rcvcat rman/rman@rcat
   ```

2. Create the stored script reco_4tblspc:

   ```
   RMAN> create script reco_4tblspc {
         Allocate channel dk1 type disk;
         Allocate channel dk2 type disk;
         Allocate channel dk3 type disk;
         Allocate channel dk4 type disk;
         Sql 'alter tablespace user_data1 offline immediate';
         Sql 'alter tablespace user_data2 offline immediate';
         Sql 'alter tablespace user_data3 offline immediate';
   ```

16

```
Sql 'alter tablespace user_data4 offline immediate';
Restore tablespace user_data1;
Restore tablespace user_data2;
Restore tablespace user_data3;
Restore tablespace user_data4;
Recover tablespace user_data1;
Recover tablespace user_data2;
Recover tablespace user_data3;
Recover tablespace user_data4;
Sql 'alter tablespace user_data1 offline immediate';
Sql 'alter tablespace user_data2 offline immediate';
Sql 'alter tablespace user_data3 offline immediate';
Sql 'alter tablespace user_data4 offline immediate';
}
```

This script will be stored in the recovery catalog and be associated with only one target database: prod.

3. Execute the script:

```
RMAN> run {
      Execute script reco_4tblspc;
      }
```

You can execute a stored RMAN script from the command line by using the command-line option `cmdfile`:

```
C:> rman target internal/oracle@prod rcvcat rman/rman@rcat
    ↪cmdfile reco_4tblspc
```

To perform parallelization of redo, set the init.ora parameter RECOVERY_PARALLELISM.

Looking at Sample Scenarios

Suppose you've been taking backups with the following schedule:

- Level 0 full backup on Sunday
- Level 2 incremental backup on Monday
- Level 2 incremental backup on Tuesday
- Level 2 incremental backup on Wednesday

- Level 1 incremental backup on Thursday
- Level 2 incremental backup on Friday
- Level 2 incremental backup on Saturday

Figure 16.3 shows the entire schedule.

FIGURE 16.3

Using incremental backups for point-in-time recovery.

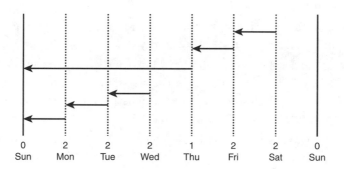

| 0 | 2 | 2 | 2 | 1 | 2 | 2 | 0 |
| Sun | Mon | Tue | Wed | Thu | Fri | Sat | Sun |

Case 1: Failure Occurs on Wednesday Before Backup

If a database failure occurs on Wednesday but before the database is backed up that day, the following steps would recover the database:

1. Apply the level 0 backup from Sunday.
2. Apply the level 2 backup from Monday.
3. Apply the level 2 backup from Tuesday.

Case 2: Failure Occurs on Friday Before Backup

If a database failure occurs on Friday but before the database is backed up that day, the following steps would recover the database:

1. Apply the level 0 backup from Sunday.
2. Apply the level 1 backup from Thursday.

Case 3: Failure Occurs on Saturday Before Backup

If a database failure occurs on Saturday but before the database is backed up that day, the following steps would recover the database:

1. Apply the level 0 backup from Sunday.
2. Apply the level 1 backup from Thursday.
3. Apply the level 2 backup from Friday.

Useful RMAN Commands

Frequently, you will use the following RMAN commands:

- `set duplex` creates up to four copies of the same backup set concurrently. `set duplex on` defaults to one copy. For `set duplex N`, N specifies the number of copies (1, 2, 3, or 4).
- `crosscheck backupset` can be used to verify that a backup piece listed as available in the recovery catalog is really available.
- `allocate channel` establishes a link between RMAN and the target database. RMAN tries to use as many channels as it can concurrently. A single channel can work on only one file copy or backup set at any given time. You can specify several parameters when allocating a channel:

connect	Specifies the connect string to use when connecting to the target database. Used by Oracle Parallel Server to run database backups across multiple instances.
format	Specifies the format of the filenames to use for this channel.
name	Specifies the device name to be used to perform the backup or restore.
parms	Sets port-specific parameters for the device to be used.
type	Specifies the type of device, such as `"disk"` or `"SBT_TAPE"`.

- `deallocate channel` deallocates or releases the channel that was allocated with the `allocate channel` command.
- `setlimit channel` controls the usage of resources for a channel. Parameters specified include the channel name and any or all of the following:

readrate	Controls the read I/O rate and thereby prevents disk contention
kbytes	Specifies a maximum limit for the output files created during a backup operation
maxopenfiles	Controls the number of files that can be opened by the channel concurrently

- `resync catalog` causes the recovery catalog to be compared to the control file of the target database. It then updates the recovery catalog with new or changed information. You should execute this command once daily or at least when the physical database structure changes, such as when a tablespace is dropped or a new datafile is added.

- change updates the recovery catalog with the availability information of backup pieces such as an archive log. For example, to make an archive log unavailable, use this command:

```
RMAN> change archivelog 'c:\backups\al_prod_1.rdo' unavailable;
```

A quick way to synchronize the recovery catalog and control file with the disk is to validate the catalog. For example, if you delete a lot of archive logs from disk and want to make sure that the catalog is aware of this, use this command:

```
RMAN> change archivelog all validate;
```

When this command is executed, it verifies that the files the catalog believes to exist really do exist on disk. Otherwise, those files will be marked as deleted in the catalog.

- list queries the recovery catalog to produce a list of its contents as specified in the command. To obtain a list of all databases the recovery catalog is aware of, use this command:

```
RMAN> list incarnation of database;
RMAN-03022: compiling command: list
RMAN-06240: List of Database Incarnations
RMAN-06241: DB Key Inc Key DB Name DB ID        CUR  Reset SCN
Reset Time
RMAN-06242: ------ ------- ------- ----------- ---- ---------
---------
RMAN-06243: 127    128     PROD    1957829059  YES  1
17-JAN-99
RMAN-06243: 133    134     DEV     1850267933  YES  1
18-JAN-99
```

To obtain a list of file copies containing a backup of any datafile that's a member of a tablespace, use this command:

```
RMAN> list copy of tablespace user_data1;
RMAN-03022: compiling command: list
RMAN-06210: List of Datafile Copies
RMAN-06211: Key    FILE  S Completion time Ckp SCN  Ckp Time
NAME
RMAN-06212: ----- ----- - --------------- -------- ---------
--------------
RMAN-06213: 212    1     D 17-JAN-99       389120   17-JAN-99
C:\ORANT\DATABASE\PROD\USER1PROD.ORA
RMAN-06213: 219    1     D 17-JAN-99       389120   17-JAN-99
C:\ORANT\DATABASE\PROD\USER1PROD.ORA
RMAN-06213: 232    1     D 17-JAN-99       389120   17-JAN-99
C:\ORANT\DATABASE\PROD\USER1PROD.ORA
RMAN-06213: 239    1     D 17-JAN-99       389120   17-JAN-99
C:\ORANT\DATABASE\PROD\USER1PROD.ORA
```

16

List the backup sets that contain archive logs within the sequence 131–138 with this command:

```
RMAN> list backupset of archivelog
from logseq 131 until logseq 138 thread 1;

RMAN-03022: compiling command: list
RMAN-06220: List of Archived Log Backups
RMAN-06221: Key  Thrd  Seq  Completion time
RMAN-06222: ----  -----  ----  ---------------
RMAN-06223: 160  1     131  17-JAN-99
RMAN-06223: 209  1     132  17-JAN-99
RMAN-06223: 311  1     133  17-JAN-99
RMAN-06223: 313  1     134  17-JAN-99
RMAN-06223: 325  1     135  17-JAN-99
RMAN-06223: 342  1     136  17-JAN-99
RMAN-06223: 357  1     137  17-JAN-99
RMAN-06223: 362  1     138  17-JAN-99
```

- `report` queries the recovery catalog to find more information than that provided by the list command. You can use such information to determine the files that require backup and obsolete backups. For example, to find the files that need to be backed up, use this command:

RMAN> **report need backup**

To find obsolete backups that can be deleted, use this command:

RMAN> **report obsolete**

- The database has been opened with reset logs, and you need to inform the recovery catalog about it. Use this command:

RMAN> **reset database;**

When you open a database with reset logs, the recovery catalog should be updated with this information before further attempts to back up the database are made. This command will cause RMAN to create a new incarnation of the database in the recovery catalog and make the new incarnation as current. Subsequent backups will belong to this new and current incarnation.

Suppose that you're performing a point-in-time recovery and want to recover to a time before the database was opened with reset logs. Essentially, you're trying to use an older incarnation. Follow these steps:

1. Obtain the incarnation you want to revert to:

   RMAN> **list incarnation of database *identifier*;**

   In this syntax, *identifier* represents the database SID.

2. Reset the database to an older incarnation:

   RMAN> **reset database to *incarnation*;**

   In this syntax, *incarnation* is a number indicating the database version (not the software database version, but more like the database copy number).

16

Troubleshooting RMAN Problems

Typically, RMAN performs many operations automatically. However, problems do occur, and you should understand the cause of the problems by running RMAN in debug mode. You can redirect output of the debug operation to a trace file instead of the log file or screen output.

When RMAN is run in debug mode, you can use it to

- See the PL/SQL generated
- Determine where RMAN is hanging
- Determine where the problem occurs in RMAN

The following example demonstrates how RMAN can be used in the debug mode and a trace file generated:

```
C:> Rman target internal/oracle@prod rcvcat rman/rman@rcat
    ➥debug trace rmantrc.log
```

Here are some problem/solution scenarios:

- *Problem 1:* The user specifies SBT_TAPE while backing up the database. The backup succeeds but is written to disk.

  Resolution: Check the RMAN log for the cause of the error. The comment= field specifies the cause of the problem. If it shows the following, the default Oracle test disk API software is being used because either Oracle can't find the vendor library to load or there's a problem with loading the library:

  RMAN-08503: <etc> comment=API Version 1.0,MMS Version 1.0.1.2

  Make sure that the library is in the WINNT\SYSTEM32 directory.

- *Problem 2:* The RMAN log indicates the following RPC errors:

```
RMAN-10030: RPC call appears to have failed to
start on channel c4
RMAN-10036: RPC call ok on channel c4
```

Resolution: These errors indicate that the target database is slow in responding. Also check the network for any errors.

- *Problem 3:* The backup process hangs.

Resolution: Follow these steps:

1. Check the progress of the backup by querying v$session_longops from the Server Manager prompt:

```
Svrmgrl> SELECT sid,
    2> round(sofar/totalwork*100,2) '% Complete",
    3> substr(to_char(sysdate,'yymmdd hh24:mi:ss'),1,15)
    4> "Present Time"
    5> FROM v$session_longops
    6> WHERE compnam = 'dbms_backup_restore';
```

OUTPUT

```
SID    % Complete        Present Time
---    ----------        ---------------
14     82                990118 19:04:08
```

If the % Complete isn't increasing for several minutes, a problem exists with the backup. Check v$session_wait view to identify the cause of the wait:

```
SELECT *
FROM v$session_wait
WHERE wait_time = 0;
```

2. Check the Media Manager log and trace files for errors or "waiting for" events such as waiting for the tape to be changed.

> You can determine the Media Manager library in use by querying the comments field in v$backup_piece.

3. Run RMAN in debug mode, and check for errors or waits.

4. If the RMAN log shows messages in the Additional information section, contact the media vendor for clarification of the error, and take appropriate steps.

Summary

Oracle provides Recovery Manager (RMAN) to simplify and automate your backup and recovery needs. It can be used to perform backups with a variety of strategies and also eliminates most of the manual intervention that might be necessary during a database recovery. In this hour, you looked at various uses of RMAN. We also saw how easy it is to write RMAN scripts to automate your tasks.

16

Q&A

Q What happens if the tablespace is in hot backup mode and I use RMAN to take a backup with the database open?

A The backup will still occur without any problems.

Q Do I still have to keep track of the archive logs when I use RMAN to perform all the backups?

A No. When using RMAN for all your backups, you don't have to track your archive logs because RMAN will do that for you.

Workshop

The Workshop contains quiz questions and activities to help reinforce what you've learned in this hour. You can check Appendix A for the answers (but don't peek!).

Quiz

1. Which view can be used to monitor the progress of your backups done through RMAN?

2. How can you determine the databases that the recovery catalog is aware of?

3. What does `resync catalog` do?

4. How can file copy operations be parallelized?

Exercises

1. Write a batch file to determine obsolete files and then delete these files.

2. Write an RMAN script to perform point-in-time recovery to 10 p.m. on April 1, 1999.

PART V

Tuning and Troubleshooting Databases

Hour

HOUR 17

Managing Contention

Contention can occur when multiple processes try to access the same resource simultaneously, resulting in some processes waiting for access to the database structures. This lesson focuses on identifying contention for the following structures:

Rollback segments	Redo log buffer latches
Shared servers	Database buffer cache LRU latches
Dispatchers	Library cache latches
Parallel servers	Free lists

This lesson also discusses several actions that you, as an Oracle DBA, can take to manage contention effectively.

Identifying Contention for Rollback Segments

Every time a transaction begins, it's assigned to a rollback segment. This occurs automatically or manually:

- *Automatic*—Oracle automatically assigns a transaction to a rollback segment when the first DDL or DML statement is issued.
- *Manual*—The SET TRANSACTION command with the USE ROLLBACK SEGMENT parameter can be used to manually specify a rollback segment to use for a transaction.

A transaction is assigned to a rollback segment for the duration of the transaction. By manually assigning a rollback segment, you have more control over the size of the assigned rollback segment. Queries are never assigned to rollback segments; therefore, rollback segments are more important for OLTP-type situations.

Two issues must be considered when you are deciding whether your rollback segment is large enough:

- Rollback segments are written in a circular manner. You should have large rollback segments so that the transactions do not wrap around.
- The rollback segment shouldn't wrap around and prevent the construction of a read-consistent view for long-running transactions.

One or more transactions can concurrently use rollback segments, so any delays caused by contention on rollback segments affect performance. Contention for rollback segments occurs when transactions request rollback segment buffers and those buffers are still busy with rollback information from previous transactions. This usually shows up as contention for undo headers because rollback segments hold transaction tables in their headers.

 More transactions per rollback segment cause more contention and use space more efficiently, whereas fewer transactions per rollback segment cause less contention and waste more space.

Interleaving the order of the rollback segments in the initialization parameter ROLLBACK_SEGMENTS can reduce contention for rollback segments. In other words, the first rollback segment is in one tablespace, the second is in another, and so on.

> You should have at least two rollback tablespaces on separate disks to achieve interleaving.

The following classes of blocks are tracked through the v$waitstat view for rollback information:

Block Class	Description
System undo header	Buffers containing header blocks of the SYSTEM rollback segment
System undo block	Buffers containing blocks of the SYSTEM rollback segment other than header blocks
Undo header	Buffers containing header blocks of the rollback segments other than the SYSTEM rollback segment
Undo block	Buffers containing blocks other than header blocks of the rollback segments, other than the SYSTEM rollback segment

Symptoms of contention for rollback segments include the following:

- Frequent occurrence of ORA-01555, Snapshot too old.
- Transaction table waits are much greater than zero.

The following queries can help you determine the number of data requests and waits for each class of block over a period of time.

- The first query:

```
SELECT SUM(value)  "DATA REQUESTS"
FROM V$SYSSTAT
WHERE name IN ('db block gets', 'consistent gets');

DATA REQUESTS
- - - - - - - - - - - - - - - - - - - - - -
        328951
```

- The second query:

```
SELECT class, count
FROM V$WAITSTAT
WHERE class LIKE '%undo%'
AND COUNT> 0;
```

17

```
CLASS                    COUNT
- - - - - - - - - - - - - - - -    - - - - - - - - - -
system undo header       6191
system undo block        102
undo header              1973
undo block               621
```

The output from these two queries indicates that the number of waits for the system undo header is (6191/328951)×100 = 1.88%, and the number of waits for the undo header is (1973/328951)×100 = 0.6%. This means contention for the system undo header because the number for waits is greater than 1% of the total number of requests.

Reducing Rollback Segment Contention

Rollback segment contention can be reduced by adding more rollback segments. These new rollback segments should be referenced in the init.ora ROLLBACK_SEGMENTS parameter and also brought online.

Depending on the anticipated number of concurrent transactions, you can use the following table to determine the number of rollback segments to create:

Number of Concurrent Transactions	Number of Rollback Segments
Fewer than 16 concurrent transactions	4
Concurrent transactions between 16 and 32	8
More than 32 concurrent transactions	Number of transactions divided by 4

Determine the rollback segment size from the activity during normal processing of the database, not from less frequently occurring large transactions.

To Do: Determine Whether the OPTIMAL Setting for Rollback Segments Is Proper

Choose the proper value of the OPTIMAL parameter for rollback segments to minimize the dynamic expansion and reduction of rollback space. Contention can also be minimized by manually assigning long-running queries and updating intensive transactions to large rollback segments.

▼ 1. From Server Manager, execute the following query:

```
Svrmgrl> SELECT substr(name, 1,20), extents, rssize, aveactive,
      2> aveshrink, extends, shrinks
      3> FROM v$rollname rn, v$rollstat rs
      4> WHERE rn.usn = rs.usn;
```

The output of this query might look like this:

```
substr(name, 1,20) extents rssize aveactive aveshrink extends shrinks
------------------ ------- ------ --------- --------- ------- -------
SYSTEM                 4    205291 0        0         0       0
RB1                    2    205197 0        0         0       0
RB2                    4    204982 0        0         0       0
```

2. If the average size is close to the size set for OPTIMAL, the parameter is set properly; otherwise, you must change its value. With v$rollstat, determine the
▲   optimal setting set for these rollback segments.

> Don't create more rollback segments than *N*/4, where *N* is the maximum number of concurrently active transactions for your instance.

The following guideline can help reduce contention for rollback segments:

- Set NEXT to INITIAL.
- Set MINEXTENTS to be greater than or equal to 20.
- Set OPTIMAL to INITIAL × MINEXTENTS.
- Determine the amount of undo generated by transactions as follows, and then set INITIAL to be greater than or equal to MAX(USED_UBLK):

```
SELECT MAX(USED_UBLK)
FROM v$transaction;
```

Managing Contention for Multi-Threaded Server Processes (MTS)

When using MTS, the main sources of contention can be the shared servers and the dispatchers used in the system.

Identifying Contention for Dispatcher Processes

Contention for dispatcher processes occurs when they're overworked. This can be identified by very busy dispatchers (v$dispatcher) or by a steady increase in the wait time for responses in the response queues of the dispatchers (v$queue).

17

The following query can be useful in determining the efficiency of dispatchers after running the application for a period of time:

```
Svrmgrl> SELECT name, owned, status, (busy /(busy + idle)) * 100
      2>        "% of time busy"
      3> FROM   v$dispatchers;

NAME     STATUS     % of time busy
-----    -------    --------------
D000     WAIT        .039876202
D001     CONNECT     .117402373
D002     WAIT        .004920195
```

This instance uses three dispatchers, of which two are in the WAIT state while D001 is servicing a client request. None of the dispatchers are very busy, so you can do with fewer dispatchers.

Reducing Contention for Dispatcher Processes

You can reduce dispatcher contention with one of the following methods:

- *Adding more dispatcher processes*—By using the ALTER SYSTEM command, you can add more dispatchers and consequently allow more dispatchers to share the workload.

- *Enable connection pooling*—This Net8 feature uses a time-out mechanism to temporarily release an idle transport connection while maintaining its network session. To enable connection pooling, use the optional attribute POOL (or POO) with the MTS_DISPATCHERS parameter. For example, in the init.ora file,

  MTS_DISPATCHERS = "(PROTOCOL=TCP) (DISPATCHERS=3) (POOL)"

  enables the connection pooling feature and starts 3 TCP dispatchers.

Identifying Contention for Shared Server Processes

A steady increase in the waiting time for requests in the request queue of shared servers (as shown by v$queue and v$shared_servers) indicates contention for shared servers. Use the following query on v$shared_servers to monitor shared servers:

```
Svrmgrl> SELECT name, status, requests, (busy /(busy + idle)) * 100
      2> "% of time busy"
      3> FROM v$shared_servers;

NAME     STATUS           REQUESTS      % of time busy
------   --------------   ----------    --------------
S000     WAIT(COMMON)     1122          .002876
S001     WAIT(COMMON)     0             .018973
S002     WAIT(ENQ)        1             99.739028
```

The output indicates that servers S000 and S001 are pretty much idle, whereas server S002 is very busy servicing a client request that might benefit from a dedicated server connection rather than MTS.

The average wait time for queued requests can be determined with the following query:

```
Svrmgrl> SELECT DECODE( totalq, 0, 'No Requests',  wait/totalq )
      2> "Average wait time per requests (hundredths of seconds) "
      3> FROM v$queue
      4> WHERE type = 'COMMON';

Average wait time per requests (hundredths of seconds)
------------------------------------------------------------
                    0.541084671
```

Reducing Contention for Shared Servers

When using MTS, the number of shared servers are automatically adjusted by Oracle to improve performance. You can get the maximum benefit, however, in a mixed environment that uses MTS connections as well as non-MTS (dedicated) connections. The success to this strategy is to identify (as shown in the preceding queries) those processes that will benefit from using a dedicated connection and those that would benefit from going through a shared server. In general, short transactions that don't tie up the server for a long time are suited for MTS connections, whereas those that require prolonged connections and perform intensive operations are suited for dedicated connections.

Managing Contention for Parallel Server Processes

Contention for parallel server processes can be identified by looking at the following statistics from the v$pq_sysstat dictionary view:

- SERVERS BUSY
- SERVERS IDLE
- SERVERS STARTED
- SERVERS SHUTDOWN

If these statistics indicate that servers are frequently being started and shut down, you should consider increasing the PARALLEL_MIN_SERVERS parameter.

```
Svrmgr> SELECT STATISTIC, VALUE
      2> FROM v$pq_sysstat
      3> WHERE statistic = "Servers Started "
      4> or statistic = "Servers Shutdown";
```

```
STATISTIC             VALUE
================      ======
Servers Started       59
Servers Shutdown      47
```

> PARALLEL_MAX_SERVERS should be set to the maximum number of concurrent
> parallel server processes that your machine can manage.
> PARALLEL_MIN_SERVERS should be set to the number of concurrent parallel
> operations multiplied by the average number of parallel server processes
> used by a parallel operation.

Use the following query to find out whether the servers are really busy:

```
Svrmgr> SELECT STATISTIC, VALUE
     2> FROM v$pq_sysstat
     3> WHERE statistic = "Servers Busy";
```

```
STATISTIC           VALUE
============        ======
Servers Busy        20
```

Compare the output of the preceding query with the value of PARALLEL_MIN_SERVERS. If
the number of busy servers is much less than the value of PARALLEL_MIN_SERVERS, you
should consider reducing this initialization parameter.

Identifying Latch Contention

Oracle uses various locking mechanisms internally to control access to various types of
structures:

- Latches
- Enqueues
- Distributed locks
- Global locks (used in parallel instance implementations)

In general, Oracle automatically uses these latches; you don't really have control over
which latch is used and when it's used. However, by using certain init.ora parameters,
you can optimize Oracle's latch usage and ultimately get better system performance.

NEW TERM   *Latches* provide a way to protect internal data structures by controlling access to
             these structures. If a process can't obtain a latch immediately, it "spins" while
waiting for the latch. Spinning processes can lead to additional CPU usage and system
slowdown and therefore should be minimized.

The following data dictionary views can be very helpful in identifying latch contention:

- v$latch
- v$latchholder
- v$latchname

Several valuable queries provide useful information about latches:

- This query provides the name of the latch by using the latch address:

```
Svrmgr> SELECT name
     2> FROM v$latchname ln, v$latch l
     3> WHERE l.addr = '&addr'
     4> AND l.latch# = ln.latch# ;
```

- This query provides system-wide latch statistics:

```
Svrmgr> SELECT ln.name, l.addr, l.gets, l.misses, l.sleeps,
     2> l.immediate_gets, l.immediate_misses, lh.pid
     3> FROM v$latch l , v$latchholder lh , v$latchname ln
     4> WHERE l.addr = lh.laddr (+)
     5> AND l.latch# = ln.latch#
     6> ORDER BY l.latch# ;
```

- This query provides statistics for any latch "Z":

```
svrmgr> SELECT ln.name, l.addr, l.gets, l.misses, l.sleeps,
     2> l.immediate_gets, l.immediate_misses, lh.pid
     3> FROM v$latch l , v$latchholder lh , v$latchname ln
     4> WHERE l.addr = lh.laddr (+)
     5> AND l.latch# = ln.latch#
     6> AND ln.name like '%Z%'
     7> ORDER BY l.latch# ;
```

The most important latches that you should be concerned about are the following:

Latch Number	Name	Latch Number	Name
0	Latch wait list	22	Sequence cache
1	Process allocation	23	Sequence cache entry
2	Session allocation	24	Row cache objects
3	Session switching	25	Cost function
4	Session idle bit	26	User lock
5	Messages	27	Global transaction mapping table
6	Enqueues	28	Global transaction
7	Trace latch	29	Shared pool

continues

Latch Number	Name	Latch Number	Name
8	Cache buffers chain	30	Library cache
9	Cache buffers LRU chain	31	Library cache pin
10	Cache buffer handles	32	Library cache load lock
11	Multiblock read objects	33	Virtual circuit buffers
12	Cache protection latch	34	Virtual circuit queues
13	System commit number	35	Virtual circuits
14	Archive control	36	Query server process
15	Redo allocation	37	Query server freelists
16	Redo copy	38	Error message lists
17	Instance latch	39	Process queue
18	Lock element parent latch	40	Process queue reference
19	DML lock allocation	41	Parallel query stats
20	Transaction allocation		
21	Undo global data		

Some of the most important latches from the preceding list are explained as follows:

Latch	Purpose	Reducing Contention
Cache buffers chains latch	Needed when the SGA is scanned for database cache buffers	Increase `DB_BLOCK_BUFFERS`
Cache buffers LRU chain latch	Needed when the LRU chain containing all the dirty blocks in the buffer cache is scanned	Increase parameters `DB_BLOCK_BUFFERS` and `DB_BLOCK_WRITE_BATCH`
Row cache objects latch	Needed when the cached data dictionary values are being accessed	Increase the `SHARED_POOL_SIZE`

Managing Contention for the Redo Log Buffer

A bottleneck for redo buffers can affect all system processes because redo information must be written before a transaction completes. Managing contention of the redo log buffers and the redo log buffer latches should therefore be a very high priority.

Identifying Contention for Space in a Redo Log Buffer

REDO BUFFER ALLOCATION RETRIES in the v$sysstat view indicates the number of times a user process waits for space in the redo log buffer. Usually, this indicates that the LGWR process isn't fast enough to write entries from the redo log buffer to the redo log file.

To determine contention for space in the redo log buffer, use this query:

```
Svrmgr> SELECT name, value
     2> FROM V$SYSSTAT
     3> WHERE name = 'redo buffer allocation retries';
```

Consistently increasing output from this query indicates contention.

Reducing Contention for Space in a Redo Log Buffer

You can reduce contention for space in a redo log buffer by using several strategies, all of which provide some help to the LGWR process:

- Increase the LOG_BUFFER parameter in the init.ora file to increase the size of the redo log buffer.
- Speed up the checkpointing process by using the checkpoint process and distributing files properly on the disk in order to minimize disk contention.
- Speed up the archiving process by increasing the number of redo log groups.

Identifying Contention for Redo Log Buffer Latches

A process can request a latch in one of two ways:

- *Willing to wait*—The process waits for the requested latch if it's unavailable and requests it again later. The process remains in the wait-request cycle until the latch becomes available.
- *Immediate*—The process doesn't wait and continues processing if the requested latch is unavailable.

17

The v$latch table shows values accumulated since instance startup. Willing-to-wait requests are shown by the following v$latch columns:

GETS	Number of successful willing-to-wait requests for a latch
MISSES	Number of unsuccessful, initial willing-to-wait requests for a latch
SLEEPS	Number of times a process waited and requested a latch after an initial request

Immediate requests are shown by the following v$latch columns:

IMMEDIATE GETS	Number of successful immediate requests for a latch
IMMEDIATE MISSES	Number of unsuccessful immediate requests for a latch

To monitor contention of redo allocation and the redo copy latch, use the following query:

```
Svrmgr> SELECT ln.name, gets, misses, immediate_gets,
    2> immediate_misses
    3> FROM V$LATCH l, V$LATCHNAME ln
    4> WHERE ln.name IN (' redo allocation', 'redo copy')
    5> AND ln.latch# = l.latch#;
```

The output of this query might look like this:

```
NAME                GETS   MISSES   IMMEDIATE_GETS    IMMEDIATE_MISSES
----------------    -----  -------  ----------------  ----------------
redo alloc...       11098  129      14                0
redo copy           21     0        1293              2
```

If either of the following is true for a latch, it indicates contention:

- The ratio of MISSES to GETS exceeds 1%.
- The ratio of IMMEDIATE_MISSES to the sum of IMMEDIATE_MISSES and IMMEDIATE_GETS exceeds 1%.

For the redo allocation latch shown in the preceding output:

- The ratio of MISSES to GETS is 129/11098, or 1.16%.
- The ratio of IMMEDIATE_MISSES to the sum of IMMEDIATE_MISSES and IMMEDIATE_GETS is 0.

For the redo copy latch:

- The ratio of MISSES to GETS is 0.
- The ratio of IMMEDIATE_MISSES to the sum of IMMEDIATE_MISSES and IMMEDIATE_GETS is 2/(2+1293), which is less than 1%.

Therefore, you have contention for the redo allocation latch.

Identifying Contention for Redo Allocation Latches

Only one redo allocation latch controls the allocation of space for redo entries in the redo log buffer. This redo allocation latch must be obtained before an Oracle process can allocate space in the redo log buffer.

The LOG_SMALL_ENTRY_MAX_SIZE parameter determines the number and size of redo entries copied on the redo allocation latch. Decreasing the value of LOG_SMALL_ENTRY_MAX_SIZE can minimize the copying on the redo allocation latch; effectively, each process holds it for a small amount of time. The end result is that contention for this latch is minimized.

Identifying and Reducing Contention for Redo Copy Latches

A user process obtains the redo copy latch before the redo allocation latch. The redo allocation latch is released as soon as space is allocated. However, the copy is then performed under the redo copy latch, which is then released. As a result, the redo copy latch is held for a longer time. On multiple CPUs, the LOG_SIMULTANEOUS_COPIES parameter determines the number of redo copy latches.

Contention for redo copy latches can be reduced by increasing the value of LOG_SIMUL-TANEOUS_COPIES, because having multiple redo copy latches allows multiple processes to concurrently write the redo entries. The default value of this parameter is the number of CPUs available to the instance; the maximum value is twice the number of CPUs.

You can also reduce contention for redo copy latches by prebuilding the redo entry before requesting the latch. You can set the LOG_ENTRY_PREBUILD_THRESHOLD parameter (default value 0) to achieve this result. This parameter causes the prebuilding of redo entries that are smaller than this parameter.

Identifying Contention for the LRU Latch

The least recently used (LRU) latch protects the least recently used list of cache buffers. Before Oracle can move around buffers on this list, it needs the appropriate LRU latch. Several situations can lead to contention of LRU latches:

- Using excessive cache-based sorts when SORT_DIRECT_WRITES is set to FALSE
- Generating extended statistics by using DB_BLOCK_LRU_STATISTICS and DB_BLOCK_LRU_EXTENDED_STATISTICS

Contention for the LRU latch can be identified by querying v$latch, v$session_event, and v$system_event.

Reducing Contention for the LRU Latch

Each LRU latch controls a set of buffers. The maximum LRU latch on the system is specified by the initialization parameter DB_BLOCK_LRU_LATCHES, the value of which can be determined by following these guidelines:

- DB_BLOCK_LRU_LATCHES can range from 1 to twice the number of CPUs in the system.
- There should be at least 50 buffers in a set controlled by an LRU latch.
- Only one LRU latch is used by Oracle in the single-process mode.

Setting SORT_DIRECT_WRITES to TRUE and SORT_WRITE_BUFFER_SIZE can also help avoid cache-based sorts by allocating additional buffers in memory.

Increasing DB_BLOCK_BUFFERS can also minimize LRU latch contention.

For SMP machines, the number of LRU latches is automatically set to half the number of CPUs on the system.

The design of your applications can have a significant influence on LRU contention depending on how the application accesses the tables and indexes.

Identifying Contention for Library Cache Latches

The three types of library cache latches control access to shared library cache entries:

- *Library cache latch*—This highest latch level is needed before getting a lock on a handle.

- *Pin latch*—This latch is needed by a process before pinning a heap. (*Pinning a heap* refers to pinning variables in memory while the program is running.)

- *Load-lock latch*—This latch is needed to load a library cache entry.

To identify contention for a library cache latch, use the following query from Server Manager:

```
Svrmgr> SELECT count(*) number_of_waiters
    2> FROM v$session_wait sw, v$latch l
    3> WHERE sw.wait_time = 0
    4> AND sw.event = 'latch free'
    5> AND sw.p2 = l.latch#
    6> AND l.name like 'library%';
```

A large number of waits in the output of the preceding query indicates that you have contention.

Reducing Library Cache Latch Contention

To minimize contention for library cache latches, follow these guidelines:

- Minimize the fragmentation of the shared pool.

- Increase the usage of shared SQL statements, and thereby decrease the reloads.

- Identify the SQL statements that are receiving many parse calls with the following query:

```
Svrmgr> SELECT sql_text, parse_calls, executions
    2> FROM v$sqlarea
    3> WHERE parse_calls > 100
    4> AND executions < 2*parse_calls;
```

Then, try to use sharable SQL wherever possible.

- Set CURSOR_SPACE_FOR_TIME to TRUE to keep shared SQL areas pinned in the shared pool. They're not aged out of the pool as long as an open cursor references them. The end result is faster execution.

17

CURSOR_SPACE_FOR_TIME should be set to TRUE only if the shared pool is large enough to hold all the cursors; otherwise, it can result in contention.

- Use fully qualified table names.

Identifying Free List Contention

NEW TERM Oracle maintains certain information in memory to allow instantaneous access to information on disk. During table creation, you can specify how much information is to be kept in memory for the purpose of tracking blocks available for the creation of new records. This is referred to as the *free list* for that table.

To Do: Create a Table with 10 Free Lists

The following query executed from Server Manager creates such a table. Make sure you don't use SYSTEM tablespace as the default tablespace for the users:

```
Svrmgr> create table employees ( empid number,
    2> title varchar2(20),
    3> salary number)
    4> freelist 12;
```

Free list contention is generally indicated by excessive disk I/O for block ID requests while creating new rows. It shows up as contention for free data blocks in the buffer cache.

The following queries use v$waitstat and v$sysstat to determine how much percentage of the total requests was actually waiting for free blocks:

- The first query:

```
Svrmgrl> SELECT class,count
    2> FROM V$WAITSTAT
    3> WHERE class = 'free list';
```

The output of this query might look like this:

```
CLASS          COUNT
------------- -----------
free list      51
```

- The second query:

```
Svrmgrl> SELECT name, value
    2> FROM v$sysstat
    3> WHERE name in ('db block gets', 'consistent gets');
```

The output of this query might look like this:

```
NAME                      VALUE
------------------------  ----------
db block gets             13097
consistent gets           12765
```

In the preceding example:

```
free list wait events
    = ( (free list count) / (db block gets + consistent gets)) * 100
    = (51/ (13097 + 12765 ) * 100
    = 0.197%
```

Use the following steps to identify free list contention:

1. Query v$waitstat for contention on DATA BLOCKS and v$system_event to determine BUFFER BUSY WAITS. A high value for BUFFER BUSY WAITS indicates contention.

2. By using v$session_wait, determine the FILE, BLOCK, and ID for each BUFFER BUSY WAIT.

3. By using the following query, determine the segment_name and segment_type for the objects and free lists with BUFFER BUSY WAITS:

```
Svrmgrl> SELECT segment_name "segment" , segment_type "type"
    2> FROM dba_extents
    3> WHERE FILE_ID = file
    4> AND BLOCK BETWEEN block_id and block_id + blocks;
```

4. By using the following query, determine the free lists having contention:

```
Svrmgrl> SELECT FREELISTS
    2> FROM DBA_SEGMENTS
    3> WHERE SEGMENT_NAME = segment
    4> AND SEGMENT_TYPE = type;
```

Reducing Contention for Free Lists

Re-creating the table with a larger value of the FREELISTS storage parameter should be enough to reduce free list contention. This can be done using several alternatives:

> To increase performance of INSERT operations, make the number of free lists at least equal to the number of concurrent inserts on the table.

Alternative 1: Using Export/Import

Export/Import can be used to change the FREELISTS associated with a table:

1. Export the table with the grants and indexes.
2. Drop the table.
3. Re-create the table by using the desired value for FREELISTS storage parameter.
4. Import the table with the option IGNORE=y. This will use the new storage settings for the table.

Alternative 2: Smoke and Mirrors

The "smoke-and-mirror" technique demonstrated here is a dynamic method of changing FREELISTS associated with a table:

1. Create a new table with the desired value for FREELISTS but with the same structure as the old table.
2. Select data from the old table into the new table.
3. Drop the old table.
4. Rename the new table.

Summary

Overall system performance depends on tuning the hardware, Oracle server, operating system, application, and network. One of the most important tasks involved in tuning the performance of Oracle on Windows NT is effectively managing contention for various system resources. This lesson focuses on the top sources of contention. Hour 18 concentrates on tuning Windows NT for Oracle8i, and Hour 19 involves tuning the database for different configurations, such as DSS and OLTP. For hardware tuning, the best source is the documentation provided by your hardware vendor. For application tuning, refer to the Oracle Server Application Developer's Guide.

Q&A

Q When should I gather the statistics to determine the contention occurring in my system?

A You should gather statistics for contention generally at times of normal loads. During normal operations, determine what causes performance degradation. Also, give enough time for the operations to proceed so that the memory structures have been used properly.

Q **Is any tool available that provides all the relevant contention sources in one file rather than me having to execute multiple queries?**

A Hour 20, "Diagnosing Problems," discusses `utlbstat/utlestat` scripts, which are provided by Oracle for this purpose. These scripts generate a report, which provides valuable information you can use for analyzing database contention. Keep in mind, however, that most contention occurs because of improperly written applications.

Workshop

The Workshop contains quiz questions and activities to help reinforce what you've learned in this hour.

17

Quiz

1. What are the most common sources of contention when using Oracle8i on Windows NT?

2. How is a latch different from a lock?

3. In a multi-threaded server environment, what can you control—shared servers, dispatchers, or both?

Exercises

1. Determine whether the `FREELISTS` setting of your tables is set properly.

2. Write a Server Manager query to determine whether you will benefit by using a multi-threaded server in addition to your current dedicated connections.

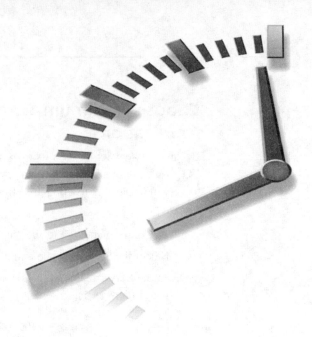

Hour 18

Tuning Windows NT for Oracle8i

This lesson focuses on tuning Windows NT and on the various strategies that can effectively and quickly improve the overall system performance. Specifically, this lesson covers

- Basic Windows NT tuning for improving Oracle8i performance
- Tuning the process priority and scheduling
- Tuning the Registry parameters
- Tuning the file system

Improving Oracle8i Performance with Basic Windows NT Tuning

You can follow several basic guidelines to tune Windows NT, knowing that the particular machine is intended for use as an Oracle database server.

Choose Maximum Throughput for Network Applications

Because Oracle Server uses its own memory management for caching file and network I/O, you can optimize server memory by changing the relationship of memory allocated to network connections compared to that allocated to applications. This can be done as follows:

1. In Control Panel, go to the Network tool's Services page.
2. Select the Server service and click Properties.
3. In the Server dialog box, select Maximize Throughput for Network Applications (see Figure 18.1).

FIGURE **18.1**

Optimize performance by allocating more memory to network applications.

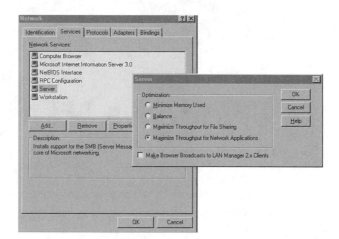

No Performance Boost for Foreground Applications

The default choice of throughput setting (for Windows NT Server) devotes much memory for file system buffers, which is unnecessary because you will use the system as a database server, not as a file server. The performance boost can be set as follows:

1. In Control Panel's System tool, go to the Performance page.
2. Choose None for the performance boost for foreground applications (see Figure 18.2).

FIGURE 18.2

Don't set performance boost for foreground applications.

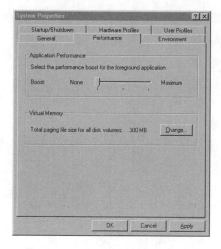

Disable Unneeded Services

The services that can be disabled include the following (see Figures 18.3 and 18.4):

- License Logging Service
- Plug and Play
- Remote Access AutoDial Manager
- Remote Access Connection Manager
- Remote Access Server
- Telephony Service

18

FIGURE 18.3

Disable the services you don't need.

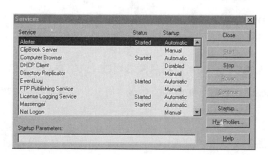

FIGURE 18.4

Disable the unneces-sary services by choosing the Disabled option.

Several services shouldn't be disabled, including the following:

- Alerter
- Browser
- EventLog
- Messenger
- OracleService*XXXX* (where *XXXX* is an instance name)
- OracleTNSListener
- Server
- Spooler
- Workstation

Use One Oracle8 Instance per System

Ideally, you should use only one instance of Oracle8i per system. This not only simplifies administration but also helps trouble-shooting performance problems.

Limit Local Users to DBAs and SysAdmins

Limiting local access to only administrators will help keep changes to the system under check and also improve security.

Disable Screen Savers

Screen savers take up valuable system resources, and their use should be minimized on the server. Especially avoid OpenGL versions of screen savers.

Don't Use the Machine for Other Purposes

To reduce contention for system resources, it's important to use a dedicated machine for your database server. Specifically, the system shouldn't also be used as

- Network file server
- Primary or backup domain controller
- Print server
- Router
- Bridge
- Remote access server
- Active workstation for desktop processing

Understand that these configurations would work with Oracle on the same machine and that this recommendation is only for performance reasons.

Apply Microsoft's Latest Service Pack

Microsoft is committed to releasing quarterly OS patches, called *service packs*. These service packs are a cumulative collection of bug fixes and product enhancements to the base Windows NT release. The service packs are free and can be downloaded from Microsoft's Web site at www.microsoft.com.

18

Using the Windows NT Resource Kit for Tuning

The Windows NT Resource Kit has a wealth of information and commands you can use to manage an Oracle database on Windows NT. The following commands help tune performance (each can be invoked from the command prompt). Before using these commands, you must install the Resource Kit on the system.

- Process Viewer (pviewer.exe) summarizes resource usage by an individual process (see Figure 18.5). Also, you can click the Memory Detail button to see a detailed description of memory usage.

FIGURE 18.5

Process Viewer can be used to determine the resource utilization per process.

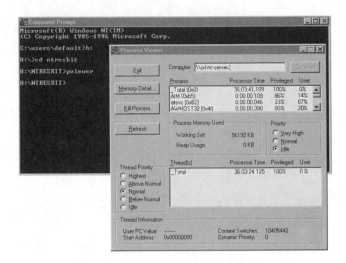

• Process Explode (`pview.exe`) provides information similar to `pviewer.exe`, except that it's more detailed (see Figure 18.6).

FIGURE 18.6

Process Explode can be used to obtain detailed process information.

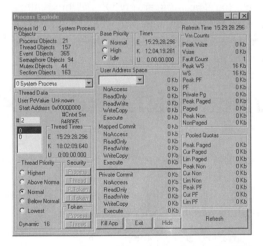

• QuickSlice (`qslice.exe`) is one of the most useful tools you can use to obtain a quick system analysis (see Figure 18.7). It has a lower overhead compared with Performance Monitor. It also uses color coding to show the time spent in kernel mode and the time spent in user mode.

FIGURE **18.7**

QuickSlice can be used to obtain a quick overview of system utilization.

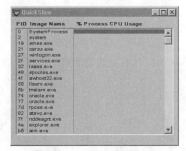

- Process Stat (`pstat.exe`) provides process statistics on several screens. The first screen provides process information (see Figure 18.8), and later screens provide details about the threads.

FIGURE **18.8**

Process Stat can display process and thread information.

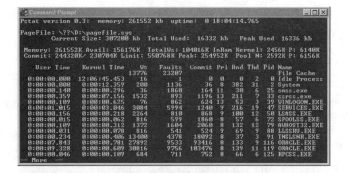

18

- Task List (`tlist.exe`) provides details about the various tasks going on in the system (see Figure 18.9). A very useful feature of this tool is its capability to show relationships between the processes in terms of which process was called by a certain process. To obtain details of a process and its threads, provide a process ID or process name:

```
c:> tlist oracle80
```

FIGURE **18.9**

Task List displays information about all the tasks in the system.

- The `drivers` command (`drivers.exe`) shows detailed information about the various drivers in use (see Figure 18.10).

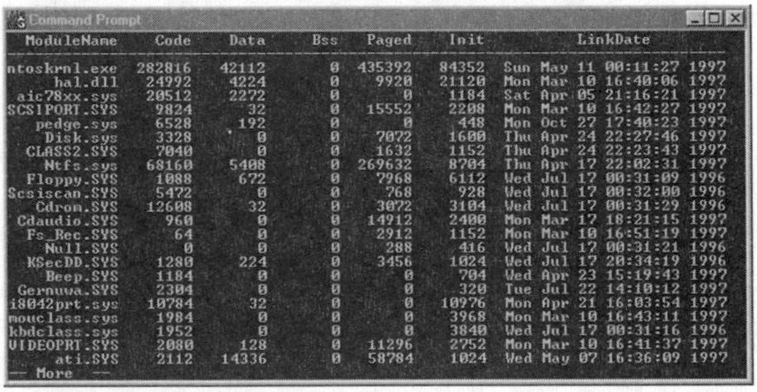

```
Command Prompt
  ModuleName      Code      Data        Bss    Paged      Init                LinkDate
------------------------------------------------------------------------------------------
ntoskrnl.exe    282816     42112          0   435392     84352   Sun May 11 00:11:27 1997
     hal.dll     24992      4224          0     9920     21120   Mon Mar 10 16:40:06 1997
 aic78xx.sys     20512      2272          0        0      1184   Sat Apr 05 21:16:21 1997
SCSIPORT.SYS      9824        32          0    15552      2208   Mon Mar 10 16:42:27 1997
   pedge.sys      6528       192          0        0       448   Mon Oct 27 17:40:23 1997
    Disk.sys      3328         0          0     7072      1600   Thu Apr 24 22:27:46 1997
  CLASS2.SYS      7040         0          0     1632      1152   Thu Apr 24 22:23:43 1997
    Ntfs.sys     68160      5408          0   269632      8704   Thu Apr 17 22:02:31 1997
  Floppy.SYS      1088       672          0     7968      6112   Wed Jul 17 00:31:09 1996
Scsiscan.SYS      5472         0          0      768       928   Wed Jul 17 00:32:00 1996
   Cdrom.SYS     12608        32          0     3072      3104   Wed Jul 17 00:31:29 1996
 Cdaudio.SYS       960         0          0    14912      2400   Mon Mar 17 18:21:15 1997
  Fs_Rec.SYS        64         0          0     2912      1152   Mon Mar 10 16:51:19 1997
    Null.SYS         0         0          0      288       416   Wed Jul 17 00:31:21 1996
  KSecDD.SYS      1280       224          0     3456      1024   Wed Jul 17 20:34:19 1996
    Beep.SYS      1184         0          0        0       704   Wed Apr 23 15:19:43 1997
 Gernuwa.SYS      2304         0          0        0       320   Tue Jul 22 14:10:12 1997
i8042prt.sys     10784        32          0        0     10976   Mon Apr 21 16:03:54 1997
mouclass.sys      1984         0          0        0      3968   Mon Mar 10 16:43:11 1997
kbdclass.sys      1952         0          0        0      3840   Wed Jul 17 00:31:16 1996
VIDEOPRT.SYS      2080       128          0    11296      2752   Mon Mar 10 16:41:37 1997
     ati.SYS      2112     14336          0    58784      1024   Wed May 07 16:36:09 1997
-- More --
```

FIGURE 18.10

The `drivers` command shows information about the various drivers.

- The Process User List (`pulist.exe`) obtains information about which user is running a particular process (see Figure 18.11).

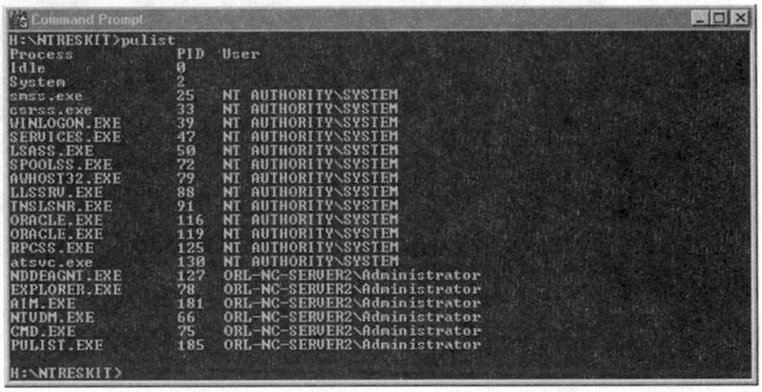

```
Command Prompt
H:\NTRESKIT>pulist
Process              PID  User
Idle                 0
System               2
smss.exe             25   NT AUTHORITY\SYSTEM
csrss.exe            33   NT AUTHORITY\SYSTEM
WINLOGON.EXE         39   NT AUTHORITY\SYSTEM
SERVICES.EXE         47   NT AUTHORITY\SYSTEM
LSASS.EXE            50   NT AUTHORITY\SYSTEM
SPOOLSS.EXE          72   NT AUTHORITY\SYSTEM
AVHOST32.EXE         79   NT AUTHORITY\SYSTEM
LLSSRV.EXE           88   NT AUTHORITY\SYSTEM
TNSLSNR.EXE          91   NT AUTHORITY\SYSTEM
ORACLE.EXE           116  NT AUTHORITY\SYSTEM
ORACLE.EXE           119  NT AUTHORITY\SYSTEM
RPCSS.EXE            125  NT AUTHORITY\SYSTEM
atsvc.exe            130  NT AUTHORITY\SYSTEM
NDDEAGNT.EXE         127  ORL-NC-SERVER2\Administrator
EXPLORER.EXE         78   ORL-NC-SERVER2\Administrator
AIM.EXE              181  ORL-NC-SERVER2\Administrator
NTVDM.EXE            66   ORL-NC-SERVER2\Administrator
CMD.EXE              75   ORL-NC-SERVER2\Administrator
PULIST.EXE           185  ORL-NC-SERVER2\Administrator

H:\NTRESKIT>
```

FIGURE 18.11

Process User List can be used to associate processes with users.

- With the Page Fault Monitor (`pfmon.exe`), you can obtain detailed analysis of the paging activity of a particular process (see Figure 18.12). It can be very useful to identify the process that might be responsible for heavy paging occurring on the system. You can also use various flags (see Figure 18.13) to configure the display of the analysis.

FIGURE 18.12

PFMON can be used to monitor paging activity.

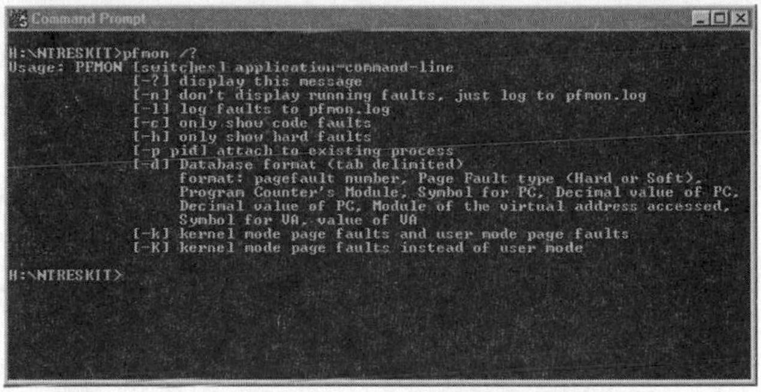

FIGURE 18.13

Using /? as a flag after the pfmon command displays the various switches available.

- Executable Type (`exetype.exe`) displays image information. You can use it to find out whether an image was originally written for Windows NT (32-bit) or Windows 3.11/DOS (16-bit).

Managing System Resources

Four major system resources can contribute to contention and performance problems. You can follow some basic guidelines to monitor them and take some action to eliminate the problems due to these resources.

System Memory

Insufficient memory is the most common cause of performance problems when running Oracle on Windows NT. Windows NT uses virtual memory to provide more memory to applications than is physically available. For I/O purposes, a page is the smallest amount of memory that Windows NT can work with.

The default page size for Intel-based Windows NT systems is 4KB; for Alpha-based Windows NT systems, it's 8KB.

By using the Windows NT Performance Monitor, you can monitor page-outs (which occur when inactive pages are moved out of memory to the paging file on disk) and page-ins (which occur when pages needed by an application are moved from the paging file into memory). Your goal should be to minimize these page faults. Table 18.1 shows other Performance Monitor counters you can use while tuning disk I/O.

TABLE 18.1 TUNING DISK I/O WITH PERFORMANCE MONITOR

Object	Counter	Symptom	Action
Memory	Pages/sec	Consistently > 10	Add more memory.
Memory	Available bytes	< 4MB	Increase page file, or add more memory.
Paging file	%Usage	> 90%	Add more memory.

By default, Performance Monitor doesn't show disk performance. To activate the disk counters in Performance Monitor, you have to execute `diskperf -y` from the command prompt and reboot the machine. Similarly, the disk counters can be deactivated by executing `diskperf -n` and rebooting the machine.

Paging is quite common unless you have a very large amount of memory. When sizing the SGA, consider the memory used by all other non-Oracle components, as well as Windows NT. Setting the SGA size very large can lead to excessive paging.

Physical memory should be greater than the sum of all memory used by Windows NT, Oracle, and non-Oracle components.

Set the initialization parameter PRE_PAGE_SGA to TRUE. That way, Windows NT keeps the pages that constitute the SGA in memory as much as possible and avoids writing them to the paging file unless absolutely necessary.

NEW TERM You should understand several important Windows NT memory management terms:

- *Working set* is the total number of pages a program requires in physical memory when it's running.
- *Soft page fault* occurs when the program requires a page found elsewhere in memory.
- *Hard page fault* occurs when the required page is obtained from the disk.

Hard page faults cause the most performance problems, but your goal should be to minimize page faults of both types—hard and soft.

To detect hard page faults, use Performance Monitor and compare the Counters Memory: Page Faults/Sec and Memory: Pages Input/Second simultaneously. More than five hard page faults per second consistently indicates a memory bottleneck.

18

Use Task Manager to identify the particular process that's causing the page faults. The Task Manager also shows the resource utilization as seen in Figure 18.14.

FIGURE 18.14

Task Manager can be used to obtain information about resources used by processes.

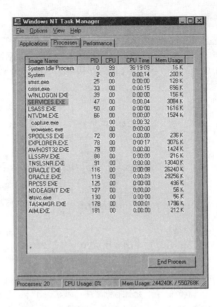

Hard page faults can be minimized by following these guidelines:

- Physical memory should be large enough to contain the entire SGA.
- Unnecessary services should be stopped.
- Unused network protocols should be removed.
- Add more memory.

Paging can reduce performance and usually occurs because of insufficient memory. Windows NT's system cache has buffers for disk I/O. On a 64MB system, approximately 8MB is allocated to the system cache. Because Oracle Server uses it own buffering scheme and bypasses the system cache, you can increase performance by setting the LargeSystemCache parameter in \HKEY_LOCAL_MACHINE\Control\SessionManager\MemoryManagement to zero.

Consider spreading the page file space across multiple disk drives. Windows NT allows a maximum of 16 page files and automatically spreads paging I/O across all page files.

To Do: Set the Page File to Four Times the Amount of Available RAM

Several people believe that having a very large page file is a problem. In my experience, however, a large page file isn't really a problem. Having said that, not having enough free space in the page file when the system needs it *is* a problem. A larger page file essentially means a slightly higher cost, but disks are cheap, and the performance benefit gained is worth the extra cost. I would also caution against a very large page file, however, because it implies overcommitting and can lead to excessive paging if the system isn't sized properly.

I recommend a page file that's 4–6 times the amount of physical RAM in the system. For example, if your system has 1,024MB of RAM, you should have a 4GB page file. Follow these steps to set the page file properly:

1. Choose Start, Administrative Tools, Windows NT Diagnostics.

2. On the Memory page, note the amount of physical RAM on the system. It is the field labeled Physical Memory...Total and is in units of kilobytes.

3. From Control Panel, double-click the System icon.

4. On the Performance page, choose the Change button in the Virtual Memory group.

5. Highlight the drive on which you want to place the paging file (see Figure 18.15). Keep in mind that you should try to spread the paging I/O across disks.

18

FIGURE 18.15

Choose the drive on which to place the paging file.

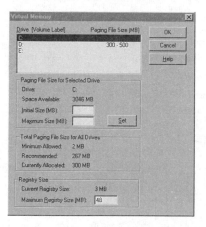

6. For the Initial Size, specify a value that's three times the physical RAM. This value is specified in units of megabytes.

▼

7. For the Maximum Size, specify a value that's four times the physical RAM.

> The total paging file size on all drives shouldn't be more than six times the physical RAM on the system.

8. Restart the computer for the changes to become effective and verify the size of the paging file (see Figure 18.16).

FIGURE 18.16

Determine the size of the paging file.

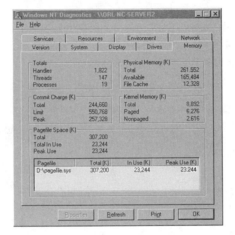

CPU

One of the most important goals for tuning system performance is to make sure that the system is CPU bound. CPU contention can occur when you run several applications concurrently. A processor's clock speed determines the maximum number of instructions that can execute per second. Several symptoms indicate that you have CPU contention in the system:

- In a multiprocessor system, if the %processor_time (as seen through Performance Monitor) is consistently greater than 80%, the CPU is bottlenecked. If the application is CPU bound and the %USER_TIME is very high, the application design should be revisited.

- The Performance Monitor Counters Processor: Interrupts/Sec and System: Processor Queue Length indicate whether the processor is spending too much time servicing interrupts or whether too many threads are waiting for the processor, respectively.

- Use the Process/%Processor time counter to identify the process using the most CPU.
- A CPU bottleneck is indicated if Processor/%Processor time or System/%total processor time is constantly more than 80%.

Currently, using more than four CPUs is a waste on Windows NT systems because too many CPUs can cause performance degradation due to the overhead for load balancing. You should determine whether you would benefit by using more CPUs or by using a faster CPU. If your system were CPU bound, you would benefit by using a faster CPU, as well as more CPUs. Performance of parallel operations can also be improved by using more CPUs.

Disk I/O

Contention for I/O results from simultaneous read/write to disk by multiple users. Try to ensure that the disk I/O is spread evenly across disks and you don't have "hot" disks. Also try to distribute the I/Os across controllers. The following query can determine whether I/O is spread evenly across multiple disk drives:

```
SELECT NAME, PHYRDS, PHYWRTS, PHYRDS + PHYWRTS "TOTAL I/O"
FROM V$DATAFILE DF, V$FILESTAT FS
WHERE FS.FILE# = DF.FILE#;
```

The output of this query might look like this:

```
NAME                              PHYRDS   PHYWRTS   TOTAL I/O
-------------------------------   -------  --------  ---------
C:\ORANT\DATABASE\SYS1ORCL.ORA    2239     201       2440
C:\ORANT\DATABASE\USR1ORCL.ORA    62909    753       63662
C:\ORANT\DATABASE\RBS1ORCL.ORA    53       21        74
```

As the output shows, the USR1ORCL.ORA file is heavily used, and a more balanced I/O can be obtained by moving it to a different disk.

Follow these simple suggestions to minimize I/O problems:

- Make sure that memory isn't a bottleneck anymore.
- Keep Oracle online redo logs on separate, nonstriped disks away from datafiles.
- Place archived redo logs on striped disks.
- Use as many disk drives and disk controllers as possible, and distribute the I/O across multiple spindles.
- Upgrade the hardware from IDE disks to SCSI and from SCSI to fast/wide SCSI.
- Files that perform sequential I/O should be separated from randomly accessed files.

18

Network

Network bandwidth may be exceeded, resulting in collisions. In addition to the strategies discussed earlier in "Improving Oracle8i Performance with Basic Windows NT Tuning," one way in which you can improve network performance is to rearrange the protocol bindings so that the protocols list is in decreasing order of protocol usage. Removing protocols and services not used by Oracle frees up memory and CPU. Refer to documentation that discusses the tuning of the NIC for Windows NT.

Hour 17, "Managing Contention," discusses several strategies used to identify and reduce contention for rollback segments, shared servers, dispatchers, parallel servers, redo log buffer latches, database buffer cache LRU latches, library cache latches, and free lists. Use those strategies to eliminate the performance problems arising from contention for these structures.

Activities of various Oracle threads, including DBWR, LGWR, PMON, and SMON, can be monitored through Performance Monitor. Use the following query to identify the Oracle threads:

```
SELECT NAME, SPID
FROM V$BGPROCESS, V$PROCESS
WHERE PADDR = ADDR;
```

The result might look something like this:

```
NAME            SPID
=========       ========
PMON            000C2
DBWR            0008A
LGWR            000B5
 . . .
```

The SPID values can be converted to their decimal equivalents. Then, you can identify the threads in Performance Monitor. The decimal SPID value matches the LAST indicator when the particular thread ID is highlighted.

Tuning Processes and Thread Priority

Oracle allows the base priority for its threads to be set by using the ORACLE_PRIORITY Registry parameter.

Don't change ORACLE_PRIORITY from its default! Setting ORACLE_PRIORITY too high can result in an unstable system because lower-priority threads might not get enough CPU.

The correct setting for ORACLE_PRIORITY is CLASS:normal;DEF:normal. The lowest priority at which any of a process's threads will run is referred to as its *base priority*. To ensure that no thread can dominate the CPU, Windows NT schedules threads by priority and dynamically adjusts the thread priorities in a range associated with the base priority of its process. When a thread runs, it runs until completion or until its time expires, at which point a context switch occurs and a new thread is scheduled. When a context switch occurs, a thread's context (registers, user mode and kernel mode stacks, and private storage area) is saved, and a new thread's context is loaded so that the new thread can execute.

By default, Oracle and its background threads run in the normal-priority class, which ranges from 1 to 15. On the other hand, real-time priority ranges from 16 to 31.

Windows NT uses the following guidelines to change thread priorities:

- A priority boost is given to threads waiting for input.
- A priority boost is given to threads that complete a voluntary wait.
- Threads receive a priority boost periodically.
- Priority is reduced for compute-bound threads.

The base priority of a process can be changed by using Windows NT's Task Manager. Select the process, and then right-click to set the base priority.

Tuning the Windows NT Registry

Changes to Registry parameters can disable your system if they aren't done properly. Changing Registry parameters also might have implications, such as performance degradation, on other applications running in the system, even if you use the proper settings.

For the purpose of running Oracle on Windows NT, the developers at Oracle didn't introduce new initialization parameters; instead, they put the Windows NT–specific parameters in the Registry. You've already seen that the Registry is a very important structure that stores system configuration information. You can use some specific Registry parameters to your benefit while running Oracle8i on that system.

Oracle has its own caching mechanism, so the system cache of Windows NT can be bypassed with the following settings in `HKEY_LOCAL_MACHINE\ SYSTEM\CurrentControlSet\Control\SessionManager\Memory Management\ LargeSystemCache` (see Figure 18.17):

```
NT Workstation Default = 0
NT Server Default =1
Optimal Setting =0
```

FIGURE 18.17

Set the value of the LargeSystemCache for optimal performance.

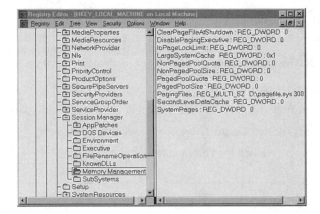

To Do: Set `LargeSystemCache` in the Registry to 0

Setting `LargeSystemCache` can have an impact on the performance of the system. The following shows how you can set it to an optimal value:

1. From the command line, run the Registry Editor:

   `C:> regedt32`

2. In the editor, go to `\HKEY_LOCAL_MACHINE\SYSTEM\CurrentControlSet\Control\SessionManager\ Memory Management\`. Double-click `LargeSystemCache` on the right, and enter `0` for that parameter.

3. Go to `HKEY_LOCAL_MACHINE\SYSTEM\CurrentControlSet\Services\LanmanServer\ Parameters\Size`. Set `Workstation Default` to 1, `Server Default` to 3, and `Optimal Setting` to 3.

> The parameters in steps 2 and 3 should be set to their optimal value when running Oracle8 on Windows NT. The settings define the working sets to a higher priority setting than Windows NT's disk cache.

4. In `HKEY_LOCAL_MACHINE\SYSTEM\CurrentControlSet\Services\LanmanServer\Parameters`, you can set several parameters that affect the working set size and, effectively, the page faults that occur. Table 18.2 describes these parameters.

TABLE 18.2   REGISTRY PARAMETERS AFFECTING THE WORKING SET

Parameter (Default)	Description
`InitConnTable` (default is 16)	Initial number of connection table entries
`InitWorkItems` (default is 255)	Initial number of work item buffers the server uses
`MinFreeWorkItems` (default is 8)	Minimum number of receive buffers the server requires before it can process an SMB
`MaxFreeConnections` (default is 8)	Number of free connection blocks maintained per end point
`MaxLinkDelay` (default is 600)	Time threshold between link delays before disabling the RAW I/O for link connections
`MaxMpxCt`(default is 16)	Maximum number of requests that can be outstanding from clients to the server
`MaxNonpagedMemoryUsage` (default is 256)	Size of nonpaged memory pool used by the Server service
`MaxPagedMemoryUsage` (default is 256)	Maximum size of memory the Server service can use
`MaxWorkItems` (default is 256)	Number of receive buffers Windows NT can allocate
`MaxWorkItemIdleTime` (default is 60)	Amount of time a receive buffer can be in the idle queue before it's reused

18

Miscellaneous System Configuration

It's not easy to determine what type of configuration you should use for the system. However, you can avoid several pitfalls and consider several alternatives with your system.

You should avoid using SIMMs from different manufacturers because this can potentially make the system unstable. Windows NT determines some internal optimal settings by timing the first memory bank on Intel systems. The system won't be optimal if a second memory bank with different timing is introduced.

Tuning the File System

You should make several considerations when determining the type of file system you want to use:

- Should I use disk striping?
- Should I use RAID 0+1 or RAID 5?
- What about RAID cache?
- Will I benefit by using RAW partitions?

The answers to these questions depend on your particular environment, but you should understand the importance of these issues because the issues relate to running Oracle on Windows NT.

Disk striping probably provides the best performance advantage over all the Windows NT disk management strategies. Stripe sets are user transparent, and all the partitions in a stripe set are the same size. Also, stripe sets are independent of the file system. Windows NT allows disk striping with parity (RAID 5), which uses 3–32 disks. The disk space used for parity equals the size of one partition.

RAID 0+1—which is essentially disk striping combined with disk mirroring—provides the best fault tolerance but is more expensive because of the hardware duplication it uses. RAID 5, on the other hand, provides a more cost-effective solution.

The following guidelines can help you determine how you should use the RAID cache in your system:

- An OLTP environment should have enough write cache to accommodate the rate of data updates.
- In a DSS environment, you don't need read or write cache.
- If the disk controller cache isn't backed by a battery, you shouldn't use disk controller write cache; otherwise, there's a potential for data loss.
- Disk controller read cache shouldn't be used because Oracle can cache its own read.

Raw partitions can be used for files accessed sequentially and for I/O-bound systems because raw devices aren't buffered by the kernel, resulting in faster I/O than FAT or NTFS file systems. Each raw partition can have one file and is represented by a drive letter. The disadvantage of using raw partitions is restricted disk configuration options.

To Do: Create a Raw Partition with Disk Administrator

▼ To Do

Raw partitions are required if you are planning to use Oracle Parallel Server. The following steps indicate how you can use the disk administrator to create raw partitions:

1. Start Disk Administrator from the Start menu's Administrative Tools submenu.

2. If free space is available, click it and go to step 4.

3. If free space isn't available, you have to delete a partition that's not necessary anymore. This can be done by selecting the unneeded partition and then choosing Partition, Delete.

4. Choose Partition, Create from the Create Primary Partition window, and then click OK.

> Make the partition equal to the size of the file desired plus 1MB.

5. Create the new unformatted partitions for the other files by repeating steps 1 through 4.

6. Choose Partition, Commit Changes Now to save the changes.

▲ Each partition is now represented by a drive letter, such as g: or h:, and one file can be located on each.

The following example, from the Server Manager prompt, shows how redo log files can be placed on a raw partition when the database is being created:

```
CREATE DATABASE CONTROLFILE REUSE
LOGFILE GROUP 1 ('\\.\g:') size 11M,
        GROUP 2 ('\\.\h:') size 11M;
```

> Raw partitions don't protect cylinder 0. Therefore, always leave at least 1MB unused on the raw partitions.

18

The following example, when run from Server Manager, creates a 19MB tablespace on raw partition \\.\f:, which has a size of 20MB:

```
CREATE TABLESPACE RAWDATA DATAFILE '\\.\f:' SIZE 19M;
```

Summary

On UNIX platforms, traditionally the tuning of UNIX is left to the system administrators. This doesn't hold true for Windows NT, however:

- Windows NT is simpler to administer than UNIX.
- Databases installed on Windows NT tend to be smaller than those on UNIX.

As a result, the same person usually ends up being the database administrator, as well as the system administrator, on Windows NT platforms. During this hour, you've looked at several strategies for tuning Windows NT to optimize the running of Oracle8i.

Q&A

Q I want to maximize the speed of Oracle processes. Should I increase the priority of Oracle threads?

A The Registry entry to change the priority of Oracle threads shouldn't be changed from its default value; otherwise, it can result in an unstable system. Work with Oracle Support Services if you have to increase the priority of Oracle threads.

Q I have two CPUs on my system. Will Windows NT automatically use both of them?

A Yes, but the best use of multiple CPUs can be made by using parallel operations.

Workshop

The Workshop contains quiz questions and activities to help reinforce what you've learned in this hour. You can check Appendix A for the answers (but don't peek!).

Quiz

1. How can you reduce the amount of disk activity when you're using Oracle8i on Windows NT?

2. Which Windows NT tool can you use to create a raw partition?

3. Which Windows NT services shouldn't be disabled?

Exercises

1. Install the Windows NT Resource Kit, and use the appropriate command to determine the amount of page faults occurring in your system.

2. Create a raw partition, and store your redo log files on it.

18

HOUR 19

Tuning Oracle8i for Windows NT

This lesson analyzes ways in which you can ensure that you've tuned the database portion of your system. When Oracle runs on Windows NT, you can perform several special tasks so that they run well together.

During this hour, you will learn the following:

- The characteristics of a well-tuned system
- How to usc Oracle's Performance Monitor for tuning purposes
- How to tune an OLTP system
- How to tune a DSS system

Characteristics of an Optimally Tuned Oracle System on Windows NT

An optimally tuned Oracle database system on Windows NT has several characteristics:

- Little or no waiting on I/O indicates that the CPU has work to do while there are outstanding I/Os. The following Performance Monitor counters can be used to determine the amount of waiting for I/O:
  - Processor usage (Processor: %Processor time)
  - Disk usage (LogicalDisk/PhysicalDisk: Disk Transfers/sec)
  - Length of processor queue (System: Processor Queue Length)
  - Threads performing I/O (Thread: %Processor time)
- Most CPU usage is allocated to shadow threads, not to background threads. Performance Monitor counters that can be used for this purpose include CPU usage at the thread level (Thread: %Processor time).
- Most CPU usage is in user mode, not privileged mode. Performance Monitor counters that you can use for this purpose include CPU time spent in the user versus privileged mode for the Oracle process (Process: %User time/%Privileged time).
- Good response time depends highly on the application and network tuning. Usually your system users tell you whether response time is satisfactory. Response time improvement generally requires tuning of the most commonly used queries.
- The system should be CPU bound. To achieve high scalability, add processors if the system is CPU bound. Verify the following to ensure that the system isn't I/O bound:
  - Use only one DBWR because Oracle8 uses Windows NT's asynchronous capabilities.
  - Isolate sequential I/Os to their own controller volumes. Components such as redo logs are accessed sequentially in a write-only manner; therefore, it helps to place them on their own disks.
  - Balance random I/Os across drives. Datafiles are usually accessed randomly and should be spread across drives to avoid hot disks. Preferably, they also should be stripped.
  - Because redo logs are an important part of the database, you should mirror them at a minimum.

- Don't exceed I/O rate capabilities. This is probably one of the most important things that you should consider because if you are somehow exceeding the I/O rates for a disk, no matter how much you tune your system you won't get a dramatic performance improvement because only so much can be communicated with the disk in a given time span. Based on Compaq testing, random I/O shouldn't exceed 60 I/Os per second for a 4GB drive, 50 I/Os per second for 2GB drives, or 40 I/Os per second for 1GB and 500MB drives.

To Do: Determine I/Os per Disk

Use the Performance monitor to determine the I/Os per disk for a non–fault tolerant system:

1. Use Performance Monitor to determine the number of disk reads and disk writes for each logical volume.

2. Because you aren't using fault-tolerance for this example, the number of I/Os per disk is given as follows:

```
I/Os per disk = (Disk reads + Disk writes)/#ofdrives
```

> If mirroring is used, the I/Os per disk equals (disk_reads + 2*disk_writes)/#_of_drives.

Using Performance Monitor to Tune Oracle

You've seen on several occasions earlier that Performance Monitor is a very important tool that provides valuable insight into the workings of the database on Windows NT. However, it displays performance information of only one instance at a time. The following script shows how you can automate the procedure of updating the Registry by using Windows NT Resource Kit commands that help you gather performance information of multiple instances.

```
@echo off
REM MULTI_PERF.CMD
REM For Hostname, use SQL*Net aliases for local and remote instances.
REM For Username, a password will be required unless you use
REM         OS authentication
REM "regchg" is a Windows NT Resource Kit command that allows
REM         changing the Registry from the command line.
setlocal

if %1.==. goto HELP
if not %2.==. SET O_USER=%2
if %2.==. SET O_USER=/
```

19

```
REM Set the Registry entries to be used by Performance Monitor
regchg "SYSTEM\CurrentControlSet\Services\Oracle8\Performance"
➥Hostname REG_SZ "%1">nul
regchg "SYSTEM\CurrentControlSet\Services\Oracle8\Performance"
➥Username REG_SZ "%OS_USER%">nul
regchg "SYSTEM\CurrentControlSet\Services\Oracle8\Performance"
➥Password REG_SZ "%3">nul

REM Launch the perfmon utility
start c:\winnt\system32\perfmon c:\orant\dbs\oracle81.pmw

endlocal
goto END

:HELP
echo Usage: multi_perf ALIAS USERID PASSWORD
echo.
echo where, ALIAS is a local or remote SQL*Net Alias.
echo and USERID is a valid
echo database userid or / for OS authentication.
echo and PASSWORD is a valid password for USERID
echo or null for OS authentication.

:END
```

This script can be used as follows from the command prompt (assuming that OS authentication is used):

```
C:> multi_perf ins1
C:> multi_perf ins2
```

This will launch Performance Monitor twice: once for the instance ins1 and then for instance ins2.

Table 19.1 provides some general guidelines for tuning the database based on information obtained from Performance Monitor.

TABLE 19.1 USING PERFORMANCE MONITOR TO TUNE THE DATABASE

Performance Monitor Statistics	Indication	Resolution
Oracle8 Library Cache: %Reloads/Pins> 1%.	Library cache needs tuning.	Increase SHARED_POOL_SIZE.*
Oracle8 Data Dictionary Cache: %Getmisses/Gets > 15%.	Data dictionary cache needs tuning.	Increase SHARED_POOL_SIZE.
(O8logical reads-physical reads)/(O8logical reads) ratio is less than 0.90.	Database buffers need tuning.	Increase DB_BLOCK_BUFFERS.

Performance Monitor Statistics	Indication	Resolution
Oracle8 Buffer Cache/ %Phyreads/Gets is greater than 10%.	Database buffers need tuning.	Increase DB_BLOCK_BUFFERS.
Oracle8 Redo Log Buffer/ Redo Log Space Requests is not approximately zero.	Redo log buffers need tuning.	Increase LOG_BUFFERS.
Oracle8 sorts: (Sorts in Memory/sec)/(Sorts on Disk/sec) is less than 10%.	Sorting operations need tuning.	Increase SORT_AREA_SIZE.
Oracle8 Free List/%Freelist Waits/Requests is greater than 1%.	Free lists need to be tuned.	Increase the number of free lists.
For ORACLEXX.EXE, (1)Process> %Privileged (2)Processor> % User Time. *User time* is the application time usage, whereas *privileged time* is the time spent in the kernel. More time should be spent by the Oracle threads/processes in the user time than in the kernel time.	Application needs to be tuned.	Perform query tuning.
Processor : %Processor Time is more than 80%.	CPU contention.	Add more CPU.

*   *SHARED_POOL_SIZE should be large enough to hold a copy of the most frequently used queries.*

To Do: Check That SGA Size Can Fit in Memory

To determine SGA size and verify that it can fit in physical memory, follow these steps:

1. Choose Start, Administrative Tools, Windows NT Diagnostics.

2. On the Memory page, note the total physical memory.

3. Start Server Manager from the command prompt:

```
C:> svrmgrl
Svrmgr> connect internal/oracle
Svrmgr> show sga
```

▼   4. Note the total SGA available.

> For queries that do many full table scans, consider boosting the block size to 8KB.

▲

Tuning Online Transaction Processing (OLTP) Systems

Online transaction processing (OLTP) systems such as airline reservation systems and banking applications have several characteristics you must consider when dealing with them:

- Throughput is usually very high.
- They are usually insert/update intensive.
- The number of concurrent users is usually large.
- A rapid increase in the amount of data is usually involved.

When designing an OLTP system, take care to ensure that the large numbers of concurrent users don't adversely affect system performance. Some goals you should strive for when building OLTP systems include

- High availability
- High speed
- Ease of recoverability

You should consider several issues when using OLTP systems:

- Rollback segments
- Indexes, clusters, and hashing
- Transaction modes
- Data block size
- Transaction processing monitors
- Multi-threaded servers
- Well-tuned memory structures

Tuning Rollback Segments

An OLTP environment is generally composed of numerous short transactions and can benefit from using numerous rollback segments. In such an environment, you can benefit from using unlimited rollback segments or a very high value for MAXEXTENTS. Rollback segments become more important when you use parallel DML, and you should have a lot of free space in the rollback tablespace. (For more information on tuning rollback segments, see Hour 17, "Managing Contention.")

Using Discrete Transactions

Transactions with certain characteristics can benefit from using discrete transactions:

- Short and nondistributed transactions do not perform a lot of processing.
- Very few database blocks are modified by the transactions.
- An individual database block isn't changed more than once per transaction.
- Data required by long-running queries for read consistency isn't modified by the transaction.
- After the transaction modifies the data, the new value isn't required immediately.
- Modified tables don't contain any LONG values.

> Standard and discrete transactions can be used concurrently.

19

Because discrete transactions don't generate undo information, you can get Snapshot too old errors if you use discrete transactions that modify blocks used by long-running queries. However, redo information is generated, and all the changes made to any data are deferred until the transaction commits.

Follow these steps to use discrete transactions:

1. In the initialization file, set DISCRETE_TRANSACTIONS_ENABLED to TRUE. This allows the use of discrete transactions; otherwise, all transactions are standard.
2. Use the BEGIN_DISCRETE_TRANSACTION procedure as the first statement in the transaction you want as the discrete transaction. After the discrete transaction commits or rolls back, the next transaction is treated as a standard transaction.

You can't use discrete transactions to perform inserts or updates on both tables involved in a referential integrity constraint. This is because discrete transactions can't see the changes they make.

Consider an example that uses a movie theatre application. The name of the movie, show time, and number of tickets are passed as arguments to this procedure. This procedure uses a discrete transaction, which checks the database for ticket availability. If the desired number of tickets are available, it issues the tickets; otherwise, `discrete_transaction_failed` is raised, the transaction is rolled back, and it informs the user of the number of tickets available for the desired movie and show time.

```
CREATE PROCEDURE PURCHASE_TICKETS (movie_name IN VARCHAR(25),
              Num_tickets IN NUMBER(10),
              movie_datetime IN DATETIME,
              status OUT VARCHAR(5))
AS
DECLARE
  tickets_available  NUMBER(3);
BEGIN
  dbms_transaction.begin_discrete_transaction;
  FOR i IN 1 . . 2 LOOP
    BEGIN
      SELECT tickets_avail
      INTO tickets_available
      FROM movies
      WHERE movie_title = movie_name
      AND showtime = movie_datetime
      FOR UPDATE;
  IF tickets_available <= num_tickets
  THEN
    status := "Sorry. Only " & tickets-available &
        "tickets are available";
  ELSE
    UPDATE movies
    SET tickets_avail = tickets_avail - num_tickets
    WHERE movie_title = movie_name
    AND showtime = movie_datetime;

    status := "Requested number of tickets issued. Enjoy!!"
  END IF;
  COMMIT;
  EXIT;
    EXCEPTION
  WHEN dbms_transaction.discrete_transaction_failed THEN
    ROLLBACK;
  END;
      END LOOP;
    END;
```

While using Oracle8 on Windows NT, you should set aside 40MB each for Oracle and for Windows NT from the available system RAM. From the remainder, reserve enough for each concurrent user (.5MB per user determined from the ORASTACK utility). You should allocate two-thirds of whatever is left to the SGA. In other words,

```
Initial SGA size = ((RAM - 80) - 0.5*NUM_CON_USERS)*0.66
```

For example, if a system has 1,024MB of physical RAM and the system must support 200 OLTP users, how should you size the SGA initially? By using the preceding formula,

```
((1024 - 80) - 0.5*200)*0.66 = (960-100)*0.66 @ 560MB
```

you can see that the SGA has to be sized at 560MB.

Tuning Decision Support Systems (DSS) and Data Warehousing

In general, OLTP systems gather huge amounts of data. A DSS system then performs large queries on this data and generates various reports. Some critical issues that you should consider when using DSS systems include

- Index usage
- Data block size
- Star queries
- Parallel execution

Using Indexes

Indexes generally provide a fast access path to the data. In a DSS environment, the amount of data involved is very large, so special steps must be taken to use indexes efficiently:

- Indexes should be created after the data is inserted into the table, by using SQL*Loader or the Import utility. You can further speed up index creation by creating them in parallel.
- Identify the type of queries being used and the objects being accessed. In a DSS cnvironment, data changes don't occur frequently, so you can have a sufficiently large number of indexes (as needed) and still have index management under control.

19

- To speed up index creation, use the UNRECOVERABLE option because it won't generate any redo log records. However, you should back up after the index is created.

Managing Sort Space

Several initialization parameters can affect sorting operations, of which the following are the most important:

- SORT_AREA_SIZE specifies the amount of memory to allocate per parallel server process for sort operations. Setting a large value for SORT_AREA_SIZE can improve sort operation performance because the entire operation can be performed in memory. A small sort area size increases disk I/O because of the necessity to perform merges of numerous sort runs.

> If you can't set SORT_AREA_SIZE to a high value because of insufficient memory, you can still improve performance by increasing the buffer cache size, which will allow blocks from temporary sort segments to be cached.

- Setting SORT_DIRECT_WRITES this parameter to AUTO and having SORT_AREA_SIZE greater than 10 times the buffer size causes the buffer cache to be bypassed for the writing of sort runs. This improves performance by reducing the path length, memory bus usage, and LRU latch contention on SMP machines.
- SORT_AREA_RETAINED_SIZE specifies the maximum amount of User Global Area (UGA) memory retained after a sort run completes. If a sort operation requires more memory, a temporary segment is allocated and becomes an external sort.

Managing Hash Join Space

When hash join operations are performed, the smaller table is used to build an in-memory table, and the hash table probe is used to scan and join the larger table.

If you have sufficient memory, the cost to perform a hash join can be represented as follows:

$$C_{hj}(T1,T2) < C_{read}(T1) + C_{read}(T2) + C_{hash}(T1,T2)$$

In this formula, $C_x(Y)$ represents the cost to perform operation x on table Y.

Suppose that you have two tables, germans and engineers, and want the names of all the German engineers:

```
SELECT /*+ use_hash(germans) */ germans.name
FROM germans, engineers
WHERE germans.name = engineers.name
```

Suppose also that germans is the smaller of the two tables. As you can see in Figure 19.1, an area of memory called as hash memory is allocated.

FIGURE 19.1

Hash filters and hash area memory. The Ps stand for partitions, and the Ts for tables.

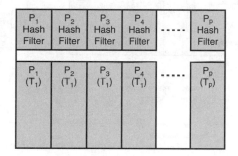

During the first stage of the join, the germans table (referred to as the *build input*) is scanned, partitioned, and used to build an in-memory hash filter and hash table. Hash partitioning is used to partition the germans table into smaller chunks to accommodate at least one hash partition. For each partition, a hash filter is created and stays in memory even if the partition doesn't fit. Rows that don't join are discarded by the hash filter. After the germans table is scanned completely, as many partitions as possible are loaded into memory. A single hash table is then built by using the in-memory partitions. Based on how much hash memory is required, the following situations can occur:

- Enough hash memory is available to contain all the partitions of the germans table. This causes the entire join operation to be completed by simply scanning the engineers table and probing the build.

- All partitions of the germans table can't fit into hash memory. In this case, the engineers table is scanned and each row is partitioned, as you can see in Figure 19.2:

  1. The hash filter can be used to discard the "No Hope" rows.

  2. Rows that can be joined with an in-memory germans partition are joined, whereas those that can't be joined are placed on a temporary segment on disk that corresponds to an engineers partition.

19

FIGURE 19.2

Hash join operations.

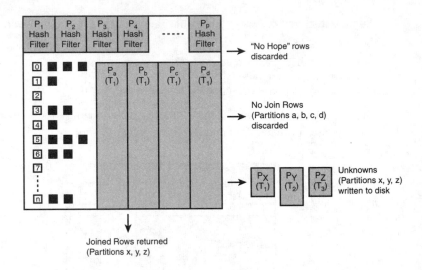

 Setting HASH_AREA_SIZE to a large value can cause excessive paging in the system, and setting it too small can degrade performance.

Phase 2 begins as soon as the engineers table is scanned. In this phase, a hash table is built by scanning the smaller of the germans and engineers partition into memory, and the join is completed by scanning the larger partition and probing the hash table.

The join will degenerate to a nested loop type mechanism if a partition won't fit in memory.

Table 19.2 shows the parameters you can set in the initialization file or set by using Server Manager's alter session command.

TABLE 19.2 PARAMETERS AFFECTING HASH OPERATIONS

Parameter	Default	Usage
HASH_JOIN_ENABLED	TRUE	Allows hash joins to be used.
HASH_AREA_SIZE	2 times SORT_AREA_SIZE	Specifies the size of hash memory. The value should not be less than 1MB. It should be approximately half the square root of S, where S is the size (in MB) of the smaller of two tables involved in the join.

Parameter	Default	Usage
HASH_MULTIBLOCK_IO_COUNT	DB_FILE_MULTIBLOCK_IO_COUNT	Specifies the number of blocks a hash join should read and write concurrently.

Designing Tables for Star Queries

Many data warehousing applications are represented as a star schema, which consists of one very large fact table and many smaller dimension tables. The name *star* refers to the representation that arises from each dimension table being related to the fact table through a primary key/foreign key constraint, yet the dimension tables aren't related to one another.

A B*-tree concatenated index is usually created on the columns of the fact table that are related to the dimension tables.

Figure 19.3 shows a retail environment that uses a star schema.

FIGURE 19.3

An example of a star schema.

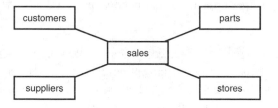

The retail environment could consist of the following tables:

- SALES, with Customer_key, Supplier_key, Part_key, Store_key, Date, Quantity, and Total_price columns
- SUPPLIERS, with Supplier_key, name, address, and telephone columns
- CUSTOMERS, with Customer_key, name, and address columns
- PARTS, with Part_key, name, and cost columns
- STORES, with Store_key, address, and telephone columns

In this scenario, the SALES table contains numerous records for the different sales transactions and can be the fact table. The other tables provide additional information about a sale and are usually small. These accessory tables can be the dimension tables.

Suppose you want to find the total sales of a specific item made by a specific customer from a specific store and sort the results by suppliers:

```
SELECT supplier.name, sum(total_sales)
FROM sales, customers, parts, suppliers, stores
Where
sales.customer_key = customer.customer_key and
sales.part_key = parts.part_key and
sales.supplier_key = suppliers.supplier_key and
sales.store_key = stores.store_key and
customers.name ='DELL' and
parts.name = 'notebook' and
stores.name = 'COMPUSA'
GROUP BY suppliers.name;
```

Tuning Star Queries

Star queries can be used efficiently when both the following are true:

- The cost-based optimizer is used. (Star schemas aren't recognized by Oracle's rule-based optimizer.)
- All the tables involved in the star query are analyzed with compute statistics. A table can be analyzed by executing the following from Server Manager:

  ```
  SVRMGR> ANALYZE TABLE tablename COMPUTE STATISTICS;
  ```

You can improve the performance of star queries in several other ways.

Hints

Because star schemas aren't recognized by Oracle's rule-based optimizer, you can use the star hint (/*+ STAR */) to force the optimizer to use a star query. Use the star hint in the query, and order the tables in the FROM clause of the query in the order of the keys in the index (on the fact table) with the large table last.

Indexes

You must create additional indexes if you use queries that omit the leading columns of the concatenated index on the fact table.

Denormalized Views

Denormalized views can be effective when too much normalization of information can cause the optimizer to consider many permutations and result in very slow queries. For example, you have two tables, brands and manufacturers, which can be combined into a view, product, as follows:

```
CREATE VIEW product AS SELECT /*+ NO_MERGE */ *
FROM brands, manufacturers
WHERE brands.mfkey = manufacturers.mfkey;
```

This will improve performance by caching the result of the view and reducing the executions of the small table joins.

Star Transformation

The star transformation uses bitmap indexes on individual fact table columns rather than compute a Cartesian product of the dimension tables. It generates new subqueries that drive a bitmap index access path for the fact table.

Star transformations can be useful when

- The fact table is sparse.
- There are many dimension tables.
- Queries don't use all the dimension tables in their constraining predicates.

Follow these steps to use star transformations:

1. In the init.ora file, set STAR_TRANSFORMATION_ENABLED to TRUE.
2. Use the STAR_TRANSFORMATION hint (/*+ STAR_TRANSFORMATION */) in the query.

You can't reap the benefit of star transformation under certain conditions:
- Tables with very few bitmap indexes
- Anti-joined tables
- Tables used as dimension tables in a subquery
- Remote tables
- Tables that are unmerged views

19

Tuning Parallel Operations

Queries that operate on a large number of records or those with a high elapsed time can be improved by using Oracle's parallel capabilities. The following operations can be performed in parallel:

- Parallel query
- Parallel DML (INSERT, UPDATE, DELETE, APPEND hint, and parallel index scans)
- Parallel DDL
- Parallel recovery
- Parallel loading
- Parallel propagation (for replication)

You can use several techniques to improve the performance of parallel operations:

- Adjust the degree of parallelism by using the ALTER TABLE command or hints. Follow these guidelines when adjusting the degree of parallelism:
    - For memory-bound operations, decrease the degree of parallelism.
    - For I/O-bound operations, data should be spread over more disks than there are CPUs, and then the parallelism should be increased in stages till it becomes CPU bound.
- Make sure that SQL statements operating on huge amounts of data are performing most operations in parallel. This can be done by obtaining the explain plan for the query and verifying that the plan steps have an OTHER_TAG of PARALLEL_TO_ PARALLEL, PARALLEL_TO_SERIAL, PARALLEL_COMBINED_WITH_PARENT, or PARALLEL_COMBINED_WITH _CHILD. If the OTHER_TAG shows any other keyword or null, it indicates serial execution.

    The following guidelines can help improve parallelism of SQL statements:
    - Convert your subqueries into joins because joins are parallelized more efficiently.
    - PL/SQL functions should be used instead of subqueries in the WHERE clause of the main query.
    - Rewrite queries with distinct aggregates as nested queries.
- Create tables by using the PARALLEL and NOLOGGING options of the CREATE TABLE statement:

```
CREATE TABLE table_new PARALLEL NOLOGGING
AS SELECT col1,col2 FROM table_old;
```

    Likewise, create indexes by using the PARALLEL and NOLOGGING clauses of the CRE- ATE INDEX statement. When using the NOLOGGING clause, the index can become unrecoverable if corruption occurs; therefore, you should back up the database after you have created indexes with NOLOGGING.
- Use initialization parameters properly. Table 19.3 shows some commonly used parameters with parallel operations.

TABLE 19.3 PARAMETERS AFFECTING PARALLEL OPERATIONS

Parameter	Recommended Value	Usage
OPTIMIZER_ PERCENT_ PARALLEL*	100 divided by the number of concurrent users	The default value, 0, causes the least resource usage and increases response time. A value of 100, however, favors a parallel plan unless the optimizer decides that a serial plan would be faster.
PARALLEL_MAX_ SERVERS	2 times CPUs times the number of concurrent users	
PARALLEL_MIN_ SERVERS	Same as PARALLEL_ MAX_SERVERS	
SHARED_POOL_SIZE	(CPUs + 2) times PARALLEL_MIN_ SERVERS times 1.5 times BLOCK_SIZE	

* *A nonzero setting of* OPTIMIZER_PERCENT_PARALLEL *is overridden if you use a* FIRST_ROWS *hint or set* OPTIMIZER_MODE *to* FIRST_ROWS.

> Generally, when parallel operations are used, some sorting invariably occurs. Therefore, you would benefit by using a large SORT_AREA_SIZE.

19

Summary

After you determine that the application and the operating system are well tuned, you should focus on tuning the database. This lesson discusses several counters provided by Performance Monitor that you can use for tuning purposes. Realize that database tuning is never complete because your goal should be to tune the database for a particular environment. The amount of effort spent on tuning should justify the performance gain obtained.

Q&A

Q **When using Performance Monitor, how can I simultaneously analyze the performance of my development and production instances?**

A You have to change the Registry parameter HOSTNAME before each invocation of Performance Monitor because this is the value it will look at for determining the Oracle SID you want to analyze.

Q **What should I place on my RAID drives?**

A Randomly accessed files such as datafiles can be placed in RAID drives. Don't place sequentially accessed files such as redo logs on RAID drives.

Workshop

The Workshop contains quiz questions and activities to help reinforce what you've learned in this hour. You can check Appendix A for the answers (but don't peek!).

Quiz

1. What are the characteristics of an optimally tuned Oracle8i system on Windows NT?

2. What's the difference between the NOLOGGING and UNRECOVERABLE options?

3. What conditions must be true to use star queries?

Exercises

1. You are using five disks on your DSS system and your reports are running very slow. Spread the data, and choose the correct degree of parallelism for your reports.

2. You are planning to use an OLTP system with 600 concurrent users. Determine the initial size of the SGA that would be appropriate for this system.

Hour 20

Diagnosing Problems

When you run Oracle8i on Windows NT, the problems you encounter can fall into one of the following categories:

- *Database crash*—An error message such as ORA-600, access violations, or other error messages that appear in the alert log or in the application usually indicate a database crash. When an ORA-600 error or an access violation occurs, the offending process generates a trace in the dump destination and places an entry in the alert log that you can use to find the name and location of the trace file. The trace file contains the stack trace, memory dump, process state dumps, and other diagnostic information that can help you diagnose the problem.

Not all error messages generate a trace file. To generate a trace file when a particular error occurs, set the appropriate event that will generate a trace file with the desired diagnostic information when the error occurs. (Setting events is discussed later this hour.)

- *Hung process*—A process is considered hung when it's waiting for an event that will never happen. If CPU time is being consumed, the process isn't hung. Usually, the hung process isn't the cause of the problem, but the hang results from a problem elsewhere in the system. System state dumps and `v$session_wait` output are useful in diagnosing a process/system hang.

- *Endless looping*—A process is considered to be in an endless loop when it's repeating the same task and using all the available CPU. The process is waiting for a condition to occur so that it can exit the loop; however, that condition never occurs. Because the target is continuously moving in such situations, an endless loop is difficult to diagnose. This type of problem can be diagnosed by obtaining multiple stack traces and process state dumps to identify the problem's source.

- *Slow process*—A slow system (indicating poor performance) is usually the result of insufficient tuning. Tuning is an art and requires thorough understanding of the database, operating system, and the application environment. Hours 17, 18, and 19 discussed several aspects of tuning the system.

  Oracle's UTLBSTAT/UTLESTAT scripts generate reports that give you an idea of how the system is performing in a specified time period. The UTLBSTAT/UTLESTAT report provides valuable information that you can use to identify problem sources. You learn more about these scripts later this hour.

- *User errors*—Many problems in the database are due to user errors in configuring the database and the system, or even improper use of the system. Oracle generates appropriate error messages that can help you diagnose such problems.

This lesson explains how to diagnose each of these errors.

Using the Alert Log and Trace Files

Oracle uses several types of logs and trace files you can use for diagnosing problems with the database/system:

- Alert log
- Process trace files
- Core files
- Application logs
- System logs
- Network logs
- Dr. Watson logs generated by Windows NT when an exception occurs in the system

Discussion of core files, application logs, system logs, network logs and Dr. Watson logs is out of the scope of this lesson. You should work with Oracle Support Services to analyze these files.

Oracle Alert Log

Threads belonging to Oracle background and shadow processes record valuable information in the alert log. The alert log records the various states through which the database instance passes during the use of the database. Information recorded in the alert log include

- Error messages
- The progress of the database instance as it goes through various stages, such as startup, shutdown, tablespace creation and drop, and rollback segments creation
- The name and location of generated trace files
- Parameters that are set to nondefault values

Oracle Trace Files

A process generates a trace file when it encounters an error during its processing. You can set events to generate trace files with different levels of detail when a certain error occurs. The trace file header contains information that can be used to verify system details such as

- Timestamp when the trace file was generated
- Version of Oracle in use
- Version of the operation system in use
- Installed database options
- Name of the instance where the error was encountered
- Oracle process ID
- Operating system process ID

Other information the trace file can include depends on the type of error and any events that might have been set.

20

Dealing with Data Block Corruption

Each Oracle data block is written in a proprietary binary format. Before an Oracle data block is used, Oracle checks it for possible block corruption. A block corruption is considered to exist if the format of the data block doesn't confirm to its format.

Checking for data block corruption is performed at the cache and other higher layers of the Oracle code. Information checked at the cache layer include

Block type	Block incarnation
Block version	Block sequence number
Data block address	Block checksum

If an inconsistency in block format is identified at the cache layer, the block is considered to be *media corrupt*, whereas an inconsistency identified at a higher layer of Oracle code marks the block as being *software corrupt.*

Information in the corrupt block is more or less lost; you will have to re-create it by using some data backup or export. Oracle has several tools—such as the Data Unloader (DUL) utility, which you can use to extract the data out of bad blocks—but typically, using these techniques is very expensive. You have to weigh the cost of using those tools (which aren't guaranteed to be completely successful) and the cost of re-creating the lost information.

Usually you see an error message such as ORA-1578 or ORA-600 when Oracle encounters corrupt blocks. You can use several techniques to determine whether the database is corrupt and also understand the nature and extent of the corruption.

Analyze the Table

By analyzing the table structure and its associated objects, you can perform a detailed check of data blocks to identify block corruptions:

```
Analyze table table_name validate structure cascade;
```

Data blocks are checked at the cache and higher levels. Index blocks are also checked, and the one-to-one association between the table data and its index rows is verified.

Use DB_VERIFY

Oracle provides the DB_VERIFY utility to validate datafiles even when a datafile is offline or the database is unavailable. DB_VERIFY is an external command-line utility that verifies the integrity of database files and the physical structure of an offline database. The executable of DB_VERIFY that comes with Oracle8i is dbverif81.exe:

```
dbverif81 parameters
```

You can use the following parameters with DB_VERIFY:

FILE	The datafile to run DB_VERIFY against.
START	The starting block address (by default, the first block of the file).
END	The ending block address (by default, the last block of the file).
LOGFILE	The name of the file that should contain the output of running DB_VERIFY.
BLOCKSIZE	The logical block size (by default, 2,048 bytes).
FEEDBACK	0 indicates that no feedback exists, but if a number n is used, a . is displayed for every n pages verified.
HELP	Indicates whether online help is needed.
PARFILE	The parameter file to use for DB_VERIFY, which contains the parameters you would have specified on the command line.

When using DB_VERIFY to verify a datafile on a raw partition, you should use the START and END parameters; otherwise, the nondatabase blocks on the raw partition will be unrecognized and marked as corrupt:

INPUT/ OUTPUT

```
C:> deverif81 rawdata1.ora

DBVERIFY: Release x.x.x.x.x - date

Copyright........

DBVERIFY - Verification starting: FILE =  rawdata1.ora
Page 28631 is marked software corrupt
Page 28841 is marked software corrupt
Page 28842 is marked software corrupt
Page 28843 is marked software corrupt
Page 28844 is marked software corrupt
Page 28845 is marked software corrupt
Page 28846 is marked software corrupt
Page 28847 is marked software corrupt
Page 28848 is marked software corrupt
Page 28849 is marked software corrupt
Page 28850 is marked software corrupt
Page 28851 is marked software corrupt
Page 28852 is marked software corrupt
Page 28853 is marked software corrupt
Page 28854 is marked software corrupt
Page 28855 is marked software corrupt
Page 28856 is marked software corrupt
```

20

```
Page 28857 is marked software corrupt
Page 28858 is marked software corrupt
Page 28859 is marked software corrupt
Page 28860 is marked software corrupt
Page 28861 is marked software corrupt
Page 28862 is marked software corrupt
Page 28863 is marked software corrupt
Page 28864 is marked software corrupt
Page 28865 is marked software corrupt
Page 28866 is marked software corrupt
Page 28874 is marked software corrupt

DBVERIFY - Verification Complete

Total Pages Examined..............................: 11086
Total Pages Processed....(Data)...................: 0
Total Pages Failing.........(Data)................: 0
Total Pages Processed....(Index)..................: 324
Total Pages Failing.........(Index)...............: 0
Total Pages Empty.................................: 12396
Total Pages Marked Corrupt........................: 28
Total Pages Influx................................: 0
```

To Do: Use DB_VERIFY to Validate a Datafile

At the command prompt, type the following:

INPUT/OUTPUT

```
C:> dbverif81 file=meghdata1.ora
                        ➥logfile=dbvlog.out feedback=10
DBVERIFY: Release x.x.x.x.x - date
Copyright......

DBVERIFY - Verification starting: FILE = meghdata1.ora
.........................................................

DBVERIFY - Verification complete

Total Pages Examined...........................: 4608
Total Pages Processed....(Data)................: 952
Total Pages Failing......(Data)............     : 0
Total Pages Processed....(Index)...............: 348
Total Pages Failing......(Index)...........     : 0
Total Pages Empty..............................: 2138
Total Pages Marked Corrupt.....................: 0
Total Pages Influx.............................: 0
```

As you can see, the meghdata1.ora datafile is verified for corruption. DB_VERIFY starts the verification process from the first block of the datafile to the last block. A block size of 2,048 bytes is used. A period (.) is displayed for every 10 pages verified. The output from DB_VERIFY is stored in dbvlog.out.

To Do: Use DB_VERIFY to Verify a Datafile on a Raw Partition

When using DB_VERIFY on a raw partition, be aware of the structure of the datafiles on raw partitions. When a raw partition contains a datafile, its structure can be as follows:

¦D¦D¦D¦D¦D¦D¦0¦0¦X¦

In this structure,

- D is the space used by data in the datafile.
- 0 is the space available in the datafile.
- X is the space reserved for non-datafile usage.

The following steps demonstrate how you can run db_verify a raw partition:

1. Connect to Server Manager as internal.

2. Determine the number of bytes in the datafile:

   ```
   SVRMGR> select bytes DFB
           from v$datafile
           where name = 'datafile_name';
   ```

3. Determine the block size used:

   ```
   SVRMGR> show parameter size
   ```

4. Determine the number of blocks by using the following equation:

   ```
   Number of blocks (NB) = DFB / BLOCKSIZE
   ```

5. Verify the datafile by using the START and END parameters so that nondatabase blocks aren't verified (otherwise, they would be marked as corrupt):

   ```
   C:> Dbverif81 file=datafile start=1 end=NB
   ```

   In this syntax, NB represents the number of blocks as calculated earlier.

Using Oracle Checksum Facilities

Oracle provides a number of checksum facilities that you can use to identify corrupt blocks. Checksum facilities are enabled by setting parameters and events in the init.ora file:

20

- Setting _block_checksum to TRUE causes checksums to be calculated for all data blocks on their next update. The database writer performs the task of calculating checksums. The checksum for a data block is stored in its cache header when writing it to disk.

> After a checksum is generated for a block, the block always use checksums even if the parameter is later removed.

- Setting `log_block_checksum` to `TRUE` causes checksums to be calculated for all redo log blocks.
- Set events 10210, 10211, 10212, and 10225 by adding the following line for each event in the init.ora file:

  ```
  Event = "event_number trace name errorstack forever, level 10"
  ```

  When event 10210 is set, the data blocks are checked for corruption by checking their integrity. Data blocks that don't match the format are marked as soft corrupt.

  When event 10211 is set, the index blocks are checked for corruption by checking their integrity. Index blocks that don't match the format are marked as soft corrupt.

  When event 10212 is set, the cluster blocks are checked for corruption by checking their integrity. Cluster blocks that don't match the format are marked as soft corrupt.

  When event 10225 is set, the `fet$` and `uset$` dictionary tables are checked for corruption by checking their integrity. Blocks that don't match the format are marked as soft corrupt.

> Use event 10225 to diagnose the problem if your `create segment` statement hangs.

- Setting `_db_block_cache_protect` to `TRUE` protects the cache layer from becoming corrupted. It might crash the database instance, but the corruption isn't written to the disk.

Salvaging Data from a Corrupt Database

A database can become corrupt for various reasons, such as

- Bad hardware
- Operating system bugs
- I/O or caching problems
- Running unsupported disk repair utilities

- Memory problems
- Oracle bugs
- A computer virus

Database corruption frequently results from problems with the hardware, so you should first resolve any hardware problems or reported operating system errors. When all the non-Oracle problems are resolved, you can embark on the adventure of recovering the data from the corrupt database. Follow these steps to recover a corrupt database:

1. Determine the extent of the damage. The information in the alert log, trace files, and the complete error message(s) reported by Oracle can provide enough information to determine the extent of database damage. Suppose that the error message indicates that the damage is done to file# (F) and block# (B).

2. Connect to Server Manager as internal.

3. Determine the file identified as corrupt:
```
Svrmgr> SELECT name
        FROM v$datafile
        WHERE file# = F;
```

4. Determine the damaged object:
```
Svrmgr> SELECT owner, segment_name, segment_type
        FROM dba_extents
        WHERE file_id = F
        AND B BETWEEN block_id AND block_id + blocks - 1;
```

5. Perform the recovery. The recovery approach depends on the damaged segment as determined by the query in step 4:

- For rollback segments and the data dictionary table, use the recovery approach described in Hour 15, "Performing Database Recovery," to recover from this situation.

- For index segments, determine the table the index belongs to, as follows:
```
Svrgmgr> SELECT table_owner, table_name
         FROM dba_indexes
         WHERE index_name = 'segment_name';
```

- For cluster segments, determine the table associated with the cluster, as follows:
```
Svrmgr> SELECT owner, table_name
        FROM dba_tables
        WHERE cluster_name = 'segment_name';
```

- For user tables, note the name of the table and its owner.

20

6. Make sure that the problem isn't intermittent by running the ANALYZE command on the segment at least twice. At the Server Manager prompt, use the following for a table:

```
Svrmgr> analyze table owner.tablename validate structure cascade;
```

Use this command for an index:

```
Svrmgr> analyze table owner.tablename validate structure cascade;
```

Use this command for a cluster:

```
Svrmgr> analyze cluster owner.clustername validate
➥structure cascade;
```

7. If a particular hardware or controller is identified as being bad, relocate the files to a good disk:

- For a database in archivelog mode, offline the corrupt datafile, and then restore it from backup onto a good disk. Recover the datafile, and then put it back online. The file can now be used.

- For a database in noarchivelog mode, offline the corrupt datafile, and then restore it from backup onto a good disk. Put the datafile back online; the file can now be used.

8. Perform the analysis on the object again to make sure that it's no longer corrupt.

At this point, data from the damaged blocks can be salvaged by using several techniques:

- You can perform media recovery (described in Hour 15, "Performing Database Recovery,") to recover the database to a state before the corruption.

- You can drop and re-create the object (table or index) by using a valid export.

- If the file# and the block# indicating the corruption are known, you can salvage the data in the corrupt table by selecting around the bad blocks.

- Set event 10231 in the init.ora file to cause Oracle to skip software and media corrupted blocks when performing full table scans:

```
Event="10231 trace name context forever, level 10"
```

- Set event 10233 in the init.ora file to cause Oracle to skip software and media corrupted blocks when performing index range scans:

```
Event="10233 trace name context forever, level 10"
```

> Oracle Support Services has access to several tools, such as Data Unloader
> (DUL) and BBED (Block Editor), that you can use to extract data from bad
> blocks. The use of these tools is expensive, and there's no guarantee that all
> the data can be salvaged.

To Do: Salvage Data from a Corrupt Table

Suppose that the test table is corrupt. Follow these steps:

1. Connect to Server Manager as internal.

2. Create a table to contain the salvaged data:

```
CREATE TABLE salvage_test AS
SELECT * FROM test WHERE 1 = 2;
```

3. Select around the corruption, and insert into the salvage table:

```
INSERT INTO salvage_test
SELECT /*+ ROWID(test) */ * FROM test
WHERE rowid <= 'low_rowid_of_corrupt_block';

INSERT INTO salvage_test
SELECT /*+ ROWID(test) */ * FROM test
WHERE rowid>= 'high_rowid_of_corrupt_block';
```

Tuning with the `utlbstat` and `utlestat` Scripts

Oracle provides two scripts that you can use to analyze the performance of an Oracle database:

- The script `utlbstat.sql` gathers the initial performance statistics and places them in temporary tables.

- The script `utlestat.sql` gathers the performance at the end of the observation period and places them in temporary tables. It then compares the information in these temporary tables with the set of temporary tables generated by `utlbstat` and generates a report named report.txt in the current directory.

You will see later how to interpret the report generated by these scripts and understand the various ways in which to improve the performance.

20

To Do: Generate a `utlbstat/utlestat` Report

The report will contain database performance. Follow these steps:

1. Choose an observation period for the analysis. The period should represent normal workload. Enough time should have passed since database startup so that the cache is loaded appropriately and the type of activity occurring in the database reproduces the performance problem being experienced.

2. Set initialization parameter `TIMED_STATISTICS`:

   `TIMED_STATISTICS = TRUE`

3. Restart the database.

> Alternatively, `TIMED_STATISTICS` can be set without restarting the database, as follows:
>
> Svrmgr> **alter session set timed_statistics = true**

4. Run utlbstat.sql at the start of the observation period:

   SVRMGR> **@%ORACLE_HOME\admin\utlbstat.sql**

5. Run utlestat.sql at the end of the observation period:

   SVRMGR> **@%ORACLE_HOME\admin\utlestat.sql**

▲ The report.txt file is generated in the current directory.

Interpreting the Report Generated from `utlbstat/utlestat`

The report generated from running `utlbstat/utlestat` contains a lot of valuable information regarding system usage during the observation period. Information in the report appears in several sections.

Library Cache Statistics

When analyzing the library cache statistics, you should look at several statistics:

- For each row, `GETHITRATIO` should be greater than 0.9.
- For each row, `RELOADS` shouldn't be more than 1% of `PINS`.

The library cache can be tuned by

- Reducing parsing
- Enabling sharing of statements
- Reducing aging out
- Making sure that large objects can be cached
- Increasing the shared pool

Systemwide Statistics

Systemwide statistics provided by the report indicate useful information such as use of table scans, sorts, row chaining, and the cache hit ratio.

Cache hit ratio can be calculated using the following formulas:

```
LOGICAL READS = CONSISTENT GETS + DB BLOCK GETS

HIT RATIO = (LOGICAL READS - PHYSICAL READS) / LOGICAL READS
```

If the cache hit ratio is less than 80%, increase the db_block_buffers parameter in the init.ora file.

You can check whether your applications are effectively using the indexes by using the following formula:

```
Non-Index lookups ratio = table scans (long tables) /
(table scans (long tables) + table scans (short tables))
```

Wait Events

The section on wait events indicates the resources that have contention:

- Waits for data blocks indicate free-list contention. You should increase the FREELISTS parameter for the heavily inserted table.
- Waits for undo segments indicate rollback segment contention. You should add more rollback segments.
- If the in-memory sorts are less than 90% of the total sorts, you should increase the SORT_AREA_SIZE parameter in init.ora.
- Waits for enqueues indicate that the enqueues aren't sufficient. You should increase the parameter ENQUEUE_RESOURCES in init.ora.

20

DBWR Statistics

This section gives you information that can be used to identify the load on the database writer. The statistics to check include DBWR Buffers Scanned Row and DBWR Checkpoints. You can increase DB_BLOCK_WRITE_BATCH to reduce the number of times the DBWR is signaled to perform a write operation. This should reduce the load on the database writer.

Latch Statistics

A hit ratio that's less than 90% indicates latch contention. Follow the steps described in Hour 17 to reduce contention for the particular latch.

Rollback Segment Contention

Contention can be identified by looking at TRANS_TBL_WAITS and TRANS_TBL_GETS. A waits-to-gets ratio of 5% or more indicates contention, and you should consider adding rollback segments. Also, a large number of SHRINKS indicates that the optimal setting isn't used properly.

Shared Pool Statistics

If GET_MISSES divided by GET_REQS is greater than 15%, consider increasing the SHARED_POOL_SIZE.

I/O Statistics

Check for the number of READS occurring against each file and tablespace to identify hot spots. You should try to balance the load by

- Moving one or more database files to another disk
- Separating frequently accessed tables from other tables
- Separating your rollback segments, redo logs, and archive logs

Using System State Dumps

NEW TERM A *system state dump* is an approximate "snapshot" of the state of the database at that time. A system state dump is generated by using information from several view tables, including

- v$session_wait
- v$sysstat
- v$process
- v$lock

- v$db_object_cache
- v$librarycache
- v$latch

System state dumps are useful only when taken two or preferably three times. To obtain a system state dump, log on to Server Manager as internal, and execute the following command:

```
Alter session set event 'immediate trace name systemstate level 10'
```

This generates a system state dump in the background dump destination. The system state provides information about various types of state objects, such as process, session, and call objects. The state objects contain information about the resources used by the various processes. Performance Monitor uses them to perform process recovery and to release the resources held by a dead process.

Interpreting System State Dumps

Much information in the system state dumps can be interpreted by Oracle Support Services, but you should look at this file to make some quick analysis of the database. A system state dump can help find the cause of a hung system or to even differentiate whether a process is really hung or simply running slowly.

> To determine whether a system is hung, take three system state dumps sepa-
> rated by about 10 minutes each, and then compare them. For a hung sys-
> tem, they should be identical.

Information that can be obtained from system state dumps includes the following:

- System global information
- Resources and events that a process is waiting on
- The SQL statement being run by the various processes

20

> To obtain the system state dump when a certain error occurs, you can
> execute
>
> ```
> Alter session set events 'XXX trace name systemstate level 10'
> ```
> where XXX is the ORA error that produces the system state dump.

System state dumps can be obtained at various levels, level 1 and level 10 being the most used. Level 10 gives the most detailed information and can generate a large file, whereas level 1 provides only the global system information and process state dumps.

Working with Oracle Support

Occasionally you might have to call Oracle support for help. Several simple but important guidelines can help you get a quick resolution to your problem. You will be helping yourself by keeping all the necessary information handy and explaining the exact nature and the criticality of the problem.

- *Keep your customer support information handy.* Keep the contact telephone numbers and your Customer Support Identification (CSI) number handy. Because Oracle provides different support contracts, you should understand the contract type you have with Oracle Support Services. You will save a lot of valuable time by keeping this information handy so that an action can be taken immediately when a problem occurs (usually at the most undesirable time). If you're calling back on an existing TAR (Technical Assistance Request), you should have the TAR number handy.

- *Understand the problem and ask for the appropriate group.* Oracle Support Services contains highly trained professionals, and various groups of people handle the large number of problems. You should try to form a clear and concise definition of the problem and ask for the correct group when calling Oracle Support Services; otherwise, you might lose valuable time while TARs are transferred to the correct group.

- *Set the correct priority for your problem.* It's very important that you communicate how critical the problem is to the analyst working with you. Explain the effect of the problem on the overall system functions.

- *Have configuration information ready.* Before calling Oracle Support Services, gather as much information about your configuration as possible:
  - The hardware and operating system release number on which Oracle and the application(s) are running
  - The release number of all Oracle products involved in the problem
  - Any third-party vendor and version in use
  - If the problem can be reproduced, a step-by-step procedure (test case) that reproduces the error

Any test case you try to provide should be very simple and not application specific (if possible).

- The nature of the problem, such as a crash, hang, slow performance, and so on
- The alert log
- The trace files you've obtained in relation to the error
- The backup strategy in use
- Your administrator account and password

If you aren't the system administrator, consult your system administrator to find out any major changes that might have occurred in the system.

- *Note your Technical Assistance Request (TAR) number.* After your problem is recorded with Oracle Support Services, the analyst working with you will provide you with a TAR number (or a PMS number in some countries). New TAR numbers are created for separate issues. Use the TAR number to refer to your problem when calling back on an existing issue.

Summary

Various types of problems can occur when running Oracle8i on Windows NT. You can see the problems by the error messages generated or by observing abnormal behavior such as slow performance or the process taking up too much system resources. In this hour, you looked at several techniques you can use to diagnose and resolve some of these problems. You should contact Oracle Support Services when you have exhausted all the resources available to you to fix the problem.

20

Q&A

Q Will a trace file be automatically generated for ORA-600 errors?

A Yes. ORA-600 errors automatically generate trace files.

Q I have a procedure that is running very slowly. How will the `utlbstat/`
`utlestat` report help me?

A `utlbstat/utlestat` reports provide systemwide performance information and are not really useful for particular queries. You should get an explain plan of the queries and also get timing information (by setting `TIMED_STATISTICS` to `TRUE`) to fix the problem with the queries involved in your procedure.

Workshop

The Workshop contains quiz questions and activities to help reinforce what you've learned in this hour. You can check Appendix A for the answers (but don't peek!).

Quiz

1. What can you use to validate offline datafiles?

2. How can you generate checksums for redo log blocks?

3. How can you generate a trace file when `ORA-942` occurs?

Exercises

1. Generate a system state dump for your database.

2. Generate a `utlbstat/utlestat` report for your database.

Part VI

Windows NT Clustering Solutions and the World Wide Web

Hour

HOUR 21

Using Oracle Fail Safe

Oracle Fail Safe (OFS) is a free product you can use with Oracle7 or Oracle8/8i Server. It comes in a separate CD that you have to order from Oracle. It provides a cost-effective, high-availability solution by

- Allowing the database to be run on either of the two cluster nodes in case of planned or unplanned downtime
- Allowing cluster nodes to function independently under normal conditions, thereby eliminating the need for standby databases, which are usually idle
- Accelerating the database reconnection
- Allowing the use of multiple virtual servers
- Allowing different initialization parameters for each node
- Allowing automatic checkpointing before planned failover
- Allowing incremental checkpointing to speed up recovery in case of unplanned failovers

In this hour, you will learn about the following:

- The various components of OFS
- How to use the Oracle Fail Safe Manager to administer an Oracle Fail Safe Server
- The failover sequence
- The use of OFS for high-availability solutions

Introducing OFS

Oracle Fail Safe for Oracle8i provides several features:

- *Scripting support*—Most Fail Safe Manager commands can be placed within scripts, which can be executed through the Oracle Enterprise Manager. These commands allow you to enable remote cluster configuration, dynamic load balancing, cold backups, or verification of cluster resources and fail-safe groups.
- *Enhanced console features*—A tree view provides information about all cluster resources.
- *Enhanced failover support*—The database resource DLL is updated to provide improved failover times.
- *Single-node cluster support*—During maintenance operations when one node is unavailable, you need support for single nodes. OFS provides resource monitoring, online/offline operations, and verify operations on single nodes.
- *Clusterwide installation*—When you install products on one node, all nodes in the cluster are automatically updated.

> Microsoft Service Pack 4 has a bug that prevents the creation of new fail-safe groups and, effectively, doesn't allow the use of OFS. Microsoft is planning to come out with a hot fix for this problem sometime in early 1999. In the meantime, you can use the OFS 2.1.3.1.0 patch that you can order from Oracle, which works around this problem.

OFS is Year 2000 compliant. It's installed on a node running Windows NT Server Enterprise Edition and Microsoft Cluster Server (MSCS).

Because OFS is a shared-nothing architecture, each node has its own workload and system disk, in addition to shared NTFS disks. Table 21.1 compares shared-disk and shared-nothing approaches.

TABLE 21.1 SHARED-DISK VERSUS SHARED-NOTHING ARCHITECTURE

Shared-Disk Approach	Shared-Nothing Approach
Symmetric architecture	Asymmetric architecture
Disks are accessible by all nodes simultaneously	Disks are owned and accessed by only one node at a time
Requires a distributed control software for management of global locks	Doesn't require a distributed control software
Example: Oracle Parallel Server	Example: Oracle Fail Safe

You configure and manage OFS through the Oracle Fail Safe Manager, a GUI tool optionally integrated with the Oracle Enterprise Manager. The Fail Safe Manager includes wizards, drag-and-drop features, online help, and tutorials to perform tasks such as

- Configuring standalone databases into fail-safe databases
- Managing fail-safe databases
- Monitoring, troubleshooting, and performing load balancing for fail-safe databases

OFS provides several benefits:

- *High availability*—If a cluster node fails, the database is automatically failed over to the surviving node, and applications can continue to access the database. The failover is very fast and usually takes less than a minute. It provides failover timings that are optimized with patented checkpoint algorithms.

- *Workload sharing by the nodes*—Under normal operating conditions, you can use both nodes independently. In other words, the nodes can serve separate applications, such as manufacturing on one node and human resources on the other. Keep in mind, however, that the nodes should have enough resources to handle both applications during outages when only one node will do all the work.

- *Planned and unplanned failover*—Planned failover occurs when you try to perform node maintenance. The database on one node can be failed over on the second node, the maintenance performed, and then the database failed back to the first node. Similarly, the maintenance can now be performed on the second node. Unplanned failover occurs when a crash occurs on one node.

21

- *Ease of administration*—Usage and administration of a fail-safe database are very simple and ideal for small organizations that don't have a full-time DBA. Most customer problems can be fixed or identified by using the fail-safe VERIFY family of commands, such as VERIFY CLUSTER, VERIFY GROUP, and VERIFY DATABASE. A quick start to using fail-safe databases is made by providing CBT, online tutorial, and sample databases. Table 21.2 compares Oracle Fail Safe 2.1 with SQL Server 6.5 EE.

TABLE 21.2 SQL Server 6.5 EE Versus Oracle Fail Safe 2.1

SQL Server 6.5 EE	Oracle Fail Safe 2.1
After failover takes place, you must run the database consistency checker	After failover, you don't have to run any kind of consistency checker, and clients can quickly reconnect.
No rolling upgrades	Allows rolling upgrades.
No validation of failover	Automatic failover validation. It also provides a VERIFY family of tools to identify and fix problems.
Maximum of two virtual servers per cluster	Unlimited number of virtual servers per cluster.
"Master" is the unit of failover	"Database" is the unit of failover.
Supports only SQL Server 6.5 EE	Supports multiple Oracle7 and Oracle8 releases.
License required per node	OFS is free.

Oracle Fail Safe Components

OFS consists of the following main components:

- *Microsoft Cluster Server (MSCS)* provides the clustering features OFS needs (see Figure 21.1). It uses a shared-nothing architecture and a private network between nodes. Version 1.0 of the cluster uses TCP/IP over standard interconnects such as Ethernet or ServerNet. SCSI-based clusters usually are low-cost solutions, but the length of the cable restricts the cluster nodes and storage arrays to be in close physical proximity. As a result, a wide-area disaster such as a hurricane can destroy both nodes. This approach has other disadvantages, such as the storage arrays being a single point of failure.

FIGURE 21.1

OFS components.

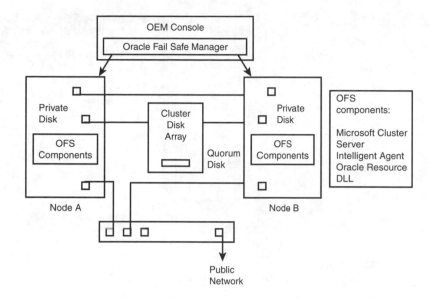

Higher-end solutions use a Fiber Channel RAID array, which is mirrored and separated by longer distances. It provides an active/active configuration, allowing both nodes to support independent applications during normal operations. (See the later section "OFS Configurations" for more information on the types of configuration available.) For each application, there's one preferred node and a backup node. The backup node comes into play only when the preferred node becomes unusable.

Now, OFS configuration supports only two nodes. This is a limitation due to MSCS and will likely change in the future.

- *Oracle Fail Safe Manager* uses GUI features such as wizards, drag and drop, and dialog boxes to automate the configuration and management of Oracle on Windows NT clusters (see Figure 21.2). It also allows you to start and stop OFS databases and define failover and failback conditions.

21

FIGURE 21.2

Cluster Administrator can be used to configure Windows NT clusters.

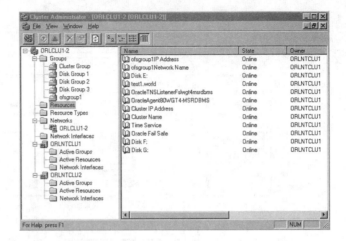

Use Oracle Fail Safe Manager to start and stop fail-safe databases.

Oracle Fail Safe Manager is integrated with Oracle Enterprise Manager version 1.5 (see Figure 21.3). Oracle Fail Safe Manager version 2.1.2 also has a command-line interface, FSCMD, that you can use to execute scripts that perform batch administration.

FIGURE 21.3

Oracle Fail Safe Manager is integrated with Oracle Enterprise Manager.

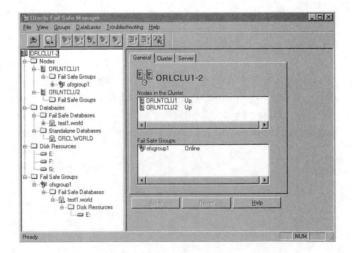

Fail Safe Manager version 2.1.2 comes with a command-line interface to support scripting and batch automation of administration tasks (such as backups).

Fail Safe Manager is integrated with OEM version 1.5. Use the Oracle Fail Safe Manager to perform cluster-related configuration and management operations of fail-safe databases. Use the Oracle Enterprise Manager (OEM) to perform other administrative tasks, such as taking backups, scheduling jobs, and tuning fail-safe databases.

- *Oracle Fail Safe Server* works with the Windows NT cluster software and cluster resource DLLs to provide fast, automatic failover for planned and unplanned outages. It runs on both cluster nodes and performs the following functions:
  - Provides the details of the Oracle database and dependencies to the Cluster Server
  - Updates all nodes with the database and fail-safe configuration
  - Fails over the database to the backup node
- The *collection of cluster resource DLLs* works with the Oracle Fail Safe Server to provide automatic application failover. The resource DLLs perform several tasks:
  - Start up and shut down the database.
  - Used by MSCS to monitor the database.
  - Query the database to perform an all-well check by performing "is alive" polling.
  - Automatically change the database timing parameters (such as `Pending Timeout`), depending on the database workload.

OFS Terminology

NEW TERM Several terms are associated with OFS:

- *Resource*—Any physical or logical component that can be managed by the cluster.
- *Cluster*—A group of systems that's accessed and managed as a single system. Clients access the cluster as a single system and can benefit from the addition of processor and storage resources to the cluster.

21

- *Preferred node*—The cluster node that hosts the database resources during normal operations.
- *Backup node*—The cluster node that hosts the database resources after the preferred node becomes unavailable and failover occurs.
- *Cluster alias*—The IP address that refers to the cluster and is used by the Fail Safe Manager for cluster management. (Keep in mind that each node still has its own IP address used by the clients to connect.)

> The cluster alias is used by the Cluster Administrator and the Fail Safe Manager, whereas the virtual server address is used by the client applications.

- *Virtual server*—Used by the clients to access the service provided by the fail-safe group. It represents the node (preferred or backup) now hosting the group. An IP address is associated with the virtual server. It looks like a physical node to the clients and OEM.
- *Fail-safe group*—A collection of resources that can be managed as a single unit of failover. At a minimum, it consists of a virtual server, a network name chosen during the installation of OFS, and an IP address used by the clients to connect to it. All resources that are part of a group have the same availability characteristics and can be owned and accessed by only one cluster node at a time. At any time, only one node will host the fail-safe group.

> Resources within a fail-safe group can have dependencies among each other, but they can't depend on resources that belong to other groups.

- *Failover (planned and unplanned)*—The process of switching database resources from one cluster node to the surviving node during a planned or unplanned downtime.
- *Failover time*—The time period in which a database becomes unavailable on one node and available on the surviving node. Usually, this time is very short (less than a minute). The actual time depends on the amount of resources that need failover.

- *Failover policy*—A set of user-defined parameters used to specify how the failover occurs. Failover policy can specify several things:

    - The maximum number of times the group is allowed to fail over during a period of time

    - Automatic failback

    - Automatic restart of the resource when a resource failure is detected

    - The maximum number of times to retry the restart of a resource over a time period

- *Failback*—The process of switching database resources from the backup node to the preferred node when the failed node comes back online.

Using OFS

You must answer several questions while deciding to use a fail-safe database:

- What business functions will this database provide?

- What's the cost of downtime?

- How often do you lose access to the database because of planned and unplanned outages?

- What resources are needed in the fail-safe group?

- What's the interdependency among the resources in the fail-safe group?

- Can your nodes support the additional resources that fail over to it, as well as their normal workload?

- Is the performance degradation that occurs during a system crash acceptable?

- Are you expecting scalability?

Keep in mind that OFS provides reliability but not scalability. Also, there will be a performance degradation when the fail-safe database is functional.

Prerequisites to Using OFS

To use OFS on Windows NT, you must install the following software on both nodes:

- Windows NT version 4.0 Enterprise Edition, with Service Pack 3 or higher

- MSCS version 1.0

- Any of the following Oracle releases:

    Oracle7 Workgroup Server release 7.3.3.2 or higher

21

Oracle7 Server release 7.3.3.2 or higher

Oracle8 version 8.0.4 or higher

Oracle8i (Oracle 8.1.5 or higher)

On nodes that will run the Oracle Fail Safe Manager, you should install Windows 95, Windows 98, or Windows NT version 4.0 with Service Pack 3.

The components should be installed on the nodes in the following order:

- Windows NT and Service Pack on node 1
- Windows NT and Service Pack on node 2
- MSCS on node 1
- MSCS on node 2
- Oracle database on the local disk of node 1
- Oracle database on the local disk of node 2
- Oracle Fail Safe under %ORACLE_HOME% on the local disk of node 1
- Oracle Fail Safe under %ORACLE_HOME% on the local disk of node 2

Hardware Requirements

OFS can be used with any cluster configuration (hardware and software) that's validated for MSCS. Use the following URL to find the list of cluster configurations that are validated against MSCS:

```
http://www.microsoft.com/isapi/hwtest/hcl.idc
```

With the release of OFS 2.1.2, you can use any shared disk resource type that's implemented with an MSCS API and registered with MSCS. It also allows you to use additional resource DLLs for specific storage-class resource types that might be supplied by other vendors or resellers.

In an OFS configuration, the initialization file can be placed on a private disk.

Failover Sequence

The sequence of events that occur during a failover depends on whether the failover is planned or unplanned.

During a planned failover, such as a scheduled downtime of the nodes, the following events occur:

1. OFS issues a checkpoint.

2. After the checkpoint completes, the database is shut down normally.

3. OFS requests MSCS to move the resources of the fail-safe group from the preferred node to the backup node.

4. MSCS starts the database instance on the surviving node.

5. Client applications connect to the OFS database on the new node using the same virtual server address.

During an unplanned failover, such as an operating system crash of the preferred node, the following events occur:

1. MSCS detects a problem on a node.

2. An action you specify as a failover policy for the fail-safe group is taken. Usually, one or more attempts are made to restart the database before taking a decision to fail over, in which case the following steps occur:

    1. MSCS starts the database instance on the surviving node.

    2. Typically, the database had a shutdown abort, so instance recovery is performed.

    3. Client applications connect to the OFS database on the new node using the same virtual server address.

Effect of Failover on Database Applications

When a failover occurs, a shutdown abort is issued on the instance running on the failed node. As a result, running transactions are rolled back when database recovery is performed on the backup node.

Database applications aren't affected much by a failover. The failover appears after a brief network outage. Because OFS uses the new ODBC and OCI features available with Oracle8i, applications can reconnect automatically and restart a query from the point of failure. Updates are rolled back automatically and users are notified about it so that they can reissue the update statement. Applications using other ODBC drivers or those using Oracle7 ODBC or OCI, however, have to perform all reconnection and transaction recovery tasks on their own. Figures 21.4 and 21.5 show the virtual server before and after failover.

21

FIGURE 21.4

The virtual server before failover.

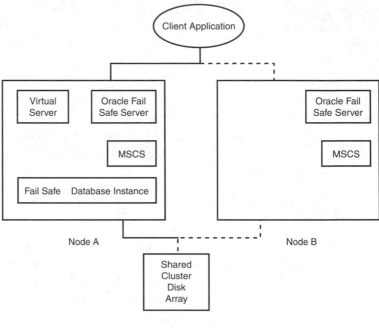

FIGURE 21.5

The virtual server after failover.

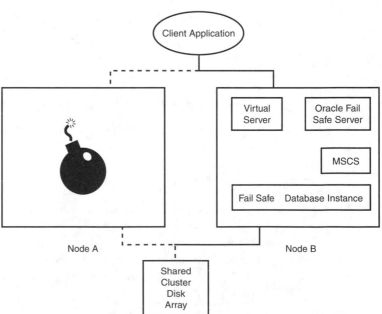

> When using a client application against a fail-safe database, you don't have to change the code. However, you should register the virtual server address for the OFS database.

Online Maintenance Operations

Oracle8i enables you to perform many maintenance operations while the database is online, such as the following:

- Adding, rebuilding, or defragmenting indexes
- Managing index-organized tables
- Making a tablespace read-only
- Performing full or incremental backups

This minimizes the necessity of taking the database offline and thereby allows continuous 24-hour, 365-days-a-year operation for mission-critical databases. Oracle8i Fail Safe provides high availability for business solutions on Microsoft Windows NT clusters. It provides fast failover support for various Oracle Server releases: Oracle8i, Oracle8, Oracle7, and Oracle Developer 6.0 Forms and Reports servers.

> When Oracle Enterprise Manger discovers a fail-safe database, it's managed just like a standalone database with OEM components such as Tablespace Manager and Schema Manager.

To Do: Discover a Fail-Safe Cluster

Before you can create a fail-safe database, you must prepare the cluster. The cluster has to be "discovered," which is essentially going to verify that the cluster has been set up properly. The following steps demonstrate how the discovery of the cluster is performed:

1. Start the intelligent agent on one of the nodes.

> If an intelligent agent is added to a fail-safe group, the agent and its associated jobs will fail over with the database so that a job scheduled to run on the preferred node will run on the backup node after failover.

▲ To Do

21

▼   2. Run OEM Discovery on the cluster node where the intelligent agent is started.

▲   3. Verify that the fail-safe cluster alias appears in the OEM console.

Performing Basic Administrative Operations with the Fail Safe Manager

From OEM, launch the Fail Safe Manager, and perform basic administrative tasks by using menu options as specified in Table 21.3.

TABLE 21.3 USING ORACLE FAIL SAFE MANAGER

Task	Menu Options
Create sample database	Database, Create Sample Database
Create fail-safe group	Group, Create
Add database to fail-safe group	Database, Add to Group
Add intelligent agent to group	Group, Intelligent Agent
Verify cluster	Troubleshooting, Verify Cluster
Verify group	Troubleshooting, Verify Group
Verify standalone database	Troubleshooting, Verify Standalone Database
Remove database from group	(Highlight the fail-safe group, right-click, and then choose Remove.)
Delete sample database	(Highlight the database, right-click, and then choose Delete Sample Database.)
Remove fail-safe group	(Highlight the fail-safe group, right-click, and then choose Delete.)

Creating a Fail-Safe Database

A standalone database can be created on either cluster node so that the database files are placed on the shared cluster disk(s). You can create a fail-safe database by following several simple steps, using the commands listed in Table 21.3:

1. Use Oracle's Database Assistant or the Oracle Fail Safe Manager's Create Sample Database command.

2. Use the Fail Safe Manager's Create Fail Safe Group Wizard to create a fail-safe group. A virtual server network name and IP address must be supplied during the creation of the fail-safe group.

3. Invoke the Add Database to Group Wizard by dragging the standalone database to the fail-safe group. The wizard performs the following tasks:

- Starts the configuration on database node
- Validates the disk information
- Configures SQL*Net version 2 or Net8 files to work with the virtual server
- Adds the database resources to MSCS
- Brings the fail-safe group online on the first node
- Starts the configuration on the second node
- Configures SQL*Net version 2 or Net8 files to work with the virtual server
- Brings the fail-safe group online on the second node
- Returns the fail-safe group on the first node
- Tests that the fail-safe database works correctly on each node

To Do: Create a Sample Database

Oracle Fail Safe Manager can be used to create a sample database that you can use to test your configuration:

1. Launch Fail Safe Manager from OEM.
2. Choose Database, Create Sample Database. The Create Sample Database dialog box appears (see Figure 21.6).

FIGURE 21.6

Specify the database information in the Create Sample Database dialog box.

3. In the Database Info section, provide the following information:

- *Service Name*—This should be a unique name for the database service.
- *Disk Resource*—The database will be created on the cluster node where the disk resides.
- *Version/Home*—The version and Oracle home should be identical cluster-wide.

21

▼ 4. Provide the password for the internal account, and confirm the password. Click OK.

▲ 5. Make sure that the clusterwide operation completes successfully, and then click Close to confirm the operation completion (see Figure 21.7).

FIGURE 21.7

Verify the clusterwide operation.

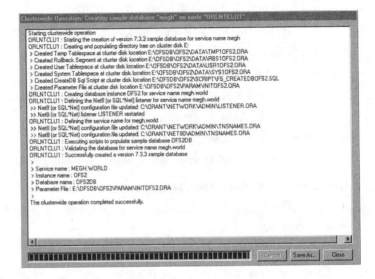

To Do: Create a Fail-Safe Group

A fail-safe group is a minimal virtual server and is populated with a network name and IP address. The fail-safe group specifies the resources used for the fail-safe configuration. The following steps demonstrate the creation of a fail-safe group:

1. Launch Fail Safe Manager from OEM.

2. Choose Group, Create.

3. On the first screen of the Create Fail Safe Group Wizard (the General page in Figure 21.8), provide a unique group name and an optional group description. Then click Next.

4. On the Virtual Server page (see Figure 21.9), click Show Networks Accessible by Clients, and then select the network on which the virtual server is defined. Enter the network name of the virtual server, the IP address for the network name, and a valid subnet mask (as specified in Control Panel). Then click Next.

▼

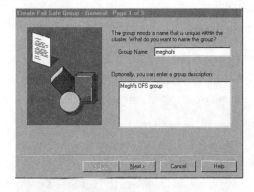

FIGURE 21.8

Specify the fail-safe group name in the General page.

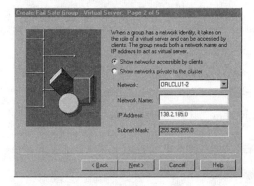

FIGURE 21.9

Specify the network information for the virtual server.

5. On the Failover Policy page, provide the following settings and then click Next:

   - *Failover Period*—Duration of the failover period
   - *Failover Threshold*—The number of times the cluster software allows the group to fail over during the failover period

6. On the Failback Policy page, specify a failback policy (Prevent Failback, Immediate Failback, or Failback During Specific Hours), and then click Next:

7. On the Preferred Nodes page, specify the preferred node for failback operations from the available nodes, and then click Next.

8. On the summary page, verify the options you chose, and then click OK.

9. Make sure that the clusterwide operation completes successfully, and then click Close.

21

Clusterwide operations are atomic, and clusters are brought to the original state if an error occurs.

To Do: Add a Database to a Fail-Safe Group

After a fail-safe group has been created, you should add a database to this group so that it can act as a fail-safe database, as shown here:

1. Launch Fail Safe Manager from OEM.

2. Choose Database, Add to Group. Alternatively, you can drag the database icon and drop it on the fail-safe group icon.

3. On the first screen of the Add Database to Fail Safe Group Wizard (the General page in Figure 21.10), provide the following information and then click Next:

   - The name of the fail-safe group to which you want to add the database
   - The service name of the database to be added
   - The database instance
   - The name of the database to be added
   - The location and name of the initialization file

FIGURE 21.10

In the General page, associate the fail-safe group with the fail-safe database.

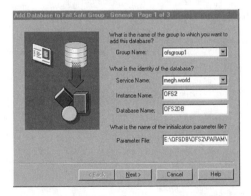

4. On the Authentication page (see Figure 21.11), supply the password of Internal and confirm by retyping the password. Then click Next.

FIGURE 21.11

Provide a valid administrative account in the authentication page.

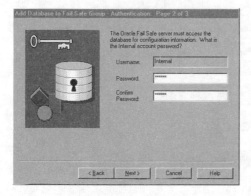

5. On the Failover Policy page (see Figure 21.12), provide the following settings:

   • *Pending Timeout*—The amount of time that the database takes to resolve a pending state before the cluster software puts the database in a failed state.

   • *Is Alive Interval*—The amount of time that the cluster software takes to determine whether the database is online.

   Then, determine whether the cluster software should automatically restart the database. Click Next.

FIGURE 21.12

Specify the failover policy.

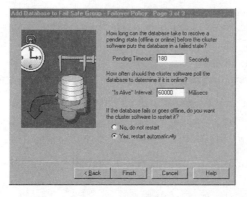

6. On the summary page, verify the options you chose, and then click OK (see Figure 21.13).

21

▼

FIGURE 21.13

Verify the configuration that you specified for the fail-safe database.

7. Confirm that during this addition of the database to the fail-safe group, all the databases in the group will be shut down and the users disconnected.

8. Make sure that the clusterwide operation completes successfully, and then click Close.

9. After the database is successfully added to the group, you are prompted to add the intelligent agent to the group. An intelligent agent should be associated with every fail-safe group so that OEM can perform discovery and job scheduling.

▲

> The intelligent agent can be added to a fail-safe group any time by choosing Groups, Add Intelligent Agent from Oracle Fail Safe Manager.

To Do: Remove a Database from a Fail-Safe Group

If a node crashes, you might want to make a fail-safe database standalone so that you can continue working against it. To make a fail-safe database standalone and place it on the same node where the group resides, follow these steps:

1. Highlight the database to be removed in the fail-safe group, right-click, and choose Remove.

2. Make sure that the clusterwide operation completes successfully, and then click Close.

▲

To Do: Delete a Standalone Database

When you want to completely eliminate a database, the Fail Safe Manager provides a simple method for achieving this task:

1. Highlight the database to be removed in the standalone database folder, right-click, and choose Delete Sample Database.

2. In the Delete Sample Database dialog box, provide the password for the internal account (see Figure 21.14) and then click OK.

FIGURE 21.14

Delete the database by providing a valid administrative account.

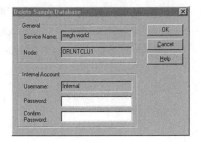

At this point, the clusterwide operation does the following:

- Validates the password
- Cleans up the SQL*NET/Net8 configuration
- Deletes the database instance
- Cleans up the database files

3. Make sure that the clusterwide operation completes successfully, and then click Close.

To Do: Delete a Fail-Safe Group

A fail-safe group should be deleted when you no longer want to include the node in a fail-safe configuration. This task can be achieved using the Fail Safe Manager:

1. Highlight the fail-safe group to be removed in the fail-safe group folder. Right-click it and choose Delete.

2. Confirm the deletion.

3. Make sure that the clusterwide operation completes successfully, and then click Close.

21

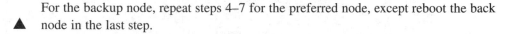

To Do: Remove OFS from a Windows NT Cluster

From the preferred node, execute the following steps:

1. Launch Oracle Fail Safe Manager.

2. Remove all the fail-safe databases from the fail-safe groups, and then remove all the fail-safe groups.

3. Exit the Fail Safe Manager.

4. Choose Start, Programs, Oracle8i for Windows NT, Oracle Universal Installer.

5. Remove Oracle Fail Safe Manager and Oracle Fail Safe Server.

6. Choose Yes when prompted to unregister the Oracle database resource from the cluster.

7. Reboot the preferred node.

For the backup node, repeat steps 4–7 for the preferred node, except reboot the back node in the last step.

Troubleshooting OFS

OFS provides a group of functions that can be used to identify problems with the fail-safe configuration and fix determinate problems. These functions, known as the Verify family of commands, consist of Verify Cluster, Verify Group, and Verify Standalone Database and can be found in the Verify menu.

Verify Cluster

This should be run after installing OFS or when the cluster configuration changes. When this command is run (see Figure 21.15), it performs the following tasks:

- Validates fail-safe installation by ensuring that the OFS and Fail Safe Manager versions are identical on all cluster nodes, that fail safe is installed on only one Oracle home, and that the fail-safe resource DLL is registered in MSCS.

- Reports the status of Oracle installations. When using multiple Oracle homes, you must have symmetry in the Oracle home names and versions.

- Reports the status of the cluster network and ensures that the network name and IP address resolution are consistent.

FIGURE 21.15

*Validate the cluster
after the configuration
is changed.*

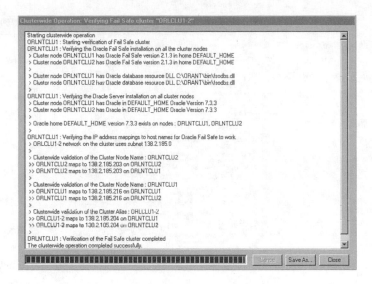

If Verify Cluster reports a problem, you should update the hosts and lmhosts files on
each cluster node. These files are located in the Winnt\system32\drivers\etc directory. For
example, for a virtual server OFSSERVER, the entry could be as follows:

```
121.3.98.16 OFSSERVER
```

Verify Group

This command can be run anytime and is usually used to validate configuration changes
and fix any problems detected. When this command is run (see Figure 12.16), it starts on
the node where the fail-safe group resides and performs the following tasks:

- Detects disk drive changes
- Verifies resources and their interdependencies
- Verifies the network name and IP address resolution
- Verifies SQL*Net and Net8 configurations
- Reconfigures the second node by performing the same operations on it

21

FIGURE 21.16

Verify the fail-safe group after changes are made to the configuration.

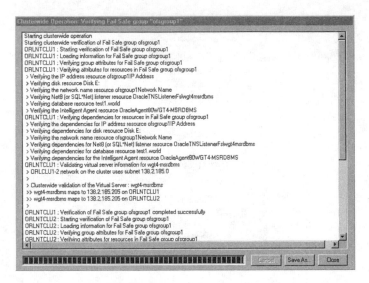

Verify Standalone Database

NEW TERM This command can be run (see Figure 21.17) to verify that the database is ready to be converted into a fail-safe database. It should also be run when the *quorum disk* (shared disk) becomes corrupted or MSCS is uninstalled. When this command is run, it starts on the node that hosts the database and performs the following tasks:

- Configures SQL*Net/Net8

FIGURE 21.17

Verify that the database can be converted back to a standalone database.

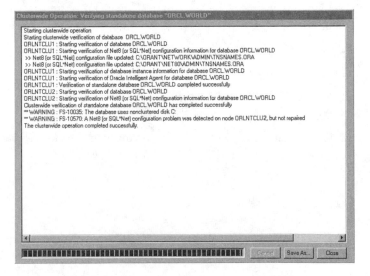

- Verifies the database instance
- Verifies that the disks are located on a shared interconnect that's accessible by both nodes
- Mounts the disk on the database node and verifies that the disks won't be moved on the standalone database
- Verifies intelligent agent information
- Cleans up references on the second node

Common Problem Scenarios

Problem: You can't make the Oracle database fail safe during the Add the Database to Group operation.

Solution:

1. Verify that the cluster network is correct by running Verify Cluster.
2. Verify that SQL*Net or Net8 is correct by running Verify Standalone Database.
3. Retry the Add Database to Fail Safe Group operation.

Problem: The quorum disk is corrupt or MSCS is uninstalled on both cluster nodes.

Solution: If the quorum disk is corrupt, run the CHECKDISK utility. If this doesn't fix the problem, or if MSCS is uninstalled on both nodes, follow these steps:

1. Reinstall MSCS.
2. Make the database standalone.
3. Verify that SQL*Net or Net8 is correct by running Verify Standalone Database.
4. Verify that the cluster is configured correctly by running VERIFY CLUSTER.
5. Retry the Add Database to Fail Safe Group operation.

Problem: The fail-safe group can't be created.

Solution: Validate cluster networking by running Verify Cluster.

Problem: The clients can't access the database.

Solution:

1. Update tnsnames.ora to use the virtual server.
2. Run Validate Group.
3. Run Validate Standalone Database and verify the SQL*Net and Net8 configuration.

21

Problem: While running Add Database to Fail Safe Group, the cluster crashes.

Solution: In this case, the solution depends on whether the database is in MSCS. If the database isn't in MSCS, follow these steps:

1. Run Verify Standalone Database.
2. Run Add Database to Fail Safe Group.
3. Run Verify Group.

If the database is in MSCS, run Verify Group.

Problem: You get a bad network name or IP address resolution.

Solution:

1. Make sure that the network name and IP address of the virtual server are in the tnsnames.ora file.
2. Make sure that public IP addresses are used in listener.ora and tnsnames.ora on the cluster nodes.

Table 21.4 shows some more OFS errors and solutions.

TABLE 21.4   OFS COMMON ERRORS AND SOLUTIONS

Error	Cause	Action
FS-10008: Unable to open the cluster node %s	The Fail Safe Server can't open the specified cluster node.	Verify that the node name is specified accurately and that the node is part of the cluster.
FS-10006: Unable to open the resource %s.	The Fail Safe Server can't open the specified cluster resource.	Verify that the resource name is specified accurately.
FS-10003: Failed to add the TCL file %s to the configuration list directory	The TCL file can't be added to the nmiconf.lst file in the $ORACLE-HOME Network\Agent\Config.	This is usually accompanied by another error that should be checked for more information.

Summary

Oracle provides a high-availability solution in Oracle Fail Safe. It's simple to implement and can be configured by using various strategies. You can administer OFS by using Oracle Fail Safe Manager, a GUI tool that's integrated with Oracle Enterprise Manager.

Unlike using a standby database, you can use a fail-safe server concurrently with the primary database, but for different applications. However, the fail-safe server doesn't provide scalability similar to that provided by Oracle Parallel Server.

Q&A

Q Can I use any Windows NT cluster to implement an Oracle fail-safe server?

A You should check with Oracle Support Services to determine whether your Windows NT cluster is valid for OFS implementation.

Q Why is the number of nodes limited in the Windows NT cluster that can be used for OFS?

A The current limitation is due to Microsoft Cluster Services and should be removed in later releases of MSCS.

Q Can I use OFS with UNIX machines?

A No. OFS is a clustering solution provided by Oracle only for Windows NT.

Workshop

The Workshop contains quiz questions and activities to help reinforce what you've learned in this hour. You can check Appendix A for the answers (but don't peek!).

Quiz

1. What are some troubleshooting utilities provided by Oracle Fail Safe Manager?
2. Can you convert a fail-safe database back to a standalone database?
3. What are some configurations in which OFS can be implemented?

Exercises

1. Implement an active/active fail-safe configuration.
2. Convert a fail-safe database back to a standalone database.

21

HOUR 22

Using Oracle Parallel Server

Oracle Parallel Server (OPS) allows multiple Oracle instances running on multiple nodes to access a single shared Oracle database. An Oracle instance exits on each node. The nodes share the same physical databasc and have common datafiles and control files but separate SGAs, log files, and rollback segments.

Each instance in a parallel server is identified by its ORACLE_SID.

In this hour, you will

- Understand Oracle Parallel Server as a clustering solution
- Understand the types of locks used in Oracle Parallel Server
- Understand the effect of pinging
- Understand how database recovery occurs in an Oracle Parallel Server environment

Using Windows NT Clusters

Windows NT clusters can exist in different configurations:

- *Tightly coupled systems* use multiple CPUs that share memory through a common memory bus. The bus's bandwidth limits the performance of such machines.

- *Loosely coupled systems* use a node that contains one or more CPUs and communicates with other nodes through a high-speed common bus. The nodes don't share memory, but they do share disk and other resources.

- *Massively parallel processors* are also referred to as a *shared-nothing architecture* (see Table 22.1). Each node usually contains an inexpensive CPU, and high scalability is achieved by the use of hundreds of nodes. Neither memory nor disk resources are shared between nodes. The nodes communicate by using a high-speed interconnect.

OPS runs on loosely coupled systems, as well as massively parallel processors. OPS isn't supported on tightly coupled systems because of the performance problem that would occur as a result of maintaining the distributed lock manager (DLM) and cache coherency.

TABLE 22.1 COMPARING SHARED-DISK AND SHARED-NOTHING ARCHITECTURES

Feature	Shared Disk	Shared Nothing
Direct access to disks from all nodes	Yes	No
Provides load balancing	Yes	No, this can result in "hot" nodes
Flexibility in resource allocation	Yes	No, resource usage can be skewed
Uses node-to-disk affinity	No	Yes
The bandwidth of the shared bus can cause performance problems	Yes	Maybe
Internode communication	Can be excessive if applications aren't well designed	Minimal
Fault tolerance	High	Low
Scalability	Low	High
Coherence control	Global, uses DLM	Local

OPS provides several advantages:

- *High performance and scalability*—You can use an OPS environment to improve the performance of well-designed database and application environments. If a single instance environment isn't properly designed and is performing poorly, using OPS can actually further degrade performance. Therefore, you have to put a lot of effort into designing your database and applications before you use OPS.

- *High availability*—By using the fault-tolerance and failover capabilities of the operating system and the DLM, you can achieve high availability. The various nodes that are part of OPS are isolated from one another, so failure in one node doesn't affect other nodes. The other nodes can keep running and can help in the recovery of the failed node.

- *Support a large number of users*—Each node has its own memory and can therefore support users. As more nodes are added, more users can be supported.

Oracle8i Parallel Server running on Windows NT has the following characteristics:

- Each node in the Windows NT cluster can run its own instance.
- All instances share the same set of database files and control files.
- Instances can use different init.ora files but must have some common parameters.
- Each instance has its own shared global area (SGA) and background threads.
- Each instance has its own redo thread accessible by other instances, because they will use this redo during instance recovery.
- Archived redo logs can be separate but are available to all instances so that media recovery can be performed.
- Each node can support multiple users who can execute multiple transactions simultaneously.

The SGA in each instance contains the following structures:

- Database buffer cache that contains the data blocks
- Redo log buffer cache that contains redo entries
- Shared pool that contains the shared SQL and PL/SQL
- Data dictionary cache that caches the data dictionary information
- Distributed lock area that contains locks used for coordinating access to shared resources

Oracle Parallel Server Architecture

Oracle has defined the requirements and interfaces for the operating system–dependent (OSD) components to provide valuable service during the operation of OPS. Each hardware vendor provides its own OSD layer. Some modules are required according to Oracle's specification, whereas others are optional and used by individual vendors to obtain competitive advantage. Figure 22.1 provides a quick overview of the OPS architecture.

FIGURE 22.1

Oracle Parallel Server architecture.

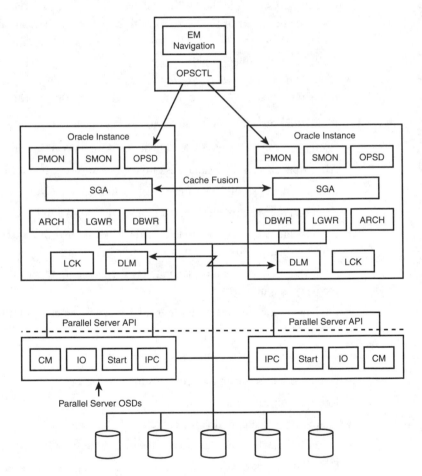

22

The OSD layer contains several modules that provide a range of functionality:

- *Cluster Manager (CM)* is used to discover and access the cluster's state. Oracle Parallel Server's fault-tolerance capabilities depend on the cluster resources' fault-tolerance capabilities. In case a cluster node fails, the CM reconfigures a cluster. CM has several restrictions:

| Cluster members are aware of one another's existence. | Cluster members can access the shared resources. |
| Nonmembers can't access the shared resources. | Nonmembers can't communicate with members. |

- *Inter-Process Communication (IPC)* provides reliable communication between instances. The DLM performs all its functions through an asynchronous messaging model supported by the IPC. An OPS system's performance depends heavily on the usage of a fast interconnect between nodes.

- *Input/Output* provides access to shared devices from all nodes to a cluster disk farm. Shared disks are accessed with the use of Win32 and Windows NT I/O calls via the Windows NT raw file system. To increase performance, use high-speed storage devices connected to the nodes in the cluster via fiber-channel links.

- *Startup* initiates the OPS components in a particular order during instance startup. It initializes vendor-specific structures and allocates the resource components.

NEW TERM
Oracle8i allows the use of *cache fusion*, a very low-cost cache coherency scheme. Now implemented in Phase I, this feature allows the transfer of requested blocks between instances via the high-speed interconnect, instead of writing the block to disk by one instance and then reading by another instance.

Cache fusion should take care of the following scenarios:

- *Read/read*—The user on one node wants to read a block just read by the user on another node.

- *Read/write*—The user on one node wants to read a block just modified by the user on another node.

- *Write/write*—The user on one node wants to modify a block just modified by the user on another node.

Phase I takes care of only the read/write case, whereas future releases will also deal with the write/write case. Cache fusion makes it possible to obtain high scalability for online transaction processing (OLTP) applications with a medium level of update activity.

> Oracle8i uses the concept of a *service*, which clients use (instead of an instance name) to make a connection. tnsnames.ora specifies the multiple nodes associated with a particular service. The service can be used to achieve automatic failover because the client connects to the service, not to a particular node. The connection is satisfied by using any available node belonging to that service. If a node fails, the connection is satisfied by a surviving node of the service.

System Requirements

Running OPS on Windows NT requires many components from the hardware vendor. Oracle has a certification plan for PC vendors so that they can support OPS on Windows NT. Using OPS on Windows NT requires the use of raw partitions, in addition to other requirements.

Hardware Requirements

Each node requires the following in the cluster:

- One or more 80486 or higher processors or Alpha processors.
- A network interface card (NIC), which must be on the hardware compatibility list for Windows NT as specified by Microsoft
- A local hard disk to store the operating system and Oracle relational database management system (RDBMS)
- A CD-ROM drive
- At least 96MB of RAM
- A high-speed intra-cluster interconnect

Software Requirements

The following is required by each node in the cluster:

- Windows NT 4.0 with Service Pack 3
- Microsoft TCP/IP
- Oracle 7.3.3 or higher
- SQL*Net 2.3 or Net8
- Vendor-specific cluster software
- Any version of Netscape Navigator or Internet Explorer (to view the online documentation)

You also have to use a shared disk subsystem. All Oracle datafiles, control files, and log files are placed on this shared disk system, which have to use raw partitions for each file.

Parallel Cache Management and Locking

Cache coherency is the key to the functioning of OPS. Cache coherency keeps the changes to data blocks synchronized across multiple memory caches (Table 22.2 shows a mapping of DLM locks to Oracle locks). Cache coherency is necessary because multiple copies of the data block are required to be kept consistent across the different instances.

TABLE 22.2   MAPPING DLM LOCKS TO ORACLE LOCKS

DLM	Oracle	Interpretation
NL	NULL	No lock acquired
CR	SS	Read concurrently
CW	SX	Write concurrently
PR	S	Read protection
PW	SSX	Write protection
EX	X	Exclusive write

The DBWR writes dirty blocks to the disk when

- A checkpoint occurs.
- A server process moves a buffer to the dirty list, and a threshold length is reached.
- A certain number of blocks are searched in the Least Recently Used (LRU) list without finding a free block.
- Another instance requests a copy of the block for write purposes.

> In an Oracle Parallel Server environment, cache coherency is done on demand.

Cache coherency provides the following benefits:

- Disk I/O operations are avoided, resulting in time savings.
- Operating system context switching is minimized, which minimizes CPU.

Distributed Lock Manager (DLM)

The DLM coordinates the access to shared resources in an OPS environment. The DLM is external to Oracle and resides on each node. It performs several functions:

- Coordinates the requests for locks on shared resources such as data blocks, data dictionary entries, and rollback segments by the various Oracle processes running on the different instances
- Keeps track of the resource owners
- Informs the resource owner when another process requests the resource owned by it
- Accepts requests for resources, grants the resources, keeps track of requests in case the requested resource is unavailable, and notifies the process when the resource becomes available
- Communicates with Oracle via the Lock (LCK) processes

During the configuration of a DLM, you can use the following formulas to determine the settings for the resources, locks, and processes:

```
resources = total_PCM_locks + (total_non_PCM_locks * num_instances)

locks = (total_PCM_locks * num_instances) +
        (total_non_PCM_locks * num_instances)

processes = processes * num_instances
```

Types of Locks in Oracle Parallel Server

Oracle uses several lock types to keep access to shared resources synchronized between the different instances:

- *PCM locks*—Parallel cache management locks are instance locks used to manage the data blocks in datafiles. They ensure cache coherency by requiring an instance to acquire the lock before reading or making any changes to the block. At any time, only one instance is allowed to modify a block. Typically, one PCM lock will cover several data blocks.

The smallest PCM lock granularity that can be achieved is one PCM lock per data block.

- *Non-PCM locks*—These locks aren't used for cache coherence.
- *DFS (Distributed File System) Enqueue locks*—These instance]locks act as global locks when in parallel mode. When not running in parallel mode, they act as normal enqueues.
- *DFS locks*—These instance locks are used only in parallel mode.

Methods of PCM Locking

PCM locks can be used in two ways, hashed locking and fine-grain locking.

Hashed Locking

Locks are preallocated. At instance startup, locks are statically hashed to blocks, so instance startup time is slower.

The association between the number of locks to datafiles is specified by the init.ora parameter `gc_files_to_locks`.

Locks are released only when the instance shuts down.

Hashed locking is suitable for read-only datafiles and when data is well partitioned.

Fine-Grain Locking

Locks are acquired and released on demand. The instance starts up faster, but time is consumed when a DLM resource is requested.

Fine-grain locking is suitable for frequently updated files.

> It's possible to use hash locking and fine-grain locking with different datafiles.

Pinging

Pinging occurs each time a data block is written to disk by one instance so that it can be read by another instance. On the other hand, false pinging occurs when a block is written to disk by one instance not because the particular block is requested, but because another block that's managed by the same lock is requested. In other words, for true pinging, the block requested is the same as the blocked pinged; in false pinging, the block requested isn't the same as the block pinged.

A ping is considered to be a hard ping if it results in a block being written to disk; it's considered to be a soft ping if it simply involves lock conversion.

Pinging always occurs by virtue of the nature of the parallel server mechanism. Therefore, your goal shouldn't be to eliminate pinging but to minimize the pinging activity. You should especially reduce the amount of false pinging.

As an example of false pinging, you have a PCM lock that manages data blocks 1–4:

1. Instance 1 is updating block 2.

2. Instance 2 requests block 4 for update.

3. All the blocks (including block 2) are written back to disk before being converted. As a result, you have false pinging because block 2 is written to disk even though it isn't really being requested.

4. When the write is completed, instance 2 acquires the lock and can update block 4.

False pinging is determined by the lock granularity.

Row-Level Locking

Row-level locking is still maintained when using OPS. This is evidenced from the following example, which assumes that there's one PCM lock per block (although it's very well possible that one PCM lock is covering multiple blocks):

1. Instance A requests to update row 1, which is in block n covered by a PCM lock.

2. Instance A becomes the owner of the PCM lock that's covering block n.

3. Instance A updates row 1 in block n.

4. Instance B requests to update row 3 in block n.

5. The DLM passes the notification to instance A.

6. Instance A writes the data block to disk and releases its ownership of the associated PCM lock.

7. Instance B acquires the ownership of the PCM lock covering block n.

8. Instance B updates row 3.

9. Instance A requests to update row 7 in block n.

10. The DLM passes the notification to instance B.

11. Instance B writes the data block to disk and releases its ownership of the associated PCM lock.

12. Instance A acquires the ownership of the PCM lock covering block n.

13. Instance A updates row 7.

Figures 22.2, 22.3, and 22.4 can further help you understand cache coherence.

FIGURE 22.2

Node 1 has a PCM lock on block n and a row lock on row i.

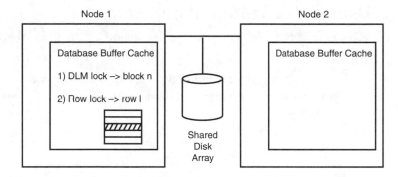

FIGURE 22.3

Node 2 requests to update row j in block n. Block n is written to disk, and the PCM lock is release by node 1.

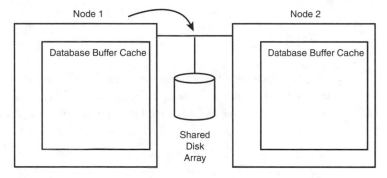

FIGURE 22.4

Node 2 acquires the PCM lock on block n and row lock on row j.

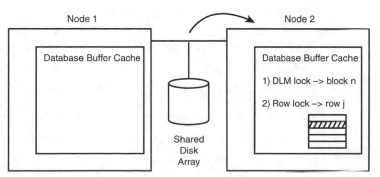

PCM locks are managed by the LCK processes associated with an instance. At least one LCK process is associated with an instance, but there can be more. If multiple LCK processes are associated with an instance, they will share the management of PCM locks so that each LCK process is responsible for a subset of the PCM locks. The LCK processes are also responsible for lock conversion in case of hash locks and acquiring, conversion, and release of fine-grained locks.

Using Initialization Parameters

You can use several init.ora parameters to control the use of PCM locks in an OPS environment:

- GC_FILES_TO_LOCKS specifies the mapping of hashed and database access (fine-grained) locks to datafiles. All instances involved in OPS must use the same value for this parameter.

> The default is to use hash locks. You can use fine-grained locking by setting a GC_ parameter to 0. For example, GC_DB_LOCKS = 0 sets fine-grained locking for data blocks, whereas GC_ROLLBACK_LOCKS = 0 sets fine-grained locking for undo blocks.

- GC_LCK_PROCS specifies the number of LCK processes used by an instance (LCK0 through LCK10 are possible 10 LCK processes). The default value is 1. This parameter is used during shared mode but ignored during exclusive mode. All instances involved in OPS must use the same value for this parameter.

- GC_RELEASABLE_LOCKS specifies the number of locks used by fine-grained locking. The default value is the same as the value for DB_BLOCK_BUFFERS. Different instances can use a different value for this parameter.

- GC_ROLLBACK_LOCKS specifies the number of locks to control the simultaneous modification of rollback segment blocks. By default, DBA locks are used for each rollback segment.

- GC_FREELIST_GROUPS specifies the number of locks to use for free-list groups.

> You can use the v$ping and v$lock_activity view tables to monitor pinging activity.

PCM resources and locks used by an OPS environment depend on the following parameters:

- `GC_DB_LOCKS`
- `GC_SEGMENTS`
- `GC_FREELIST_GROUPS`
- `GC_SAVE_ROLLBACK_LOCKS`
- `GC_ROLLBACK_SEGMENTS`

Non-PCM resource usage depends on

- `PROCESSES`
- `DLM_LOCKS`
- `TRANSACTION`
- `GC_LCK_PROCESSES`
- `ENQUEUE_RESOURCES`

Mapping Blocks to PCM Locks

PCM locks are mapped to blocks in the datafiles as specified by the `GC_FILES_TO_LOCKS` parameter. Use the following guidelines to set this parameter:

- All instances accessing the database should have the same value for `GC_FILES_TO_LOCKS`.
- "Hot" files concurrently accessed by many instances should be assigned a large number of locks to reduce pinging. At the same time, files not accessed simultaneously by many instances can have fewer locks so that the overhead for managing them is reduced.
- Indexes should be placed in their own tablespaces or in datafiles separate from their data so that they're assigned PCM locks separately. PCM locks on indexes are usually fewer than those on datafiles.
- Use only one PCM lock for a read-only index.
- If possible, specify all the datafiles in `GC_FILES_TO_LOCKS` so that they aren't assigned "leftover" locks.
- Don't assign any locks to undo blocks.
- Don't assign any locks to temporary/sort blocks.
- Place all read-only objects in one file, and then assign one hash lock to that file.

22

The syntax for `GC_FILES_TO_LOCKS` is as follows:

```
GC_FILES_TO_LOCKS = "{file_list=lock_count[!blocks][EACH][:]}..."
```

> No spaces should be used in the specification of `GC_FILES_TO_LOCKS`.

In this syntax,

- `file_list` specifies the files affected by the locks. You can specify a single file, range of files, or multiple files separated by commas.
- `lock_count` specifies the number of PCM locks to be assigned to the specified file list.
- `!blocks` optionally specifies the number of contiguous data blocks to be covered by each PCM lock.
- `EACH` optionally specifies that each file in the `file_list` should have `lock_count` locks.

> If you omit `EACH` and `!blocks` in the specification, the locks specified by `lock_count` are collectively allocated to the files specified by `file_list` so that an individual PCM lock covers data blocks across each file in the `file_list`.

The following examples assume the following datafile sizes:

- Datafile 1 has 80 blocks.
- Datafile 2 has 100 blocks.
- Datafile 3 has 120 blocks.
- Datafile 4 has 240 blocks.

Example 1:

```
GC_FILES_TO_LOCKS = "1=40:2-3=60:4=240"
```

Interpretation:

- In datafile 1, 40 PCM locks map to 80 blocks. Therefore, each PCM lock covers 2 blocks.
- For datafiles 2 and 3, a total of 220 blocks is covered by 60 blocks. Therefore, a PCM lock can cover two or three data blocks in datafile 2 and two blocks in datafile 3. Thus, one PCM lock may cover four or five data blocks across both datafiles.
- In datafile 4, each PCM lock maps to a single data block.
- The total PCM locks are 40+60+240 = 340.

Example 2:

```
GC_FILES_TO_LOCKS = "1-2,4=40EACH:3=100"
```

Interpretation:

- Datafiles 1, 2, and 4 will have 40 PCM locks.
- Datafile 3 will have 100 PCM locks.
- The total PCM locks are 40*3 + 100 = 220.

Example 3:

```
GC_FILES_TO_LOCKS = "1-4=45"
```

Interpretation:

- Because this example doesn't use the keyword EACH, 45 PCM locks are allocated to datafiles 1–4.
- The total number of data blocks are 80+100+120+240 = 540.
- Each PCM block covers 12 blocks (540/45 = 12), which are spread across the four datafiles. In other words, each PCM lock will cover three blocks in each datafile.

Example 4:

```
GC_FILES_TO_LOCKS = "1=20:2=0:3=40:4=100"
```

Interpretation:

- Datafile 1 gets 20 hash locks.
- Datafile 2 will use fine-grained locking.
- Datafile 3 gets 40 hash locks.
- Datafile 4 gets 100 hash locks.

The value of GC_DB_LOCKS must be greater than or equal to the locks speci-fied by GC_FILES_TO_LOCKS.

Application Features That Cause Contention in OPS

Several application features can cause contention in an OPS environment. Make sure that if your application uses these features, you make the appropriate changes to the environment to avoid excessive pinging:

- *Multiple nodes inserting in the same table concurrently*—This will cause contention for the free blocks of that table and effectively slow the insert operation.

  Resolution: Use free-list groups and multiple tables. Also, partition the application.

- *Use of sequence numbers and maintaining ordering*—In an OPS environment, sequence numbers can't be cached in the SGA of multiple instances and still be used to maintain order.

  Resolution: Use multiple sequences, and change the application to eliminate the necessity of maintaining ordering.

- *Multiple nodes inserting in the same indexed table concurrently*—This will cause contention for the free blocks of the index and effectively slow the insert operation.

  Resolution: Use free-list groups.

- *Performing full table scans at the same time that the blocks are being updated by another instance*—This will cause pinging of the rollback segments to provide a valid read-consistent image of the data.

  Resolution: Avoid full table scans.

- *Use of referential integrity constraints that propagate across nodes*—This refers to situations in which a transaction performs an operation, such as cascading a DML operation. This will cause pinging if the tables involved in the transactions are used by other nodes. Your transaction might not necessarily update the child tables directly, but they will be affected behind the scenes.

  Resolution: Redesign your applications to minimize the use of cascade operations. Also, partition the applications.

- *Use of triggers*—Triggers can do many things behind the scenes that might not be obvious when performing a DML. These "extra" operations can result in significant pinging.

22

Resolution: Understand the operations performed by triggers, and validate whether they are all necessary or can be performed by some alternative means. Also, partition the application.

- *Use of tables that hold transient information*—If an application uses tables to hold transient information such as the state of the transaction, progress of the transaction, and so forth, such tables will have much DML activity, even though the actual amount of information they store might not be significant.

  Resolution: Tune the locks and use the minimum number of such tables that hold transient information.

- *Performing large, range-based deletes from multiple nodes*—On the surface, it might seem a good idea to perform a large delete operation from multiple nodes where each node is working on a range of rows. However, this operation will cause lots of pinging unless the application is well partitioned.

  Resolution: Perform the range-based delete operation from only one node, instead of multiple nodes simultaneously. Also, partition the table so that the range-based deletion conforms with the partitioning strategy in use.

- *Packing too many rows in a block*—Although space is saved when you use a large number of rows in a block, the potential for pinging greatly increases in this situation.

  Resolution: Spread data as much as possible without wasting too much space (this is a challenge!). Also, partition the application, and use fine-grained locking to avoid false pinging.

Space Transaction (ST) Lock Contention

When using OPS, you will commonly encounter contention for ST locks because of the serialization of space management. The following guidelines can help minimize contention for ST locks:

- Disable SMON on all but a few instances.
- Initial and next extent sizes should be almost equal and large enough to avoid a lot of extension by the segments.
- Set PCTINCREASE to 0.
- DML operations on the same file must be performed from the same instance.
- Increase SORT_AREA_SIZE.
- Use fine-grained locking to block granularity on the system tablespace.
- Set event 10269 to disable coalescing.

- Don't perform frequent creation and deletion of objects.
- Minimize the number of sort space management transactions by using dedicated temporary tablespaces.

 Contention for space management resources can be indicated by the occurrence of ORA-1575.

Administering OPS on Windows NT

OPS on Windows NT can be managed by using Server Manager or Oracle Parallel Server Manager (OPSM), which is part of Oracle Enterprise Manager. OPSM provides several capabilities, including

- Startup and shutdown of an instance
- Gathering performance statistics per instance or for the entire cluster
- A GUI interface to simplify administration

You also can use command-line utilities to perform some administration in an OPS environment:

- opsconf can be used to create the topology files in the Enterprise Manager.
- opsctl uses the opsd daemon to send commands and queries to the instance.

To Do: Use the opsconf Utility to Create Configuration Files

Oracle provides a useful utility, opsconf, that allows you to quickly and easily create the configuration files required for Oracle Parallel Server as demonstrated here:

1. From the command prompt, run opsconf.
2. When prompted, provide the following information:
    - Name of your OPS database (TMx)
    - The ports for the listener and intelligent agent
3. The tnsnames.ora and listener.ora files are created under the %ORACLE_HOME%\ops directory. Copy these files to the %ORACLE_HOME%\network\admin directory on each node.
4. Verify that the listener.ora file is okay by stopping and starting the listener.
5. Verify that the tnsnames.ora file is okay by connecting to Server Manager with the TMx alias for your instance.

To Do: Use the `opsctl` Utility

The syntax for the use of `opsctl` utility to start instances is as follows:

```
OPSCTL START -Cconnect string -Nops_name [-ISID, SID]
      [-F] [-T] [-U] [-M] [-Y¦-E] [-v] [-h]
```

To start instances with this utility, follow these steps:

1. Start all the instances:

   ```
   c:\> OPSCTL START -Csystem/manager -Nops_name
   ```

2. Start the "test" instance, where *test* is the SID of the instance:

   ```
   c:\> OPSCTL START -Itest -Csystem/manager -Nops_name
   ```

The syntax to use the `opsctl` utility to stop instances is as follows:

```
OPSCTL STOP -Cconnect string -Nops name [-ISID, SID]
      [-F]  [-M] [-v] [-h]
```

To stop instances with this utility, follow these steps:

1. Stop all the instances:

   ```
   c:\> OPSCTL STOP -Csystem/manager -Nops_name
   ```

2. Stop the "test" instance:

   ```
   c:\> OPSCTL STOP -Itest -Csystem/manager -Nops_name
   ```

Backup and Recovery

You can perform online backups of multiple tablespaces in parallel from different nodes. This can be very efficient for very large databases. If an instance fails, another instance will detect the failure and perform recovery. Failure of one or more instances doesn't affect the operation of the other instances. Recovery of a failed instance is performed by coordinating the SMON process from the other instances.

> At least one instance has to be running in order to perform recovery of the other failed instances.

Instance recovery is performed by applying the redo logs, rolling forward the committed transaction, and then applying rollback on uncommitted transactions. If all the instances go down, the recovery is started when any instance starts up. All instances should have access to the redo logs from other instances so that recovery can be performed successfully. Media recovery can be performed with the instance mounted in the exclusive or parallel mode but not open.

Traditional backup and recovery strategies used in a single instance database environment also hold good in an OPS environment. For performing backups in an OPS configuration, note the following points:

- Backups (online and offline) can be started from any node. When performing a hot backup, the tablespaces must be put in hot backup mode in only one instance.
- You can start two different backups from two different nodes simultaneously.
- To prevent one set of redo logs from having their SCN too much behind the current SCN, log switches will be forced on instances that lag behind in SCNs.
- The amount of redo generated in an OPS configuration is generally much higher than a single instance.

To Do: Perform Media Recovery in an OPS Configuration

▼ To Do

To recover from the loss of a datafile, follow these steps:

1. Shut down the database by using the shutdown command from any instance:

   Svrmgr> **shutdown immediate**

2. Restore the lost datafile from a valid backup.

3. Startup mount the database from any one instance:

   Svrmgr> **startup mount**

4. Recover the database:

   Svrmgr> **recover database**

5. Apply the redo logs from all the instances, or make all the redo logs available in the same directory so that the recovery will be automatic.

6. Open the database in the shared mode:

   Svrmgr> **alter database open shared**

▲ 7. Restart all the instances. Now users can log on to the database from any instance.

Identifying Problems in OPS

Identifying a performance problem in an OPS environment shouldn't start with the database. This is because most of the time the problem is with the application of the configuration of the O/S or DLM. To pinpoint the problem to the database, follow these guidelines:

- Examine the O/S statistics for problems.
- Examine the DLM statistics for problems.

22

- Check v$session_wait for waits on `buffer busy` or `lock element cleanup`.
- Determine the type of lock converts occurring in the system by using v$lock_activity.
- Determine the amount of pinging activity by using v$ping.
- Identify problem blocks by using v$bh.
- Identify objects in problem blocks by using v$ping and v$cache.

Run catparr.sql to create the views related to OPS.

OPS loads individual DLLs at runtime. The DLLs are specified in the HKEY_LOCAL_MACHINE\software\oracle\osd Registry hive. DLM parameters can be seen under the HKEY_LOCAL_MACHINE\Software\Oracle\OSD\PM\OPS Registry hive.

Summary

Oracle Parallel Server is a clustering solution that provides not only reliability but also good scalability, as long as the applications are written to take advantage of the parallel architecture. Application design plays an important role in the overall system performance, and you should make sure that the pinging in the system is minimized. Although you might not be able to completely avoid pinging, you should definitely focus on minimizing false pinging.

Oracle Parallel Server can potentially improve system performance tremendously, but it also requires careful configuration.

Q&A

Q My application is performing very poorly. Can I use an OPS environment to improve the performance?

A Not really. An application that performs badly in a non-OPS environment usually performs worse in an OPS-environment if it is used as is. You should change the application design and code to take advantage of the OPS environment. Only then will you achieve better performance.

Q Can I use OPS with MS Wolfpack?

A No. OPS does not use MS Wolfpack.

Workshop

The Workshop contains quiz questions and activities to help reinforce what you've learned in this hour. You can check Appendix A for the answers (but don't peek!).

Quiz

1. What is pinging?
2. What is the function of the Distributed Lock Manager?
3. How can you minimize contention for ST locks?

Exercises

1. Modify the init.ora parameters to implement fine-grained locking in your OPS environment.
2. In an OPS environment, you have dropped a table by mistake and want to recover it. Perform point-in-time recovery in the database.

Hour 23

Performing Parallel Operations

SQL performance can be greatly increased by executing statements in parallel. Unless specified, Oracle executes each SQL statement sequentially. Oracle8i can perform several operations in parallel:

- Table scans
- Create table as select (CTAS)
- Create index
- Rebuild index
- Update
- Insert
- Delete
- Star transformation
- Partition management such as moving and splitting of partitions
- Order-by operations

- Group-by operations
- Select distinct
- Union operations
- Join operations such as hash joins, sort merge joins, and nested loop joins

> Both query and Data Manipulation Language (DML) portions of a SQL state-
> ment can be parallelized.

In this hour, you will learn the following:

- The parallel query architecture
- How to use parallel operations
- How to troubleshoot parallel operations
- How to perform parallel data loads
- How to perform database recovery in parallel
- The initialization parameters that affect parallel operations

> The parallel operations described this hour are available only with the
> Enterprise Edition of Oracle8i Server.

Parallelization Methods

SQL statements are parallelized by several methods:

- *Parallelize by means of ROWID*—A query is parallelized dynamically at the time
  of execution. SELECTs and subqueries that are part of a DML or DDL statement are
  parallelized by using ranges of ROWIDs. The table or index on which the operation will be performed is split into ranges of ROWIDs, and the operation is performed in parallel on the different ranges. If the table or index is partitioned, a
  range of ROWIDs can't span partitions.

> The table or index on which a parallel operation is performed in ROWID
> ranges can be partitioned as well as nonpartitioned.

- *Parallelize by using partitions*—Operations on partitioned tables and indexes can be performed in parallel by assigning different parallel query server processes to the various partitions. You must execute the ALTER SESSION ENABLE PARALLEL DML command before using this method. This method is used only when more than one partition is affected by the operation and more than a predetermined number of table or index pages are being accessed.

> There is no parallelism within individual partitions, but a parallel server process can span multiple partitions.

- *Parallelize by using slave processes*—Insert operations for nonpartitioned tables are partitioned by using slave processes. You use the parallel slave processes to insert the new rows into the free space.

> You don't have to use the Oracle Parallel Server feature to be able to execute SQL statements in parallel.

Restrictions on Using Parallel Operations

There are several restrictions on the use of parallel operations:

- When used in a transaction, the parallel DML (PDML) must be the only statement in the transaction.
- A commit or rollback should immediately follow a PDML statement.

> If you place a PDML statement after a serial statement in a transaction, the PDML will also be executed serially.

- PDML can't be used on tables that have Long Objects (LOBs) or abstract datatypes.
- PDML can't be used on clustered or replicated tables or on bitmap indexes.

23

- Each PDML slave runs in its own transactions. The changes made by the slave aren't visible to subsequent statements in the top-level transaction. In the following example, the Select statement will see only changes made by the serial update, not those made by the parallel update. This is because the parallel update runs in a separate transaction, which isn't committed when the Select statement is run.

```
Begin transaction
Update table1 (serial)
Update table1 (parallel)
Select * from table1
Commit;
```

> If SERIALIZABLE = TRUE is set in the init.ora file, the PDML will be serialized.

- There's no trigger support for the table affected by PDML.
- Integrity constraints have several restrictions—namely, delete cascade, deferred integrity, and self-referential integrity aren't used.
- The PDML can't reference the remote table.
- Embedded functions that read or write database state or package state aren't allowed.
- Parallel updates can't use global unique indexes.

Parallel Query Architecture

In a dedicated server environment (non-MTS), each Oracle user session uses a single, dedicated server thread. The shadow thread is responsible for processing the client request and communicates with the client via some interprocess communication method.

Parallel operations use a query coordinator (QC), which performs several tasks:

- Divides the workload between PQ slave processes
- Manages the work
- Returns the query results back to the client

When an Oracle database instance starts, it starts a number of parallel query slave processes that are coordinated by the master query process as specified by the PARALLEL_MIN_SERVERS parameter. These servers keep running as background threads waiting for work. The coordinator can spawn additional query slaves on demand as required by a parallel operation, up to the maximum limit specified by PARALLEL_MAX_SERVERS.

Workload is balanced between the query slaves as follows: The query coordinator divides the target table into roughly equal-sized partitions so that the number of partitions equals the degree of parallelism (see Figure 23.1). Each partition is then further subdivided into three subpartitions: One is 9/13ths of the original; another, 3/13ths of the original partition; and the remaining, 1/13th of the original partition (see Figure 23.2). For example, if you're performing a full table scan on a table using a query of degree 6, the QC will divide the table into six partitions. Each partition is further subdivided into three subpartitions sized 9/13, 3/13, and 1/13, as shown in Figure 23.3. One of the larger 9/13ths of each partition is assigned to each query slave.

23

FIGURE 23.1

Original partitioning of table ABC.

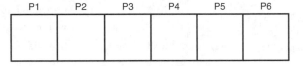

FIGURE 23.2

Subpartitioning of table ABC.

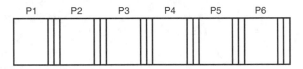

FIGURE 23.3

Large 9/13 subpartitions assigned to each query slave.

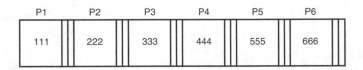

When a query slave finishes with a partition, the QC assigns the next biggest (3/13ths) partitions to the query slave. After the second round is over, the query slave works on the smallest (1/13th) partitions as they become available.

This kind of multitiered scheme of workload distribution allows a balance to occur between the query slaves. Also, the effect of skewed data is minimized.

 Inserts can be parallelized within partitions, but updates and deletes can be parallelized only across partitions.

Performing Parallel Operations

You can take advantage of the Oracle8 parallel DML features right after the installation of Oracle8i Server Enterprise Edition. Table 23.1 describes several initialization parameters you can use to reap the maximum benefit from using parallel operations.

TABLE 23.1 INITIALIZATION PARAMETERS USED WITH PARALLEL OPERATIONS

Parameter	Default Value	Description
parallel_min_servers	0	Specifies the number of query slaves to start when Oracle instance is started. 0 indicates that query slaves will be started on demand.
parallel_max_servers	Depends on cpu_count, parallel_automatic_ tuning, and parallel_adaptive_ multi_user	Specifies the maximum number of parallel query or recovery processes It determines the size of the memory structures used by parallel operations.
parallel_min_percent	0	Specifies the minimum percent of threads required for parallel query. It prevents an operation from running serially if enough resources aren't available.
parallel_automatic_ tuning	FALSE	When set to TRUE, Oracle tunes the parallel operations. The DBA should set the target tables to PARALLEL, and then Oracle will tune the parallel operations. User-specified hints will be ignored.
parallel_adaptive_ multi_user	parallel_automatic_ tuning	When set to TRUE, an adaptive algorithm is used to tune parallel queries in multiuser environments.
parallel_threads_ per_cpu	2	Specifies the number of threads a CPU can handle while executing a parallel query.

Several data dictionary views (see Table 23.2) are available for monitoring and tuning parallel operations.

TABLE 23.2 DATA DICTIONARY VIEWS USED WITH PARALLEL OPERATIONS

Data Dictionary View	Use
v$parallel_degree_limit_mth	Displays the available parallel degree limit resource allocation methods
v$pq_sesstat	Displays the statistics of parallel operations for the current session
v$pq_slave	Displays the information about active parallel query slaves
v$pq_sysstat	Displays systemwide statistics for parallel operations
v$session	Determines whether PDML is enabled for a session
v$transaction	Determines the status of a transaction
v$pq_tqstat	Displays detailed information about the execution of each parallel query slave and can be used to identify problems with skewed data

For a partitioned table, the number of query slaves can't exceed the number of partitions.

Hints Used with Parallel Queries

You can use several hints with parallel queries:

- PARALLEL can be used to specify the degree of parallelism for parallel operations. The syntax for a parallel hint is

  PARALLEL (*table*,*x*,*y*)

  where *table* is the table on which the parallel operation is to be performed, *x* is the desired degree of parallelism, and *y* is used only for a parallel server environment, specifying the number of instances that should run the SQL statement.

  For example, the following when executed from Server Manager selects from the dept table with a parallel degree of 3:

  ```
  Svrmgr> select /*+PARALLEL(dept,3)*/ *
          From dept;
  ```

- NOPARALLEL specifies that the operation is to be performed serially by ignoring the parallel degree associated with the target object.

- APPEND, during an insert operation, uses new free blocks to insert the data and ignores existing free space in the blocks.

- NOAPPEND, during an insert operation, uses existing free space in the blocks.
- PARALLEL_INDEX specifies parallel execution of a partitioned index during an index range scan.

To Do: Perform Parallel DML on a Partitioned Table

The amount of parallelism in your system can be increased by combining parallel operations with partitioned tables. The following steps demonstrate how to perform a parallel insert operation on a partitioned table:

1. Start Server Manager and connect as SCOTT:

```
C:\> svrmgrl
Svrmgr> connect scott/tiger
```

2. Create a partitioned table:

```
Svrmgr> CREATE TABLE megh (col1 number)
        PARTITION BY RANGE (col1)
        PARTITION P1 VALUES LESS THAN (5),
        PARTITION P2 VALUES LESS THAN (10),
        PARTITION P3 VALUES LESS THAN (15),
        PARTITION P4 VALUES LESS THAN (maxvalue);
```

3. Enable parallel DML for the session:

```
Svrmgr> alter session enable parallel dml;
```

4. Verify that parallel DML was enabled:

```
Svrmgr> select username, pdml_enabled
        From v$session
        Where username = 'SCOTT';

USERNAME      PDM
--------      ----
SCOTT         YES
```

5. Insert sample rows into the table by using parallel insert:

```
Svrmgr> insert /*+parallel (megh,3) */ into megh
        Select /*+parallel (dept,6) */ dept_id from dept;
```

6. Commit the parallel insert:

```
Svrmgr> commit;
```

> You must commit after a parallel DML. Otherwise, you will get error ORA-12830: Must COMMIT or ROLLBACK after executing parallel INSERT/UPDATE/DELETE.

▼   7. Determine the degree of parallelism:

```
Svrmgr> select * from v$pq_sysstat
        Where statistic in ('Servers Busy','Server Sessions');


STATISTIC            VALUE
--------------       -------
Servers Busy         3
Server Sessions      3
```

The output verifies the precedence rule for insert..select, which is as follows:

- Insert hint directive > parallel directive on insert

- Table > max query directive

8. Modify the values in the table by using parallel update:

```
Svrmgr> update /*+parallel (megh,6) */ megh
        Set col1 = col1 * 5;
```

9. Commit the parallel update:

```
Svrmgr> commit;
```

10. Determine the degree of parallelism:

```
Svrmgr> select * from v$pq_sysstat
        Where statistic in ('Servers Busy','Server Sessions');


STATISTIC            VALUE
--------------       -------
Servers Busy         4
Server Sessions      6
```

As seen from the output, although you specified six parallel query slaves, only four are busy—one for each partition.

11. Delete the values in the table by using parallel delete:

```
Svrmgr> delete /*+parallel (megh,3) */ megh;
```

12. Commit the parallel delete:

```
Svrmgr> commit;
```

13. Determine the degree of parallelism:

```
Svrmgr> select * from v$pq_sysstat
        Where statistic in ('Servers Busy','Server Sessions');


STATISTIC            VALUE
--------------       -------
Servers Busy         2
Server Sessions      2
```

▲   As seen from the output, you can have parallel query slaves spanning across partitions.

23

To Do: Create an Index in Parallel

▼ To Do

Indexes can be created in parallel by using the PARALLEL clause in the CREATE INDEX statement. You can also use the NOLOGGING clause to prevent the generation of redo.

> If you use the NOLOGGING clause for index creation, back up the index after creation because the index is essentially unrecoverable. Alternatively, you could also export the table.

Use these commands to create an index in parallel:

1.
```
CREATE INDEX megh_p_idx
ON megh (col1)
        PARALLEL (degree 2);
```

2.
```
commit;
```

▲

To Do: Determine the Degree of Parallelism for Join Operations

▼ To Do

When using parallelism with join operations the number of query slaves used is based on the maximum number specified in a query hint or the maximum degree of parallelism of all the tables in the particular SQL statement as shown here:

1. Connect to the database as SCOTT.

2. Change the degree of parallelism for the employees table to 4:
```
Svrmgr> alter table employees (parallel degree 4);
```

3. Change the degree of parallelism for the dept table to 6:
```
Svrmgr> alter table dept (parallel degree 6);
```

4. Verify the degree of parallelism set for the tables:
```
Svrmgr> SELECT table_name, degree
        FROM user_tables
        WHERE table_name in ('EMPLOYEES','DEPT');
```

TABLE_NAME	DEGREE
EMPLOYEES	4
DEPT	6

▼

▼   5. Perform the join operation:

```
Svrmgr> SELECT *
        FROM EMPLOYEES E, DEPT D
        WHERE E.dept_id = D.dept_id;
```

6. Determine the degree of parallelism:

```
Svrmgr> select * from v$pq_sysstat
        Where statistic in ('Servers Busy','Server Sessions');
```

```
STATISTIC              VALUE
- - - - - - - - - - - - - -    - - - - - - -
Servers Busy           4
Server Sessions        4
```

As seen from the preceding output, the number of query slaves used is based on the maximum number specified in a query hint or the maximum degree of parallelism of all the tables in the particular SQL statement.

7. Perform the join operation with hints:

```
Svrmgr> SELECT /*+ PARALLEL (employees,8) */ *
        FROM EMPLOYEES E, DEPT D
        WHERE E.dept_id = D.dept_id;
```

8. Determine the degree of parallelism:

```
Svrmgr> select * from v$pq_sysstat
        Where statistic in ('Servers Busy','Server Sessions');
```

```
STATISTIC              VALUE
- - - - - - - - - - - - - -    - - - - - - -
Servers Busy           8
Server Sessions        8
```

▲

Determining the Degree of Parallelism

The degree of parallelism for a parallel operation is the number of query slaves used by that operation. The degree of parallelism depends on several factors:

- User-supplied hints
- Initialization parameters
- The number of CPUs in the system
- The number of disks or files on which the target object is spread

The precedence rule for determining the degree of parallelism is determined as follows:

- *Using hints at the SQL statement level*—Hints can be used in SQL statements to specify the degree of parallelism desired:

```
SELECT /*+ PARALLEL (employees,4) */ *
FROM employees
ORDER BY dept_id;
```

  When this operation is performed in parallel, it uses nine processes: four parallel query slaves for the full table scan, four parallel query slaves for the sort operation, and one shadow process for the coordinator.

- *At the object level*—The degree of parallelism can be set at the object level for tables, clusters, indexes, and so on by using the CREATE and ALTER statements. You can view the degree of parallelism associated with an object by looking at the USER_TABLES table:

```
Svrmgr> Alter table employees parallel(degree,8);
Svrmgr> select table_name, degree
        From user_tables
        Where table_name = 'EMPLOYEES';


TABLE_NAME        DEGREE
- - - - - - - - - - -     - - - - - - -
EMPLOYEES         8
```

- *At the instance level*—The default degree of parallelism depends on your system resources, such as CPU, memory, I/O bandwidth, initialization parameters (such as parallel_automatic_tuning), and spread of data across disks.

If you don't have enough system resources to sustain the desired degree of parallelism, you might experience excessive paging, I/O bottlenecks, and performance degradation.

Parallel Load

The direct path SQL*Loader option allows you to load data into a table or partition in parallel:

```
C:\>Sqlload scott/tiger control=employee1.ctl parallel=TRUE direct=TRUE
C:\>Sqlload scott/tiger control=employee2.ctl parallel=TRUE direct=TRUE
C:\>Sqlload scott/tiger control=employee3.ctl parallel=TRUE direct=TRUE
C:\>Sqlload scott/tiger control=employee4.ctl parallel=TRUE direct=TRUE
```

Several characteristics are associated with the use of parallel data loads:

- There shouldn't be any local or global indexes on the table; otherwise, the parallel load fails. You have to drop the indexes before the parallel load and re-create them after the load is complete.
- The loading sessions run independently and don't communicate with each other.
- Each SQL*Loader session loads data into a new extent. Therefore, you should control the size of new extents by using the FILE and STORAGE keywords of the options clause in the controlfile.

Parallel Recovery

Oracle uses the redo log to record changes made to an Oracle block. The redo log can be used during media recovery to restore the blocks to their state before the media failure. During media recovery, you can restore the lost datafiles from a good cold backup and then perform recovery by applying the changes to the data blocks as indicated by the redo log.

You can perform recovery in parallel by setting the initialization parameter RECOVERY_PARALLELISM or using the PARALLEL clause of the RECOVER command. When performing the recovery in parallel, the redo log is read, and the information is passed to the slave processes. The slave processes then read the datafiles in parallel and apply the changes suggested by the redo log.

Performing Parallel Operations in a Parallel Server Environment

Use parallel operations to improve the performance of a parallel server environment. If you use an OPS environment with two instances and a degree of parallelism of 4 for an operation, four parallel query slaves are used in each instance when the statement executes. You can control the involvement of instances in parallel execution by using

- The PARALLEL hint, as described earlier in the section "Hints Used with Parallel Queries"
- The PARALLEL_INSTANCE_GROUP parameter

Instances can be grouped as desired so that during parallel executions you can specify the instance groups that participate by using the parallel_instance_group parameter.

Suppose you have three instances in an OPS environment with the following specifications:

- Instance 1 has `instance_groups = g_12, g_13`.
- Instance 2 has `instance_groups = g_23`.
- Instance 3 has `instance_groups = g_13, g_23`.

To perform a SQL operation in parallel on instances 1 and 3 while connected to instance 1, you should log on the instance 1 and execute

```
alter session set parallel_instance_group g_13;
```

Then, perform the parallel operation.

Transaction Recovery and Rollback Segment Issues

Oracle uses rollback segments to record "undo" information for transactions. This information is used during the recovery of a transaction from a system failure or a user-issued rollback of the transaction. Rollback segments are also used to provide read consistency for transactions so that changes made by one user aren't seen by another user until the transaction commits.

Long-running DML statements can have problems if the rollback segments aren't set properly. If you have a DML statement generating a lot of redo information, you may get an error if one of the following occurs:

- The rollback tablespace runs out of space, and the rollback segment can't extend.
- The MAXEXTENTS are reached for the rollback segment and can't extend further.

Because of these problems, when running parallel DML statements, you should set MAX-EXTENTS for rollback segments to be UNLIMITED and create the rollback segments in a tablespace that has enough space to expand as needed.

 Bring enough rollback segments online so that no more than two parallel transactions are assigned to each rollback segment.

A parallel DML statement can potentially use multiple rollback segments. Parallel operations use multiple slave processes, which generate their own undo information and therefore can potentially use different rollback segments. This brings up an issue regarding committing the transaction because it should be committed in each participating rollback segment. Oracle uses a two-phase commit mechanism to commit the transaction in each participating rollback segment. A COMMIT or ROLLBACK statement is therefore required after each parallel DML statement. The user isn't aware of the multiple commits going on in the background and is notified of a successful commit only when all query slaves can commit successfully.

If you attempt to issue another SQL statement in the same transaction as the parallel DML, you will get ORA-12830.

In Oracle8i, the time required to rollback a parallel DML is about the same as the time required to perform the forward operation. This is provided by a special form of the parallel transaction recovery feature called *intra-transaction recovery*.

Parallel transaction recovery wasn't available before Oracle8i.

When the parallel transaction recovery feature is enabled, SMON acts as a coordinator and rolls back multiple transactions in parallel by using multiple server processes. Multiple server processes are automatically used to recover transactions if the amount of work is above a certain threshold determined by SMON. The threshold is the point at which parallel recovery will be faster overall, compared with serial recovery.

Intra-transaction recovery—a special form of parallel transaction recovery—rolls back parts of a long-running transaction. The PARALLEL_TRANSACTION_RECOVERY parameter can be set to specify the number of processes used during transaction recovery. It can be set to one of the following values:

FALSE	Disable parallel transaction recovery.
LOW	The maximum number of parallel recovery servers is twice the value of CPU_COUNT.
HIGH	The maximum number of parallel recovery servers is four times the value of CPU_COUNT.

Advantages of Parallel DML Over Manual Parallelism

A DML statement can be manually parallelized by issuing multiple DML statements simultaneously over different datasets—for example, by issuing multiple UPDATEs and DELETEs using different ranges of ROWIDs. Using parallel DML instead of manual parallelization has several advantages:

- It's easy to use because Oracle performs the parallelization for you.
- Transactional atomicity can be achieved because all the query slaves will work on a read-consistent snapshot of the target object and commit simultaneously.
- Load balancing can be achieved.

Locking in Parallel DML

A parallel DML holds many more locks and enqueue resources compared with a serial DML; therefore, you should increase the value of DML_LOCKS and ENQUEUE_RESOURCES parameters so that the extra need can be satisfied.

When a parallel DML statement is executed, the coordinator acquires

- One table-level SX lock
- One partition lock X per partition (unless a parallel update or parallel delete includes a where clause that limits the partitions involved)

whereas each slave process acquires

- One table-level SX lock
- One partition-level NULL lock per partition
- One partition-wait lock X per partition

For example, if you perform a parallel update (degree 4) on a table with eight partitions, the number of locks held are as follows:

- The coordinator has one table lock SX and eight partition locks X
- The slave processes have four table locks SX, eight partition NULL locks, and eight partition-wait locks X

Using Event 10046 to Diagnose a Parallel Query

You've seen thus far that while running a parallel operation, you can encounter performance problems because the demand on system resources is very high. Usually, when the system is overloaded and you try to perform a parallel operation, you will get ORA-12800, which indicates that you should lower the degree of parallelism or perform the operation later, when the load on the system isn't very high.

Several events can be set in the system to diagnose the behavior of a parallel query. The most important event, 10046, basically performs a SQL_TRACE on the parallel query and provides more detailed information based on the level set for the event. The various levels that can be set for event 10046 and their corresponding level of detail displayed is as follows:

- Level 1, the default level, enables standard SQL tracing for the operation.

- Level 4 displays SQL_TRACE information and trace bind values.

- Level 8 is probably the most useful tracing level because it indicates the SQL_TRACE information and wait events that can be used to see whether the operation is waiting on some event.

- Level 12 is the most detailed level, which includes SQL_TRACE information, trace bind values, and wait events. This level can generate a large file, so make sure that you have enough space in the dump destination.

The event can be set at the session level or at the instance level. If you set the event at the instance level, the generated trace information will be huge but not necessarily very clear. Therefore, you should set the event at the session level just before executing the parallel operation.

- To set event 10046 at the instance level, set the following line in init.ora, and restart the database instance:

  ```
  Event="10046 trace name context forever, level X"
  ```

  X is the level that you want to set for the event.

- To set event 10046 at the session level, use

  ```
  Svrmgr> alter session set events '10046 trace name
      2> context forever, level X'
  ```

  X is the level you want to set at the session level.

Interpreting the Output of Event 10046

After you set event 10046 and execute a parallel query, a trace file is generated that contains SQL_TRACE information for the query, as well as other diagnostic information. If level 8 is in use, for example, you will receive wait information, which can be interpreted as follows:

```
WAIT#A: nam="B" ela=C p1=D p2=E p3=F
```

In this interpretation,

- A is the wait event number.
- B is the event being waited on.
- C is the time elapsed for the operation.
- D is the file number of the file in use.
- E is the block number in use.
- F is the number of blocks read by the operation.

For example,

- A wait for full table scan is as follows:
  ```
  WAIT #1: nam="db file scattered read"
       ela= 4 p1=3 p2=1264 p3=20
  WAIT #1: nam="db file scattered read"
       ela= 4 p1=3 p2=1285 p3=32
  WAIT #1: nam="db file scattered read"
       ela= 4 p1=3 p2=1318 p3=32
  ```

  This output indicates that a full table scan is being performed because of "db file scattered read". The first line indicates that only 20 blocks of the object are being read—because the object is only 20 blocks long or because these are the last 20 blocks. The next two lines indicate that you're reading the number of blocks specified by the db_file_multiblock_read_count parameter.

- A wait for index scans is as follows:
  ```
  WAIT #1: nam="db file sequential read" ela= 4 p1=3 p2=1819 p3=1
  WAIT #1: nam="db file sequential read" ela= 4 p1=3 p2=2901 p3=1
  WAIT #1: nam="db file sequential read" ela= 4 p1=3 p2=3104 p3=1
  ```

  These waits indicate an index scan due to "db file sequential read". Only one block is being read at a time.

Summary

Symmetric multiprocessing systems (SMP), clustered systems, and massively parallel processing systems (MPP) can benefit tremendously by executing SQL statements in parallel. The workload can be shared by multiple processes that can simultaneously work on the SQL statement and achieve scalability. You can perform several operations in parallel, but it's important to properly configure the initialization parameters that can affect these parallel operations.

23

Q&A

Q Why should I issue a COMMIT or ROLLBACK after a parallel DML?

A During a parallel DML, Oracle can use multiple rollback segments. A two-phase commit mechanism is used to commit or roll back the transaction in all rollback segments. If this isn't done, data inconsistency can result. Oracle gives error ORA-12830 if you don't execute a COMMIT or ROLLBACK after a parallel DML.

Q If I don't enable parallel DML, can I still perform parallel queries?

A Yes.

Workshop

The Workshop contains quiz questions and activities to help reinforce what you've learned in this hour. You can check Appendix A for the answers (but don't peek!).

Quiz

1. What is *degree of parallelism*?
2. What are the advantages of using parallel DML?
3. What happens if the init.ora parameter SERIALIZABLE is set to TRUE and you perform a parallel DML operation?
4. How do you determine whether parallel DML is enabled for a session?

Exercises

1. You have a very large database system. Implement a recovery strategy for this database in order to reduce mean time to recover (MTTR).
2. You get ORA-12800 when running an application that you wrote. How do you resolve this error?

Hour **24**

Integrating Oracle and the World Wide Web

Oracle recognizes Java as a very powerful language that's quickly gaining acceptance in the development community for deploying enterprise applications. Several important characteristics of Java contribute to its success:

- It's an object-oriented language.
- It uses an open standard for application development.
- It uses JavaBeans and Enterprise JavaBeans (EJB), which can improve productivity by allowing code reuse.
- It enables you to develop portable applications.
- It can execute in browsers, application servers, and databases. Thus, developers can write applications by using just one language. It's widely accepted as *the* language to develop Internet applications.

In this hour, you will

- Understand the Java Virtual Machine
- Create and use Java stored procedures
- Understand the Internet file system
- Understand Enterprise JavaBeans

Oracle's Java Strategy

Java is a key component to Oracle's strategy of a network computer model (see Figure 24.1) that will ultimately result in a low cost of ownership. Oracle has implemented Java into Oracle8i with two major approaches:

- Providing an enterprise-class Java server platform with fast access and manipulation for online transaction processing systems and decision support systems, support for a large number of concurrent users, high availability and fast failover, integration with system management tools such as Oracle Enterprise Manager, and integration of a Java virtual machine (JVM).

FIGURE 24.1

Oracle's Java strategy.

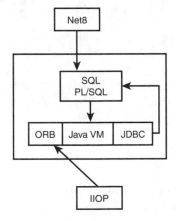

- Providing a set of Java tools that can be used to quickly develop efficient Java applications: JDBC drivers that provide database connectivity from Java; an SQLJ translator, which allows the use of embedded SQL in Java; JDeveloper, which allows the development of Java programs and integrates JDBC and the SQLJ translator into a complete development environment; CORBA connectivity; Oracle Application Server; the ability to create and load Java stored procedures and triggers; and component-oriented development, supported with the use of JavaBeans and EJB.

Applications written in Java can be deployed in two-tier and multitier configurations.

Using Java Database Connectivity (JDBC)

JDBC is a standard set of classes that allow application developers to access and manipulate relational databases from within Java programs. JDBC supports SQL92 syntax and allows vendors to provide extensions to improve performance.

JavaSoft modeled Java on open database connectivity (ODBC), an open standard developed by Microsoft for accessing databases.

24

JDBC Drivers Provided by Oracle

Oracle provides two types of JDBC drivers, which you can use for different types of applications:

- *Thin JDBC driver*—Written completely in Java, this is ideal for Java applets that can be used with a browser. The thin driver is only 300KB and can be downloaded. When you download an applet from an HTML page, the thin JDBC driver is downloaded with it. When the applet is fired, the thin driver establishes a direct Net8 connection between the applet and the Oracle database. Scalability is achieved by the use of the Net8 Connection Manager, which should reside on the same host as the Web server. The Connection Manager multiplexes several inbound physical connections onto a single database connection, thereby saving server memory.

The thin JDBC driver supports only Net8 running over the TCP/IP protocol. Also, client-side libraries aren't required when using the thin JDBC driver.

- *JDBC/OCI driver*—This provides OCI calls to access the database, using Oracle client libraries such as OCILIB, CORE, and Net8. These are written in C, so the driver isn't downloadable. You have to perform client installation of the JDBC/OCI driver. It can be used for client/server Java applications, as well as middle-tier Java applications running in a Java application server.

> The Java code you write to access Oracle is the same no matter which driver you use. The only difference is in the connect string used.

Both drivers are JDBC 1.2.2 compliant and support Oracle-specific features:

- Support for Oracle7 and Oracle8 object-relational data types
- Support for manipulating LOB data
- Performance enhancement features such as array interface, prefetching, and batch SQL statement execution
- Access to PL/SQL and Java stored procedures
- Support for all Oracle character sets

> Current security restrictions require that the database and Web server be on the same host. This restriction is lifted for applets signed with JavaSoft JDK1.1.

Embedding SQL in Java with SQLJ

Oracle allows developers to write efficient and compact programs with the use of SQLJ. SQLJ, built on top of JDBC, allows application developers to embed SQL statements in Java programs, and to run a preprocessor to translate SQLJ to Java code that makes JDBC calls to the database by using a JDBC driver from any vendor. SQLJ programs can be developed and debugged by using Oracle's JDeveloper, which is a standard Java development tool. Because the SQLJ runtime environment runs on top of the JDBC driver, it can be deployed by using the same configuration as JDBC programs—namely, the JDBC/OCI driver with middle-tier applications and the thin JDBC driver for Java applets. The biggest advantage you gain by using SQLJ is increased productivity and manageability of Java code by providing the following:

- Code that's significantly compact compared to JDBC
- Strong typed queries with the use of typed cursors
- Compile-time checking of SQL statements to identify errors at an earlier stage and quickly debug and deploy applications

You can use SQLJ programs by following these generic steps (see Figure 24.2):

1. Write a SQLJ Java program.

FIGURE **24.2**

Using SQLJ to develop Java applications.

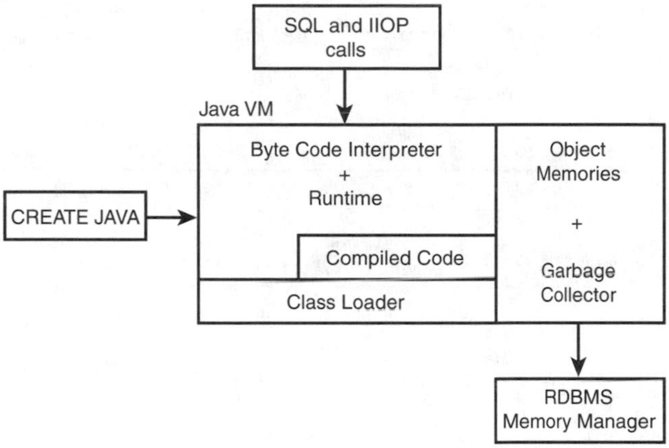

2. Run the SQLJ program through the SQLJ translator. The translator preprocesses the SQLJ program and generates standard Java code with JDBC calls.

3. Compile the Java code.

4. Run the Java program.

Listings 24.1 and 24.2 show a JDBC program and its equivalent SQLJ program. From these examples, you can easily see that the use of SQLJ results in compact and simpler code.

INPUT   **LISTING 24.1**   A SAMPLE JDBC PROGRAM

```
Java.sql.CallableStatement stmt;
Connection conn;
ResultSet res;

/* Declare the objects for a callable statement,
connection, and the result set*/

Conn = DriverManager.getConnection("jdbc:default");

/* Initialize the connection object with the default connection */
Stmt = conn.prepareStatement
("SELECT ename FROM emp WHERE ecity = ? AND deptno = ?");

/* Prepare the statement to execute */
```

continues

LISTING 24.1   CONTINUED

```
Stmt.setString(1,city_p);
Stmt.setInteger(2,deptno_p);

/* Use positional parameters to set the variables*/

Res = stmt.executeQuery();

/* Execute the query and store the results in the result set */
```

INPUT   **LISTING 24.2**   A SAMPLE SQLJ PROGRAM

```
ResultSet res;

/* Define an object to store the result set */

#sql res = (SELECT ename FROM emp
           WHERE ecity = :city_p AND deptno = :deptno_p);

/* Pass the program through the SQLJ translator and execute the program.
The result set is stored in "res" */
```

Stored Java procedures and triggers are SQL intensive and can benefit from the use of SQLJ during their development.

Oracle8i provides a SQLJ translator embedded in its Java machine.

Oracle8i offers several features that make it an open and extensible platform for application development:

- An open protocol CORBA/IIOP (in addition to Net8)
- Java as an open server programming language (in addition to PL/SQL)
- The capability to use data cartridges
- The Internet File System (IFS)

Understanding the Java Virtual Machine

Oracle's Java virtual machine (JVM) is a very important component of the Oracle Java strategy, providing high performance and scalability while running Java applications. Oracle's JVM is tightly integrated with the database and runs on the Multi-Threaded Server. The JVM has several characteristics (see Figure 24.3):

- It supports shared Java byte codes and lightweight Java threads.

FIGURE 24.3

Components of the JVM.

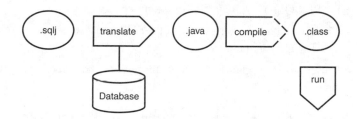

- It provides a well-tuned memory manager and garbage collector that optimize the use of the SGA (40KB per user session) and the operating system's virtual memory manager.
- It allows Java classes to be stored in the database as database library units.
- It provides the NCOMP Java compiler to translate Java byte code to C executables, which can be run very efficiently.
- It supports standard Java libraries such as Java.lang, Java.io, and Java.util.
- It supports JDBC driver and SQLJ translator approaches.
- It provides a CORBA 2.0–compliant ORB (Object Request Broker) that can be used to call in and out of the database with the CORBA/IIOP protocol.
- It provides utilities to load and unload Java programs into the database.
- It allows you to use Java stored procedures and triggers.
- It's 100% JDK 1.1.6 compliant.
- It allows the use of Enterprise JavaBeans (EJB 1.0 compliant) by taking various approaches: pure Java clients, CORBA/IIOP clients, and D/COM clients.
- It provides a standard JDBC driver, which offers the same interfaces as OCI, and thin JDBC drivers, which allow Java applications to be easily loaded into and used in the database.
- It efficiently uses Oracle Multi-Threaded Server (MTS). The Net8 Connection Manager also can multiplex CORBA/IIOP connections, in addition to Net8 connections.

24

- It provides mission-critical high availability and transparent application failover.
- It supports efficient load balancing on SMP and MPP architectures.
- It allows ease of management through the use of Oracle Enterprise Manager. OEM allows centralized monitoring and management of distributed Oracle8 servers and Java stored programs, use of standard Oracle utilities such as SQL*Loader, and Export/Import for Java procedures.
- It allows the use of existing database security mechanisms such as roles and grants for PL/SQL, as well as Java stored procedures.
- The use of "invoker" rights with PL/SQL and Java stored procedures simplifies security management.
- It uses security features available through the advanced networking option against Java procedures.

Using Enterprise JavaBeans and CORBA

EJBs allow the use of a component-based model for implementing Java systems. They can be completely developed in Java and deployed by using execution containers such as databases, TP-Monitors (also known as Transaction Processing Monitors), and application servers. The use of EJBs offers several advantages:

- They use a high level of abstraction, making them simple to program.
- They are developed completely in Java.
- They are compatible with CORBA, D/COM, and so on.
- They allow the use of transactional applications as modular components.

Oracle8i provides a CORBA 2.0 – compliant ORB, which allows applications to access Java stored procedures and EJBs through the IIOP protocol. It also allows you to write Java applications that can call out of the database and communicate with other ORBs through IIOP. Using CORBA/IIOP with Oracle8i now requires the use of MTS.

 Now, only Java-Java communication is supported with the ORBs.

The mechanism to use CORBA/IIOP is very simple:

1. Write your Java stored procedures and EJBs.

2. Publish the procedures and EJBs so that they can be accessed as a stored procedure via Net8 and as a CORBA server.

3. Client applications (CORBA and D/COM) can access the published procedures through IIOP.

Java Stored Procedures

You can build applications in Java by using three methods:

- Write Java stored procedures and triggers.
- Implement CORBA servers in the database in Java.
- Execute Enterprise JavaBeans.

Oracle8i lets you write stored procedures by using PL/SQL and Java. Although PL/SQL is seamless with SQL, using Java provides an open, general-purpose platform to develop and deploy applications. Java stored procedures can be written efficiently by using SQLJ, which allows SQL to be embedded in Java code. Java stored procedures can run in different runtime contexts:

- You can write top-level SQL functions and procedures that allow you to implement business logic in a manner similar to PL/SQL.
- All types of triggers supported by Oracle can be implemented using Java.
- Methods associated with objects can be implemented by using Java, in addition to PL/SQL or C/C++. The body of an object type also can be implemented as a Java class.

Java stored procedures implemented in Oracle8i are standards compliant, which consist of two main parts:

Part 0	The specification of SQLJ that lets you develop efficient applications by embedding SQL statements into Java programs.
Part 1	The specification of Java stored procedures that provides standard DDL extensions to "publish" or register Java programs with SQL so that the Java stored procedure is callable from SQL. It also provides standard DML extensions to call Java from SQL.

Java stored procedures can be replicated between Oracle8i servers and from Oracle8i servers to mobile clients by using Oracle Lite.

The use of Java stored procedures provides several benefits to OLTP applications:

- Network traffic can be reduced because result sets can be processed on the database server and only the results are sent across the network. This allows efficient usage of server resources because transfer of large quantities of data across the network isn't necessary.

- Business rules can be enforced centrally and by allowing Java stored procedures to be replicated between, say, the headquarters and the branch offices.

- Various configurations can be supported, such as client/server and multitier configuration.

- The use of Java in the development of stored procedures provides an open and ANSI/ISO-compliant standard environment. This allows the stored procedures to be portable across various platforms.

- Java and PL/SQL can interoperate very well to allow application reuse.

You develop Java stored procedures by following these general steps:

1. By using a standard Java tool, develop a Java program that you want to make a stored procedure. Oracle provides JDeveloper and SQLJ, which you can use to develop efficient Java programs quickly.

2. After the Java program is written, load it into Oracle8i's JVM. Java source text can be loaded as standard Java .class files or as Java .jar files. To load Java class files in Oracle8i, issue the CREATE JAVA DDL command, or use the LOADJAVA utility to automate the loading process.

3. Register the Java program with SQL by exposing the top-level entry point, which SQL can use to call Java. These exposed entry points are the only calls that SQL can make to this Java program. Subsequent Java-to-Java calls can be made within the JVM as needed. You should also make sure that the data types are appropriately mapped between Java and SQL.

4. Give appropriate rights to the users so that they can call and run this procedure.

5. Call the Java stored procedure from SQL DML, PL/SQL, or triggers.

Loading Java Classes into the Database

Java developers write Java programs by using a standard Java tool such as AppBuilder for Java. They debug the programs locally and then load them into the database. Oracle8i accepts two input sources:

- A binary file on the operating system level
- A LOB column in the RDBMS

The two input sources can be obtained in three formats:

- Standard Java source texts automatically recompiled by the Oracle Java byte code compiler
- Java binaries
- Java resources

 Java programs are stored as database library units (*libunits*). The JVM's class loader loads Java from any input source in any format into an RDBMS libunit. Three types of libunits are provided, one for each type of input.

> One libunit is created per Java class, and the name of the libunit is derived from the Java class. For example, if the fully qualified name of a Java class is `com.oracle.sqlj.TestClass`, the libunit's name is `com/oracle/sqlj/TestClass`.

Using the LoadJava and DropJava Utilities

LoadJava is a utility that Oracle provides to automate loading Java programs into the database. LoadJava is written in Java and uses the JDBC drivers (thin JDBC or JDBC/OCI) to communicate with the database. It can take input, which can be Java source texts, Java binaries (.class), and Java archives. It doesn't load Java resources directly, but you can archive (.jar) the Java resources and then load the JARs via the LoadJava utility.

DropJava is a complimentary utility you can use to drop Java binaries and archives from the libunits.

24

When LoadJava is run, it performs the following tasks:

1. It creates a system-generated table, `create$Java$lob$table`, that can be used to load Java.

2. The Java binaries and JARs are loaded into a BLOB column of this system-generated table.

3. `CREATE JAVA` is invoked to load Java from the BLOB column into database libunits.

The syntax for LoadJava is as follows:

```
LoadJava [-user connectstring] [options]
```

In this syntax,

- `connectstring` is of the form `username/password@database` and is used to specify the database schema to load Java into.

- Options that can be specified include the following:

`-o`	Use the JDBC/OCI driver.
`-t`	Use the thin JDBC driver.
`-v`	Use verbose mode to indicate the status of the load as it occurs.
`-f`	Force loading of classes by replacing existing classes. The default is to load only those that don't exist and those that have been modified.
`-r`	The resolver spec to use during the load.
`-s`	Create public synonyms for the loaded classes.
`-g`	Grant permissions on loaded classes.
`-h`	Obtain help on the syntax.

The following code example loads a Java class named `Test.class` into the schema SCOTT in the specified server using thin JDBC drivers. The class is forced, and status information is provided as the loading proceeds.

```
LoadJava -user scott/tiger@myserver:5521:ORCL -t -f -v Test.class
```

Registering Java Programs

Unlike PL/SQL procedures, Java procedures aren't automatically available to SQL. You have to register the Java programs by publishing the Java entry points so that SQL can call the Java methods. These Java methods can, in turn, make Java-to-Java calls within the JVM. Publishing Java to SQL can be accomplished in two steps:

1. Create a PL/SQL program that provides a type system wrapper for the Java method. Known as the *call descriptor*, this program specifies the mapping from Java types to SQL types, the mapping of the parameter modes, and so on.

2. At runtime, the SQL and PL/SQL code can call the "wrapper" program. This call is intercepted by the JVM, which executes the Java method in the database's address space.

Oracle8i provides a new SQL DDL syntax that you can use to specify the PL/SQL call descriptor. The PL/SQL call descriptor consists of two parts:

- The PL/SQL procedure PSEC declaration, which represents a proxy for the Java method

- The body of the PL/SQL program, which is composed of the Java method signature

> Arguments between the proxy program and the Java method signature are mapped by position.

The oracle.sql package provides automatic datatype conversion between Java, SQL, and PL/SQL. Table 24.1 shows the mapping between the datatypes.

TABLE 24.1 MAPPING JAVA TO SQL AND PL/SQL DATATYPES

Java	SQL and PL/SQL
String, oracle.sql.CHAR	CHAR, VARCHAR2
Oracle.sql.DATE	DATE
Int, Integer, float, Float, double, Double, oracle.sql.NUMBER	NUMBER, DECIMAL, INTEGER, FLOAT, REAL, DOUBLE PRECISION
Oracle.sql.BLOB	BLOB
Oracle.sql.CLOB	CLOB

continues

24

TABLE 24.1 CONTINUED

Java	SQL and PL/SQL
Oracle.sql.BFILE	BFILE
Oracle.sql.RAW	RAW and LONG RAW
Oracle.sql.ROWID	ROWID
Oracle.sql.OracleObject	Oracle8 objects
Oracle.sql.REF	Oracle8 REF

When you use Java stored procedures, you should be careful about using different modes for the parameters. Java accepts only IN arguments by reference, whereas SQL and PL/SQL use IN, OUT, and IN OUT modes of parameter passing. When using IN parameters, consult Table 24.1 to determine the data type mapping that can be used between Java and PL/SQL types. While using OUT and IN OUT parameter modes in SQL and PL/SQL, the corresponding Java parameter should be a one-element array of the appropriate Java type so that no mismatch occurs with the use of parameters in the Java stored procedures.

Here's the syntax for declaring the PL/SQL call descriptor:

```
CREATE [OR REPLACE]
PROCEDURE proc_name [([sql_parameters])] ¦
FUNCTION func_name [([sql_parameters])]
    RETURN sql_type
AS LANGUAGE JAVA NAME 'Java_fullname ([Java_parameters])
    [return Java_type_fullname]'
```

In this syntax,

```
sql_parameters := sql_type> [, sql_parameters]
Java_parameters := Java_type_fullname [, Java_parameters
```

Listing 24.3 is a sample Java stored procedure.

INPUT **LISTING 24.3** A JAVA STORED PROCEDURE

```
/* The Java method 'greetings' takes a String argument and returns
a string value. This method needs to be published in SQL */
Java Class Welcomejava:
    Public class welcome {
    Static public String
    Greetings(string firstname) {
        Return "Welcome " + firstname;
        }
    }
```

```
/* PL/SQL proxy for welcomejava
It maps the string datatype to SQL VARCHAR2 */
CREATE FUNCTION greetings(fname VARCHAR2) RETURN
VARCHAR2 AS
    LANGUAGE JAVA NAME
    'Welcome.greetings(Java.lang.String)
    return Java.lang.String'
```

Java methods called from SQL or PL/SQL execute under the definer's privileges. Java methods called from other Java methods can execute under definer's or invoker's privileges, but by default, they execute under the invoker's privileges. This is a marked difference from execution of PL/SQL procedures that execute under the definer's privileges. In order to execute a Java method, users must have the following privileges:

- EXECUTE rights on the PL/SQL call descriptor for the Java method
- EXECUTE rights on the Java class
- EXECUTE rights on the Java classes and resources used by the Java class being called

24

> Oracle GRANT and REVOKE statements can be used to manage privileges on Java stored procedures.

To Do: Write a Java Stored Procedure

▼ To Do

Now you have a chance to write a Java stored procedure that modifies an employee record to give the employee a raise and change the employee's location. This example uses JDeveloper, but you can use any Java tool or editor to write the Java program. Follow these steps:

1. Start JDeveloper.
2. Choose File, New Project.
3. Write the Java programs as shown in Listings 24.4 (updjava) and 24.5 (empjava), one in each Java source file.
4. Compile both source files: updjava and empjava.
5. From the toolbar, select the New button.
6. On the Deployment page, choose Stored Procedure Profile.
7. Click OK to start the Stored Procedure Wizard.
▼ 8. For the wizard's first two dialog boxes, click Next.

▼ 9. In the next dialog box, select only the updjava file.

10. Click Next in the Step 3 dialog box.

11. In the next dialog box, select Thin JDBC Driver and then click Next (also see Listing 24.6, which shows how to use JDBC drivers with Java applications).

12. Specify the connection parameters: username, password, host ID, Oracle SID, and port number. Click Next.

13. Click Next for the Step 6 dialog box.

14. In the next dialog box, select the method that has to be published, and click Next.

15. Click Finish. The Java method is now loaded and published to SQL.

16. Select the Project pull-down menu from the menu bar.

17. On the Run/Debug page, provide the appropriate connection parameters, for example,

    ```
    jdbc:oracle:thin:@myserver:5521:ORCL scott tiger
    ```

18. Choose Send Run Output to Execution Log.

19. Click OK.

20. Compile the empjava file.

▲ 21. Run empjava to invoke the procedure.

INPUT   **LISTING 24.4**   UPDJAVA—USING SQLJ TO WRITE JAVA STORED PROCEDURES

```
package modify_emp;

import sqlj.runtime.*;
import sqlj.runtime.ref.*;

public class update_emp {

  public static int update_emp (String name,
         int raise, String location) {

    int newsal = -1;
    String newloc = "UNKNOWN";

    try{
      #sql {UPDATE emp
            SET sal = sal + :raise
            WHERE ename = :name};

      #sql {UPDATE emp
            SET city = :location
            WHERE ename = :name};
```

```
    #sql {SELECT sal INTO :newsal
          FROM emp
          WHERE ename = :name};

    #sql {SELECT city INTO :newloc
          FROM emp
          WHERE ename = :name};

  }
  catch (Java.sql.SQLException e) {};

  return newsal;
 }
}
```

24

LISTING 24.5   EMPJAVA—CALLING JAVA STORED PROCEDURES

```
//Title:      Using SQLJ with Java Stored Procedures
//Author:     Megh Thakkar
//Description: This Java program modifies the employee record by
// giving the employee a raise and changing the employee's location
package modify_emp;
import Java.sql.*;
import Java.io.*;

class maintain_emp
{
  public static void main (String args [])
      throws SQLException, IOException
  {
    String cstring = args[0];
    String uname = args[1];
    String pwd = args[2];

    // Load JDBC Drivers
    DriverManager.registerDriver
        (new oracle.jdbc.driver.OracleDriver());

    // Connect to the database using the specified parameters
    Connection conn =
      DriverManager.getConnection (cstring, uname, pwd);

    // Prepare to call the stored procedure
    CallableStatement cstmt =
        conn.prepareCall ("{? = call
            modify_emp_update_emp (?, ?, ?, ?)}");
```

continues

LISTING 24.5   CONTINUED

```
        // We are using positional arguments
        // The first argument is declared as an OUT parameter
        cstmt.registerOutParameter (1, Types.INTEGER);

        // The second argument is SCOTT
       //   The third argument is the raise
     // The fourth argument is the city
       cstmt.setString (2, "SCOTT");
       cstmt.setInt (3, 50000);
       cstmt.setString(4,"MIAMI");

        // Execute the command
        cstmt.execute ();

        // The first argument returns the new salary
        int new_salary = cstmt.getInt (1);

      System.out.println ("The new salary for SCOTT is: " + new_salary);
    }
  }
```

INPUT   **LISTING 24.6**   USING THE JDBC DRIVER WITH JAVA APPLICATIONS

```
//Title:       Using JDBC
//Author:      Megh Thakkar
//Description: This Java program queries the emp table to find the
// location of each employee

package package1;

import Java.sql.*;

public class find_location

{
  public static void main (String args [])
       throws SQLException
  {
    String cstring = args[0];
    String uname = args[1];
    String pwd = args[2];

    // Load JDBC Drivers
    try
    {
      Class.forName ("oracle.jdbc.driver.OracleDriver");
```

```
    }
    catch (ClassNotFoundException e)
    {
      System.out.println ("Unable to load driver");
    }

// Connect to the database using the connection parameters
    Connection conn =
      DriverManager.getConnection (cstring, uname, pwd);

    // Create JDBC Statement
    Statement stmt = conn.createStatement ();

    // Query the employee locations and store
    // the output in the result set
    ResultSet rset = stmt.executeQuery
            ("select empno, ename, city from emp");

    while (rset.next ())
    {
      // Get Employee Number
      int eno = rset.getInt(1);
      // Get Employee Name
      String ename = rset.getString(2);
      // Get Employee city
     double loc = rset.getString(3);

      System.out.println (eno + "   " + ename + "   " + city);
    }
    conn.close();
  }
}
```

Oracle Internet File System

It has been found that most companies store very little information (only about 1% of all the data) in relational databases. Most of the information is now held in file systems. File systems basically fragment information such as documents, Web content, and so on, into separate data stores, which have their own storage and access methods. The current technique of storing information in file systems has several problems:

- *End users*—End users have to install multiple clients, each with its own configuration set to access the information in the separate data stores. Users also find it extremely difficult to keep track of the various datatypes associated with the project they're working on.

- *System administrators*—System administrators have a difficult time maintaining security, performance, and configuration; providing access to users; and maintaining the integrity of the data, which may be spread across multiple machines and data stores.
- *Application developers*—Application development is slow because of the necessity for developers to understand different operating system peculiarities; understand different APIs to access files, Web content, and relational data; and keep track of all the components of the project.

One approach to simplifying the problems associated with storing information in file systems is to move as much data as possible into a relational database such as Oracle. However, this approach also presents several problems:

- Certain types of information, such as email and simple files, aren't efficiently used and manipulated using a relational database.
- End users have to be more "SQL aware."
- In a regular file system, you double-click a file to access its contents. For a file stored in a relational database, you have to download the file, edit the file, and upload it back to the database.

Oracle8i provides the Internet File System (IFS) to merge the file system with the database. IFS is a database file system (DBFS) that stores the data in the database, rather than leave the data outside the database and provide links from the database to access the information. Placing data within the database provides several benefits:

- *Simplified data security*—Clients can access the information by using multiple protocols and client interfaces. To access IFS, you can use the following protocols:

SMB	Allows users to drag and drop files. Files can be edited within IFS. Access is possible through Windows 95, Windows 98, and Windows NT.
HTTP	Used for Web browsers.
FTP	Access to IFS is through FTP. The contents of IFS are viewed as FTP directories from which you can get and put files.
SMTP, IMAP4, POP3	Access to IFS is through email clients such as Microsoft Outlook and Eudora.

- Application developers can use a common API for programming against the database.

- Advanced search capabilities can be used to search the contents of the DBFS using SQL and provide much better search performance compared to file systems.

- Database-level security is provided to simplify administration.

- Check in and check out facilities simplify the management of information and increase productivity.

- Enhanced scalability can ease data administration.

- Document parsing and rendering make it possible to view the same document in different formats.

- Data within the database is tightly integrated with the Oracle Enterprise Manager, ConText data cartridge and Oracle8i features such as objects.

- IFS messaging can be used to simplify administration by sending email to the system administration when important events occur.

- You can write and use Java stored procedures and EJBs.

- Version control is provided so that a new version of a file can be created when you copy or edit a file. One version can be identified as "official" and will be used by all users.

- Automatic purging of files after a specified "expiration" period simplifies data management.

24

Oracle IFS runs as a Java application that runs inside a Java machine in Oracle8i, providing a flexible and easy-to-use mechanism for storing and manipulating the data. Multiple protocols can be used to access the data. Application development is achieved by using the programming APIs provided by Java, CORBA, and PL/SQL.

IFS uses a "folder" strategy to make itself appear as a mounted network drive. The contents of IFS appear in folders and subfolders, which can be easily manipulated just like a file system. In addition to the manipulation of folders provided by IFS (similar to a regular file system), you can store relational and nonrelational data in the same folder. Relational data also appears as files, and you can construct a document by merging relational and nonrelational data. The documents can further appear as files.

Another important characteristics of an IFS "file" is that it can have multiple parent directories. For example, an email document (which appears as an IFS file) can be part of two separate folders.

You can create, rename, and delete IFS folders as you would in a regular file system.

Several additional features are planned for the future release of IFS:

- Support for NFS
- Application development tools for IFS
- Portable IFS
- "File system" tablespaces
- Integration with SQL

The full production version of IFS is expected to appear in Oracle 8.1.7, which is due for release in June 1999.

Summary

Java is a key component of the Oracle8i strategy, and this chapter discusses the various ways Oracle has implemented Java. The Java Virtual Machine makes it a very easy environment to run Java applications. You have seen how to write Java stored procedures and the use of Enterprise JavaBeans.

Oracle provides two types of drives to allow Java programs to access the database: thin drivers and JDBC/OCI drivers. No matter which driver you use, the code is still the same, but you use different connect strings.

Q&A

Q How can I configure the Java Virtual Machine?

A The Java Virtual Machine is automatically configured by Oracle. You don't have to do anything special to use it.

Q Should I develop procedures using PL/SQL or Java?

A It depends on the use of the procedure. Java provides more portability to the procedure and allows you to use an open standard, whereas PL/SQL is more tightly integrated with Oracle and allows you to write more efficient code. However, object methods are implemented more effectively using Java.

Workshop

The Workshop contains quiz questions and activities to help reinforce what you've learned in this hour. You can check Appendix A for the answers (but don't peek!).

Quiz

1. Which JDBC drivers are provided by Oracle?

2. How can you use SQLJ programs?

3. What are the advantages of using EJBs?

Exercises

1. Modify the Java stored procedure in Listing 24.4 to give all employees a 25% raise.

2. Move all the Java stored procedures from the TEST database to the PROD database.

24

Appendix A

Answers to Quiz Questions

Hour 1, "Understanding the Architecture of Windows NT and Oracle8i"

1. Can Oracle8i be used with Windows NT on ALPHA platforms?

   Yes, Windows NT's HAL component hides the hardware complexities and allows Oracle8i to run on various hardware platforms, including ALPHA.

2. What file systems does Windows NT support? Which file system provides file-level security?

   FAT, HPFS, NTFS, and CDFS are supported by Windows NT. NTFS provides file-level security.

3. Which Oracle background threads are required?

   PMON, SMON, LGWR, and DBWR.

4. What does the control file contain?

   The system change number (SCN), data file locations, redo log file locations, database name, and database size.

5. Which data dictionary view can be used to determine whether a database is in archivelog mode?

   v$database

Hour 2, "Using Windows NT Tools for Oracle8i"

1. Which Windows NT tool can you use to start Oracle services?
   Control Panel.

2. Where is information about all the Oracle variables kept in Windows NT?
   Registry.

3. Which log in Event Viewer contains Oracle-related messages?
   Application log.

4. What tool can be used to create raw partitions?
   Disk Administrator.

5. What happens when the OracleServiceORCL service is started?
   A handle is provided to a location in memory where the instance for ORCL database can be initialized.

Hour 3, "Configuring a Windows NT Server for Oracle8i"

1. What do we mean by *trust* with reference to Windows NT domains?
   Trust is an administrative and communication link that allows the sharing of account information between domains.

2. Which file system provides file-level security?
   NTFS.

3. Can you use Windows NT Workstation in a domain?

Yes, but it can't be used as a primary domain controller or backup domain controller.

Hour 4, "Installing Oracle8i on Windows NT"

1. What are the main components of a multi-threaded server environment?

Network listeners, shared servers, and shared dispatchers.

2. Which file contains a list of Oracle products installed?

nt.prd

3. What happens to the MTS connections if `MTS_SERVICE=ORACLE_SID`?

Connections requesting a particular SID get an available MTS connection (unless client calls request a dedicated server). If an MTS connection isn't available, a dedicated connection is made.

4. What init.ora parameter can be used to disable multi-threaded servers?

Setting `MTS_SERVERS = 0`.

Hour 5, "Migrating from Oracle7 to Oracle8i"

1. What alternative methods can you use to perform the migration to Oracle8i?

- The MIG utility
- Oracle's Data Migration Assistant
- Export/Import
- The SQL*PLUS `COPY` command

2. How is upgrading a database different from migrating one?

An *upgrade* is usually referred to as the process of going from one Oracle release to another (the source and destination having the same major release), such as upgrading from Oracle 8.0.4 to Oracle 8.0.5. A *migration*, on the other hand, refers to the process of going from one major release to another, such as migrating from Oracle7 to Oracle8i.

A

3. What are the restrictions on the use of the MIG utility to perform a migration?

Manual migration to Oracle 8.1.5 can be performed by using the MIG utility, provided the following is true:

- You are at Oracle release 7.1.3.3.6 or greater before the migration.
- The DB_BLOCK_SIZE is to be the same on the Oracle7 database and the migrated Oracle8i database.
- The character set will be the same on the Oracle7 database and the migrated Oracle8i database.
- The database isn't to be migrated to a different operating system.

Hour 6, "Creating an Oracle Database on Windows NT"

1. What script can be used to manually create a database?

BUILD_ALL.sql

2. How can you group objects to reduce disk contention?

To help reduce disk contention, group objects based on their access and use:

- Segments with different backup needs
- Segments with different security needs
- Segments belonging to different projects
- Large segments versus smaller segments
- Rollback segments
- Temporary segments
- Data segments
- Index segments

These objects should be separated across different disk drives, as well as tablespaces.

3. What are the purposes of the catalog.sql and catproc.sql scripts?

Catalog.sql creates the data dictionary, and catproc.sql is used to create the object used by PL/SQL.

4. Changing which parameters will require the database to be re-created?

DB_BLOCK_SIZE and/or the database character set.

Hour 7, "Converting a SQL Server Database to Oracle8i with the Migration Workbench"

1. What methods are available to you for migrating from SQL Server to Oracle8i?

   - Write a program that connects to both SQL Server and Oracle8i databases, retrieves from the source database, performs conversion/translation, and then inserts into the target database.

   - Use a gateway that performs a distributed query to transfer the database.

   - Use flat files for data transfer. SQL Server provides a tool, the Bulk Copy Program (BCP), that you can use to unload the data into flat files. This flat file can be loaded into Oracle by using Oracle's SQL*Loader utility.

   - Use Oracle's GUI Migration Workbench.

2. What script can you use to create the Oracle Migration Workbench Repository?

   The mwbrinst.bat script in the %ORACLE_HOME%\mwb\admin directory.

3. Where is the redo information contained in SQL Server?

   In the SYSLOGS table.

4. How do you convert DATETIME values from SQL Server to Oracle8i?

   - Replace the DATETIME data type with a combination of the DATE and NUMBER columns, in which the NUMBER column is inserted with values returned by DBMS_UTILITY.GET_TIME.

   - Precreate the SQL Server table with an additional integer column that has a sequence associated with it.

Hour 8, "Integrating and Administering Oracle8i on Windows NT"

1. What parameters must be set to encrypt database passwords?

   - Set DBLINK_ENCRYPT_LOGIN to TRUE for the Oracle instance. Restart the instance.

   - Set ORA_ENCRYPT_LOGIN to TRUE for each user that connects to Oracle.

2. What is the advantage of running a 16-bit application in its own VDM?

   Problems in other 16-bit applications won't affect a 16-bit application running in its own NTVDM.

A

3. How can you set up a Windows NT application as a service?

Using the INSTSRV.exe and SRVANY.exe utilities.

Hour 9, "Using Oracle Utilities"

1. What Oracle utility can you use to load an ASCII text file obtained from a Sybase database into an Oracle database?

SQL*Loader.

2. What restrictions are involved in using a direct path load?

- Clustered tables can't be loaded.
- Loaded tables can't have active transaction on them.
- The control file shouldn't contain SQL functions.
- SELECT statements can't be issued against the table during the load if it contains indexes.
- Referential integrity constraints are disabled during the load but re-enabled after the load.
- Default column values aren't used.

3. Can you lose sequence numbers as part of database exports?

You can potentially lose sequence numbers if one of the following occurs:

- Users are accessing the sequence while the export is running.
- Cached sequences are used. Export gets the current value from the data dictionary; cached numbers are skipped.

Hour 10, "Using the Oracle Enterprise Manager"

1. Which files are used by OEM?

Client files	sqlnet.ora, tnsnames.ora, and topology.ora
Server files	sqlnet.ora, tnsnames.ora, listener.ora, and snmp.ora

2. What does Oracle TopSessions provide?

Oracle TopSessions displays the top sessions based on any criteria you specify, such as CPU usage and disk I/O.

3. What are the main OEM components?

- OEM console
- OEM repository
- Communication daemon
- Intelligent agents
- Common services
- Application Programming Interface (API)
- Oracle Management Server
- Integrated applications

Hour 11, "Using the Replication Manager"

1. Why is replication not ideal for OLTP environments?

   Replication isn't ideal to use with highly transactional OLTP systems because of the amount of data changes that can occur in such systems. All these changes can cause performance problems during replication.

2. What are some methods for conflict resolution?

- The additive method adds the delta value of replicated changes to the current value.
- You can use timestamps.

3. Where are replicated object groups created?

   At the Master Definition Site.

Hour 12, "Managing Objects"

1. What is a method?

   A method is basically a PL/SQL procedure or function associated with an object. It stores the logic for the actions that can be performed against the object.

2. What are the benefits of using object views?

- A gradual migration path from relational systems to object-based systems
- Coexistence of relational and object-oriented applications because you can still access the base tables directly
- Improved performance by giving you the choice of using the best available strategies for manipulating data

A

3. What are the benefits of using object types?

- It standardizes applications and promotes easy data transfer between applications.
- Methods can be defined and reused, so development of applications can be fast and efficient.
- Object types make it easy to model real-world entities.

Hour 13, "Securing the Oracle8i Database on Windows NT"

1. What are the benefits of using fine-grained access control?

- Secure—The policies set for an object can't be bypassed, irrespective of how the object is accessed.
- Flexible—Predicates are generated dynamically, based on the application's state, and can thus serve diverse requirements.
- Transparent—The security rules can be changed for the object by changing the associated policies without requiring any change to the applications accessing the object.
- Scalable—If queries are written, they're automatically optimized, and the execution plan is sharable.

2. If user John is given NO_ACCESS on a file, but the group Engineers is given READ access to the same file and John is a member of the Engineers group, what is the effective right John has on the file?

   NO_ACCESS

3. When is the ACL associated with an object checked?

   An ACL associated with an object is checked only when the object is initially opened. Subsequent changes to the ACL take effect only when the object is reopened.

Hour 14, "Performing Backups"

1. Can a cold backup be used to perform incomplete recovery?

   No, a hot backup is necessary to perform incomplete recovery.

2. How do you copy open files on Windows NT?

   OCOPY.exe can be used to copy open files on Windows NT.

3. Can you use a standby database for other applications?

No, the standby database isn't used for any other purpose while it's in the "standby" mode.

4. Which data dictionary view can be used to obtain the location of control files?

`v$controlfile`

Hour 15, "Performing Database Recovery"

1. How can you reduce MTTR?

- Use partitioning techniques.
- Design the database so that the components are small and autonomous.
- Make sure that the backup is easily accessible.
- Verify that the backups are valid by testing them against dummy recovery scenarios.
- Familiarize yourself with the recovery procedures for the various scenarios.

2. Your control files are damaged, and the database instance doesn't mount. What do you do?

Execute the `CREATE CONTROLFILE` statement, and create a new control file.

3. If you lose a datafile that contains the index tablespace, what's the quickest way to recover from this?

Re-create the indexes.

4. A read-only tablespace is lost, and you don't have valid archive logs. What do you do?

You don't need archive logs to recover from a loss of a read-only tablespace.

Hour 16, "Using Recovery Manager (RMAN)

1. Which view can be used to monitor the progress of your backups done through RMAN?

`v$session_longops`

2. How can you determine the databases that the recovery catalog is aware of?

`rman> list incarnation of database`

A

3. What does `resync catalog` do?

   `resync catalog` causes the recovery catalog to be compared to the control file of the target database. It then updates the recovery catalog with new or changed information.

4. How can file copy operations be parallelized?

   By allocating multiple channels.

Hour 17, "Managing Contention"

1. What are the most common sources of contention when using Oracle8i on Windows NT?

   Rollback segments, shared servers, dispatchers, parallel servers, redo log buffer latches, database buffer cache LRU latches, library cache latches, and free lists.

2. How is a latch different from a lock?

   Locks control access to data rows, whereas latches control memory structures.

3. In a multi-threaded server environment, what can you control: shared servers, dispatchers, or both?

   Both

Hour 18, "Tuning Windows NT for Oracle8i"

1. How can you reduce the amount of disk activity when you're using Oracle8i on Windows NT?

   To minimize I/O problems, follow these guidelines:

   - Make sure that the memory isn't a bottleneck anymore.
   - Keep Oracle online redo logs on separate, nonstriped disks away from the datafiles.
   - Place archived redo logs on striped disks.
   - Use as many disk drives and disk controllers as possible, and distribute the I/O across multiple spindles.
   - Upgrade the hardware from IDE disks to SCSI and from SCSI to fast/wide SCSI.
   - Files that perform sequential I/O should be separated from randomly accessed files.

2. Which Windows NT tool can you use to create a raw partition?

Windows NT Disk Administrator.

3. Which Windows NT services shouldn't be disabled?

- Alerter
- Browser
- Eventlog
- Messenger
- OracleService*XXXX* (where *XXXX* is an instance name)
- OracleTNSListener
- Server
- Spooler
- Workstation

Hour 19, "Tuning Oracle8i for Windows NT"

1. What are the characteristics of an optimally tuned Oracle8i system on Windows NT?

- There's little or no waiting on I/O.
- Most CPU usage is allocated to shadow threads and occurs in user mode.
- The database has a good response time.
- The system is CPU bound.

2. What's the difference between the NOLOGGING and UNRECOVERABLE options?

NOLOGGING doesn't generate redo information, and UNRECOVERABLE doesn't generate rollback information.

3. What conditions must be true to use star queries?

- The cost-based optimizer must be used.
- All tables must be analyzed with compute statistics.

Hour 20, "Diagnosing Problems"

1. What can you use to validate offline datafiles?

DB_VERIFY

2. How can you generate checksums for redo log blocks?

Setting log_block_checksum to TRUE causes checksums to be calculated for all redo log blocks.

3. How can you generate a trace file when ORA-942 occurs?

A trace can be generated when ORA-942 occurs by adding the following line in the init.ora file:

```
Event = "942 trace name errorstack forever, level 10"
```

Hour 21, "Using Oracle Fail Safe"

1. What are some trouble-shooting utilities provided by Oracle Fail Safe Manager?

   - VERIFY CLUSTER
   - VERIFY GROUP
   - VERIFY STANDALONE DATABASE

2. Can you convert a Fail Safe database back to a standalone database?

   Yes.

3. What are some configurations in which OFS can be implemented?

   - Active/Passive
   - Active/Active
   - Multitiered

Hour 22, "Using Oracle Parallel Server"

1. What is pinging?

   Pinging occurs each time a data block is written to disk by one instance so that it can be read by another instance.

2. What is the function of the Distributed Lock Manager?

   The Distributed Lock Manager performs several functions:

   - Coordinates the requests for locks on shared resources such as data blocks, data dictionary entries, and rollback segments by the various Oracle processes running on the different instances
   - Keeps track of the resource owners
   - Informs the resource owner when another process requests the resource owned by it
   - Accepts requests for resources, grants the resources, keeps track of requests in case the requested resource is unavailable, and notifies the process when the resource becomes available
   - Communicates with Oracle via the Lock (LCK) processes

3. How can you minimize contention for ST locks?

- Disable SMON on all but a few instances.
- Initial and next extent sizes should be almost equal and large enough to avoid a lot of extension by the segments.
- Set PCTINCREASE to 0.
- DML operations on the same file must be performed from the same instance.
- Increase SORT_AREA_SIZE.
- Use fine-grained locking to block granularity on the system tablespace.
- Set event 10269 to disable coalescing.
- Don't perform frequent creation and deletion of objects.
- Minimize the number of sort space management transactions by using dedicated temporary tablespaces.

Hour 23, "Performing Parallel Operations"

1. What is *degree of parallelism*?

   The degree of parallelism for a parallel operation is the number of query slaves used by that operation.

2. What are the advantages of using parallel DML?

   Using parallel DML instead of manual parallelization has these advantages:

   - It's easy to use because Oracle performs the parallelization for you.
   - Transactional atomicity can be achieved because all the query slaves will work on a read-consistent snapshot of the target object and commit simultaneously.
   - Load balancing can be achieved.

3. What happens if the init.ora parameter SERIALIZABLE is set to TRUE and you perform a parallel DML operation?

   The operation will be performed serially instead.

4. How do you determine whether parallel DML is enabled for a session?

   Query v$session.

A

Hour 24, "Integrating Oracle and the World Wide Web"

1. Which JDBC drivers are provided by Oracle?

   Oracle provides two types of JDBC drivers:

   - Thin JDBC drivers
   - JDBC/OCI drivers

2. How can you use SQLJ programs?

   You can use SQLJ programs by following these generic steps:

   1. Write SQLJ Java programs.
   2. Run the SQLJ program through the SQLJ translator. The translator pre-processes the SQLJ program and generates standard Java code with JDBC calls.
   3. Compile the Java code.
   4. Run the Java program.

3. What are the advantages of using EJBs?

   The use of EJBs offers several advantages:

   - They use a high level of abstraction, making them easy to program.
   - They are developed completely in Java.
   - They are compatible with CORBA, D/COM, and so on.
   - They allow the use of transactional applications as modular components.

INDEX

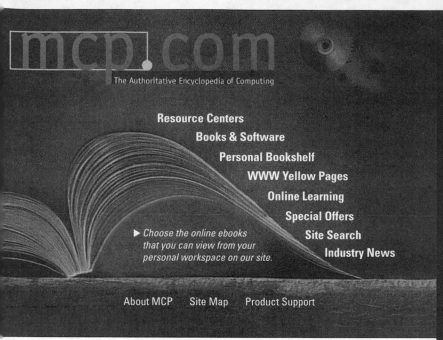

Other Related Titles

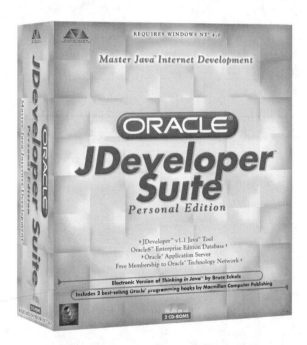